# Advanced Multimedia in the 21st Century

# Advanced Multimedia in the 21st Century

Edited by
Christopher Maxwell

MURPHY & MOORE
www.murphy-moorepublishing.com

Published by Murphy & Moore Publishing,
1 Rockefeller Plaza,
New York City, NY 10020, USA





ISBN: 978-1-63987-012-7

**Cataloging-in-Publication Data**

Advanced multimedia in the 21st century / edited by Christopher Maxwell.
p. cm.
Includes bibliographical references and index.
ISBN 978-1-63987-012-7
1. Mass media. 2. Multimedia systems. 3. Multimedia communications.
4. Communication. I. Maxwell, Christopher.

P90 .A28 2022
302.23--dc23

For information on all Murphy & Moore Publications
visit our website at www.murphy-moorepublishing.com

MURPHY & MOORE

# Contents

# Preface

Multimedia can be defined as a form of communication that employs different content forms such as text, images, animations, audio, or video into a single presentation. Video podcasts, audio slideshows, animated shows, and movies are some of the popular examples of multimedia. It can be recorded for playback on computers, smartphones, laptops, and other electronic devices, either on-demand or for live streaming. There are several applications of multimedia in the 21st century such as in creative industries, commercial purposes, entertainment, educational technology, social work, language communication, journalism, engineering, mathematical and scientific research, medicine, virtual reality, and augmented reality. This book brings forth some of the most innovative concepts and elucidates the unexplored aspects of multimedia in the 21st century. Its aim is to present researches that have transformed this discipline and aided its advancement. This book will serve as a reference to a broad spectrum of readers.

After months of intensive research and writing, this book is the end result of all who devoted their time and efforts in the initiation and progress of this book. It will surely be a source of reference in enhancing the required knowledge of the new developments in the area. During the course of developing this book, certain measures such as accuracy, authenticity and research focused analytical studies were given preference in order to produce a comprehensive book in the area of study.

This book would not have been possible without the efforts of the authors and the publisher. I extend my sincere thanks to them. Secondly, I express my gratitude to my family and well-wishers. And most importantly, I thank my students for constantly expressing their willingness and curiosity in enhancing their knowledge in the field, which encourages me to take up further research projects for the advancement of the area.

**Editor**

# 1

# Digital Camera Work for Soccer Video Production with Event Detection and Accurate Ball Tracking by Switching Search Method

Yasuo Ariki and Tetsuya Takiguchi
*Kobe University*
*Japan*

## 1. Introduction

Due to the increasing number of special channels, digital broadcasting requires a tremendous amount of video content and work associated with new interactive services. Sports video production for small spectators is a key issue associated with this problem, because such videos have not been produced to date due to the cost of producing such videos. From this viewpoint, an efficient and automatic low-cost production system for sports video content is needed even if it sacrifices a degree of professionalism.

When we watch a sports game on TV, the camera work helps us to understand the game progress owing to the panning and zooming carried out by the cameraman. This means that the camera work is strongly associated with the game events and the most suitable camera work is selected according to the events. Through camera work based on event recognition, more interesting and intelligible video content can be produced. Camera work can be classified into real camera work and virtual camera work. In real camera work, event recognition has to be carried out in real time. At present, it is difficult to do this, so virtual camera work is now the best way to produce dynamic video content with panning and zooming. This virtual camera work is sometimes called ``digital shooting,'' which is a composite of digital camera work and digital switching techniques.

We have been developing an automatic production system for commentary soccer video using digital shooting techniques based on the event (situation) recognition (Ariki et al., 2006). ``Commentary'' means intelligible and the system can produce comments on the game's progress or events because the events are recognized and digital shooting is carried out based on the events. The system is composed of image recognition techniques to track the soccer ball, event recognition, and finally digital camera work using panning and zooming. Event recognition is the key issue for digital camera work as well as for retrieving the events and summarizing the whole soccer game. However, event recognition mainly depends on the ball tracking accuracy, because events such as free kicks, goal kicks, throw ins, corner kicks and penalty kicks are strongly related to the ball. So far, ball tracking has been a difficult task, so complete event recognition and automatic video production have not been possible.

In this chapter, we describe a new technique to track the ball accurately on the Hi-vision video. Since the Hi-vision camera was located far from the soccer field in order to film half the field, the ball looks too small for tracking. At first, in the first frame, the ball is searched for using a global search with normalized cross-correlation. Although it is possible to search for the ball using global searching for all frames, the ball is lost sooner or later because of its small size and because of occlusion by the players. To solve this problem, we employed a local search with a particle filter, which can continue tracking around the area where the ball is ``lost." When the local search fails due to the disappearance of the ball (when the ball passes on and along the white line), the real ball is located far from the particles. In this case, a global search replaces the local search. After detecting the ball again, the local search continues tracking the ball. This switching of the search strategies is automatically carried out depending on the situation in which the ball is lost.
The organization of this chapter is as follows. In Section 2, the related works are described and in Section 3, the overview of the automatic production system is presented. A new ball tracking method is presented in Section 4. The camera work and the situation recognition are described in Section 5 and 6. In Section 7, the experiments of ball tracking and subjective evaluation of soccer video production with AHP are described.

## 2. Related Works

There are many aspects to a TV program sports video content production system, including generating highlights (Yow et al, 1995) (Assfalg et al, 2003), creating a summary (Ekin et al, 2003) (Nguyen et al, 2003), reconstruction (Bebie & Bieri, 1998), creating a mosaic (Kim & Hong, 2000) and other elemental technologies (Utsumi, et al, 2002). However, these produced videos are greatly subjected to limitations related to the video production staff (cameraman, editor, switcher, etc.). Also, the content inherits any mistakes in camera work and switching. Therefore, such video content has absolutely no degree of freedom (for example, adjusting the content to fit the preferences of the viewer).
Digital shooting has degrees of freedom higher than secondary usage of sports TV program content, because it is able to generate varied camera work and switching from the material video content, obtained by filming the whole soccer field using a HD (High-Definition) camera. One related topic of research in the field of automatic video shooting systems that we call a ``one-source multi-production system" is Virtual Soccer Stadium (Koyama et al, 2003), which makes it possible to show viewers a free view of the soccer field in 3D. Using this system, we can watch the game from any viewpoint, but the camera work or shooting techniques used in TV broadcasts can help the viewer to understand the game's progress more clearly.
The camera work such as panning and zooming are frequently utilized in classroom lectures, and content production systems or content summarization systems are proposed, employing the detection of lecturer-movement and voice-detection algorithms (Yokoi & Fujiyoshi, 2005) (Yokoi & Fujiyoshi, 2006). However, the event detection needed to switch between various camera works in a soccer sports video production system is much more difficult.
Event recognition depends mainly on the ball-tracking accuracy, because events such as free kicks, goal kicks, throw ins, corner kicks, and penalty kicks are strongly related to the ball. There are two procedures in soccer ball tracking. One is ball detection and the other is ball

tracking. In paper (Huang et al, 2005), the ball candidates were first detected from several consecutive frames of broadcast TV video using color, shape and size information. Then a weighted graph was constructed with each node representing a candidate and each edge linking two candidates in adjacent frames. Then a Viterbi algorithm was carried out to extract the optimal path as the ball's locations. After ball was detected, it was tracked using Kalman filter-based template matching.

In paper (Tian et al, 2003), the ball candidates were also detected in each frame of the broadcast TV video by removing non-ball objects using color, shape and size information. After obtaining the ball candidates in all the frames, the Kalman filter was applied from the first frame to estimate the ball position on the succeeding frames. If the candidate was found in the next frame near the estimated point, it was used to update the Kalman filter. Otherwise (if no candidates were found), the estimated position was considered to be the ball position.

In paper (Liu et al, 2004), the soccer field was first extracted from the broadcast soccer video. Then several simple shape features and spatial context color were evaluated, and distinct non-ball regions were removed. Further examination determined the initial position of the ball in the first frame. The ball was then tracked using a CONDENSATION algorithm (particle filter) based on the similarity of histogram intersection of the object regions. This method hypothesizes the ball's occurrence on the game field and fails under some special conditions, such as occlusion of the ball by players or white field lines, too complex of a background, or the small size of the ball due to its distance from the camera. Although our approach also employs a particle filter, it is used for the local search only and switches to a global search when the ball is lost. This means that it is not necessary to hypothesize the ball's occurrence on the field.

## 3. Overview of the System

### 3.1 Digital Shooting

Digital shooting can be assumed to be an emulation of a virtual multiple-camera system that works by clipping a frame from HD material video content and mapping it roughly to frame at low resolution, such as SD (Standard Definition).

The digital shooting technique is composed of digital camera work and digital switching technique. The digital camera work is defined as virtual panning and virtual zooming. The virtual panning is a video production technique involving clipping a size-fixed frame by controlling frame location on HD video. The virtual zooming is a video production technique involving clipping a frame by controlling frame size. Also, digital switching is defined as the change of some virtual camera by controlling rapid change of frame location or size on HD video.

Although the camera work or switching by human beings during live sports events cannot retake the scene, digital shooting is able to repeatedly produce various camera work and switching from the recorded video material, which involved the filming of the entire soccer field with a HD camera.

In our experiments, we used a Victor GR-HD1 Hi-vision camera. Figure 1 shows half the field taken by Hi-vision camera and a SD image clipped from the fixed HD image. Digital camera work is produced by changing the coordinates of the clipping window on every HD frame. For example, Figure 2 and Figure 3 show digital panning down from right to left down and digital zooming in, respectively.

Fig. 1. Clipping from the HD image to a SD image using digital camera work

Fig. 2. Panning by digital camera work

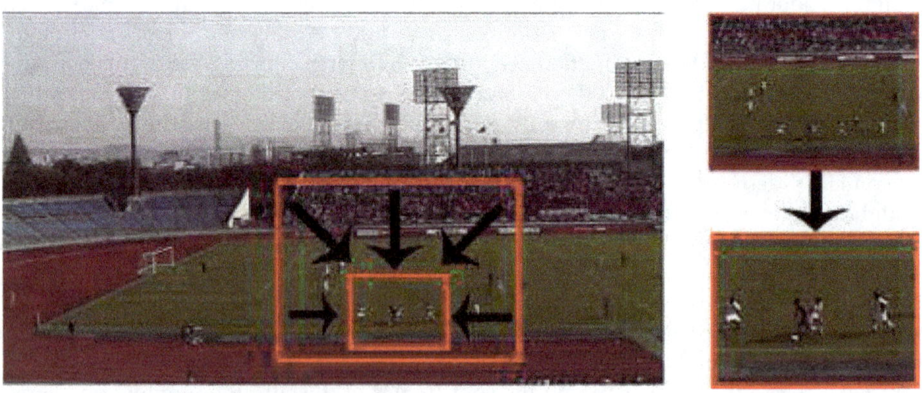

Fig. 3. Zooming by digital camera work

### 3.2 Processing Flow

Figure 4 shows the processing flow of the digital camera work system. At first, the entire image sequence is captured by the fixed Hi-vision camera.
In the image processing module, the players and the ball are tracked, and their coordinates are extracted. The image sequence is captured by the fixed Hi-vision camera so that no camera work is included in the original video content. Therefore, the background subtraction method can be applied to the material video to extract the players and ball. Background subtraction is a simple but effective method to detect moving objects in video images.

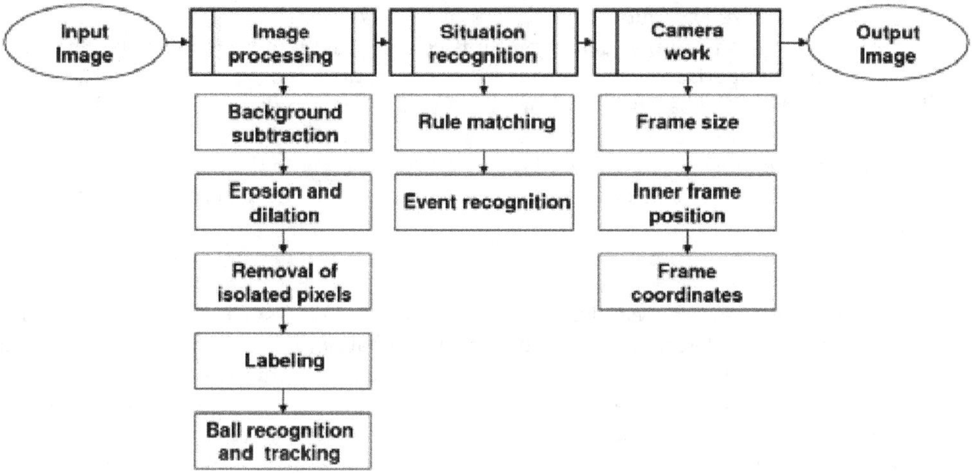


Fig. 4. Processing flow of the system

These background subtracted images do not depend on the image color. Hence, this method can be applied not only to the grass field but also to a dirt field. Furthermore, it is robust enough to handle the slow changes caused by sunshine or illumination if the background image to be subtracted is updated. The background image is updated by averaging the $M$ frames at every $N$ frames.
In the background subtraction process, each binary image is preprocessed by a morphological operator (erosion and dilation) to extract a player region, and noise reduction processing is applied. After region labeling, the ball is recognized and tracked. The players are extracted on every frame but not tracked or matched between consecutive frames.
In the situation recognition module, the events (such as throw ins, free kicks and goal kicks) are recognized based on the coordinates of the players and the ball, using the rules to recognize the event situation. In the camera work module, proper clipping size and frame coordinates are decided according to the recognized events.
The event recognition depends mainly on the ball tracking accuracy, because events (such as free kicks, goal kicks, throw ins, corner kicks and penalty kicks) are strongly related to the ball. So far, ball tracking was a difficult task so that complete event recognition and automatic video production were not successful.

In the following section, we propose an efficient and stable ball-tracking method by switching search methods back and forth between global search and local search. In the frames where the ball is lost as well as in the first frame, the global search with normalized cross-correlation is performed. Then the local search with particle filter continues the tracking. Once the system has recognized that the local search has failed by receiving a sequence of low probabilities among the ball-tracking results, the search method is switched to the global search.

## 4. Ball Tracking

In tracking a soccer ball on videos, there are several problems to be solved. The main problems are summarized as follows;

1. A ball is small and round, so sometimes it is confused with other similar objects due to its featureless properties.
2. In the case where the ball is kicked high and passes over the spectators, similar objects such as people's faces, caps or bags are confused with the ball.
3. The ball is sometimes occluded by players and confused with the players' white shoes.
4. In the case where the ball passes on the white line or white pole, it disappears for a short time.
5. The ball movement is sometimes irregular when it touches players.

To solve problems 1 and 2, background subtraction is effective because the stationary objects similar with the ball are removed. Then ball detection methods, such as normalized cross-correlation between the detected moving objects and a ball template, can be applied on the first frame. We call this the global search because the system does not know where the ball is on the first frame so that it searches the whole image.

This global search is time-consuming, so a more efficient search algorithm is required. One of the most plausible methods will be a local search, such as Kalman filter or particle filter. The Kalman tracker hypothesizes a unimodal Gaussian probability distribution function. On the other hand, the particle filter does not have such a hypothesis, so the particle filter is thought to be better than the Kalman filter. This ball search method is called a local search because the system predicts the ball's location area, and the ball is searched for within this area.

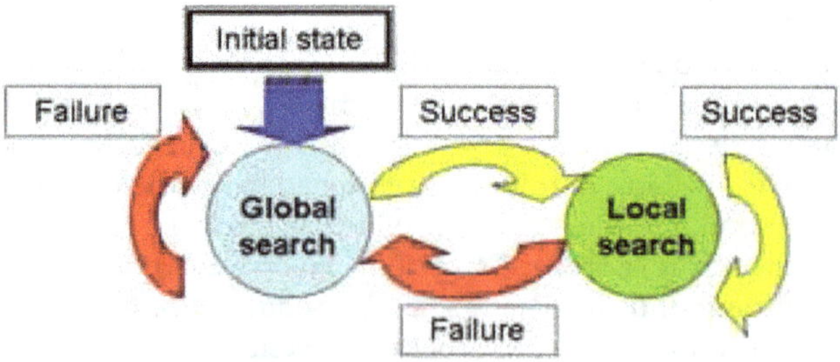


Fig. 5. Organization of a ball tracking system

A local search can solve problems 3, 4 and 5 to some degree, but it fails due to ball disappearance when the ball passes on and along the white line or a big white character

written on the wall in front of the spectators. In this case, after a few seconds, the global search should be applied to detect the ball position again.
Figure 5 shows the organization of the proposed ball-tracking system using global search and local search. In the frames where the ball is lost as well as in the first frame, the global search with normalized cross-correlation is performed. Then the local search with a particle filter continues the tracking. Once the system has recognized that the local search has failed by receiving a sequence of low probabilities of the ball tracking results, the search method is switched to the global search.

### 4.1 Global Search

In the global search for the ball, the normalized cross-correlation *R(x,y)* is computed between the ball template *T(i,j)* and the small region within the search area *I* based on the following equation:

$$R(x,y)=\frac{\sum_{i,j}\{T(i,j)-\bar{T}\}\cdot\{I(x+i,y+j)-\bar{I}\}}{\sqrt{\sum_{i,j}\{T(i,j)-\bar{T}\}^2\cdot\sum_{i,j}\{I(x+i,y+j)-\bar{I}\}^2}} \tag{1}$$

$$(\hat{x},\hat{y})=\underset{x,y}{\arg\max}\,R(x,y) \tag{2}$$

where $\bar{T}$ and $\bar{I}$ are the averaged intensity of the ball template image and the underlying small region, respectively. $(\hat{x},\hat{y})$ is the point where the ball is matched best within the search area *I*. In this study, the search area *I* is set to a whole image in the video. The ball template is prepared manually in advance.

### 4.2 Local Search with Particle Filter

#### 4.2.1 Particle Filter

In the local search for the ball, a particle filter (Isard & Blake, 1998) is employed. The ball is tracked by estimating *a posterior* probability $p(x_t\,|\,Z_t)$ of the ball state $x_t$ at time *t* after observing the image feature sequence $Z_t=(z_1,...,z_t)$ up to current time *t*.
This *posterior* probability is computed based on Bayesian theory as follows, using *a prior* probability $p(x_t\,|\,Z_{t-1})$ and likelihood $p(z_t\,|\,x_t)$ of the image feature $z_t$ at the state $x_t$.

$$p(x_t\,|\,Z_t)=k_t p(z_t\,|\,x_t)p(x_t\,|\,Z_{t-1}) \tag{3}$$

If the *posterior* probability $p(x_t\,|\,Z_t)$ is complicated, it can be computed by randomly sampling the states $x_t$ as particles $s_t^{(n)}$ (*n*=1,...,*N*) according to the *prior* probability $p(x_t\,|\,Z_{t-1})$ and estimating the likelihood $p(z_t\,|\,x_t)$ of the image feature $z_t$ at the state $x_t$ as $\pi_t^{(n)}$. It is expressed as follows:

$$p(x_t \mid Z_t) \approx \sum_{n=1}^{N} \pi_t^{(n)} \delta(s_t^{(n)}) \tag{4}$$

Here, $\delta$ indicates the delta function.

The *prior* probability $p(x_t \mid Z_{t-1})$ is computed by transferring the *posterior* probability $p(x_{t-1} \mid Z_{t-1})$ at previous time *t-1*, using the state transition probability $p(x_t \mid x_{t-1})$ as follows:

$$p(x_t \mid Z_{t-1}) = \int_{x_{t-1}} p(x_t \mid x_{t-1}) p(x_{t-1} \mid Z_{t-1}) dx_{t-1} \tag{5}$$

In this study, we employ motion dynamics.

### 4.2.2 Motion Dynamics

The motion dynamics used to move the particles from the *posterior* probability at time *t-1* to the *prior* probability at time *t* is expressed by the following equation of motion:

$$x_t = \begin{bmatrix} I & I \\ 0 & I \end{bmatrix} x_{t-1} + \omega \tag{6}$$

where $\omega$ is the Gaussian noise term, and $x_t$ is the state of the particle and expressed as follows:

$$x_t = [p_{tx}, p_{ty}, v_{tx}, v_{ty}]^T \tag{7}$$

Here, $p_{tx}$, $p_{ty}$, $v_{tx}$ and $v_{ty}$ are the positions of $x$ and $y$ and the velocities in the $x$ and $y$ directions in the image at time *t*, respectively. The velocity is estimated using the past tracked positions.

### 4.2.3 Likelihood Estimation

The likelihood of the ball is estimated at each particle by the normalized cross-correlation between the image feature at the position of the particle and the ball template, expressed in Eq. (1). When the normalized cross-correlation is applied directly, many particles are confused with non-ball objects such as spectator faces, caps and bags. To avoid such a situation, moving objects are only extracted and tracked using the particle filter. Moving objects are extracted by subtracting the background image from the present image.

## 5. Camera Work Module

In the camera work module, the digital panning and zooming are controlled. Digital panning is performed on the HD image by moving the coordinates of the clipping window, and digital zooming is performed by changing the size of the clipping window.

### 5.1 Zooming and Clipping Size

After analyzing the professional camera work on a TV soccer game, it was found that during soccer games, three sizes of the clipping window are used in zooming in: tight shot, middle shot and loose shot size. These sizes of the clipping window are selected according to the game situation. For example, the tight shot is selected for the play near the goal when the ball movement is slight. If the tight shot is used frequently, the video becomes not intelligible so the tight shot is used only for important play with duration more than two seconds.

The loose shot or middle shot camera work is selected for normal play or situations, such as free kicks, where the ball is expected to move fast. Transition from the loose shot to middle shot or vice versa is performed according to the game situation. The transition is continuously done within 0.5 seconds. If the duration of the loose shot or middle shot after the transition is less than 0.5 seconds, then a transition does not take place.

Based on these parameters, in our experiment, three clipping sizes are prepared as shown in Table 1. Figure 6 shows examples of these shot sizes on the HD image. They are continuously or abruptly switched back and forth between each other according to the game situation, as shown in Figure 7.

| Tight shot size | Middle shot size | Loose shot size |
|---|---|---|
| $120 \times 90$ | $240 \times 180$ | $480 \times 360$ |

Table 1. Three sizes of the clipping window on the HD image (pixels)

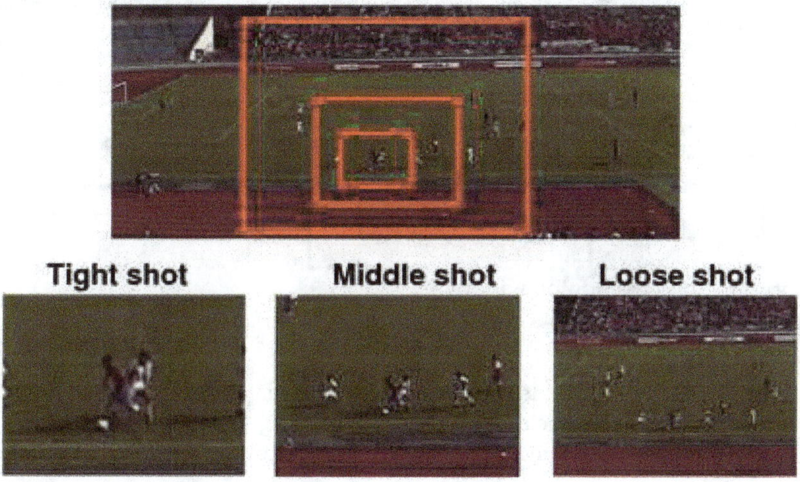


Fig. 6. Example of clipping window sizes

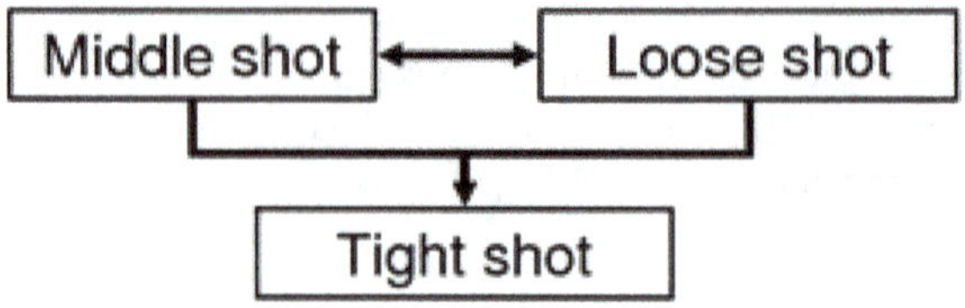


Fig. 7. Size switching of clipping window

### 5.2 Panning and Clipping Coordinates

The ball location is important because the soccer game progresses following the ball's location. However, ball trajectory cannot adequately be used directly to trigger a commencement of panning because smooth panning cannot be obtained due to the erratic movement of the ball.

In other words, the panning operation has to satisfy two contrary conditions, namely that the clipping window (frame) must follow the ball quickly if the ball moves fast, but if the ball moves erratically, the frame must not follow the ball.

To meet these two conditions, we set an inner frame within the clipping window as shown by the black frame in Figure 8. Even if the ball is moving erratically, the clipping window remains still if the ball exists inside the inner frame. If the ball moves out of the inner frame, the centroid of the clipping window moves toward the ball location as shown in Figure 9.

Fig. 8. Clipping window (white) and inner frame (black)

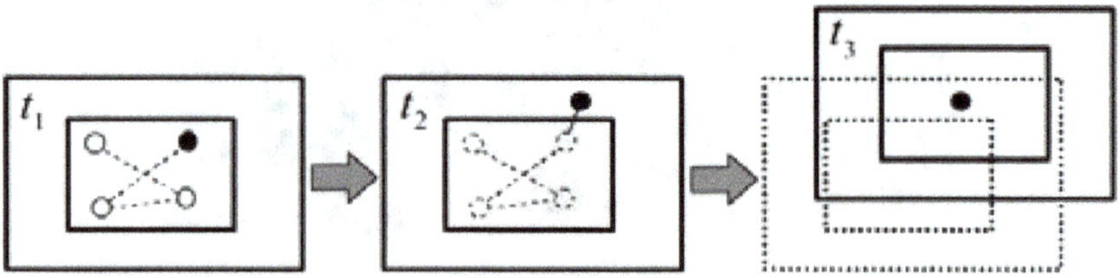


Fig. 9. Control method of clipping window

### 5.3 Inner Frame Position

The inner frame usually locates itself at the center of the clipping window. However, if the play is something like a free kick, long pass or dribbling etc., then the forward direction should be included in the clipping window to make the play formation or players remain visible.

Therefore, it is necessary to set the inner frame at the position opposite the center of the clipping window toward the ball movement direction. Figure 10 shows the inner frame in such a situation. The inner frame is shown as the small rectangle and the clipping window is shown as the large rectangle. Usually the left clipping window and the inner frame are employed. However, in the situation of a free kick by the goalkeeper, the right clipping window is selected to set the inner frame at the left position (opposite to the ball direction).

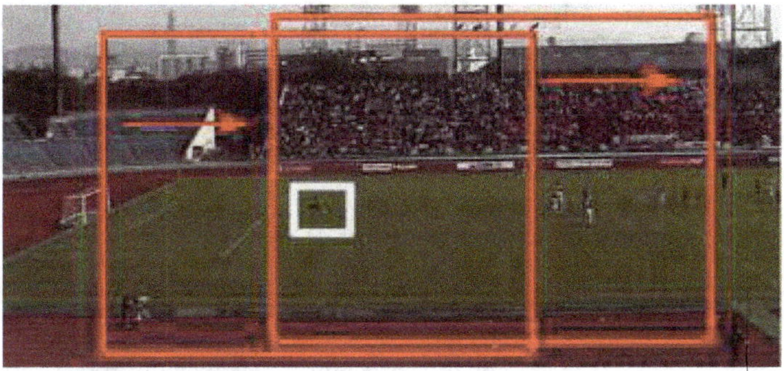

Fig. 10. Inner frame position control

## 6. Situation Recognition Module

In the situation recognition module, the game situation is recognized based on the ball and players extracted in the image-processing module and this game situation are forwarded to the camera work module. The game situations for controlling the camera work are classified into two groups. One changes the camera work among loose shots, middle shots and tight shots according to ball-player relationships. The other sets the typical camera work according to the events such as goal kicks, corner kicks and free kicks.
In order to clarify the game situation for changing the camera work, we analyzed the professional camera work of a soccer game broadcast on TV. From this analysis, rules were found for causing the camera work changes based on the game situation and the events. In this section, the rules for starting zooming and the rules for detecting events are described.

### 6.1 Zooming Rule

Rules for changing the camera work based on the game situation are described. The camera work change has already been described in Figure 7.

#### 6.1.1 Rules for Switching from Loose Shot to Middle Shot

Changing the camera work from the loose shot to the middle shot occurs when a more detailed game situation is required in order to understand play. Through analyzing TV soccer games, two types of such situations are found. One is the case where the ball approaches the goal and the other is the case where the players crowd around the ball.
One of the most important scenes in a soccer game is a goal scene so that the camera must be zooming in at this time. When the ball passes over the penalty line toward the goal, a goal

scene may be expected, so the system changes the camera work to the middle shot from the loose shot. The situation is recognized by computing the horizontal coordinate of the ball.
When a lot of players are around the ball, it is effective to zoom in to see clearly. This situation is recognized by counting the number of players around the ball on middle shot resolution. If the number is over six or seven players, then the situation is interpreted as crowded.
The accuracy of the player detection is not so high due to the overlap of the players, however, so the crowded situation is determined by counting the number of players including the player overlap.

### 6.1.2 Rules for Switching from Middle Shot to Loose Shot

Changing the camera work from middle shot to loose shot occurs when the camera field does not include the ball or the minimum number of players. Through analyzing broadcast soccer games on TV, two such situations are found. One is the case where the ball moves too fast and the other is where the players scatter very fast.
A fast-moving ball situation is detected by computing the displacement of the ball coordinates at every frame. If it is over the threshold (six pixels), the fast movement of the ball is detected. This rule may be applied even when the ball moves forward and backward around the same place. In this case the camera work may change frequently. To avoid this situation, the coordinate of the ball is checked and if it is increasing or decreasing in a constant direction for more than two seconds, the rule is applied.
When players scatter, the camera work changes from the middle shot to loose shot to catch the ball and the minimum number of players. This situation is recognized by counting the number of players around the ball.
There are some conflicts between rules for changing camera work from the middle shot to loose shot and vice versa. One conflict is when a player kicks the ball toward the goal; i.e. when the ball moves very fast near the goal. In this case, two rules may be applicable. One is the rule to change the camera work from loose shot to middle shot because the ball is located near the goal as described in Section 6.1.1. The other rule is to change the camera work from middle shot to loose shot because of the very fast ball movement. In this case, the rule to change the camera work from the middle shot to the loose shot is inhibited.
The other conflict is when the ball moves very fast over a crowd of players. In this case, two rules may be applicable. One is the rule to change the camera work from middle shot to loose shot because the ball moves very fast. The other is the rule to change the camera work form loose shot to middle shot because the crowded players are detected. In this case, the rule to change the camera work from the loose shot to middle shot is inhibited.

### 6.1.3 Rules for Tight Shots

In the professional camera work on TV soccer games, tight shots, such as famous players or players scrambling for the ball and dribbling, are sometimes inserted in the videos. These tight shots make the game interesting. The proposed system does not recognize players' faces at present, so the scrambling situation is only zoomed in on as a tight shot in our system.

This situation is recognized when the ball movement is below some threshold and there is at least one player around the ball. The threshold is set to be 1.5 pixels through the preliminary experiment.

### 6.2 Event Detection Rule

The proposed system can recognize five events; free kicks, goal kicks, throw ins, corner kicks and penalty kicks. These events are detected using a feature that notices when the ball remains still for some duration under the tight shot camera work. The detection duration for such events is set at 6 seconds.

Once the events are detected, the system zooms out to view the entire situation and recognizes the event types according to rules using the ball position and the distance between the ball and the players' average position as shown in Table 2. For example, if the ball is on the corner arc and the distance between the ball and the players' average position is medium distance, the event is recognized as a corner kick.

After the event recognition, the clipping size is determined according to the rules and the center of the clipping window is set to the players' average position.

| Events | Ball position | Distance between ball and players | Clipping size |
|---|---|---|---|
| Free kick | Field area | Far | LS or MS |
| Goal kick | Goal area | Far | LS |
| Throw in | Out of bounds | Middle | MS |
| Corner kick | Corner spot | Middle | MS |
| Penalty kick | Penalty spot | Middle | TS |

Table 2. Event recognition rules

## 7. Evaluation Experiment

### 7.1 Ball Tracking Accuracy

We selected consecutive 800 consecutive frames (26.6 sec) from a soccer game that was played during the 38th National High School Soccer Championship (Kyoto area final) in Japan. The size of the image was 1,280 x 720 pixels with 24-bit color. The background image was produced in advance by averaging the randomly selected images in the video. The ball template image size was 15 x 15 pixels and the particle image size was 30 x 30 pixels, which is larger than the ball template image size, in order to search the best position within the particle image. The number of particles re-sampled was 100.

Three tracking methods (global search, local search and switching search) were evaluated. The results are shown in Table 3. In the table, ``Tracking rate'' is the ratio of the number of correctly tracked frames to the number of total frames (800). ``Restart'' indicates the necessity of manual restart when the tracking failed. The average ``processing time'' per image was calculated on a computer with a Xeon 3.06GHz processor and 1,024 MB of memory.

In Table 3, the local search achieved a very high tracking rate with low processing time owing to the particle filter. Two failures occurred when the ball passed on and along the white line and it passed along the big white character written on the wall in front of the spectators. In these cases, a manual restart was required by specifying the true ball position. On the other hand, in the proposed method, the search was switched to the local search after the global search obtained a high cross-correlation value, and the search was switched to the global search when 40 frames continued with the low probability of the ball tracking results. The threshold of high cross-correlation and the low probability were empirically determined. It showed that the incorrect tracking caused by the particle filter was restored by the proposed switching search and the processing time was almost same as that of the particle filter.

| Method | Tracking rate [%] | Restart | Processing time [sec] |
|---|---|---|---|
| Global search | 61.1 | Not required | 3.2 |
| Local search | 91.5 | Required | 0.8 |
| Switched search | 91.8 | Not required | 0.9 |

Table 3. Experimental results

### 7.2 Subjective Evaluation by AHP

The final goal of this study is to construct a soccer video production system that meets viewer preferences and contains announcer commentary. Therefore, AHP (Analytic Hierarchy Process) (Saaty, 1997) can be used for the evaluation of the produced video contents because of its ability to represent human subjectivity.

AHP is a multi-criteria decision support method designed to select the best from a number of evaluated alternatives with respect to several criteria. It carries out pair-wise comparison judgments, which are used to decide the overall priorities for ranking the alternatives.

Three items were selected for the evaluation criteria of the video contents by AHP. They are naturalness, video quality and intelligibility. For naturalness, four camera work criteria are selected: zooming, panning, shot size, and shot duration. The video quality is adopted to judge whether or not the produced video content is inferior to TV or HD content. Also, the intelligibility of the game process is also adopted. These criteria are shown in Table 4.

| Criteria | Evaluation |
|---|---|
| 1. Zooming | Good <-> Poor |
| 2. Panning | Good <-> Poor |
| 3. Shot size | Good <-> Poor |
| 4. Shot duration | Proper <-> Improper |
| 5. Video quality | Fine <-> Coarse |
| 6. Intelligibility | High <-> Low |

Table 4. Evaluation criteria used in AHP

The video content to be evaluated by AHP are HD content, TV content, the produced content by our proposed method and the content produced by our conventional method with only panning from the original HD content (Ariki et al, 2004). All were produced from the same soccer game (38th National High School Soccer Championship).

The HD content was taken for a wide-angle half of the field by HD camera because of the limitation of camera resolution. The TV content was recorded by a video recorder when the game was broadcast on TV. The reason why the HD content was compared in this chapter was to investigate which was fundamentally more comprehensible, TV content with camera work or wide-angle HD video content.

Figure 11 shows the AHP tree map used in this experiment. The middle row shows the six evaluation criteria. The bottom row shows the four materials to be compared.

The preference weights of AHP for each type of content are shown in Figure 12. The TV content showed high score followed by the contents of the proposed method, HD and the conventional method. The result shows that the presentation of game process is the most important and, therefore, the TV content obtained a high score. It also indicates that the TV content with panning camera work by professional cameramen is important compared with the HD content with no camera work.

The proposed method showed an AHP weight similar to the TV content and improved the intelligibility of the game process compared with the conventional method because of the camera work (panning and zooming based on the situation recognition). The content produced by the proposed method is still inferior to the TV contents since the digital camera work is not so high compared with the professional cameraman and the video quality is also lower than the TV and HD contents.

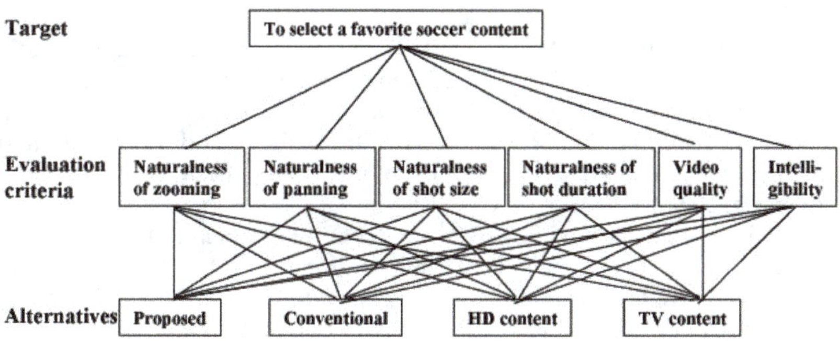


Fig. 11. AHP treemap

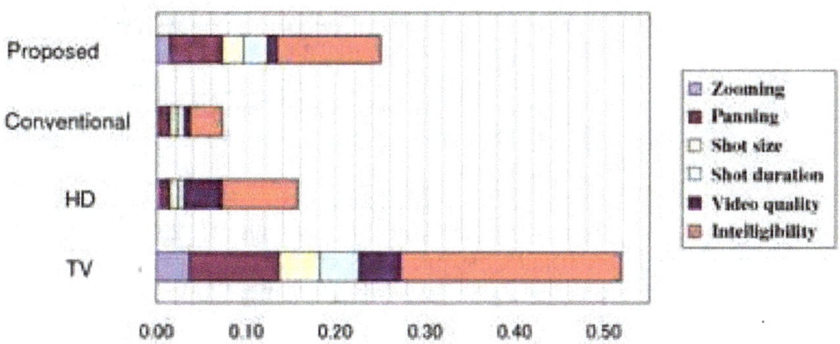


Fig. 12. Evaluation result by AHP

## 8. Conclusions

In this chapter, we proposed a system to track a small ball accurately on the fixed Hi-vision video by switching between global search and local search. This switching in search strategies is carried out automatically, depending on the situation when the ball is lost. Through the experiment, we showed that the proposed method can achieve continuous and stable ball tracking.

We also proposed a method to produce soccer video content with digital camera work based on situation recognition. AHP evaluation for our method showed a lower preference score than the TV content. However, the basic composition of the AHP scores is almost the same between the content produced by the proposed method and the TV content in terms of evaluation criteria, such as panning and zooming. This indicates that the improvement of our proposed method will lead to a degree of quality close to the technique of the TV cameramen in the future. Multiple cameras will be required to film the various shots that need to be taken from different angles rather than just the three shot types we tested. This problem will be also dealt with in the future.

## 9. References

Ariki, Y.; Kubota, S. & Kumano, M. (2006). Automatic Production System of Soccer Sports Video by Digital Camera Work Based on Situation Recognition, *Proceedings of Eight IEEE International Symposium on Multimedia*, pp. 851-858, 2006

Yow, D.; Yeo, B-L.; Yeung, M. & Liu, B. (1995). Analysis and Presentation of Soccer Highlights from Digital Video, *Proceedings of 2nd Asian Conference on Computer Vision*, pp. 499-503, 1995

Assfalg, J.; Bertini, M.; Colombo, C.; Bimbo, A. D. & Nunziati, W. (2003). Automatic Interpretation of Soccer Video for Highlights Extraction and Annotation, *Proceedings of ACM symposium on Applied computing*, pp. 769-773, 2003

Ekin, A.; Tekalp, A. M. & Mehrotra, R. (2003). Automatic soccer video analysis and summarization, *IEEE Trans. on Image Processing*, 12-7, pp. 796-807, 2003

Nguyen, N. T.; Thang, T. C.; Bae, T. M. & Ro, Y. M. (2003). Soccer Video Summarization System Based on Hidden Markov Model with Multiple MPEG-7 Descriptors, *Proceedings of the International Conference on Imaging Science, Systems and Technology*, pp. 673-678, 2003

Bebie, T. & Bieri, H. (1998). SoccerMan - Reconstructing Soccer Games from Video Sequences, *Proceedings of 2007 IEEE International Conference on Image Processing*, pp. 898-902, 1998

Kim, H. & Hong, K-S. (2000). Soccer Video Mosaicing Using Self-Calibration and Line Tracking, *Proceedings of International Conference on Pattern Recognition*, pp. 1592-1595, 2000

Utsumi, O.; Miura, K.; Ide, I.; Sakai, S. & Tanaka, H. (2002). An object detection method for describing soccer games from video, *Proceedings of 2002 IEEE International Conference on Multimedia and Expo*, pp. 45-48, 2002

Koyama, T.; Kitahara, I. & Ohta, Y. (2003). Live Mixed-Reality 3D Video in Soccer Stadium, *Proceedings of International Symposium on Mixed and Augmented Reality*, pp. 178-187, 2003

Yokoi, T. & Fujiyoshi, H. (2005). Virtual Camerawork for Generating Lecture Video from High Resolution Images, *Proceedings of 2005 IEEE International Conference on Multimedia and Expo*, pp. 45-48, 2002

Yokoi, T. & Fujiyoshi, H. (2006). Generating a Time Shrunk Lecture Video by Event Detection, *Proceedings of 2006 IEEE International Conference on Multimedia and Expo*, pp. 641-644, 2006

Huang, Q.; Liang, D.; Liu, Y. & Gao, W. (2005). A scheme for ball detection and tracking in broadcast soccer video, *Proceedings of PCM2005*, pp. 864-875, 2005

Tian, Q.; Yu, X.; Xu, C. & Leong, H. W. (2003). A ball tracking framework for broadcast soccer video, *Proceedings of 2003 IEEE International Conference on Multimedia and Expo*, pp. 273-276, 2003

Liu, Q-S.; Tong, X. F. & Lu, H. Q. (2004). An effective and fast soccer ball detection and tracking method, *Proceedings of ICPR*, pp. 795-798, 2004

Isard, M. & Blake, A. (1998). Condensation-conditional density propagation for visual tracking, *International Journal Computer Vision*, 29 (1), pp. 5-28, 1998

Saaty, T. (1997). A scaling method for priorities in hierarchical structures, *Journal of Mathematical Psychology*, 15, pp. 234-281, 1997

Ariki, Y.; Kumano, M. & Tsukada, K. (2004). A method of digital camera work focused on players and a ball, *Proceedings of 2004 Pacific-Rim Conference on Multimedia*, pp. 466-473, 2004

# 2

# Online Surface Inspection Technology of Cold Rolled Strips

Guifang Wu
*Electronic Information Engineering College, Henan University of Science & Technology*
*China*

## 1. Introduction

With enlargement of cold rolled strips' productive scale and enhancement of productive speed, traditional quality detection by human eyes becomes more and more unsuitable for surface detection of cold rolled strips, and multimedia technique such as machine vision become impendent. Recent years, CCD cameras and image processing techniques make online inspection of cold rolled strips possible (Sugimoto, T., 1998). An online surface inspection with CCD cameras and image processing techniques is a newly developed technique to detect surface defects of steels on production lines, and it can release workers from hard work and improve work efficiency.

Last century, many detection technique raised up, for example, in the early 70's, there are many new techniques in Japan such as Laser Scan Surface Defect Inspection System, and it developed continuously and can detect some of inner defects by the 80's. Till 90's, some of Japanese corporation developed a new system which can be used to detect the surface of electric steel. By the time of the end of 90's, camera techniques were used to detect the surface of metal strips, especially in German.

But because of the reason of computer technique, the techniques still stop in some normal work conditional, and the advantages of camera techniques weren't exerted fully, especially in developing countries and districts as China, India, etc. Consequently this newly developed technique becomes a hot subject, and its application problems are more and more concerned by people.

In this chapter, an automatic surface inspection system (Kim, S. M., 2006) of cold rolled strips is introduced. The system is equipped with 12 CCD area scan cameras which are used to capture surface image of strips simultaneously. With special illumination units, defects can be distinguished from backgrounds of images because of different gray levels. Many multimedia image processing algorithms are developed to decide whether there are defects on the images and to locate the defects in the whole strips. At the same time, pattern recognition algorithms are developed to classify the defects. With statistical data of defects, such as numbers, sizes, areas, classes, and so on, surface qualities of strips are evaluated.

## 2. General design of online surface inspection system

### 2.1 Requirement of System

When producing cold rolled strips, because of high speed, the surface of strips cannot be easily inspected by human eyes, if there are some defects on the surface, it cannot be found by inspector, and all the defects will be sometimes, many impurities would be embed in it, therefore, the surface condition would become too bad to be recognized. In order to inspect surface quality of hot rolled strips, the online inspection system must meet such performance indexes as followings:

1. Velocity requirement: It can work at the velocity of 5~15 m/s;
2. Detection size requirement: It can detect defects of strips with size of 0.5mm× 0.5 mm;
3. Maximum width requirement: The maximum detection width can meet 2000 mm;
4. Work condition requirement: It can work online under any inner condition;
5. Defect position requirement: It can record exact position of defects;
6. Offline requirement: It can display history process of production, and have many offline function such as offline query, offline analysis and offline statistics;
7. Detection rate requirement: The detection rate of common defects can meet 90%, and about 80% for other defects;
8. Recognition rate requirement: The recognition rate of common defects can meet 85%, and about 80% for other defects;
9. Defect types requirement: It can detect over 10 main defects.

### 2.2 Chief defect types and their causes

When producing steel plate and strip, there are always such chief defect types as scratch, felt horizontal texture, point felt, feather roll imprint, white spot, roll imprint, Edge folding, rust mark, orange texture, emulsion mark, edge crack, scale, crack, air bubble, and so on. The following will analyze the clauses of these defects detailed.

1. Scratch

Scratch is a straight imprint on the surface of steel plate and strip. It is created by the relative movement between two surfaces of steel plate and strip, or between a hard sharp object and one of surface of steel plate and strip. Commonly, scratch is concave and directional in shape, and it is a bit light in black-white image.

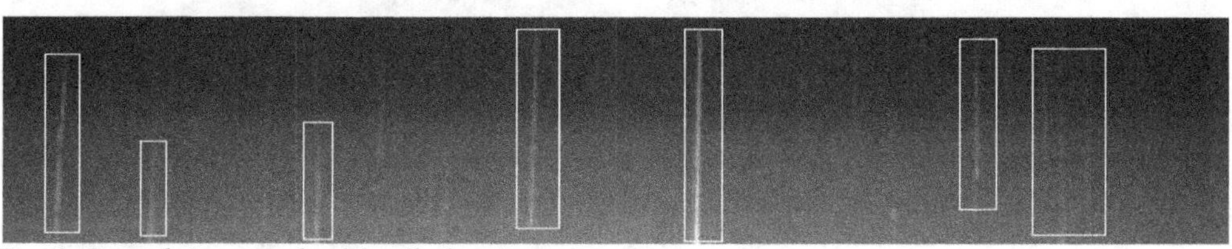

Fig. 1. Scratch image of cold rolled strips

2. Felt horizontal texture

Felt horizontal texture is horizontal wave texture along the edge of steel plate and strip, and it is also called edge pucker or edge folding mark. It is mainly caused by the sudden deduced thickness of edge before temper rolling and extending not enough at edge when temper rolling, or unfolding not enough in rolling direction .this type defect always appears in cold rolled slight sheet.

Fig. 2. Felt horizontal texture image of cold rolled strips

3. Point felt

Point felt is a felt phenomenon with a shape of point or block on the surface of steel plate and strip. The main cause is that the liquidity and plasticity of material is changed by bad shape or exceeded curl tension or bruise on surface.

Fig. 3. Point felt image of cold rolled strips

4. Feather roll imprint

Feather roll imprint is the same as a feather in shape. It is caused by linear load odds in the rolling process. At the same time, it is also related with raw material. The feather roll imprint appears generally in cold rolled steel sheet, and it is easy to form crack in bad condition.

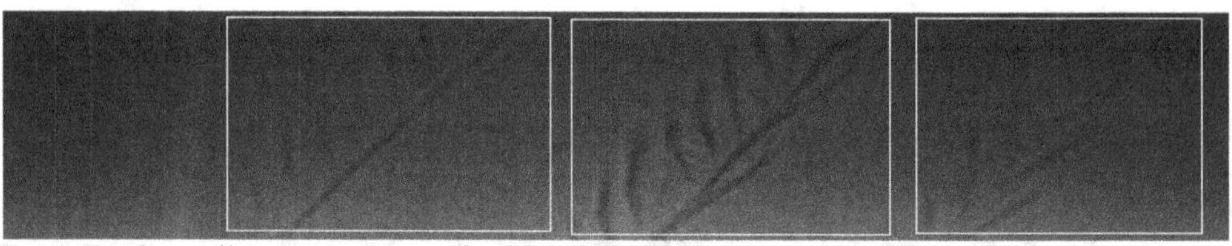

Fig. 4. Feather roll imprint image of cold rolled strips

5. White spot

White spot is a white similar circular spot block on the sur-face of steel plate and strip, its size is variable, but its border is smooth. It is primarily caused by white foam on the surface of plate and strip which has not been disposed immediately, it affect less on surface quality than surface appearance.

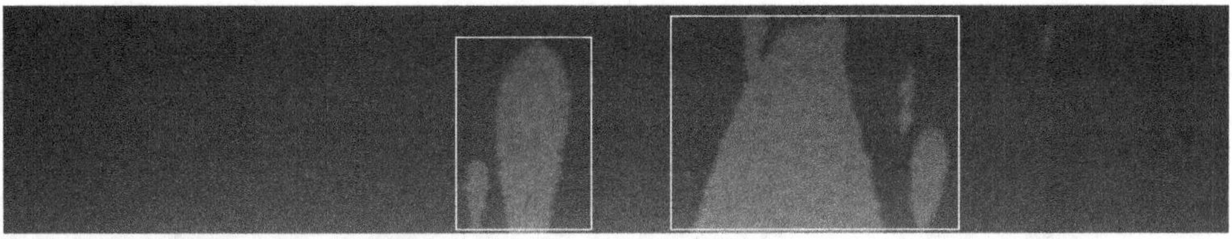

Fig. 5. White spot image of cold rolled strips

6. Roll imprint
Roll imprint is a periodic indentation on the surface of steel plate and strip, and appears more or less in a regular form. It is mainly caused by some hard and sharp foreign bodies or im-purities on work rollers, and every round the roller rolls over, there will leave a same indentation on the surface of steel plate and strip.

Fig. 6. Roll imprint image of cold rolled strips

7. Edge folding
Edge folding is a defect with a folding phenomenon on the edge of steel plate and strip. it is caused by untidy curled edge.

Fig. 7. Edge folding image of cold rolled strips

8. Rust mark
Rust mark is a thin layer of corrosion products on the surface of steel plate and strip. It is caused by high air humidity or small drips on surface under the circumstance of wide temperature fluctuations. If corrosion is very serious, the touch will be obvious, and it will be irregular light spot in image.

Fig. 8. Rust mark image of cold rolled strips

9. Orange texture

Orange texture is a block of irregular rough surface like orange skin and is touchable. It is caused mainly by incompletely removed impurities and greasy dirt on work roller during temper rolling.

Fig. 9. Orange texture image of cold rolled strips

10. Emulsion mark

Emulsion mark is a block of untouchable spot. It is caused by the incompletely washed oiliness of earlier rolling working procedure, it is hard to be removed from surface of steel plate and strip, and it generally presents dark in image.

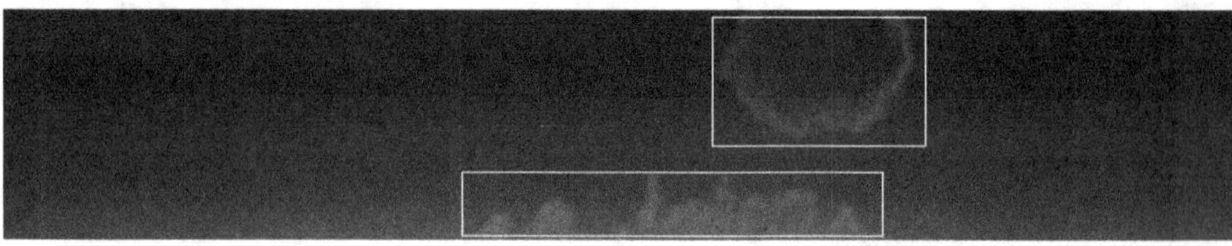

Fig. 10. Emulsion mark image of cold rolled strips

11. Edge crack

Edge crack is a phenomenon of crack or hole at the edge of steel plate and strip. It is caused by linear load odds or strong local stress when rolling or the capacity for deformation of the material is over exceeded.

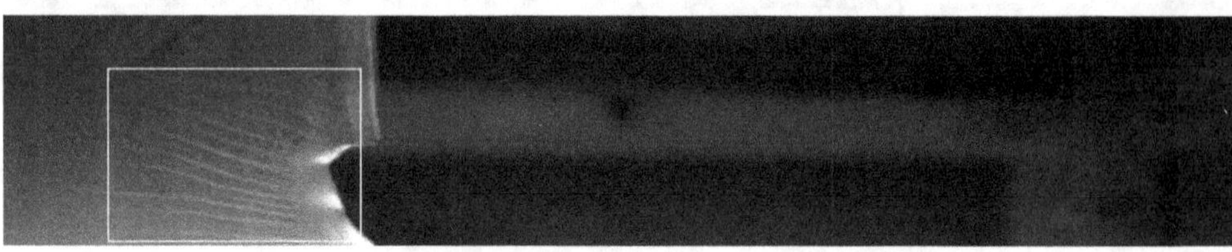

Fig. 11. Edge crack image of cold rolled strips

12. Scale

Scale is a lay of oxide covered on the surface of steel plate and strip. It is caused by high temperature and insufficient descaling when rolling. The scale can be removed by pickling, but it is hard to be completely eradicated.

Fig. 12. Scale image of cold rolled strips

13. Crack

Crack is a phenomenon of local break of steel plate and strip. Because of the surface tension odds caused by impurity inside steel plate and strip or surface stress concentration caused by surface sag of material, crack will appear while rolling. Crack is generally directional, and vertical crack is most frequent, in some special cases, star crack is occasional.

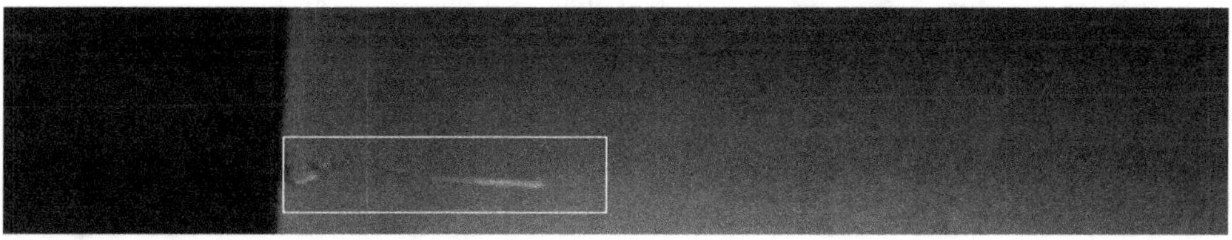

Fig. 13. Crack image of cold rolled strips

14. Air bubble

Air bubble is undischarged air inside steel plate and strip. Some air will discharge when rolling and will induce a pit in the surface of steel plate and strip. It is produced in the steel-making process.

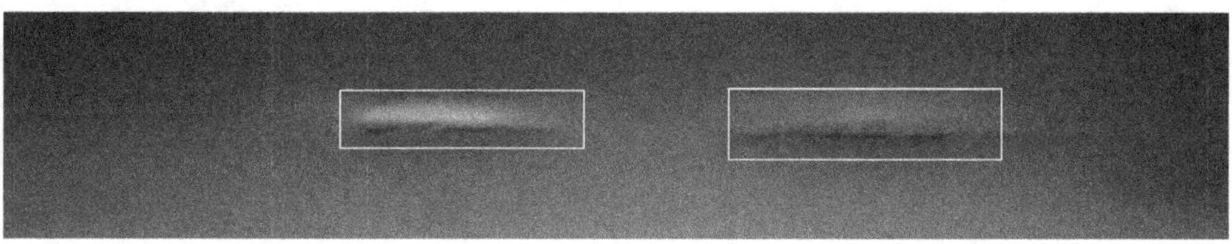

Fig. 14. Air bubble image of cold rolled strips

### 2.3 General system design

In order to content all the requirements of above, a system as Figure 15 is designed. The figure shows a general structure of an online inspection system. The system mainly includes 6 parts, such as detection devices, illumination, parallel computation system, server system, mass memory and console system.

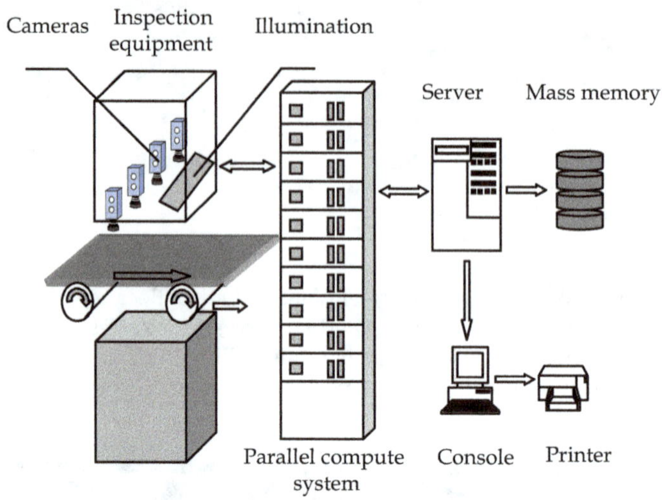


Fig. 15. General structure of an online inspection system

From Figure 15, it can be seen that detection devices are installed in the production line. One set of inspection device consists of several CCD cameras worked together with one illumination unit. Because there are two sides of strips, two sets of inspection devices are designed to meet the requirements, one is for upside inspection, the other is for down side inspection, and both sides of strips must be detected simultaneously.

Illumination part is very important and essential to the system because it determines whether defects are visualized in images captured by the cameras.

There are 2 illumination modes in this system such as dark illumination mode and bright illumination mode. The former is used to detect 3-dimensional defects, and the latter is used to detect 2-dimensional defects. Figure 16 shows these two different illumination modes, Figure 16 (a) is dark illumination mode, and Figure 16 (b) is bright illumination mode.

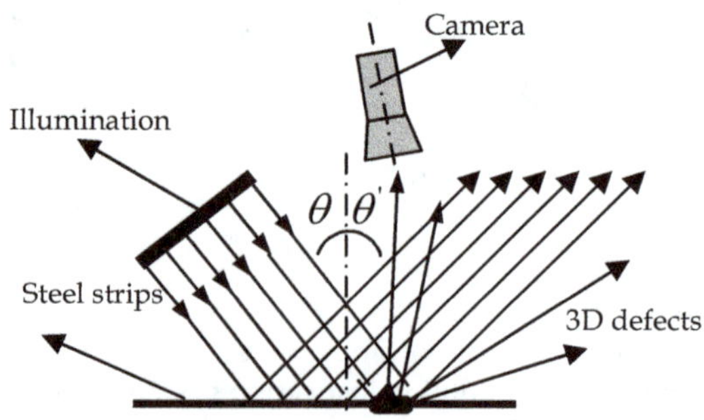


(a) Dark illumination mode

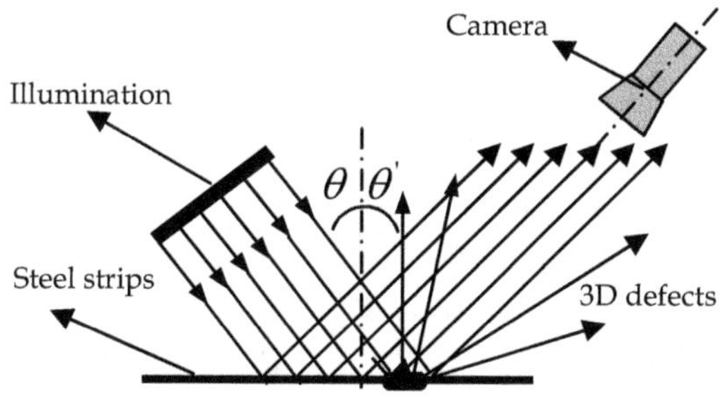


(b) Bright illumination mode

Fig. 16. Two different illumination modes

In dark illumination mode, the steel strips will reflect the light of illumination devie, and only the reflection light of 3D defects will be acquired by camera, but in bright illumination mode, most of reflection light of 3D defects will not be acquired by camera, the reflecrion light of 2D defects will enter into the camera and be acquired as object images.

All the algorithms of whole system are realized by software method, it brings conviences not only for system upgrade, but also for less outside hardware tache to reduce trouble rate. The software is mainly consist of 2 parts such as client software and server software, Figure 17 and Figure 18 are client software flow chart and server software flow chart respectively.

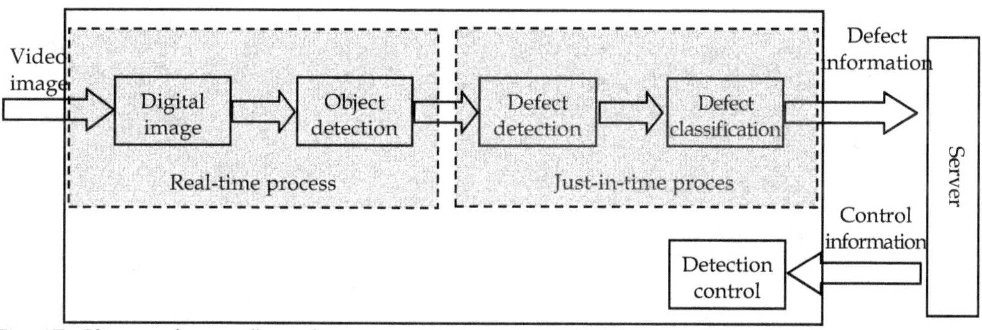


Fig. 17. Client software flow chart

Client software can meet data acquisition function of online inspection and online observation, including image acquisition, image pre-process and analysis, defect inspection, defect feature extraction and defect recognition etc, and it does not require human intervention as long as guaranteeing the veracity, high effect and stability of the client software. Server software mainly realizes offline defect data analysis, statistic report making and all the mutual control of the whole system, etc. At the same time, the server software provides visual man-machine interface, worker of quality inspection department can know about the surface quality of current coil and historic coils directly by the interface and it can make various statistic report according to the requirement of customer.

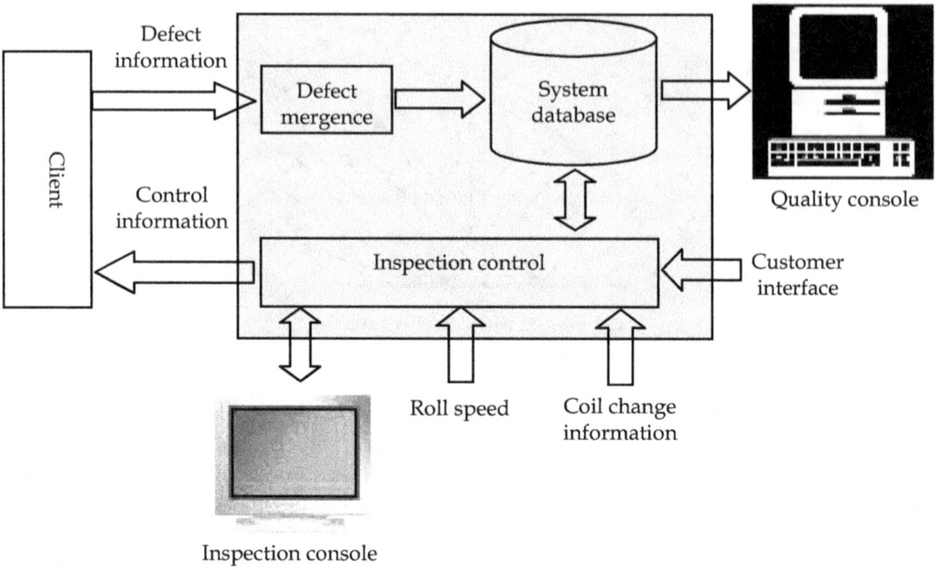


Fig. 18. Server software flow chart

In client software, there are 2 special processes in order realize high speed inspection, they are real-time process and just-in-time process. Real-time process takes charge of some immediate information process, so that the system can meet real-time requirement, and just-in-time process takes charge of other information process when CPU is not in full task, so that the system can settle large amount data problem.

## 3. Main technologies analysis

### 3.1 Image frozen techniques

When applies multimedia technologies to detect the defects of cold rolled strips with high speed, how to acquire high precision and clear image is very important, and it is a difficulty of automatic surface inspection system for online application. The image acquisition of moving objects techniques are mainly image frozen technique.

Image frozen techniques are adopted to capture surface images of strips at high speed. Shutters of cameras are set very high as 1/4000 seconds to make images jitter slightly, while the illumination units supply enough luminance intensity and make images captured by cameras clear. All cameras are synchronized to capture images simultaneously. To keep service performance and increase service life, the illumination units are not always in operation. They are synchronized with shutters of cameras to make them only lighten at the exposure of cameras.

### 3.2 Defects detection techniques of moving strips

As positions and shapes of strips vary continuously during producing, reflection of incident lights is different at different areas of strips. Therefore it leads to different backgrounds in different images captured by cameras. Moreover, gray levels of background differ everywhere in one image because of uneven illumination and reflection. It is difficult to find out defects from non-uniform and ever-changing backgrounds. However, gray levels of backgrounds are gradually changed, while gray levels between backgrounds and defects are abruptly changed. Effective algorithms of defect detection are developed which consists of 4 steps as followings:

1. Background extracted: In this step, backgrounds are found and separated from original images.
2. Gray level calculation: Differential gray levels of backgrounds and original images are calculated.
3. Thresholds decision: One or more threshold values are decided and applied on differential gray levels to determine whether pixels are in defect areas or backgrounds, and pixels in defect areas are marked as "Suspicious Pixels".
4. ROI (Region of Interest) searching and merging; "Region growing" is used to find out defect areas by merging "Suspicious Pixels", and the defect area are called as "Region of Interest", or ROI.

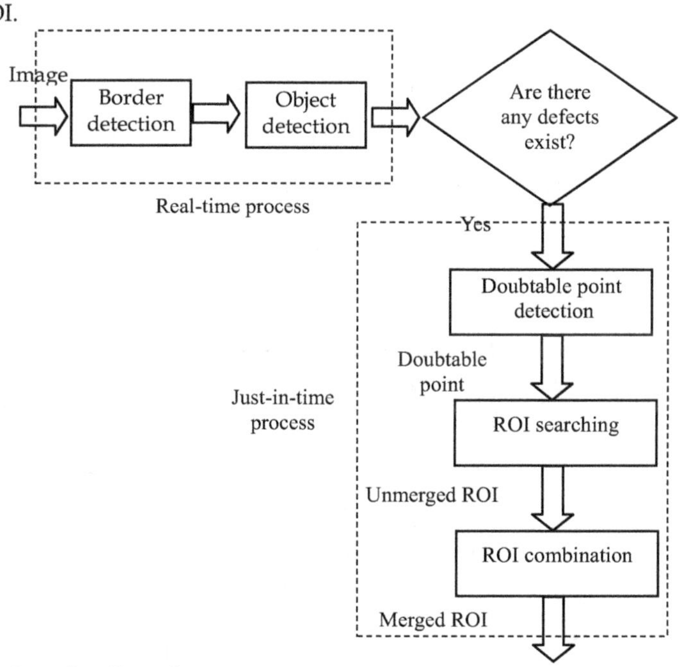


Fig. 19. Defects detection flow chart

### 3.3 Feature extraction and optimization techniques

#### 3.3.1 Space-domain feature extraction

According to the defect character of cold rolled strips, we can extract 4 types of space domain features.

1. Geometric shape features

Geometric shape features are basic features of object, and they are used to describe geometric shape such as simple descriptor, shape descriptor and fixed quadrature. Simple descriptor includes area, border perimeter, region center, etc. Suppose $x$, $y$ are coordinates of horizon and vertical orientation, $R$ is region area, $R_x$ is aggregate of horizon coordinate, $R_y$ is aggregate of vertical coordinate, $f(x,y)$ is image data, $R_d$ is aggregate of defect point in ROI, $R_b$ is aggregate of border point of ROI, some main geometric shape features can be described as followings:

1) Defect area s. It is used to describe the size of defect region as equation (1).

$$S = \sum_{(x,y)\in R_\mathrm{d}} 1 \tag{1}$$

2) Defect perimeter $P$. It is mean defect contour pixel gross as equation (2).

$$P = \sum_{(x,y)\in R_\mathrm{b}} 1 \tag{2}$$

3) Region center $\left(x_\mathrm{c}, y_\mathrm{c}\right)$. It is calculated by barycentric coordinate as equation (3).

$$\begin{cases} x_\mathrm{c} = \dfrac{1}{S} \sum\limits_{(x,y)\in R_\mathrm{d}} x \\ y_\mathrm{c} = \dfrac{1}{S} \sum\limits_{(x,y)\in R_\mathrm{d}} y \end{cases} \tag{3}$$

4) Defect compact $C$. It is calculated by equation (4).

$$C = \frac{\|P\|^2}{4\pi \cdot S} \tag{4}$$

5) Defect quadrature feature. There are total 7 quadrature features, and can be described as equation (5) to equation (11), they are fixed for shift, rotation and scale transform

$$\mathrm{IM}_1 = \eta_{20} + \eta_{02} \tag{5}$$

$$\mathrm{IM}_2 = \left(\eta_{20} - \eta_{02}\right)^2 + 4\eta_{11}^2 \tag{6}$$

$$\mathrm{IM}_3 = \left(\eta_{30} - 3\eta_{12}\right)^2 + \left(\eta_{03} - 3\eta_{21}\right)^2 \tag{7}$$

$$\mathrm{IM}_4 = \left(\eta_{30} + \eta_{12}\right)^2 + \left(\eta_{03} + \eta_{21}\right)^2 \tag{8}$$

$$\begin{aligned} \mathrm{IM}_5 = {} & \left(\eta_{30} - 3\eta_{12}\right)\left(\eta_{30} + \eta_{12}\right)\left[\left(\eta_{30} + \eta_{12}\right)^2 - 3\left(\eta_{21} + \eta_{03}\right)^2\right] \\ & + \left(3\eta_{21} - \eta_{03}\right)\left(\eta_{21} + \eta_{03}\right)\left[3\left(\eta_{30} + \eta_{12}\right)^2 - \left(\eta_{21} + \eta_{03}\right)^2\right] \end{aligned} \tag{9}$$

$$\mathrm{IM}_6 = \left(\eta_{20} - \eta_{02}\right)\left[\left(\eta_{30} + \eta_{12}\right)^2 - \left(\eta_{21} + \eta_{03}\right)^2\right] + 4\eta_{11}\left(\eta_{30} + \eta_{12}\right)\left(\eta_{21} + \eta_{03}\right) \tag{10}$$

$$\begin{aligned}\mathrm{IM}_7 = &\left(3\eta_{21}-\eta_{03}\right)\left(\eta_{30}+\eta_{12}\right)\left[\left(\eta_{30}+\eta_{12}\right)^2-3\left(\eta_{21}+\eta_{03}\right)^2\right] \\ &+\left(3\eta_{12}-\eta_{30}\right)\left(\eta_{21}+\eta_{03}\right)\left[3\left(\eta_{30}+\eta_{12}\right)^2-\left(\eta_{21}+\eta_{03}\right)^2\right]\end{aligned} \tag{11}$$

There are total 19 geometrical feature parameters extracted.

2. Gray level features

Gray level features are very useful in classification and they depict many essential characters of gray image. They are mostly consisted of average, variance, kurtosis, skewness, enrage and entropy of gray level etc., all these characters can be calculated by gray level histogram. There are total 36 gray level character parameters extracted in the software.

1) Gray level average $\bar{b}$

$$\bar{b} = \sum_{b=0}^{L-1} bP(b) \tag{12}$$

2) Gray level variance $v$

$$v^2 = \sum_{b=0}^{L-1} \left(b-\bar{b}\right)^2 P\left(b\right) \tag{13}$$

3) Gray level kurtosis $H_s$

$$H_s = \frac{1}{v^3} \sum_{b=0}^{L-1} \left(b-\bar{b}\right)^3 P\left(b\right) \tag{14}$$

4) Gray level skewness $H_k$

$$H_k = \frac{1}{v^4} \sum_{b=0}^{L-1} \left(b-\bar{b}\right)^4 P\left(b\right)-3 \tag{15}$$

5) Gray level enrage $H_p$

$$H_p = \sum_{b=0}^{L-1} P(b)^2 \tag{16}$$

6) Gray level entropy $H_E$

$$H_E = -\sum_{b=0}^{L-1} P\left(b\right)\log_2\left[P\left(b\right)\right] \tag{17}$$

At the same time, there are 3 other gray level features such as max gray level, min graylevel and gray level scope, therefore there are total 9 gray level types.

Now, we can extract up 9 gray levels for background images, defect suspicious pixel images, contrast images and defect images respectively, and can get total 36 gray level features.

3. Projection features

It is always very practical to map high-dimensional data into low-dimensional data in engineering, because low-dimensional data are much easier to analyze than high-dimensional data. Projection features are extracted by mapping two-dimensional image signal to one-dimensional digital wave signal, such as wave features, peak value features, impulse features, margin features, skewness features, kurtosis features, and so on. In Figure 20, a defect in image is projected to X direction, and formed a Gray level – X coordinate. There are total 24 projection features in the software.

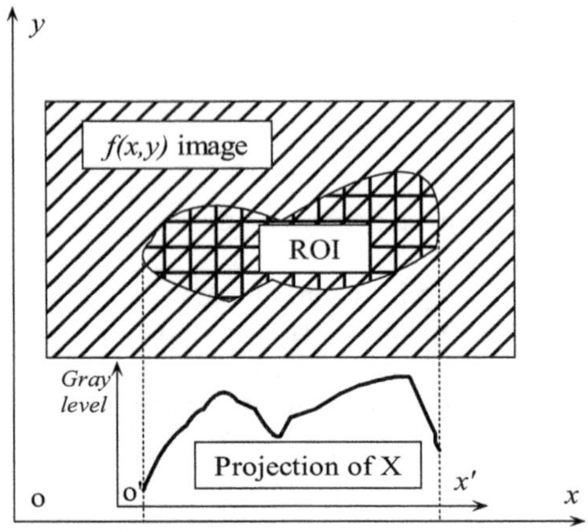


Fig. 20. X direction projection of defect in an image

Defect image can project to X aix, Y aix, 45° diagonal and 135° diagonal, they can be described as equation (18) to equation (21) .

$$p\left(0^{\circ},t\right)=\int_{R_{\mathrm{d}}} f\left(t,y\right)dy \tag{18}$$

$$p\left(90^{\circ},t\right)=\int_{R_{\mathrm{d}}} f\left(x,t\right)dx \tag{19}$$

$$p\left(45^{\circ},t\right)=\int_{R_{\mathrm{d}}} f\left(x,x-\sqrt{2}\,t\right)\mathrm{d}x \tag{20}$$

$$p\left(135^{\circ},t\right)=\int_{R_{\mathrm{d}}} f\left(x,\sqrt{2}\,t-x\right)\mathrm{d}x \tag{21}$$

According to the 4 types projection, we can get

1) Peak value $\hat{X}$ :

$$\hat{X}=\max\left(\left|x\left(t\right)\right|\right) \tag{22}$$

2) Average peak value $\overline{X}_{\mathrm{p}}$ :

$$\overline{X}_{\mathrm{p}}=\frac{1}{T}\sum_{t}\left|x\left(t\right)\right| \tag{23}$$

3) Mean square root $X_{\mathrm{RMS}}$ :

$$X_{\mathrm{RMS}}=\sqrt{\frac{1}{T}\sum_{t}x^{2}\left(t\right)dt} \tag{24}$$

4) Square root scope $X_{\mathrm{r}}$ :

$$X_{\mathrm{r}}=\left(\frac{1}{T}\sum_{t}\left|x\left(t\right)\right|^{1/2}dt^{2}\right) \tag{25}$$

Consequently, we define 6 projection features as following:

1) Projection wave features $F_{\mathrm{B}}$ :

$$F_{\mathrm{B}} = \frac{X_{\mathrm{RMS}}}{\overline{X}_{\mathrm{p}}} \tag{26}$$

2) Projection impulse features $F_{\mathrm{M}}$ :

$$F_{\mathrm{M}} = \frac{\hat{X}}{\overline{X}_{\mathrm{p}}} \tag{27}$$

3) Projection peak value features $F_{\mathrm{F}}$ :

$$F_{\mathrm{F}} = \frac{\hat{X}}{X_{\mathrm{RMS}}} \tag{28}$$

4) Projection margin features $F_{\mathrm{Y}}$ :

$$F_{\mathrm{Y}} = \frac{\hat{X}}{X_{\mathrm{r}}} \tag{29}$$

5) Projection skewness features $F_{\mathrm{S}}$ :

$$F_{\mathrm{S}} = \sum_{x} x^{3} p\left(x\right) dx \tag{30}$$

6) Projection kurtosis features $F_{\mathrm{K}}$ :

$$F_{\mathrm{K}} = \sum_{x} x^{4} p\left(x\right) dx \tag{31}$$

According to 4 direction projection, there are total 24 projection features can be extracted, and can be used to recognize the defects.

4. Textural features

For some special defects, they have obvious textural features, Figure 21 shows an image with obvious textural features.

Fig. 21. Typical defect image with obvious textural features

Textural features can be achieved by gray level co-occurrence matrix with statistics, as in equation (32).

$$P(g_1, g_2) = \frac{\#\left\{\left[\left(x_1, y_1\right), \left(x_2, y_2\right)\right] \in S \mid f\left(x_1, y_1\right) = g_1 \;\&\; f\left(x_2, y_2\right) = g_2\right\}}{\# S} \tag{32}$$

According to the gray level co-occurrence matrix, 4 textual features such as second-order moment, entropy, contrast and homogeneity can be achieved.

1) Textural second-order moment $W_{\mathrm{M}}$ :

$$W_{\mathrm{M}} = \sum_{g_1} \sum_{g_2} P^2\left(g_1, g_2\right) \tag{33}$$

2) Textural entropy $W_{\mathrm{E}}$ :

$$W_{\mathrm{E}} = -\sum_{g_1} \sum_{g_2} P\left(g_1, g_2\right)) \log P\left(g_1, g_2\right) \tag{34}$$

3) Textural contrast $W_{\mathrm{C}}$ :

$$W_{\mathrm{C}} = \sum_{g_1} \sum_{g_2} \left|g_1 - g_2\right| P\left(g_1, g_2\right) \tag{35}$$

4) Textural homogeneity $W_{\mathrm{H}}$ :

$$W_{\mathrm{H}} = \sum_{g_1} \sum_{g_2} \frac{P\left(g_1, g_2\right)}{k + \left|g_1 - g_2\right|} \tag{36}$$

### 3.3.2 Frequency-domain feature extraction

In order to extract frequency domain feature, all the defect images are given by the size of 64 × 64 shown as Figure 22.

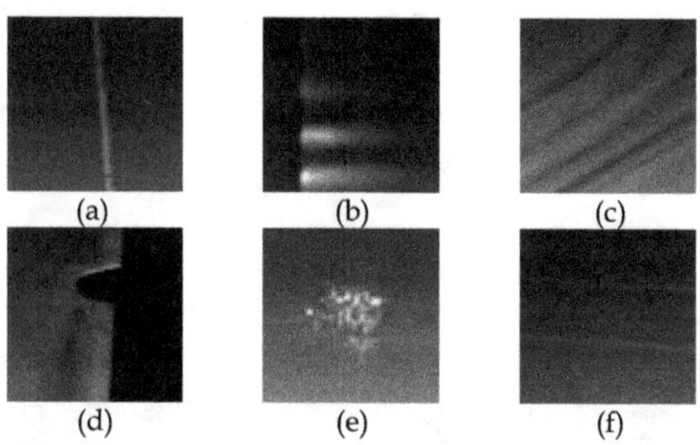

Fig. 22. Some typical defect images with size of 64× 64, (a) is scratch, (b) is edge folding, (c) is feather imprint, (d) is edge crack, (e) is point felt and (f) is felt horizontal texture.

Applying Fast Fourier Transform (FFT) (Chu, E., 2000) to the images and the spectrum images can be achieved. According to the qualities of Fast Fourier Transform, Fast Fourier Transform can transform images from space-domain to frequency-domain, and concentrated most of energies on the center, it can not only reflect gray features and geometrical features of defect images, but also make fast convolution and object recognition to become very real. Therefore, regarding gray values of spectrum images as feature information of defect images can recognize defects, especially the pixels near the central area of spectrum images. The typical spectrum images of FFT are shown as Figure 23.

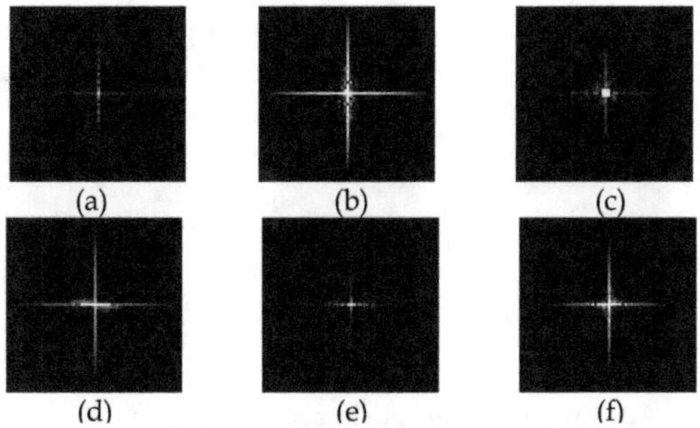


Fig. 23. Typical FFT images of Figure 22 with size of 64× 64, (a) is scratch, (b) is edge folding, (c) is feather imprint, (d) is edge crack, (e) is point felt and (f) is felt horizontal texture.

According to the result of FFT, it can be seen that nearly all energies are concentrated on the center area, and at the same time, if make all pixels of FFT image as features, the feature set will be too large and unnecessary, and will affect recognition result to some extent in fact. As a consequence, based on many experiments, the crisscross region shown as Figure 4 is taken as original feature set, and the feature number can be calculated with equation (37).

$$n = 32 \times (a + b) - ab \tag{37}$$

In the paper, parameter $a$ is 4 and parameter $b$ is 4 too. Therefore, the total chosen region includes 240 pixels, and the original feature set includes 240 features. The feature set can reflect local outstanding feature information of frequency-domain.

Fig. 24. Optimized crisscross original Feature set region. There are two parameters, parameter a is region width and parameter b is region height.

After given an original feature set, another two extended features are introduced, one is named Sum of Valid Pixels (SVP), and the other is Repletion Ratio of Centre Region (RRCR). The definition of SVP is the count of all the pixels whose values are larger than a given threshold in the full FFT images, therefore by defining SVP, the region outside the crisscross region is taken into consideration, and the feature reflects global statistic feature information of frequency-domain.

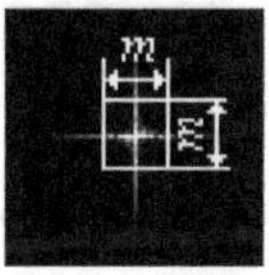

Fig. 25. Definition of Repletion Ratio of Centre Region (RRCR) and parameter m is width of centre square region.

Figure 25 shows the definition of RRCR, and it can be defined as equation (38):

$$\eta_m = N / m^2 \times 100\%, \qquad m < 64 \tag{38}$$

$N$ is amount of features whose value are greater than a given threshold value in a $m \times m$ centre region. Parameter m can be given as a needed value. This feature can reflects local statistic feature information of frequency-domain in low frequency section. In the paper, three RRCR features are extracted, they are $\eta_5$ , $\eta_{10}$ and $\eta_{15}$.

### 3.3.3 Feature optimization

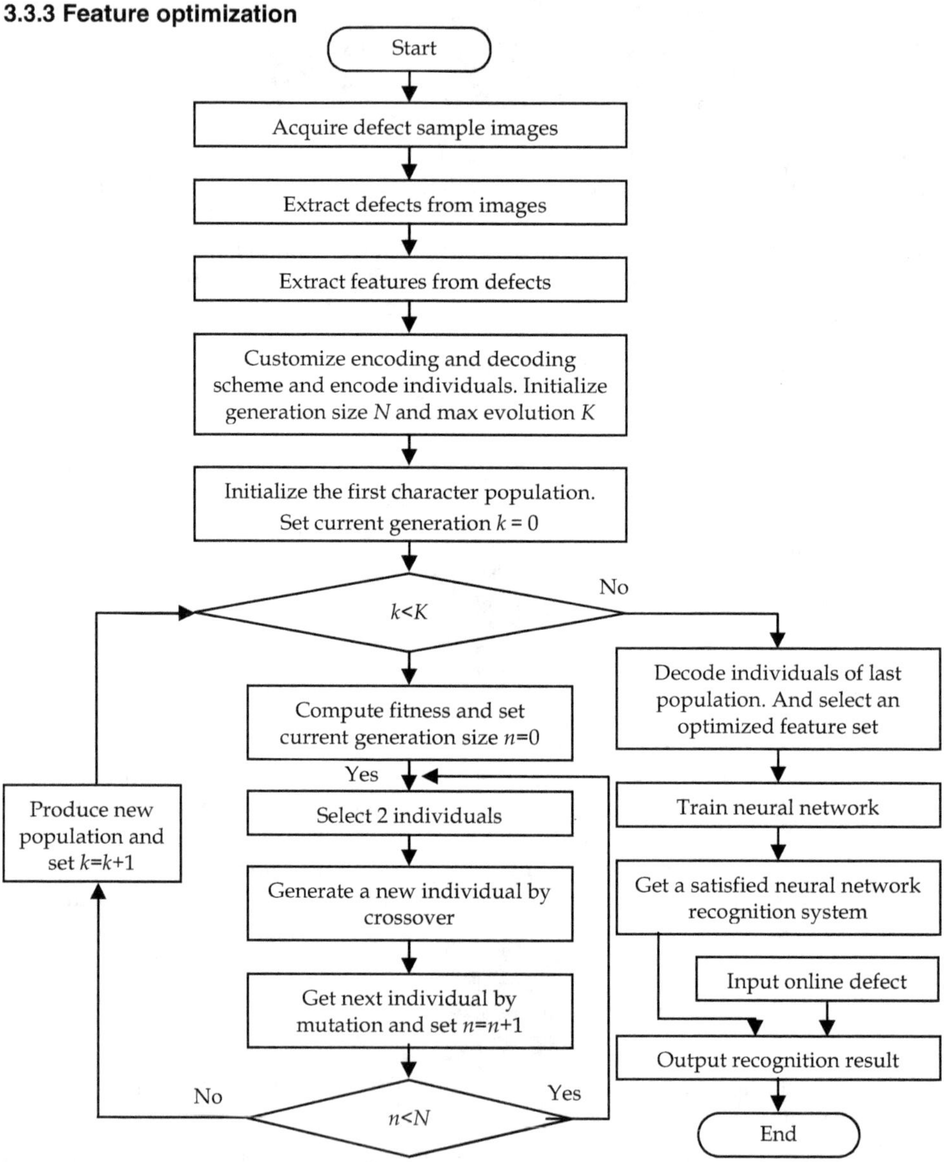


Fig. 26. Feature optimization and defect recognition of hot rolled strips

The process of using genetic algorithm (Hannes, L., 2006) to optimize the feature set is a process of setting the parameters of genetic algorithm which can describe problem best. Genetic algorithm is used to optimize the region of original crisscross frequency-domain feature set which includes 240 features and space-domain feature set which includes 82 features.

In order to find a best fitness function for genetic algorithm, we tried to use mutual information entropy as fitness function. It is known that the object function of mutual information entropy is a problem of the largest values. Based on experiments, and according to analysis of surface defects of steel strips, mutual information entropy is made as fitness function of genetic algorithm, and it is shown as equation (39);

$$\begin{aligned} I(E,F) &= \frac{1}{N}[I^*(E,F) - I(F)] \\ &= \frac{1}{N}[\sum_{i=1}^{n}\sum_{j=1}^{N} I(w_i, x_j) - \frac{1}{N-1}\sum_{i=1}^{N}\sum_{j=1, j\neq i}^{N} I(x_i, x_j)] \end{aligned} \tag{39}$$

where

$$I(w_i, x_j) = \sum_{k=1}^{K} p(w_i, x_{j,k}) \bullet \log\frac{p(w_i, x_{j,k})}{p(w_i) \bullet p(x_{j,k})} \tag{40}$$

$$I(x_i, x_j) = \sum_{h=1}^{K}\sum_{k=1}^{K} p(x_{i,h}, x_{j,k}) \bullet \log\frac{p(x_{i,h}, x_{j,k})}{p(x_{i,h}) \bullet p(x_{j,k})} \tag{41}$$

### 3.4 Local border search algorithm

According to the statistics of cold rolled strip, there are more than 30% defects in border region, therefore how to extract the border from acquired images fast and accurate is very important for defect detection. Figure 27 shows a local pixel image with a $45^\circ$ border. From the figure, it can be seen that the next border point will arise in one neighbor pixel, and if the border angle is smaller than 45o, the next border point will arise among on neighbor pixel. Therefore, , the next border point must be found if let the algorithm search a small neighbor region such as 3 pixels, and here bring forward Local Border Search Algorithm (LBSA) as follows. Figure 28 is flow chart of the new algorithm.

After the algorithm finishes, the border can be get, and every horizontal border point coordinates can be expressed with equation (42) and vertical border point coordinate can be expressed with equation (43).

$$\left(x, a[x]\right) \quad x = 0,1,2,\cdots, Width-1 \tag{42}$$

$$\left(a[y], y\right) \quad y = 0,1,2,\cdots, Height-1 \tag{43}$$

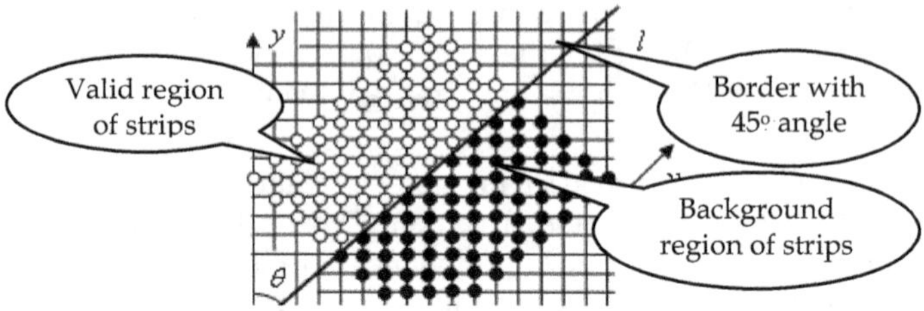


Fig. 27. A local pixel image with a 45 border

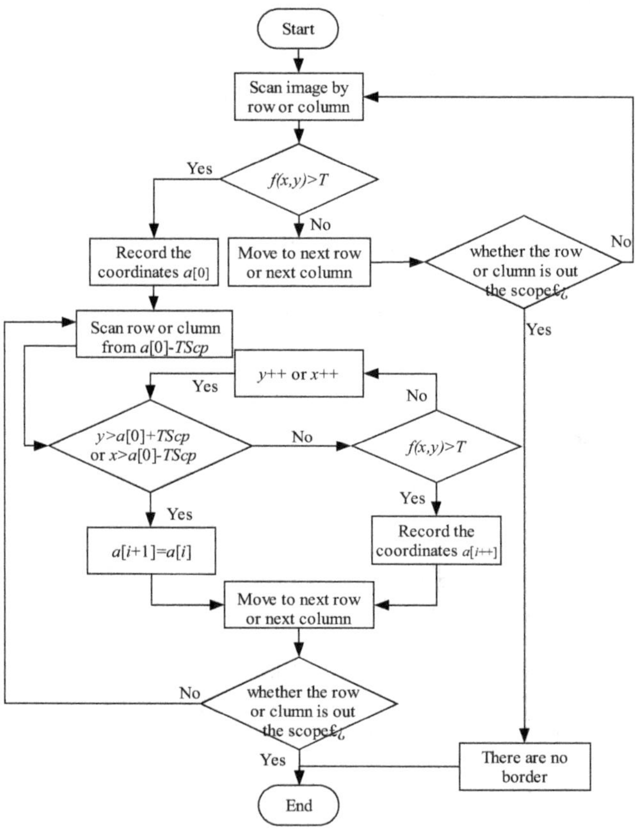


Fig. 28. Flow chart of Local Border Search Algorithm (LBSA)

For some complicated border types shown as Figure 33, it can be get both two horizontal and vertical border lines with equation (44), and then utilize the condition as equation (45) to calculate the point of intersection$(X,Y)$ of the two border line, and the valid region of strips can be achieved.

$$\begin{cases} (x, a[x]) & x = 0, 1, 2, \cdots, Width - 1 \\ (b[y], y) & x = 0, 1, 2, \cdots, Height - 1 \end{cases} \tag{44}$$

$$\begin{cases} x = b[y] \\ y = a[x] \end{cases} \tag{45}$$

Fig. 29. Left border image of cold rolled strips

For example, Figure 29 is a 756×141 cold rolled strip image, and the valid region of steel strip lies in the left part of the image. When input the image into the Local Border Search Algorithm and give its border type, the algorithm can firstly search from right of row 0 with the coordinates of $(755,0)$, till first border point is found, and records the horizontal coordinate $a[0]$, it will meet the condition $|f(a[0],0)-f(a[0]+1,0)>T|$. After that the algorithm can search the next border point with a given scope of $TScp=3$, and the search scope of row 1 is $[a[0]+3, a[0]-3)$, and the border point must be appeared in the small region, so that a point $(a[1],1)$ can be found and it will meet the condition of $|f(a[1],1)-f(a[1]+1,1)>T|$. Similarly, the algorithm can run row by row till all border point are found, and get all the coordinates $a[2]$、$a[3]$、$\cdots$、$a[139]$、$a[140]$, and at last, the search result is as Figure 30 With the same method, other border type can be achieved.

Fig. 30. Extraction result of Figure 2 (b) by LBSA

(a) Extraction result by Local Border Search Algorithm

(b) Extraction result by traditional algorithm

Fig. 31. Contrast effects of extraction results

Fig. 32. Extraction result left valid region with right border which is near the border of the image

Fig. 33. Extraction result of complicated border type of top-right border

Figure 31 is the contrast effects of extraction result for the same image with different algorithm, and Figure 31(a) is extracted by Local Border Search Algorithm (LBSA), and Figure 31(b) is extracted by traditional Gray Level Gradient Threshold Algorithm (GLGTA). It can be seen that there are some noise inside Figure 31(b) but the effect is very perfect in Figure 31(a). Figure 33 shows the extraction result of complicated border type of top-right border. Table 1 shows the contrast effects of extraction results from 300 right border images, and it can be seen that the speed of the new algorithm is increased over 22-220 times than the traditional algorithm.

| Sample image | Distance between strip border and image border (Pixels) | Time cost of Gray Level Gradient Threshold Algorithm (T1: ms) | Time cost of Local Border Search Algorithm (T2: ms) | T1/T2 (times) |
|---|---|---|---|---|
| Fig. 30 | Greater than 600 pixels | 2.0~2.2 | 0.01~0.03 | 67~220 |
| Fig. 32 | Smaller than 200 pixels | 0.65~0.75 | 0.01~0.03 | 22~75 |

Table 1. Contrast table of right border extraction

Although Local Border Search Algorithm is more advantageous in search accuracy and speed of border than traditional algorithms, it is still short in some aspects. The main shortages are: (1) It is strongly dependent on prior knowledge; (2) It is sensitive to initial point.

In order to overcome the weaknesses above, deep research is carried out mainly from following three aspects:

1. Introducing a small neighborhood to the algorithm

Changing comparison between pure pixels to two small neighborhoods, generally, the neighborhood can be selected as a $m \times n(m > 0, n > 0)$ regular area or crisscross area. Then by calculating average of neighborhood or median etc. replace old gray value with the result. After improving it, the algorithm can remove disturbance of local noise, raise accuracy of border, and make the algorithm owning a higher quality of anti-noise. The neighbors can be chose as Figure 34.

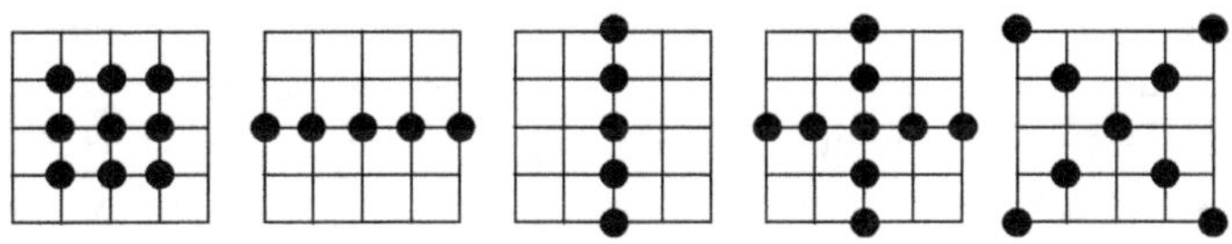

(a) (b) (c) (d) (e)

Fig. 34. Neighbor region in common use, (a) Square neighbor; (b) Horizontal neighbor; (c) Vertical neighbor; (d) 3× 3 strong connection neighbor; (e) 3× 3 weak connection neighbour

2. Modifying search rules of initial point

Whenever the gray value change reaches a given threshold value, recording the point as initial point of border. If there is no such point, enter next loop till such point appears. The advantage of this method is that we can find the border point even with no gray changes.

3. Adding judgment rule of ending point

Defining wrong permitting search times in Local Border Search Algorithm, if no border ending point is found in the scope of wrong permitting search times, the algorithm continues, when there is no border ending point is found beyond the scope of wrong permitting times, the algorithm stops.

After improving Local Border Search Algorithm from the three aspects above, the expanded algorithm can still keep the complexity as $O(n)$, and meanwhile, it can be used to detect high contrast defects of cold rolled strips fast and accurately, and can be used as fast thinning algorithm of image.

### 3.5 Defect classification techniques

Artificial neural network is a parallel distributed information processing system. It is a network constituted by many processing units which are connected each other by unidirectional signal path. These processing units are called artificial neural units, and have the abilities of local memory and local information processing. Every processing unit outputs to an expected connection unidirectionally and transmits the same signal which is called output signal of processing unit. The output signal of processing unit can be any demanded mathematic types. Under complete local constraint circumstances, information processing executed in every processing unit can be any definition, namely the information processing depends only on the memorized value of itself and current value of the input stimulated signal of the processing unit. Neural network is an abstraction and simplification of human brain in microstructure and function, and reflects some fundamental characters such as parallel processing, learning, association, pattern classification , memory, and so on.

Obviously, according to the above characters of neural network, applying neural network to surface defect recognition of cold rolled strips is a good choice. In the application, LVQ neural network (Kohonen, T., 1992) is applied to recognize the defects.

1. LVQ neural network

LVQ neural network consists of 3 parts such as input layer, hidden layers and output layer. The hidden layer is also called competitive layer or Kohonen layer, and it is completely linked between input layer and hidden layer but just partly connected between hidden layer and output layer, and every output neuron is connected with different group of hidden neuron. The training process of LVQ neural network is in fact a process of continually competition and weight updating process among all neuron units of hidden layer. Figure 35 is topological structure of LVQ neural network.

Given a sequence of input documents, an initial group of reference vectors $w_k$ is selected. In each iteration, a $x_i$ document is selected and the vectors w are updated, so that it will adapt better to xi. The LVQ algorithm works as follows.

For each class k, a weight vector wk is associated. In each repetition, the algorithm selects a xi input document and compares it with each weight vector $w_k$, using the Euclidean distance $\|x_i - w_k\|$, so that the winner will be the weight vector $w_c$ nearest to $x_i$, with c as the index of that weight vector:

$$\|x_i - w_c\| = \min_k \{\|x_i - w_c\|\} \tag{46}$$

The classes compete among themselves in order to find which is most similar to the input vector, so that the winner will be that one with less euclidean distance with respect to the input document. Only the winner class will modify its weights using a reinforced learning algorithm, either positive or negative, depending on whether the classification is correct or not. Thus, if the winner class belongs to the same class as the input vector, it will increase the weights, moving slightly closer to the input vector (prize). On the contrary, if the winner class is different from the input vector class, it will decrease the weights, moving slightly further from the input vector (punishment). Let $x_i(t)$ be an input document at time *t*, and $w_k(t)$ the weight vector for the class *k* at time *t*.

The following equations define the basic learning process for the LVQ algorithm:

$$w_c(t+1) = w_c(t) + s \cdot \alpha(t)[x_i(t) - w_c(t)] \tag{47}$$

where $s = 0$, if $k \neq c$; $s = 1$, if $x_i(t)$ and $w_c(t)$ belong to the same class; and $s = -1$, if they are not the same class. Where $\alpha(t)$ is learning rate, always between 0 and 1, is a monotonically decreasing function of time. It is recommended that $\alpha(t)$ should initially be rather small, especially smaller than 0.1, and $\alpha(t)$ continues decreasing to a given threshold *u*, very close to 0. Usually, $\alpha(0)$ is always initialized in 0.005, decreasing linearly to $u$ = 0.001, according to the following equation where *K* is the number of classes :

$$\alpha(t+1) = \alpha(t) - \frac{\alpha(0) - u}{K} \tag{48}$$

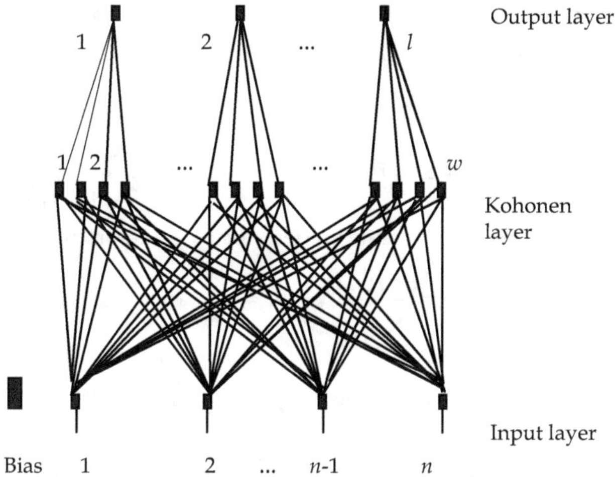


Fig. 35. Topological structure of LVQ neural network

2. Parameter optimization method of neural network

In order to choose best parameters for neural network, traditional methods are all decided by experience, but in fact, these parameters are not optimized parameters, a new parameter optimization method of neural network is put up here, and it can settle the problem perfectly.

The new parameter optimization method of neural network is aiming at finding inner parameters for describing practical problem based on small-samples(Tang, B., 2003), so that the parameters can meet the solution of the problem, and it makes possible for avoiding blindly finding possible parameters of neural network. Figure 36 shows the flowchart of the new parameter optimization method based on small-samples.

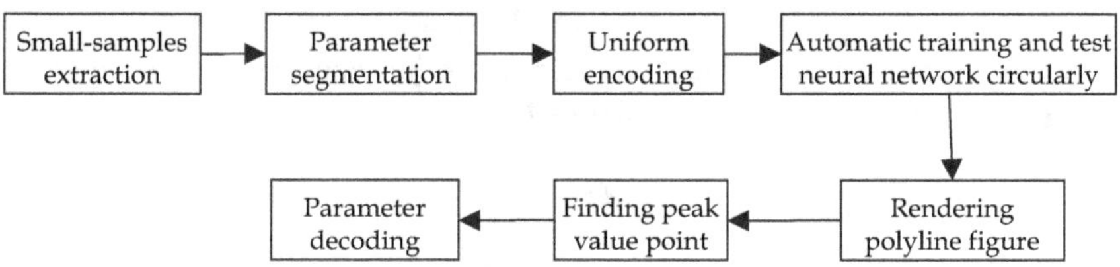


Fig. 36. Flowchart of parameter optimization algorithm

1) Extraction of small-samples

In order to make parameters reflect the essence of practical problem, a certain proportion of samples is extracted from all the samples to form a new sample aggregation, named small-samples, and let the proportion be$\eta$ . We supposed that the original sample aggregation is $P_0$ as equation (49).

$$P_0 = \{X_1, X_2, \cdots, X_n\} \tag{49}$$

The amount of every item inside the original sample aggregation is $p_0^1, p_0^2, \cdots, p_0^n$ respectively. At the same time, we supposed that the new sample aggregation is $P_s$ as equation (50)

$$P_s = \{X_1', X_2', \cdots, X_n'\} \tag{50}$$

Its amount is N, therefore the extraction rule is defined as following:
Extracting every class of samples by its proportion from sample library, and defining the number of every sample as $p_s^i$, therefore it can describe as equation (51).

$$p_s^i = \frac{p_0^i}{\sum_{j=1}^{n} p_0^j} N \qquad i = 1, 2 \cdots n \tag{51}$$

Consequently the distribution law of extracted new small-samples $P_s$ is the same as original samples $P_0$, in another word that the extracted small-samples can stand for the original samples to some extent, and the parameters of neural network selected under such small-samples can express the map relationship of the neural network under the whole original samples. Such small-samples selected by the method are so called proportional samples. A group of training small-samples $p_{s1}$ and testing small-samples $p_{s2}$ can be extracted in the practical application.

2) Parameter segmentation and uniform encoding
When applying it to practical engineering project, firstly it is necessary to know all the parameters of neural network, and choose the parameters which are related with the essence of problem among all the parameters. Now defining the number of selected parameters as p, and all parameters are independent and have no relation with samples theoretically, in another word that the selected parameter variables can reflect the essence characters of the practical problem. After determined parameters which need be optimized, it is time to segment all the parameters under a scope of experience values or theoretical values.
Supposed that all these p parameters are divided into such parts respectively as $C_1, C_2, \cdots, C_p$, then combining all the parameters under unrepeated rule, and there are total M combinations, it can be described as equation (52):

$$M = \prod_{i=1}^{P} C_{C_i}^1 \tag{52}$$

What come on next? We must encoding the parameters for every combination, and assign a number to it as 1, 2, ..., M. There are mainly 2 steps in this stage as following:
Firstly, determining the order of every parameter and fixing its position from the front to the back. Figure 37 shows the exact order of every parameter in the same group.

| $P_1$ | $P_2$ | ... | $P_M$ |
|---|---|---|---|

Fig. 37. Exact order of every parameter

Secondly, a uniform serial number is given to every combination. When a specific number is given to a front parameter, the back parameter will traverse all possible values, and the number will increase 1 step by step till all M possibilities is finished, and the encoding finished.

3) Automatic training circularly and plotting polyline figure

After encoding all the parameters, an automatic program must be developed, and every group of parameters is used as parameters of neural network respectively to do training and testing. The procedure can be described as followings:

a. Take out one specific group of parameters as parameters of neural network.

b. Training the neural network with the training small-samples of $P_{s1}$.

c. When the training finished, saved the trained neural network model for testing.

d. Testing the neural network with testing small-samples $p_{s2}$.

e. Making a statistic of its recognition rate.

f. Repeating step "a" to "e" again till all *M* group of parameters are traversed for one time.

g. Using the *M* recognition rate values under different *M* group of parameters of neural network to plot a polyline figure on a coordinate system.

h. Finding the peak recognition rate value of the figure, and writing down its related group number of parameters which is selected as the final parameters of neural network under the original samples.

## 4. Application and experiments

Table 2 is samples distribution table which are all acquired by surface defect online inspection system of cold rolled strips from locale of certain production line in China. From the table, it can be seen that there are total 12 classes of defects of cold rolled strips, and there are total 6360 original training samples and 3180 original testing samples.

According the extraction rule of small-samples of parameter selection method described in preceding part, a training small-samples aggregation $P_{s1}$ and a testing small-samples aggregation $P_{s2}$ will be get from original training samples and testing samples under a given extraction proportion of 8% and 4% respectively.

| Item | Scratches | coil Breaks | point sticks | Feathers | white spots | roll Imprints | edge Foldings | rusts | Emulsion marks | Orange peels | edge Cracks | other | sum |
|---|---|---|---|---|---|---|---|---|---|---|---|---|---|
| Number of training samples | 1223 | 1398 | 1203 | 1153 | 463 | 295 | 193 | 121 | 89 | 80 | 70 | 71 | 6360 |
| Number of testing samples | 612 | 699 | 602 | 577 | 232 | 147 | 96 | 61 | 45 | 40 | 35 | 35 | 3180 |

Table 2. Samples distribution table of system

For LVQ3 neural network, the number of neurons in compete layer must be determined firstly, and according the system, it is assigned 106. Secondly, make sure that there are three parameters which are related with the essence of described system, they are initial learn rate η (0), relative learn rate $\varepsilon$ and window width m. According to the experience of LVQ3 neural network, the experience scope of all the three parameters can be described as equation (53).

$$\begin{cases} 0.01 \leq \eta(0) \leq 0.1 \\ 0.05 \leq \varepsilon \leq 0.3 \\ 0.1 \leq m \leq 0.5 \end{cases} \tag{53}$$

After experiments, polyline will be plotted under coordinates of recognition rate and parameter combination number as shown in Figure 38. It can be seen that the coordinate (48, 96.2%) stands for the peak point in the figure, it means that No. 48 parameter combination can describe the practical problem better than other parameter combination of LVQ3 neural network, and the test result can reach the highest recognition rate of 96.2%. By decoding we can get the parameters of LVQ3 neural network as Table 3.

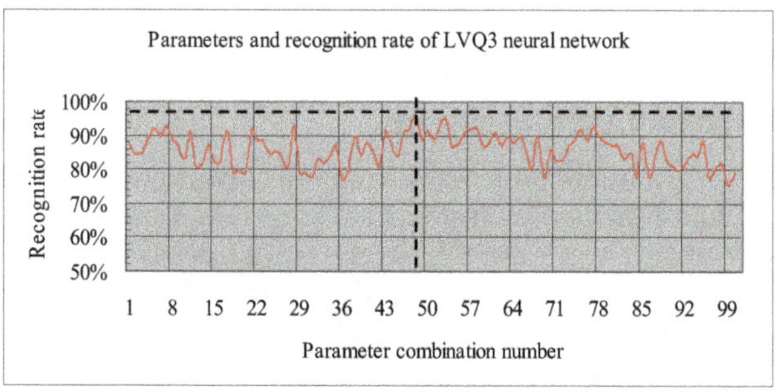


Fig. 38. Curve of optimized parameter selection of LVQ3 neural network

It can be seen from Table 4 that the recognition rate under No.1 group of parameters reaches to 89.69%, and it is the highest in table, but under other 7 group of parameters, the recognition rates are all lower than it. Therefore, the experiments here fully proved that using the optimized parameters of neural network by the new parameter selection method as the parameters of neural network, the classification information can be expressed more accurately, a higher recognition rate can be get when applying to recognize surface defect of cold rolled strips.

| Item | Neuron number of input layer | Neuron number of competion layer | Neuron number of output layer | Initial learn rate $\eta(0)$ | Relative learn rate $\varepsilon$ | Window width $m$ | Iteration times |
|---|---|---|---|---|---|---|---|
| Value | 22 | 1276 | 12 | 0.05 | 0.1 | 0.3 | 51040 |

Table 3. Parameters of LVQ3 neural network

| No. | Training condition | | | Testing result | | |
|---|---|---|---|---|---|---|
| | $\eta(0)$ | $\varepsilon$ | $m$ | Number of correct recognition | Recognition rate | Difference with No.1 |
| 1 | 0.05 | 0.1 | 0.3 | 2852 | 89.69% | 0.00% |
| 2 | 0.01 | 0.05 | 0.1 | 2493 | 78.40% | 11.29% |
| 3 | 0.1 | 0.3 | 0.5 | 2598 | 81.70% | 7.99% |
| 4 | 0.08 | 0.2 | 0.4 | 2530 | 79.56% | 10.13% |
| 5 | 0.03 | 0.3 | 0.2 | 2645 | 83.18% | 6.51% |
| 6 | 0.06 | 0.08 | 0.3 | 2791 | 87.77% | 1.92% |
| 7 | 0.01 | 0.3 | 0.1 | 2609 | 82.04% | 7.65% |
| 8 | 0.05 | 0.1 | 0.5 | 2755 | 86.64% | 3.05% |

Table 4. Recognition results under different neural network parameters

## 5. Conclusion

An online surface inspection system of cold rolled strips is researched based on multimedia technology such as image process technology and pattern recognition technology, and it is applied to a production line of a certain iron & steel corporation in China, which includes cameras, illuminations, parallel computer systems and other correlative parts, and can detect and recognize over 10 main defects of cold rolled strips real time. The application effects show that the system can meet most requirements of corporation, and it can detect defects stably for long time. With the improvement of algorithm, some difficulties will be overcome, and the system will become wider use.

## 6. References


Sugimoto, T.; Kawaguchi, T.(1998). Development of a Surface Defect Inspection System Using Radiant Light from Steel Products in a Hot Rolling Line, *IEEE Transactions on Instrumentation and Measurement*, 47, 409-416

Hannes, L.; Weuster-Botz, Dirk, (2006). Genetic algorithm for multi-objective experimental optimization, *Bioprocess and Biosystems Engineering*, vol.29, No.5-6, 385-390

Kim, S. M.; Lee, Y. C.; Lee, S. C., (2006). Vision Based Automatic Inspection System for Nuts Welded on the Support Hinge, *SICE-ICASE International Joint Conference*, pp. 1508-1512, 2006.10

Tang, B.; Luo, S. W.; Huang, H.(2003). High performance face recognition system by creating virtual sample, *Proceedings of the 2003 International Conference on Neural Networks and Signal Processing*, pp. 972 – 975, 2003. 2

Chu, E.; George, A.(2000). Inside the FFT black box: serial and parallel fast Fourier transform algorithms, In: *CRC Press*, Boca Raton, Fla.

Kohonen, T. (1992) New Developments of Learning Vector Quantization and the Self-Organizing Map, *Symposium on Neural Networks Osaka*, Alliances and Perspectives in Senri

# 3

# Testing and Evaluation System for Camera Shake and Image Stabilizers (TEVRAIS)

Kazuki Nishi
*UEC Tokyo (University of Electro-Communications)*
*Japan*

## 1. Introduction

Hand movement while taking pictures, that is called camera shake, causes undesirable image blur. A quicker shutter reduces the camera shake blur but degrades the signal-to-noise ratio of image due to insufficient exposure. The camera-shake blur is, therefore, unavoidable especially in darker situation that the shutter speed needs to be set in slower range. Increasing pixel count in recent image sensor is more susceptible to the camera shake because even a slight camera movement causes a large pixel displacement in the imaging area. Additionally the higher pixel density requires a longer exposure because the light-sensing areas in each pixel become smaller, and therefore makes the camera image more likely to be affected by the camera shake.

To prevent or reduce the camera shake, various image stabilizers (see Figure 1) have been developed in many camera manufacturers. As the traditional technology, the electronic image stabilizer (Uomori et al., 1990) has been investigated to suppress the camera shake of

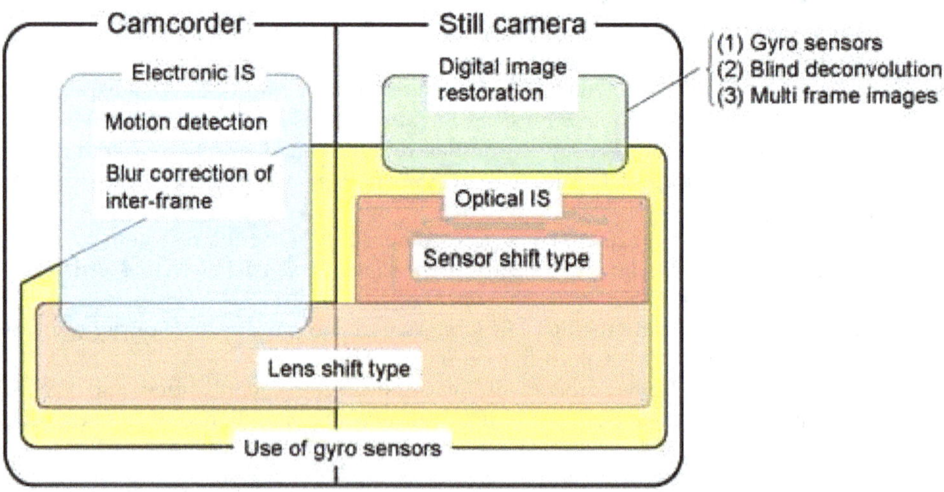


Fig. 1. Classification of image stabilizer technology

camcorders or video cameras. This technique shifts the frame image horizontally and/or vertically frame-by-frame to counteract the motion. The visible frame is limited to a narrower area inside of the maximum possible imaging area to provide a buffer for the motion. The digital image restoration technology has also been studied to recover the image blur due to camera shake of still cameras. This technique is based on the deconvolution filter that is derived from the point spread function (PSF) representing the camera motion. The PSF is estimated from the built-in gyro sensors or the camera image itself without any sensors (Fergus et al., 2006). Especially the latter type is called BLIND deconvolution. Recently, many serial images taken by the continuous shooting mode are used to realize the camera shake correction as well as the super-resolution to break out of the resolution limit (Park et al., 2003).

The most efficient technology that is employed in the most consumer products is the OPTICAL image stabilizer (Sato et al., 1993). The common architecture consists of built-in gyro sensors that identify the hand movement and the movement cancellation mechanism that precisely shifts the optical axis or image sensing device to compensate for camera motion. Since the camera motion is canceled mechanically and directly, the trail of camera shake blur does not remain in the camera image, therefore, the optical image stabilizer has superior performance. It is said that the optical image stabilizer allows us to take handheld shots at three or four-step slower shutter speed than without image stabilizers, but it is not known exactly how effective it works for cancellation of the camera shake. It is important to evaluate the performance qantitavely and objectively, because the performace will be improved if drawbacks of the present image stabilizer can be found through the evalution. This capter focuses on the measurement of camera shakes and the evalution of image stabilizers.

If the camera shake draws just a straight line, it can easily be detected by analyzing the PSF shape (Yitzhaky & Kopeika, 1998) or the spectrum distribution (Choi, et al., 1998) since it takes a simple 1D structure. Recently, the 2D trajectory corresponding to the camera motion in yaw and pitch axes, that can be estimated by shooting a point light source, have been investigated (Xiao et al., 2006). The 3D camera motion can be identified with the optical flow computed from the camera image of a stationary test pattern (Park et al., 2004), however, it is impossible to draw the trajectory in temporal sequence. The most popular method is to use the modulation transfer function (MTF) and examine how much high frequcey components of MTF are retrieved by the image stabilizer (Choi et al., 2008). Any methods has not, however, been successful detecting the 3D trajectory that corresponds actual camera motions and quantifying them.

Our proposed method makes it possible to estimate the exact 3D trajectory of camera shakes and evaluate the quantitative performance of image stabilizers (Nish & Ogino, 2007). The key idea consists of shooting the quickly changing test patterns that are displayed in the custom-made LED panel and calculating displacements between each pattern that is multiply recorded in the camera image while opening the shutter. The concept of the 3D camera shake detection and the performance evaluation results of some optical image stabilizers are presented.

## 2. How to detect camera shakes and analyze them

### 2.1 Point light source

To examine camera motions, the simplest method is to shoot a pint light source (Xiao et al., 2006). The trajectory of camera shake appears as a random curve on the camera image (see Figure 2). So we can observe directly the behavior of camera shake and the shrunk trajectory by the optical image stabilizer. However, when camera shakes are small especillay in cases of a short time exposure or after-stabilization, it is difficult to discriminate the feature and extract it numerically.

Our goal is to make it possible to detect detail of camera shakes in any case. For this purpose, not only the point light source but also any static test pattern that is commonly used for camera tests are no longer useful because they overlap densely with slight diplacements due to the camera shake and thus can not be discriminated each other.

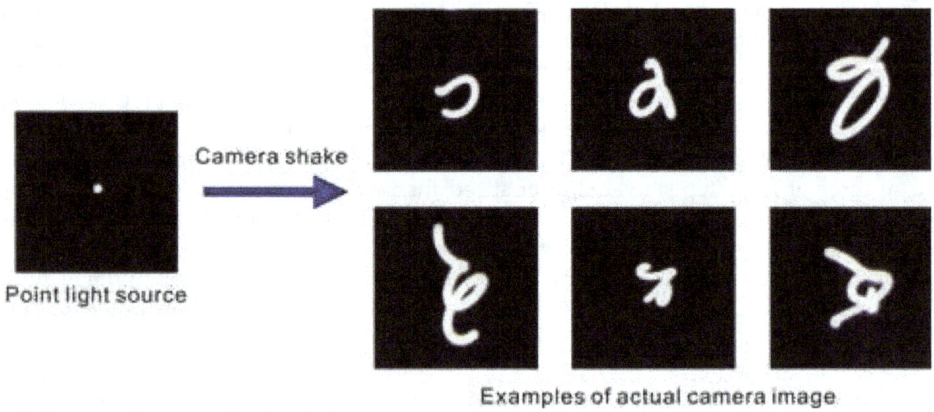


Fig. 2. Camera images of point light source

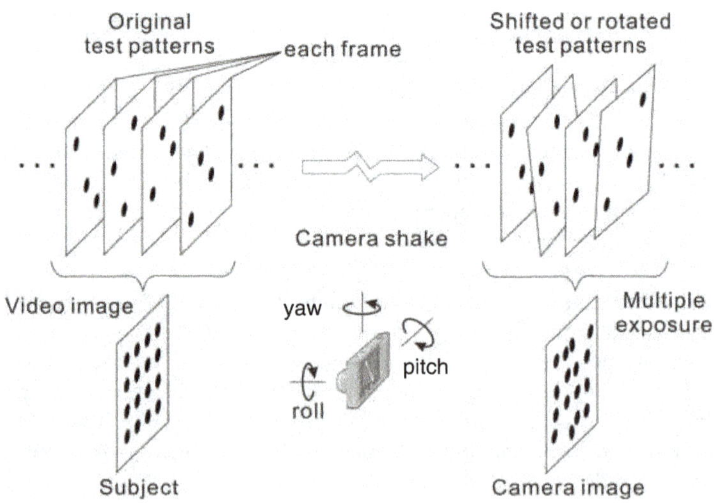


Fig. 3. Shooting of video test pattern with camera shake

## 2.2 Video test pattern

To realize precise detection of camera shakes, we propose using a VIDEO test pattern instead of static ones as the photographic subject. While the camera shutter is opening, each frame of the video test pattern is multiply recorded on an image with some shifts or rotations due to the camera shake. If those test patterns are chosen to eliminate overlap each other, each pattern can be easily discriminated from the multiply-exposed image. This is the key idea to detect camera shakes. Figure 3 shows the process from the shooting of video test pattern to the multiple exposure of them with some displacements or rotations due to the camera-shake. In this study, dot matrix patterns are used for the video test one.

For generating dot matirix patterns , we have developed a custum-designed LED panel (see Figure 4), that is comopsed of a window frame: 193mm $\times$ 193mm for the reference of pattern detection and 24 $\times$ 24 LED array with 1.5mm$\phi$ lighting holes and 7mm spacing for dot matirx patterns. By displaying dot matrix patterns repeatedly with a horizontal or vertical shift, no-overlapping video test pattern is realized (see Figure 5).

Figure 6 is a camera image of the video test pattern. If camera shakes do not exist, it becomes the distortion-free lattice pattern, or it causes a deformation due to camera shakes.

The video test pattern can also be implemented in a high-response liquid-crystal display where each video frame corresponds to each test pattern, but the frame rate is limited to 60Hz.

Fig. 4. Custum-made LED display for video test pattern

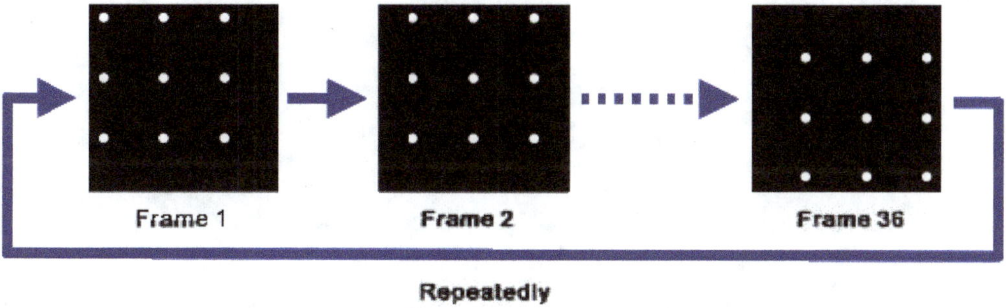


Fig. 5. Formation of video test pattern

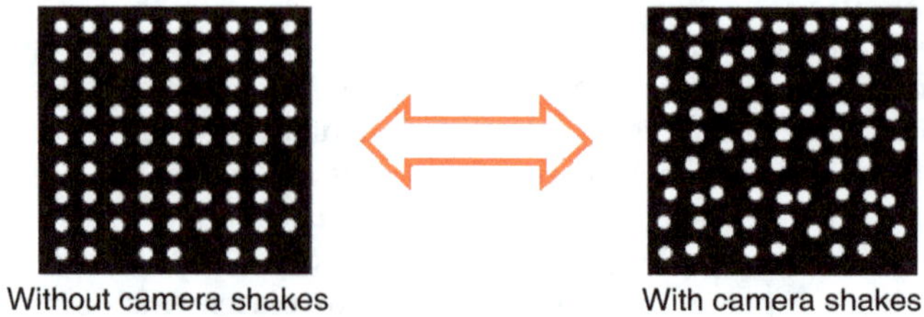


Fig. 6. Camera images of video test pattern

### 2.3 Computation of 3D trajectory based on pattern matching

The trajectory of camera shake can be obtained by computing displacements between each pattern in the multiply-exposed image. The pattern matching technique is useful for detecting positions of each test pattern from the image and computing displacements or roations between each pattern (see Figure 7). It is realized by using the shape-based pattern matching function of MVTec's machine vision tool HALCON. The shape-based pattern matching is advantageous to detecting in sub-pixel resolution and noise environment. Finally, the 3D trajectory of camera shake can be obtained by rearranging their estimates in time-sequence. Figure 8 shows examples of 2D trajectory (in yaw and pitch axes) computed through the above procedure.

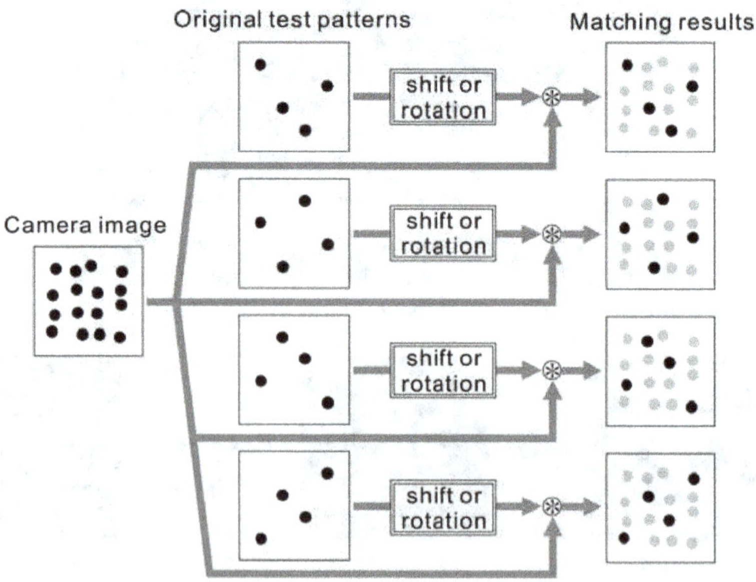


Fig. 7. Detection of displacements or rotations based on pattern matching

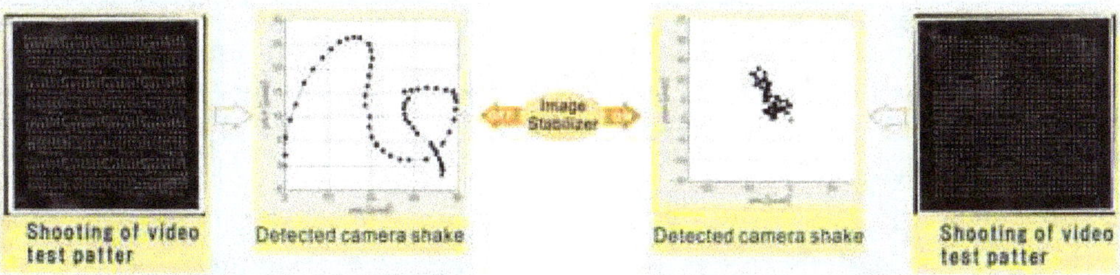


Fig. 8. Examples of detected camera shake trajectory with IS OFF and ON

### 2.4 Relation between camera motion and image plane

The actual camera shake involves random 3-axis shifts and 3-axis rotations, but the image movement is dominantly affected by rotations in 3-axis because parallel shifts make only a slight movement and are negligible in the camera image. When the camera rotates by $\theta_y, \theta_p, \theta_r$ in yaw, pitch and roll axes, respectively, an arbitrary point $(x, y)$ of the image is moved to the following point $(x', y')$:

$$\begin{bmatrix} x' \\ y' \end{bmatrix} = \begin{bmatrix} \cos\theta_r & -\sin\theta_r \\ \sin\theta_r & \cos\theta_r \end{bmatrix} \begin{bmatrix} x \\ y \end{bmatrix} + \begin{bmatrix} d_y \\ d_p \end{bmatrix}, \tag{1}$$

$$\text{where} \quad d_y = L\tan\theta_y \approx L\theta_y \qquad d_p = L\tan\theta_p \approx L\theta_p. \tag{2}$$

$d_y, d_p$ mean image shifts due to yaw and pitch rotations, respectively, where the camera-to-subject distance is $L$ and both of them are assumed to be set to the same scale for simplicity. The above implies that if the displacement or rotation of the target image can be detected from the relation between $(x, y)$ and $(x', y')$ in the camera image, then the camera rotations in 3-axis $(\theta_y, \theta_p, \theta_r)$ can be computed directly (see Figure 9). The left of Figure 10 shows a 3D trajectory of camera shake, that is obtained through the above conversion from the displacements and rotation detected by the pattern matching.

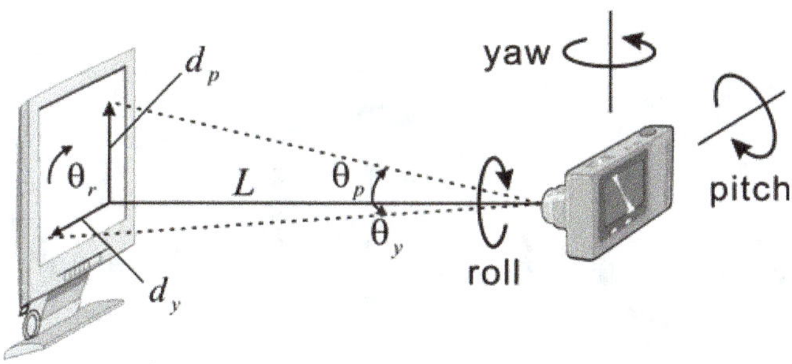


Fig. 9. Relation of camera-to-subject

## 2.5 Scatter diagram analysis

It is difficult to analyze the general trend of camera shake from just one of detected trajectories because it behaves randomly. The scatter diagram that is computed by accmulation of motion vectors between each frame interval (see the left side of Figure 10) from many images is useful for analyzing the camera shake trend. The quantification can be

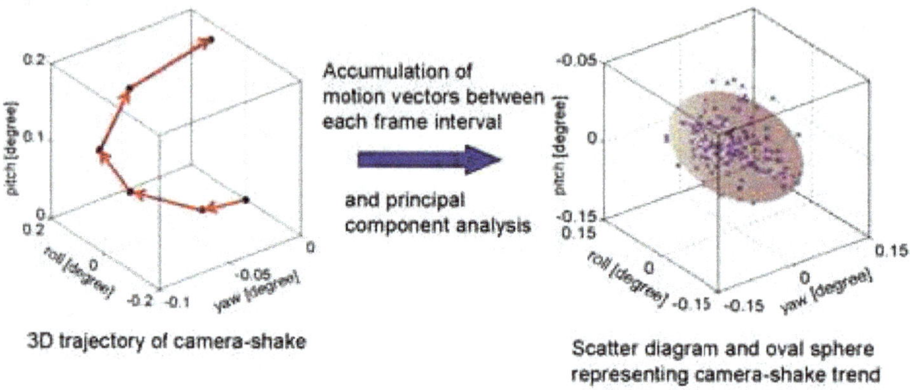


Fig. 10. 3D trajectory of camera shake and scatter diagram

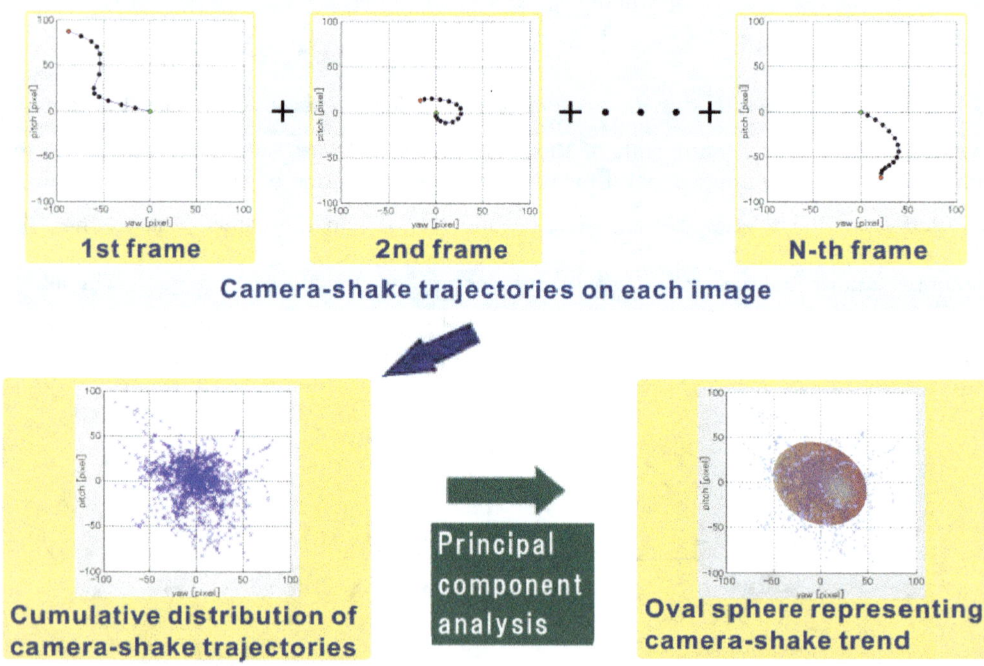


Fig. 11. Cumulative distribution of camera-shake trajectories

given by the principal component analysis, that means the average amplitude and orientation of camera shakes. The right side of Figure 10 shows an example of the scatter diagram obtained from many camera shake images. The oval sphere corresponds to the result of principal component analysis and shows the rough trend of camera shakes. So we can investigate differences of camera shake property in individuals or camera models through this analysis. When taking pictures with the image stabilizer, the distribution shrinks in origin. The degree of shrinkage shows the efficiency of image stabilizer.
Another way for quantification of the camera-shake trend is to compute the cumulative distribution of the detected trajectories, where all the start points of each trajectory are placed in origin, and apply the pricipal component analysis to that distribution (see Figure 11). The longer the shutter speed causes the larger the camera shake, therefore, more spread the distribution.
Figure 12 is an overview of developed GUI for displaying all the above results.

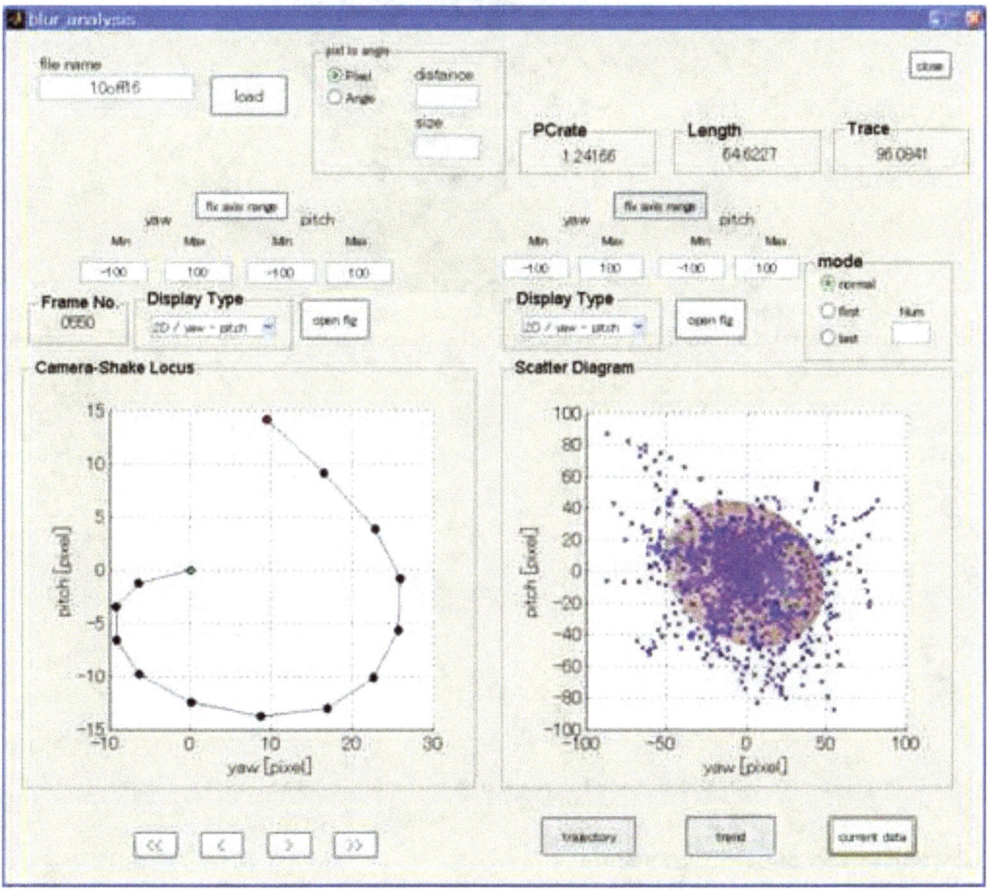


Fig. 12. Visualization and analysis tool of detected camera shakes

# 3. Experiments

## 3.1 Camera shake simulator

A camera shake simulator (see Figure 13) is used to examine the accuracy of detected camera shakes and compare the performance of image stabilizers under a definite motion. It consists of two stepping motors for vibrating in two axes chosen from among yaw, pitch and roll directions. The stage configuration for realizing arbitrary motion in yaw and pitch axes is shown in the left side of Figure 14. The case of yaw and roll axes is shown in the right side.

Fig. 13 Camera shake simulator for evaluating the detection accuracy and the effectiveness of image stabilizer

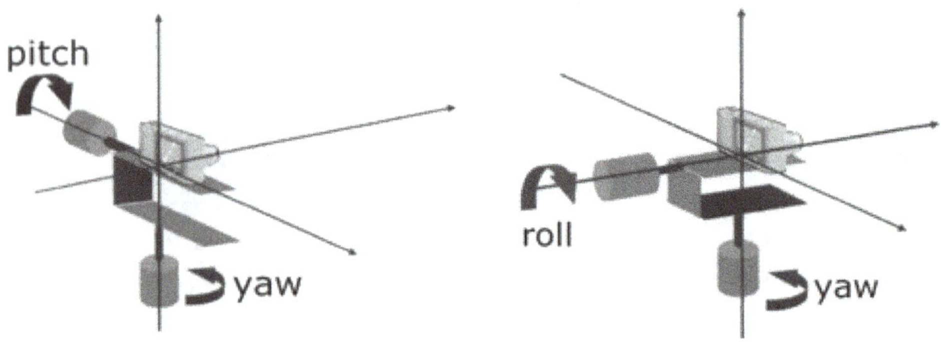


Fig. 14. Two types of vibration mode for realizing artificial camera shakes

## 3.2 Comparison of detection accuracy

A single-lens reflex camera is used to evaluate the detection accuracy in our measurement system. The left side of Table 1 shows standard deviations of detected vibrations from the camera images in static condition without any motions, where the camera is mounted on a

tripod and no mirror shocks exist. The right side of Table 1 shows measurement results under the motion by the camera-shake simulator that is controlled by an uniform circular motion in pitch and yaw axes.
This experiment is performed under the following conditions. The sizes of test pattern in the camera image are 800×800 pixels and 1200×1200 pixels, respectively. The rotation speed of the camera-shake simulator is constant at 1.68 degree/sec. The camera-to-subject distance is 3090mm.
The use of high resolution image in 1200×1200 pixels succeeds to reducing detection errors by 55%, 64% and 38% in pitch, yaw and roll axes, respectively, compared with the low resolutioni mage in 800×800 pixels. In the case of the circular motion, error reductions by 17%, 20% and 20% in pitch, yaw and roll, respectively, are also observed. These results show that the detection accuracy is improved by use of the high resolution pattern compared with the low resolution one.

| | Static | | | Moving | | |
|---|---|---|---|---|---|---|
| | **pitch** (deg.) | **yaw** (deg.) | **roll** (deg.) | **pitch** (deg.) | **yaw** (deg.) | **roll** (deg.) |
| 800×800 pix. | 0.0011 | 0.0014 | 0.0214 | 0.0030 | 0.0030 | 0.0270 |
| 1200×1200 pix. | 0.0005 | 0.0005 | 0.0133 | 0.0024 | 0.0024 | 0.0176 |

Table 1. Comparison of accuracy with standard deviation of detected camera shakes

### 3.3 Personal differences of camera shake

Here we measured camera shake amplitudes on eight photographers. Each person shot about 140 pieces with the same camera. The size of test pattern in the camera image is about 1200×1200 pixels. The camera-to-subject distance is 3600mm.
Table 2 shows minimum and maximum camera rotations on each person, that is estimated through our measurement system. It shows that average values in pitch and yaw are about 0.03 degree and the average value in roll is 0.1 degree that means greater than pitch and yaw ones.

| **Person** | **Pitch**(degree) | | **Yaw**(degree) | | **Roll** (degree) | |
|---|---|---|---|---|---|---|
| | min | max | min | max | min | max |
| A | -0.021 | 0.023 | -0.016 | 0.025 | -0.080 | 0.065 |
| B | -0.030 | 0.035 | -0.029 | 0.028 | -0.075 | 0.085 |
| C | -0.036 | 0.039 | -0.033 | 0.033 | -0.140 | 0.150 |
| D | -0.032 | 0.032 | -0.023 | 0.022 | -0.065 | 0.065 |
| E | -0.031 | 0.033 | -0.041 | 0.040 | -0.110 | 0.100 |
| F | -0.021 | 0.025 | -0.020 | 0.020 | -0.105 | 0.011 |
| G | -0.038 | 0.040 | -0.036 | 0.040 | -0.095 | 0.100 |
| H | -0.039 | 0.044 | -0.035 | 0.037 | -0.115 | 0.115 |
| **Average** | **-0.029** | **0.031** | **-0.031** | **0.034** | **-0.098** | **0.099** |

Table 2. Personal differences and average trend of camera shakes

### 3.4 Performance evaluation of image stabilizers

Next experiment results for comparing the camera-shake reduction performance on four different cameras of single-lens reflex type with image stabilizers are shown. The pattern size is set to be 1200×1200 pixels in the camera image. All cameras on the camera-shake simulator take uniform circular motion at 1.59 Hz in yaw and pitch axes. Tow cameras of them have lens shift-type stabilizers and another two have sensor shift-type ones. The camera-to-subject distance is 3160mm.

Figure 15 shows 2D distributions of motion vectors of the detected camera-shakes in the case that image stabilizers are off and on. It menas that camera A has most effective performance of image stabilization because the distribution is most concentrated in origin.

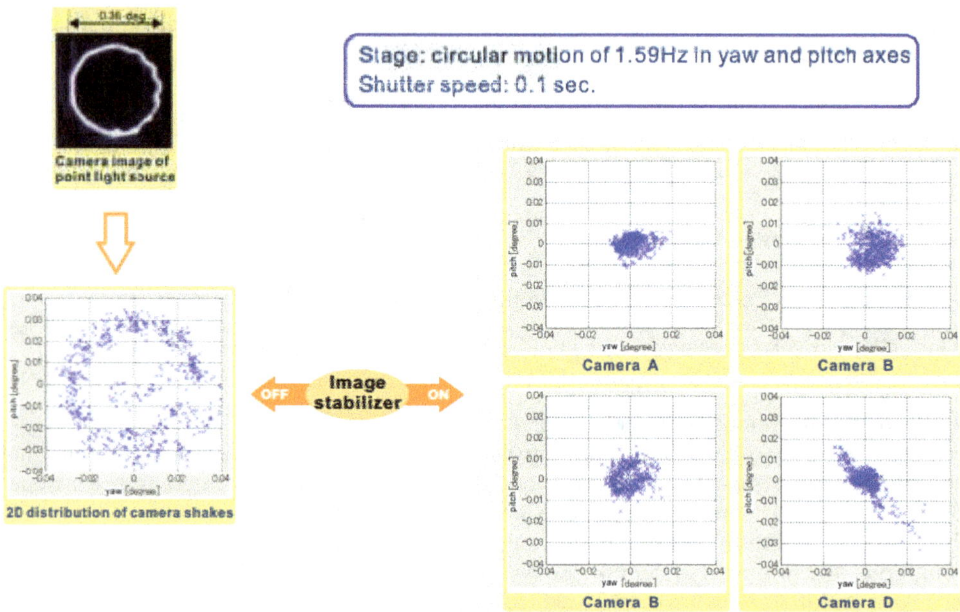


Fig. 15. Performance comparison of image stabilizers

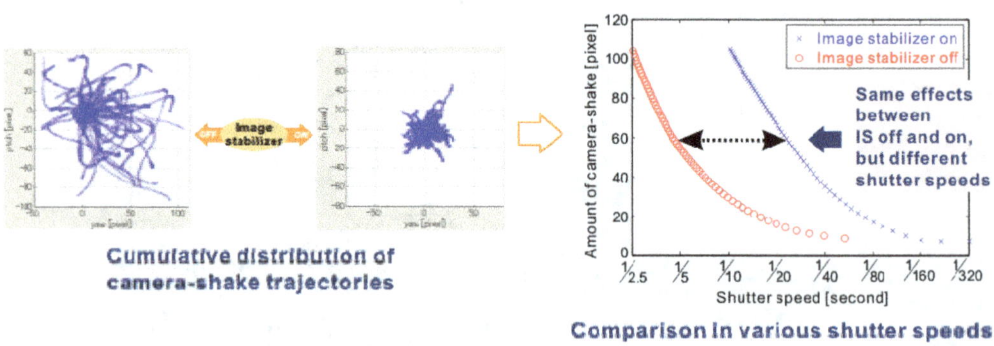


Fig. 16. Performance evaluation of an image stabilizer by means of cumulative distributions

The image stabilization of camera D becomes ineffective in 45-degree direction. Through these analyses, we can examine the tendency of image stabilization and exploit the result for the next development.
An example of evaluation using the cumulative distribution is shown in Figure 16. The distribution is widely spread due to camera-shakes, but the image stabilizer shrinks it in origin. From each distribution, amount of camera-shakes or the remainning one after the image stabilization are defined by the sum of long axis and short one of the oval sphere given by the principal compornent anaysis. The right side graph of Figure 16 is the computational results in various shutter speeds. In this graph, the shift distance between both curves of IS off and on means the total efficiency of image stabilizer.

### 3.5 Measurement of camera body and tripod vibration

Our system has a sub-pixel resolution in detection of dispacement due to camera motions. So not only camera-shakes but also slight vibrations in camera body and tripod when taking piictures can be detected.

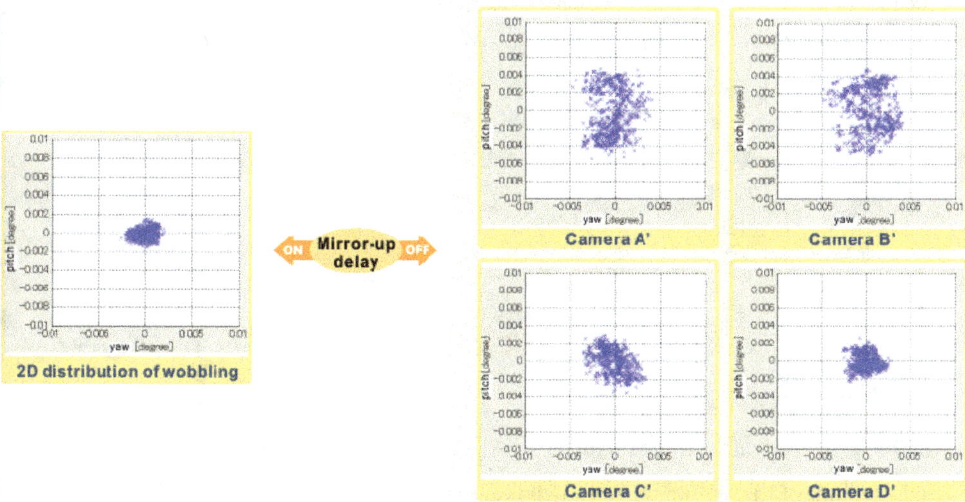


Fig. 17. Comparison of vibration suppression performance

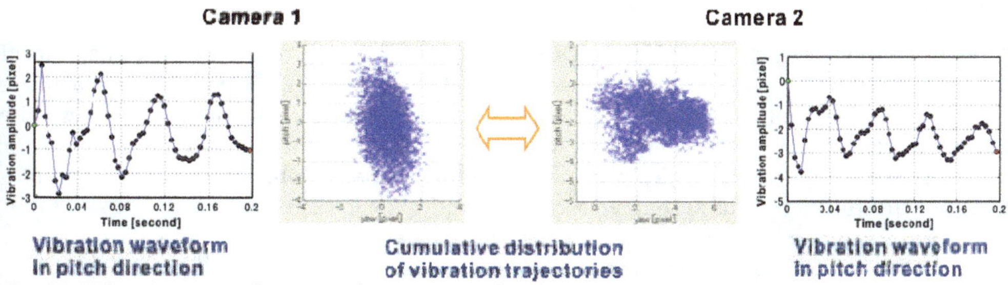


Fig. 18. Vibration waveforms at the moment the shutter opens

Figure 17 shows how much the camera vibration increases without mirror-up delay. Camera D', that the distribution is most concentrated in origin, has the most superior performmance for suppression of the camera vibration. The waveform of camera vibration on a triod can be also observed with a sub-pixel resolution (see Figure 18).

### 3.6 Measurement of camcorder-shakes and efficiency of image stabilizer in camcorder

The video image taken by camcorder is composed of sequential still images. The camera-shake in each still image, that is called *intra*-frame camera-shake, can be detected as with the above method. However the camera-shake arising in the interval between each frame, that is called *inter*-frame camera-shake, needs to be detected by another way. The inter-frame camera-shake corresponds to the image movement from previous frame to next one. Therefore the movement can be easily detected by using the pattern matching because each pattern is recored in different frame. By connecting between the estimated inter and intra-frame camera-shakes, the overall camera-shake can be obtained.
Figure 19 shows examples of detected camcorder-shake when the image stabilizer is off and on, respectively.

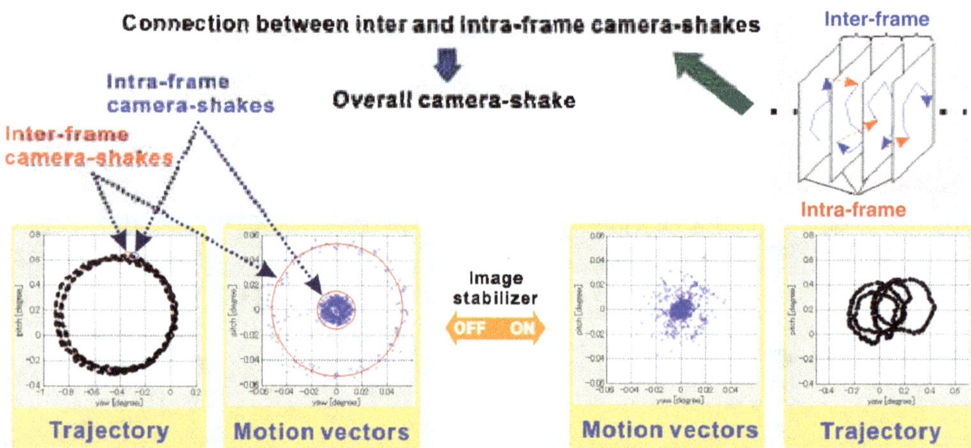


Fig. 19. Detection of the artificial camera-shake under a uniform circular motion

## 4. Conclusion and future work

A novel method for detecting the trajectory of camera-shake from the camera image itself was presented. The main feature is to use a video test pattern, detect positions of each test pattern multiply-recorded in the camera image by the pattern matching and obtain the camera-shake trajectory by connecting them. The LED display was also developed for realizing the high-response video test pattern. Many experimental resulsts and examples that show usefulness of this system were presented.
Now we are aiming at commercialization of this technology and standardization for measurement of camera-shake and evaluation of image stabilizers.

## 5. References

Choi, H.; Kim, J.P.; Song, M.G.; Kim, W.C., Park, N.P.; Park, Y.P. & Park, K.S. (2008). Effects of motion of an imaging system and optical image stabilizer on the modulation transfer function. *Optics Express*, Vol. 16, No. 25, pp. 21132-21141.

Choi, J.W.; Kang, M.G. & Park, K.T. (1998). An algorithm to extract camera-shaking degree and noise variance in the peak-trace domain. *IEEE Transactions on Consumer Electronics*, vol. 44, no. 3, pp. 1159-1168.

Fergus, R.; Singh, B.; Hertzmann, A.; Roweis, S.T. & Freemam, W.T. (2006). Removing Camera Shake from a Single Photograph. *ACM Transactions on Graphics*, vol. 25, no. 3, pp. 787-794.

Nishi, K. & Ogino, R. (2007). 3D Camera-Shake Measurement and Analysis. *Proceedings of IEEE International Conference on Multimedia & Expo (ICME)*, pp. 1271-1274.

Park, S.C.; Lee, H.S. & Lee, S.W. (2004). Qualitative estimation of camera motion parameters from the linear composition of optical flow. *Pattern Recognition*, vol. 37, pp. 767-779.

Park, S.C.; Park, M.K. & Kang, M.G. (2003). Super-Resolution Image Reconstruction -A technical Overview-. *IEEE Signal Processing Magazine*, vol. 20, no. 3, pp. 21-36.

Sato, K.; Ishizuka, S.; Nikami, A. & Sato, M. (1993). Control Techniques for Optical Image Stabilizing System. *IEEE Transactions on Consumer Electronics*, vol. 39, no. 3, pp. 461-466.

Uomori, K.; Morimura, A.; Ishii, H.; Sakaguchi, T. & Kitamura, Y. (1990). Automatic image stabilizing system by full-digital signal processing. *IEEE Transactions on Consumer Electronics*, vol. 36, no. 3, pp. 510-519.

Xiao, F.; Silverstein, A. & Farrell, J. (2006). Camera-motion and effective spatial resolution. *Proceedings of International Congress of Imaging Science*, pp. 33-36

Yitzhaky, Y. & Kopeika, N.S. (1997). Identification of Blur Parameters from Motion Blurred Images. *Graphical Models and Image Processing*, vol. 59, no. 5, pp. 310–320.

# 4

# Bit Rate Estimation for Cost Function of H.264/AVC

Mohammed Golam Sarwer[1,2], Lai Man Po[1] and Q. M. Jonathan Wu[2]
[1]*City University of Hong Kong, Hong Kong SAR, China*
[2]*University of Windsor, Canada*

## 1. Introduction

The appearance and development of various new multimedia services have need for higher coding efficiency. The ITU-T/ISO/IEC Joint Video Team established the newest video coding standard known as H.264/AVC (Joint Video Team (JVT), 2002). H.264/AVC offers a significant performance improvement over previous video coding standards such as H.263++ and MPEG-4 part 2 (Erol et al., 1998; Topiwala et al., 2001). New and advanced techniques are introduced in this new standard, such as intra prediction for I-frame encoding, multi-frames inter prediction, small block-size transform coding, context-adaptive arithmetic entropy coding, de-blocking filtering, etc. These advanced techniques make this new standard provides approximately 50% bit rate saving for equivalent perceptual quality relative to the performance of prior standards.

To achieve the best coding efficiency, H.264/AVC employs the rate-distortion (RD) optimization technique to get the best result consider of the visual quality and bit rate. For a macroblock in I-slice, RD optimization exhaustively searches the predefined 13 intra modes (9 modes for 4x4 block and 4 modes for 16x16 block) to produce the best encode mode for this macroblock. However, the latest H.264/AVC standard also defines 9 intra prediction modes for 8x8 block, for simplicity in this chapter only intra 4x4 and 16x16 blocks are considered. When a macroblock is in P-slice, it may be coded in intra mode or inter mode, so RD optimization employs a brute force algorithm to search through all possible inter modes and intra modes to find the best choice. RD optimization ofcourse will get the best encode mode for a macroblock, but it is at the great expanse of higher computational complexity at the encoder. To reduce computational complexity of H.264/AVC, a number of efforts have been made to explore the fast algorithm in motion estimation, intra mode prediction and inter mode prediction for H.264/AVC video coding (Chen et al., 2002; Feng et al., 2005; Han & Lee, 2005; Kim et al., 2006; Lim et al., 2003; Sarwer et al., 2008; Sarwer & Wu, 2009; Wu et al., 2005; Yang et al., 2004). The number of inter modes is reduced by using the amplitude of edge vector (Lim et al., 2003). To reduce the complexity of intra mode decision, H.264/AVC reference software suggested sum of absolute difference (SAD) and sum of absolute transform difference (SATD) based cost functions. These two cost functions reduce computation significantly but performance of RD characteristics is not good enough. In (Chiang & Zhang, 1997) and (Coebera & Lei, 1999) rate models were observed from the quantizer (Q)-domain. But these are considered only for rate control. To improve the RD performance, an enhanced cost function for intra 4x4 mode decisions was proposed in (Tseng et al., 2006). In this cost function, sum of absolute integer transform difference (SAITD) is used in distortion part and a rate prediction algorithm is used in rate part. The major drawback of this cost is that the bit estimation method cannot give the very good estimation.

In this chapter, we propose a shortcut way to get the number of entropy coded bits as soon as the transform coefficients are quantized. A method for estimation of rate for cost function of intra and inter mode decision is proposed. This method is based on the properties of context-based adaptive variable length coding (CAVLC) and observation of VLC tables. The total number of bits need to encode a quantized residual block is predicted by estimating the rate of each symbols of CAVLC separately.

The remainder of this chapter is organized as follows. Section 2 provides the review of intra and inter mode and rate distortion optimized mode decision technique. In section 3, Context-based adaptive variable length coding (CAVLC) is briefly described. In section 4, we present the proposed fast bit rate estimation method. The performance results of the proposed method are presented in section 5. Finally, section 6 concludes the chapter.

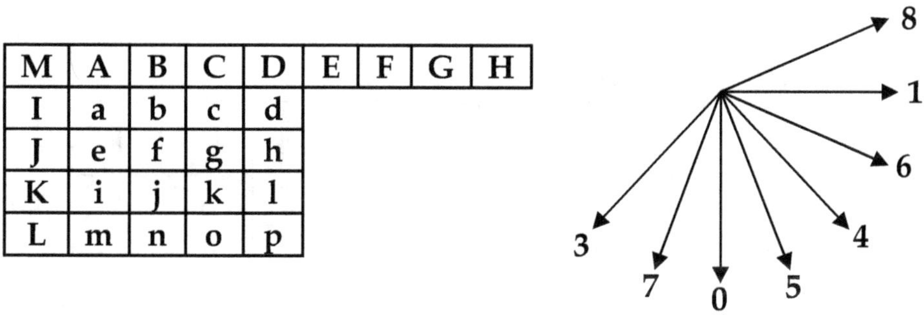


(a) (b)

Fig. 1. (a) A 4x4 block with elements (a to p) which are predicted by its neighbouring pixels (b) Eight prediction direction for I4MB prediction

## 2. Overview of Mode Decision

### 2.1 Intra mode in H.264/AVC

The H.264/AVC video coding standard supports intra prediction for variable block size. If a macroblock (MB) is encoded in intra mode, a predicted block is formed based on previously encoded and reconstructed upper and left blocks so it exploits the spatial correlation between the adjacent MB. Then the residual data between the current to be coded MB and predicted one is DCT transformed, quantized and entropy coded. For each luma samples, the prediction block may be formed for each 4x4 block (denoted as I4MB) or for an entire MB (denoted as I16MB). When using the I4MB prediction, each 4x4 block of the luma component utilizes one of the nine prediction modes. Besides DC prediction, eight directional modes are specified. When utilizing I16MB, which is well suited for homogeneous area of image, 4 prediction modes are supported. Another 4 prediction modes are used to predict the U and V 8x8 chroma blocks. Nine prediction modes of 4x4 luma block are shown in Figure 1(a) and Figure (b). In addition, the prediction block is calculated based on the samples labeled A-M.

### 2.2 Inter mode in H.264/AVC

Inter-prediction is to reduce the temporal correlation with help of motion estimation and compensation. In H.264, the current picture can be partitioned into the MBs or the smaller blocks. A MB of 16x16 luma samples can be partitioned into smaller block sizes up to 4x 4. There are altogether conceptually 7 different block sizes ( 16x16, 16x8, 8x16, 8x8, 8x4, 4x8, 4x4 ) that are used in a MB that is encoded in inter mode. These block sizes can be classified as 16x16, 16x8, and 8x16 and P8x8. Each 8x8 block of P8x8 MB can be one of the subtypes such as 8x8, 8x4, 4x8 or 4x4. Figure 2 shows the different block sizes in a MB of inter mode. The smaller block size requires larger number of bits to signal the motion vectors and extra data of the type of partition, however the motion compensated residual data can be reduced. Therefore, the choice of partition size depends on the input video characteristics. In general, a large partition size is appropriate for homogeneous areas of the frame and a small partition size may be beneficial for detailed areas.

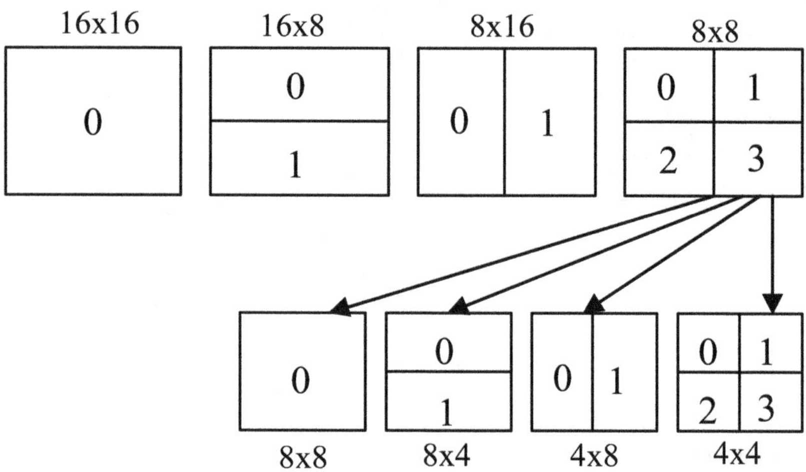


Fig. 2. Variable block sizes of macroblock of INTER mode

### 2.3 Rate Distortion optimized mode decision

To take the full advantages of all modes, the H.264 encoder can determine the mode that meets the best RD tradeoff using RD optimization mode decision scheme. The optimization approach is based on the assumption that the distortion and rate incurred in coding a MB are independent each other. Let us denote $S_t$ as a block of any rectangular size in a frame at time $t$; while $C_{t-\tau}$ is a reconstructed block of the same block size as $S_t$ located in the previously coded frame at time $t-\tau$ ($\tau=0$ in intra frame coding). Then the best mode for every block that produces the minimum rate-distortion cost is given by

$$J_{RD}(S_t, C_{t-\tau}, m \mid QP, \lambda_m) = SSD(S_t, C_{t-\tau}, m \mid QP) + \lambda_m R(S_t, C_{t-\tau}, m \mid QP) \tag{1}$$

where QP is the MB quantization parameter, $\lambda_m$ is the Lagrangian multiplier and $m$ is the candidate mode. In (Sullivan & Wiegand, 1998), a strong connection between the local Lagrangian multiplier and the QP was found experimentally as

$$\lambda_m = 0.85 \times 2^{(QP-12)/3} \tag{2}$$

In (1), SSD is the sum of squared difference between original block and reconstructed block, defined separately in terms of intra and inter frame coding

$$SSD_{\text{intra}}(S_t, C_t, m \mid QP) = \sum_i \sum_j \left| S_t(i,j) - C_t(i,j,m \mid QP) \right|^2 \tag{3}$$

$$SSD_{\text{inter}}(S_t, C_{t-\tau}, m \mid QP) = \sum_i \sum_j \left| S_t(i,j) - C_{t-\tau}(i+mv_i, j+mv_j, m \mid QP) \right|^2 \tag{4}$$

where $(i, j)$ represent the $i$th and $j$th element and $(mv_i, mv_j)$ represents the motion vector in the inter-frame case.
The $R$ in (1) reflects the number of bits associated with choosing the mode which includes the bit consumption of quantized transform coefficients, motion vector data and the header. Thus $R$ can be written as

$$R = R_{header} + R_{motion} + R_{res} \tag{5}$$

where $R_{header}$ and $R_{motion}$ means the number of bits need for header information and motion vectors respectively. It should be noted that in case of intra frame coding $R_{motion}=0$. $R_{res}$ indicates the number of bits need to encode a quantized residual block.

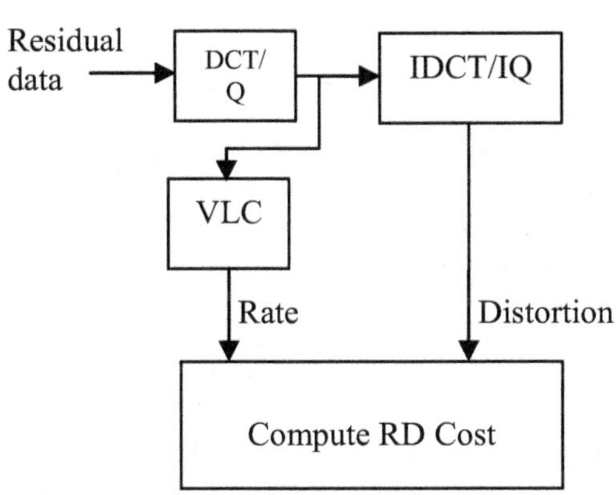


Fig. 3. Computation of RD cost

In intra-frame coding, the final mode decision is selected by the member (either from *I4MB* or *I16MB*) that minimizes the Lagrangian cost in (1). In inter-frame coding, motion estimations with 7 different block-size patterns, as well as the other members in three members (*I4MB*, *I16MB*, and *SKIP*), are calculated. The final decision is determined by the mode that produces the least Lagrangian cost among the available modes. Figure 3 shows the computational process of RD cost of H.264 video coding standard. As indicated in Figure 3, in order to compute RD cost for each mode, same operation of forward and inverse transform/quantization and variable length coding is repetitively performed. All of these processing explains the high complexity of RD cost calculation.
In order to calculate RD cost using (1), 4×4 integer *DCT+Q*, CAVLC, and *(DCT+Q)-1* in units of 4×4 blocks should be performed. If the amount of RD cost computation in P8×8 mode and Inter16×16 mode and I4MB mode in a MB unit are calculated, it is shown that those computations in Inter16×16 mode are performed 16 times, while those computations in P8×8 mode are performed 64 times and those computations in I4MB mode are performed 144 times. To reduce computation, several fast mode-decision approaches proposed in (Feng et al., 2005; Kim et al., 2006; Yang et al., 2004) focused on how to eliminate unnecessary modes. However, it is noted that the remaining modes should be performed RD optimization. So it still introduces a great deal of computation complexity because of the transform, quantization/inverse quantization and entropy coding to get distortion and bit-rate. A bit rate estimator by modeling the coded bits consumption as a function of the number and levels of the nonzero quantized transform coefficients is introduced in (Yu et al., 2006). In (Tseng et al., 2006), a rate predictor for 4x4 quantized residual blocks is proposed as follows

$$R_{e(res)} = \alpha T_c - \beta T_o + 4P \tag{6}$$

where $T_c$ is the total number of non-zero coefficients, $T_o$ is the number of trailing +/-1 values, $\alpha$ and $\beta$ are the positive constants and the P equal to 0 for the probable mode and 1 for the other modes. From simulation it is shown that this method cannot achieve very good rate estimation. This is because only two parameters are not enough to estimate the bit rate. In this chapter a rate prediction scheme is introduced based on the properties of CAVLC entropy coding method. Before we propose the new estimation method, review of the CAVLC encoding method is described at following section.

## 3. Review of Context based adaptive variable length coding (CAVLC)

Context based Adaptive Variable Length Coding (CAVLC) is designed to take advantage of several characteristics of quantized 4x4 blocks. The block is encoded by five syntax elements. These elements are described as follows:

1. *coeff_token:* Both the total number of nonzero coefficients and the number of trailing +/- 1s are coded as combined event. If number of trailing +/- 1s is greater than 3, last 3 trailing +/-1s of zig-zig ordered block are consider as trailing +/-1s and remaining trailing +/-1s are consider as normal coefficient. One out of 4 VLC tables is used (ITU-T Rec., 2002). Since the number of non-zero coefficients in neighboring blocks are usually correlated, the selection of VLC table is depends on the number of non-zero coefficients in neighboring blocks (Richardson, 2003).

2. *Sign of trailing +/- 1:* One bit is used to signal sign information of trailing +/- 1s. 0 is used for positive and 1 is used for negative.
3. *Level:* The magnitude (level) of non-zero coefficients gets larger near the DC coefficient and gets smaller around the high frequency coefficients. CAVLC takes advantage of this by making the choice of the VLC look-up table for the level adaptive in a way where the choice depends on the recently coded levels (Richardson, 2003). One out of 7 VLC tables is used to encode the level information (ITU-T Rec., 2002).
4. *Total_zeros:* The codeword Total_zeros is the number of zeros between the last non-zero coefficient of the zig-zag scan and its start. One out of 15 VLC tables is chosen based on the number of non-zero coefficients (ITU-T Rec., 2002).
5. *Run_before:* Run_before means the number of preceding zeros before each non-zero coefficient and Zeros_left called the number of zeros left before each non-zero coefficient. Based on Run_before and Zeros_left, one out of 7 VLC tables is used to encode this element (ITU-T Rec., 2002).

| Element | Value | Code |
|---|---|---|
| coeff_token | TotalCoeffs=6, T1s=3 (use VLC0) | 00000100 |
| T1 sign (5) | + | 0 |
| T1 sign (4) | - | 1 |
| T1 sign (3) | + | 0 |
| Level (2) | +1 (use Level_VLC0) | 1 |
| Level (1) | -2 (use Level_VLC1) | 011 |
| Level (0) | +4 (use Level_VLC1) | 00010 |
| TotalZeros | 2 | 111 |
| run_before(5) | ZerosLeft=2; run_before=0 | 1 |
| run_before(4) | ZerosLeft=2; run_before=0 | 1 |
| run_before(3) | ZerosLeft=2; run_before=1 | 01 |
| run_before(2) | ZerosLeft=1; run_before=1 | 0 |
| run_before(1 & 0) | ZerosLeft=0; run_before=0 | No code required |

Table 1. Example of CAVLC

For example, the coefficients in the zig-zag order of a 4x4 block are [4,-2,0,1,0,1,-1,1,0,0…]. Here total number of non-zero coefficients ($T_c$) is 6, total number of zero before the last nonzero coefficients ($T_z$) is 2, number of trailing one's ($T_o$) is 3. Based on the VLC tables (ITU-T Rec., 2002) as shown in Table 1, the transmitted bit stream for this block is 000001000101011000101111010.

## 4. Proposed Fast Bit Rate estimation Method

To estimate the bits for quantized transform coefficients, we estimate the number of bits for each of five different types of symbols of CAVLC separately.

1. *The coefficient token (the number of coefficients, the number of trailing ones):* Four VLC tables are used for encoding coefficient token. Selection of VLC table is context adaptive.

Figure 4(a) shows the plot of actual bit rate to encode the coefficient token versus the number of coefficients of foreman video sequence at QP=28. Similar results were found for other video sequences. It is clearly shown that bit consumption to encode the coefficient token is increased with number of coefficients. Based on VLC tables (ITU-T Rec., 2002), it is also shown that bit rate for coefficient token is decreased with number of trailing ones. Based on this criteria, we propose the number of bits require to encode the coefficient token is

$$R_{coff} = w_1 T_c - w_2 T_o + w_3 \tag{7}$$

where $T_c$ and $T_o$ are same as equation (6). These $w_1, w_2$ and $w_3$ are weighting constants. In order to set the weighting factors, we have done several experiments for different video sequences (akiyo, foreman, stefan, mobile, table tennis, paris) with QCIF format at different QP values. We have observed rate-distortion performance of these video sequences at different combinations of weighting factor. Better rate-distortion performance was found at $w_1 = w_2 = 1, w_3 = 0$.

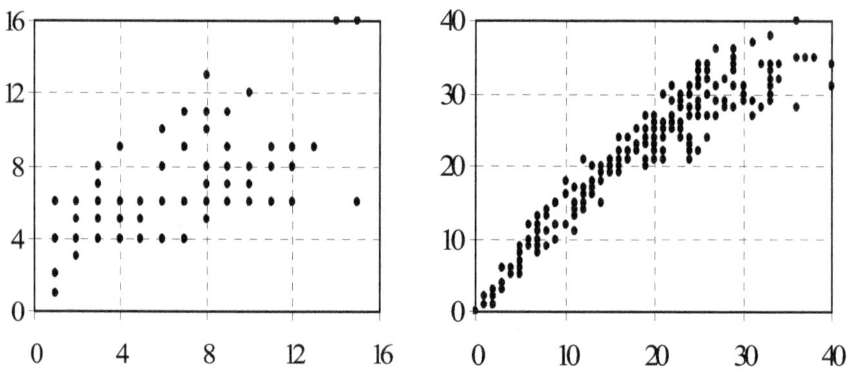


(a) (b)

Fig. 4. Plot of (a) no. of non-zero coefficients vs true value of coefficient token ( X-axis: $T_c$, Y-axis: True rate of Coeff_token) (b) $SAT_l$ vs actual rate of level ( X-axis: $SAT_l$, Y-axis: True rate of level)

2. *The sign of trailing ones:* For each $T_o$, a single bit encodes the sign ( 0=+, 1=-). So bit consumption to encode the trailing ones as follows:

$$R_{trail1} = T_o \tag{8}$$

3. *The level of nonzero coefficients:* From the observation of level-VLC tables (ITU-T Rec., 2002), it is shown that bit requirement is increased with magnitude of non-zero coefficients. Number of bits to encode the level information is proposed as follows:

$$R_{level} = w_4 SAT_l \tag{9}$$

with the $SAT_l$ given by

$$SAT_l = \sum_{k=1}^{Tc} |L_k| \tag{10}$$

where $|L_k|$ is the absolute value of $k_{th}$ non-zero coefficient, $SAT_l$ is the sum of absolute values of all levels of quantized transform residual block. $w_4$ is a positive constant. Suppose two coefficients are encoded using same level_VLC table. If the magnitude of first coefficient $(|L_1|)$ is larger than that of second coefficient $(|L_2|)$, from level_VLC table it is shown that rate for first coefficient $R(L_1)$ also greater than that of second coefficient $R(L_2)$. So equation (9) is valid. Let us consider two coefficients are encoded using multiple level_VLC tables. If the earlier coefficient is not larger than the other coefficient, by observing the all level_VLC tables (ITU-T Rec., 2002) there is $R(L_1) > R(L_2)$ if $|L_1| > |L_2|$. In some times, $R(L_1) > R(L_2)$ if $|L_1| < |L_2|$ but fortunately this event does not occur high frequently and is slightly influence the estimation result. Figure 4(b) shows the plot of actual bit rate to encode the level information with $SAT_l$ of foreman video sequence at QP=28. Similar results were found for other video sequences. By changing the value of $w_4$, we have observed RD performance of different sequences. Better results were found with $w_4$=1.

4. *Encode the total number of zeros before the last coefficient:* From the observation of total zero VLC tables, it is shown than bit consumption to encode the total zero is increased with number of total zero. So we can propose the estimated bits for total zero is as follows

$$R_{zero} = w_5 T_z \tag{11}$$

where $w_5$ is a positive constant and $T_z$ is the total number of zeros before the last non zero coefficients. Here $w_5$=1, which is found in similar way of $w_4$.

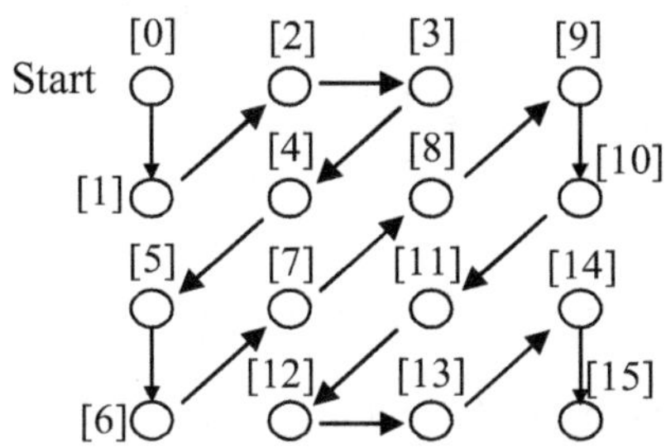


Fig. 5. Zig-zag scan and corresponding frequency of 4x4 luma block

5. *Encode each run of zeros:* After the DCT transform, the high frequency coefficient usually has small energy. By quantization, more zeros are found at the high frequency position of quantized transform block. So the value of *Run* for the high frequency non-zero coefficients is larger. From the observation of run VLC tables, it is shown that more bits

are required for large value of run. So bit consumption is higher to encode the run of high frequency non-zero coefficients. Based on this idea, we propose the rate for run of each non-zero coefficients as follow:

$$R_{run_{(k)}} = w_6 f_k \ , \ 0 \geq f_k \leq 15 \tag{12}$$

where, $f_k$ is the frequency of $k_{th}$ non-zero coefficient of recorded block and $w_6$ is the positive constant. For example, given a string of coefficients [0, 3, 0, 1,-1,-1, 0, 1, 0, 0…], frequency of first non-zero coefficient (3) is 1 and frequency of last non-zero coefficient (1) is 7. The weighting factor $w_6$=0.3 is found in similar way of $w_4$. Figure 5 shows the zig-zag scan of a residual block with corresponding value of frequency.

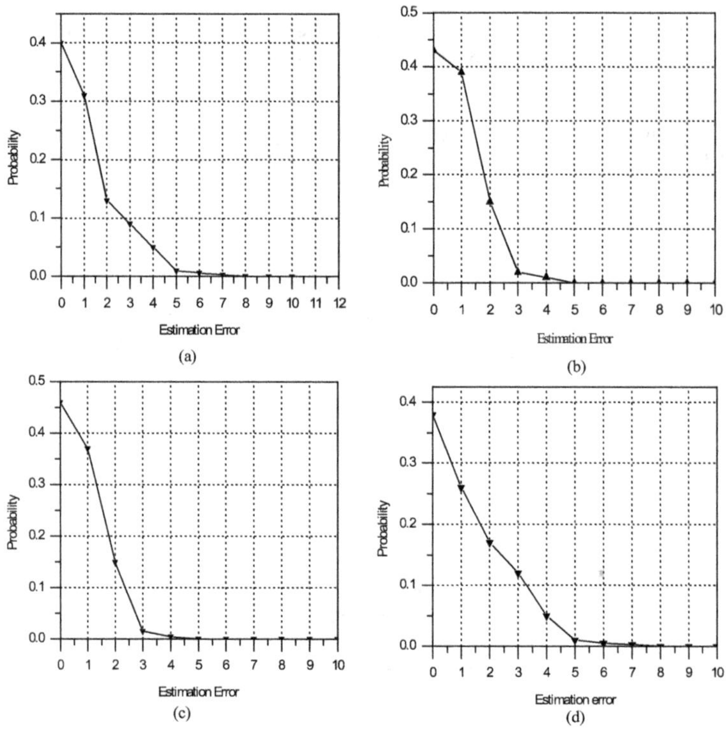


Fig. 6. Probability of estimation error of (a) Coeff_token (b) level (c) total zero (d) run

From above analysis, we have estimated the bits needed to encode a 4x4 residual block ($R_{est_{(res)}}$) is

$$R_{est_{(res)}} = R_{coeff} + R_{trail1} + R_{level} + R_{zero} + \sum_{k=1}^{T_c} R_{run_{(k)}}$$

$$= w_1 T_c - w_2 T_o + w_3 + T_o + w_4 SAT_l + w_5 T_z + \sum_{k=1}^{T_c} (w_6 f_k) \tag{13}$$

By putting the values of different constants, the proposed rate estimator becomes

$$R_{est_{(res)}} = T_c + T_z + SAT_l + 0.3\sum_{k=1}^{T_c} f_k \tag{14}$$

Figure 6 shows the probability of estimation error of four different types of symbols. Estimation error of the symbol is the absolute difference between actual bit rate and estimated bit rate of that symbol. Y-coordinate of Figure 6 is the probability of corresponding estimation error. It is shown that most of the estimation errors of each symbol are between 0 to 4 and the probability of each symbol that the estimated rate perfectly match with CAVLC is about 40%.

## 5. Simulation Results

To verify the proposed technique, JM 8.3 reference software is used in simulation. Six well known video sequences are used as test materials. The test conditions are as follows:

a) Hadamard transform is used
b) RD optimization is enabled
c) CAVLC is enabled.
d) Frame rate is 30
e) MV search range is ±32 pels for QCIF and CIF
f) Fast motion estimation algorithm is used (Chen et al., 2002).

A group of experiments were carried out on the test sequences with different quantization parameters. Comparison results were produced based on the percentage of difference of coding time (Δ T %), the PSNR difference (Δ $P_{snr}$) and percentage of the bit rate difference (Δ Bit %). In order to evaluate complexity reduction, Δ T (%) is defined as follows

$$\Delta T = \frac{T_{original} - T_{proposed}}{T_{original}} \times 100\% \tag{15}$$

where, $T_{original}$ denotes the total encoding time of the JM 8.3 encoder with rate distortion optimization and $T_{proposed}$ is the total encoding time with proposed fast rate estimation technique.

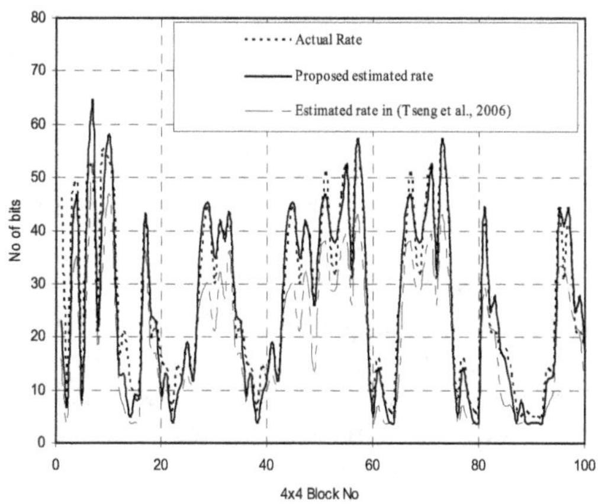


Fig. 7. Comparison of our proposed method with rate estimation method described in (Tseng et al., 2006)

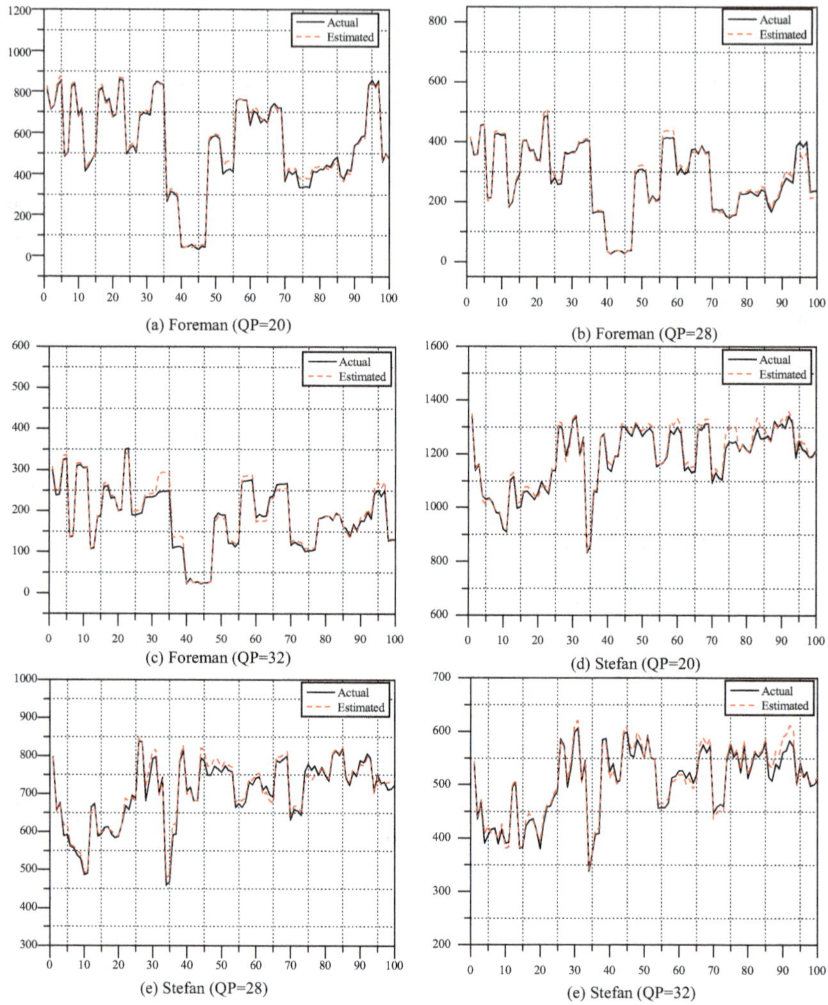


Fig. 8. Curves of the estimated and the actual rates of first 100 macroblocks of I frame of intra coding of foreman and Stefan sequences ( X-axis: Macroblock number, Y-axis: number of bits)

### 5.1 Experiments with all intra frame sequences

In this experiment, a total number of 100 frames are used for each sequence, and period of I-frame is set to 1, i.e., all the frames in the sequence are intracoded. In (Tseng et al., 2006), a rate predictor for 4x4 intra mode decisions is introduced based on the number of non-zero coefficients and number of trailing ones. Figure 7 shows the comparison of our proposed method with actual rate and the rate predictor described in (Tseng et al., 2006) for the Foreman sequence. Data is collected from the first 100 4x4 block of first frame of IIIIII sequence. QP factor is set as 28. It is shown that the proposed method is very closely matched with actual rate as compared to rate predictor in (Tseng et al., 2006). By using the proposed estimation method, Figure 8 shows the predicted rates $R_{est}(= R_{header} + R_{motion} + R_{est(res)})$ and actual rates $R(= R_{header} + R_{motion} + R_{res})$ are very closely identical, which are obtained from first 100 MBs of IIIIII sequence of Foreman-QCIF and Stefan_CIF at three different (20, 28, 32) QP values. The proposed estimation achieves a precise prediction in intra frame coding.

| Sequence | QP | $\Delta$ P$_{snr}$ | $\Delta$ Bit% |
|---|---|---|---|
| Akiyo (QCIF) | 20 | -0.06 | +0.64 |
| | 24 | -0.05 | +0.50 |
| | 28 | +0.02 | +0.53 |
| | 32 | +0.17 | +0.70 |
| | 36 | +0.12 | +1.49 |
| | 40 | +0.16 | +2.59 |
| Foreman (QCIF) | 20 | -0.06 | +0.49 |
| | 24 | -0.05 | +0.89 |
| | 28 | -0.02 | +1.16 |
| | 32 | +0.10 | +1.75 |
| | 36 | +0.11 | +2.35 |
| | 40 | +0.15 | +3.86 |
| Mobile (QCIF) | 20 | -0.16 | +0.85 |
| | 24 | -0.09 | +0.78 |
| | 28 | -0.10 | +0.54 |
| | 32 | -0.08 | +0.27 |
| | 36 | -0.06 | +0.70 |
| | 40 | +0.03 | +1.83 |
| Paris (CIF) | 20 | -0.16 | +0.46 |
| | 24 | -0.11 | +0.25 |
| | 28 | -0.10 | +0.45 |
| | 32 | -0.06 | +0.88 |
| | 36 | -0.02 | +0.64 |
| | 40 | +0.04 | +1.61 |
| Table Tennis (CIF) | 20 | -0.14 | +0.31 |
| | 24 | -0.12 | +0.36 |
| | 28 | -0.04 | +1.01 |
| | 32 | +0.01 | +0.88 |
| | 36 | +0.02 | +1.48 |
| | 40 | +0.06 | +2.23 |
| Stefan (CIF) | 20 | -0.19 | +0.62 |
| | 24 | -0.12 | +0.44 |
| | 28 | -0.11 | +0.42 |
| | 32 | -0.02 | +0.68 |
| | 36 | -0.02 | +1.69 |
| | 40 | +0.13 | +3.15 |

Table 2. Performance of PSNR and bit rate of proposed plgorithm while all frames are intra coded

| Sequence | Quantization Parameter, QP | | | | | |
|---|---|---|---|---|---|---|
| | 20 | 24 | 28 | 32 | 36 | 40 |
| Akiyo_QCIF | 51.21 % | 47.29 % | 44.11 % | 39.34 % | 35.35 % | 30.42 % |
| Foreman_QCIF | 55.20 % | 51.16 % | 46.66 % | 42.42 % | 37.28 % | 33.33 % |
| Mobile_QCIF | 62.87 % | 61.78 % | 59.45 % | 57.14 % | 51.21 % | 47.14 % |
| Paris_CIF | 58.11 % | 54.96 % | 52.81 % | 47.94 % | 43.30 % | 41.08 % |
| Table_tennis_CIF | 57.04 % | 53.56 % | 49.54 % | 43.41 % | 39.11 % | 35.21 % |
| Stefan_CIF | 57.41 % | 54.12 % | 50.55 % | 44.96 % | 39.20 % | 34.52 % |
| Average = 47.36 % | | | | | | |

Table 3. Computational complexity reduction of proposed algorithm while all frames are intra coded

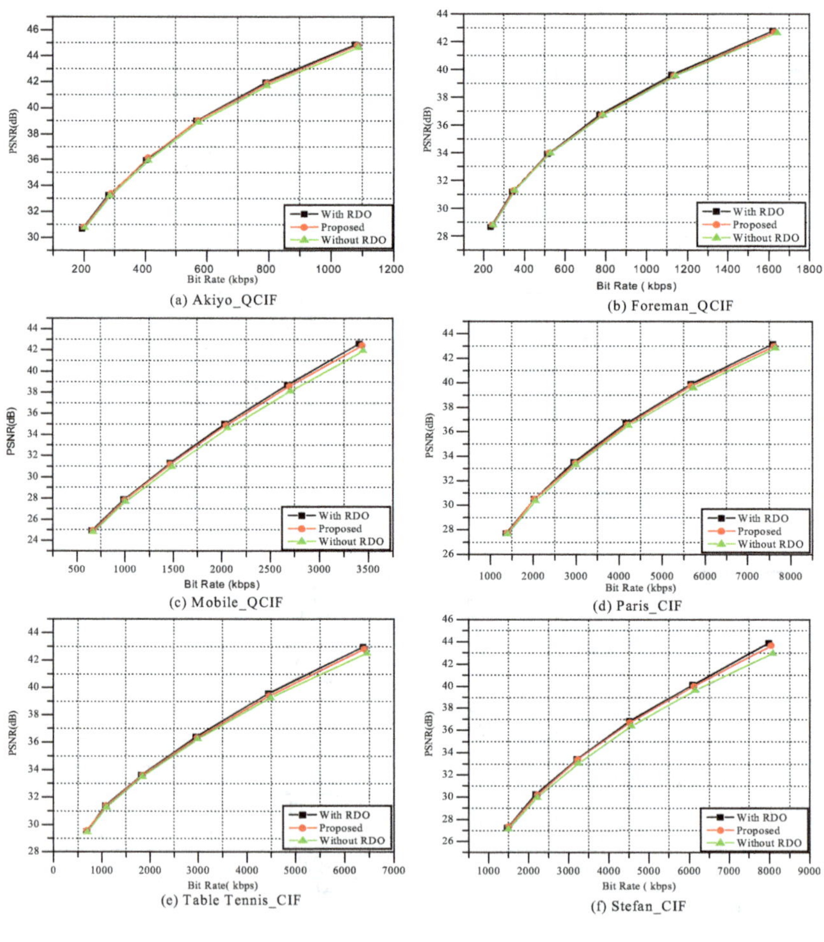


Fig. 9. Rate-distortion performance of proposed rate estimation method of different video sequences while all frames are intra coded.

To evaluate the rate distortion performance six different sequences (Akiyo, Foreman, Mobile, Paris, Table tennis and Stefan) are used in simulation. As shown in Table 2, it is clear that PSNR loss and bit rate increment is negligible. Figure 9 shows the rate-distortion curves of different sequences. The proposed method is very close with RD optimized curve. Comparing with the original H.264/AVC encoder with RD optimization, the proposed algorithm achieves about 47% time reduction of total encoding time on average. As shown in Figure 10, for the sequence "Mobile" and "Paris", the coding speed is high because both the sequences contains high detail such as different books in bookshelf of "Paris". On the other hand sequence "Akiyo" show strong spatial homogeneity and low detail. Therefore, the time saving of this sequence is not much as compared to other sequences. Figure 10 also indicates that percentage of complexity reduction is decreased with increasing the QP values. This is because there is large number of non-zero coefficients at small QP values. If true encoding process is used large entropy coding time is spent at small QP values whereas in our proposed method no entropy coding is required during mode-decision process.

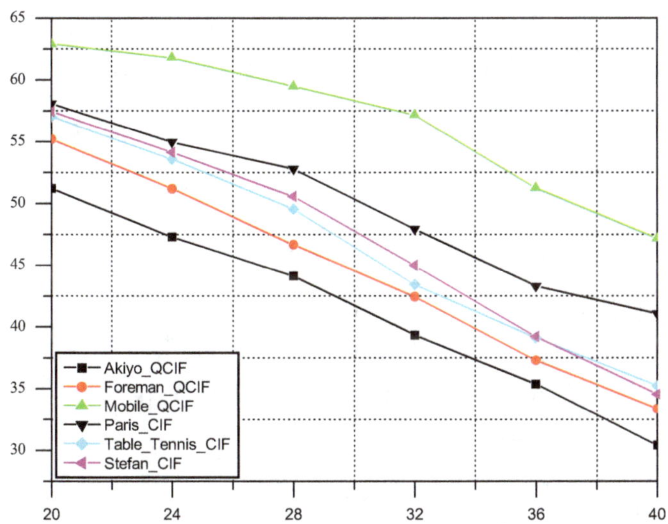


Fig. 10. Complexity reduction of proposed algorithm during intra frame coding (X-axis: QP; Y-axis: % of complexity reduction)

### 5.2 Experiments with IPP sequences

To evaluate the performance of proposed method during inter frame coding, several test video sequences are used. In this experiment total number of frames is 100 for each sequence, and the period of I-frame is 3. Figure 11 shows the actual and predicted rates of foreman and Stefan at different QP values. Data is generated as similar ways of intra frame coding.

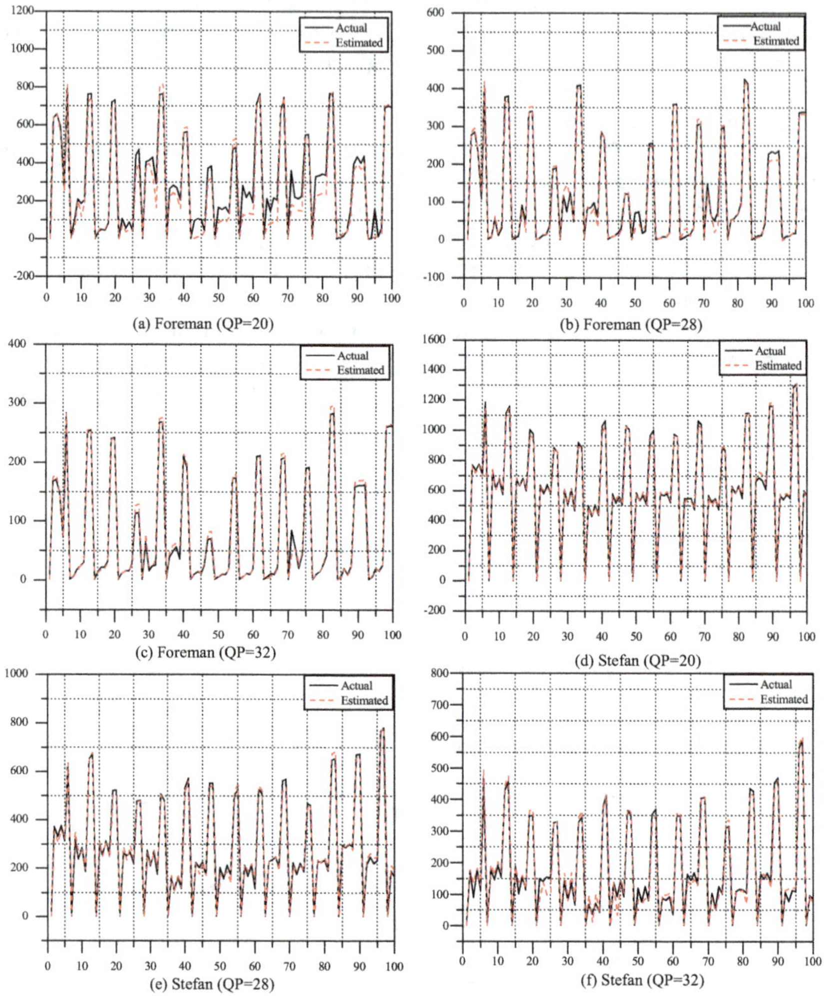


Fig. 11. Curves of the estimated and the actual rates of first 100 macroblocks of P frame of inter coding of foreman and Stefan sequences (X-axis: Macroblock number, Y-axis: number of bits)

Experimental results are tabulated as Table 4 which means that PSNR reduction and bit rate increments are negligible. The positive values mean increments whereas negative values mean decrements. From the experimental results in Table 5, it is observed that the proposed approach has reduced the encoding time by 34% on average. RD performances are given in Figure 12 which shows that the proposed method is closely matched with actual RD curves. Figure 13 presents the plot of computational complexity with quantization parameter of different sequences. Figure 13 show the general tendency that time saving increases as QP decreases. This is understandable that at small QP, coding quality is high and many detailed are retained. From this figure it is also shown that computation saving is large for those sequences which have high motion and large detail.

| Sequence | QP | $\Delta P_{snr}$ | $\Delta$ Bit% |
|---|---|---|---|
| Akiyo (QCIF) | 20 | +0.01 | +1.47 |
| | 24 | +0.01 | +1.38 |
| | 28 | +0.09 | +1.97 |
| | 32 | +0.14 | +2.79 |
| | 36 | +0.11 | +3.00 |
| | 40 | +0.16 | +2.89 |
| Foreman (QCIF) | 20 | +0.02 | +2.12 |
| | 24 | +0.03 | +2.23 |
| | 28 | +0.05 | +2.57 |
| | 32 | +0.07 | +3.01 |
| | 36 | +0.13 | +3.05 |
| | 40 | +0.15 | +4.44 |
| Mobile (QCIF) | 20 | -0.05 | +0.95 |
| | 24 | -0.04 | +0.99 |
| | 28 | -0.03 | +1.17 |
| | 32 | -0.01 | +2.39 |
| | 36 | +0.02 | +2.89 |
| | 40 | +0.07 | +2.94 |
| Paris (CIF) | 20 | -0.05 | +1.17 |
| | 24 | -0.05 | +1.37 |
| | 28 | -0.02 | +1.43 |
| | 32 | +0.00 | +2.38 |
| | 36 | +0.02 | +2.33 |
| | 40 | +0.08 | +3.21 |
| Table Tennis (CIF) | 20 | -0.03 | +2.20 |
| | 24 | +0.01 | +2.33 |
| | 28 | +0.04 | +2.52 |
| | 32 | +0.06 | +2.88 |
| | 36 | +0.06 | +2.95 |
| | 40 | +0.06 | +3.11 |
| Stefan (CIF) | 20 | -0.10 | +1.17 |
| | 24 | -0.09 | +0.08 |
| | 28 | -0.03 | +1.97 |
| | 32 | -0.02 | +3.01 |
| | 36 | +0.07 | +3.65 |
| | 40 | +0.14 | +4.74 |

Table 4. Performance of PSNR and Bit Rate of Proposed Algorithm of Inter frame (IPP sequences) coding

| Sequence | Quantization Parameter, QP | | | | | |
|---|---|---|---|---|---|---|
| | 20 | 24 | 28 | 32 | 36 | 40 |
| Akiyo_QCIF | 36.63 % | 31.91 % | 28.73 % | 23.45 % | 22.07 % | 21.33 % |
| Foreman_QCIF | 41.66 % | 37.85 % | 33.33 % | 29.47 % | 27.58 % | 22.22 % |
| Mobile_QCIF | 53.08 % | 50.99 % | 46.71 % | 40.49 % | 34.57 % | 29.89 % |
| Paris_CIF | 45.15 % | 41.82 % | 38.39 % | 33.98 % | 28.64 % | 24.29 % |
| Table_tennis_CIF | 41.61 % | 36.59 % | 32.45 % | 28.16 % | 25.94 % | 23.87 % |
| Stefan_CIF | 46.19 % | 42.65 % | 38.61 % | 35.13 % | 30.56 % | 25.14 % |
| Average = 34.20 % | | | | | | |

Table 5. Computational complexity reduction of proposed algorithm during Inter frame (IPP sequences) coding

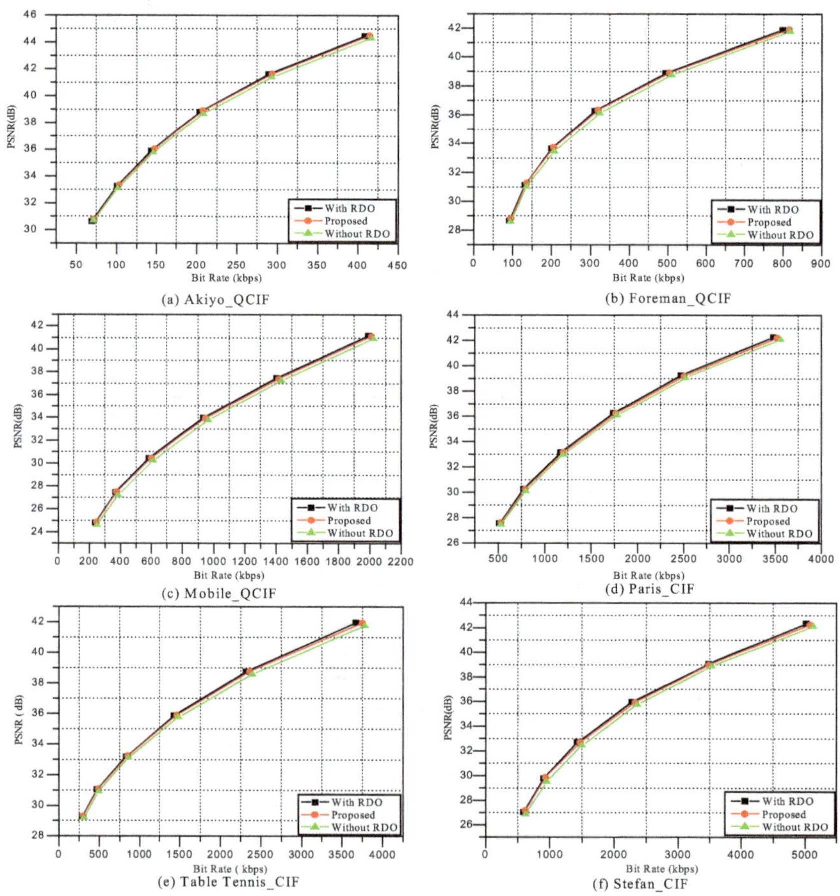


Fig. 12. Rate-distortion performance of proposed rate estimation method of different video sequences during Inter frame (IPP sequences) coding

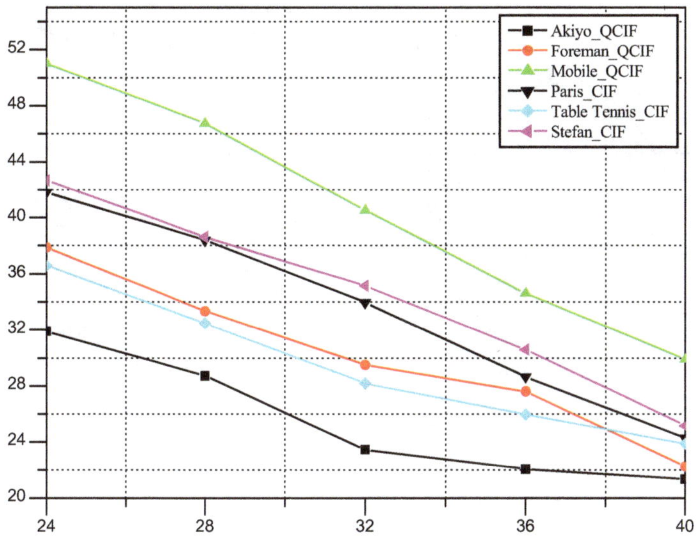


Fig. 13. Complexity reduction of proposed algorithm during IPP sequences (X-axis: QP; Y-axis: % of complexity reduction)

| Sequence | Frame Skip | QP | Δ $P_{snr}$ | Δ Bit% | Δ T% |
|---|---|---|---|---|---|
| Akiyo (QCIF) | 1 | 20 | +0.09 | +3.84 | 30.41 |
| | | 28 | +0.14 | +3.00 | 20.84 |
| | | 32 | +0.06 | +3.02 | 17.76 |
| | 2 | 20 | +0.11 | +2.85 | 33.20 |
| | | 28 | +0.14 | +3.55 | 25.99 |
| | | 32 | +0.10 | +3.67 | 20.46 |
| Foreman (QCIF) | 1 | 20 | +0.09 | +3.24 | 36.86 |
| | | 28 | +0.11 | +3.96 | 29.60 |
| | | 32 | +0.10 | +2.98 | 23.88 |
| | 2 | 20 | +0.06 | +2.03 | 34.51 |
| | | 28 | +0.10 | +4.13 | 26.25 |
| | | 32 | +0.13 | +4.41 | 20.27 |
| Mobile (QCIF) | 1 | 20 | +0.01 | +3.04 | 46.26 |
| | | 28 | +0.11 | +2.82 | 39.67 |
| | | 32 | +0.08 | +3.33 | 35.35 |
| | 2 | 20 | +0.04 | +1.60 | 47.46 |
| | | 28 | +0.11 | +3.10 | 40.06 |
| | | 32 | +0.08 | +2.87 | 36.51 |

Table 6. Experimental results of IBPBP sequences

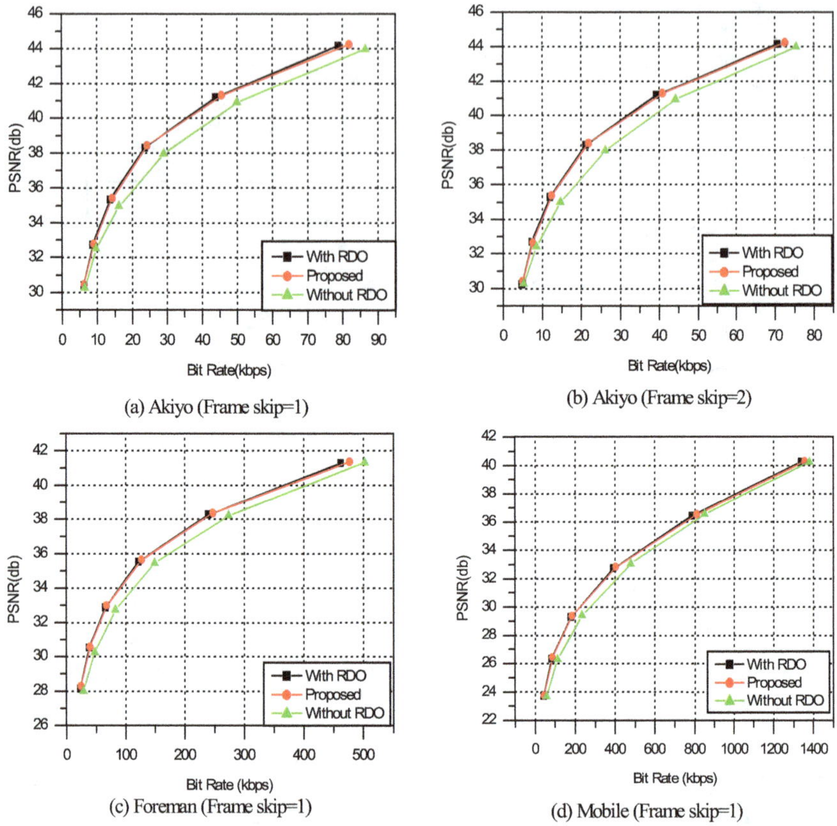


(a) Akiyo (Frame skip=1)

(b) Akiyo (Frame skip=2)

(c) Foreman (Frame skip=1)

(d) Mobile (Frame skip=1)

Fig. 14. Rate distortion performance of proposed method with IBPBP sequences

### 5.3 Experiments with IBPBP sequences

In this experiment, there is one B-frame between any two I- or P-frames with different frame skip values. Period of I-frames is set to 100. Number of frames is 100. Experimental results were tabulated at table 6. As shown in table 6, the proposed algorithm achieves time saving of about 32% (on average) with slight increment in bit rate. Rate-distortion performances of different sequences are shown in Figure 14 with different frame skip value.

### 5.4 Experiments with Full Search Motion Estimation

It is well known that motion estimation requires major portion of the processing power. In all of the previous experiments, fast motion estimation technique described in (Chen et al., 2002) is utilized. In order to show the complexity of proposed method with full search motion estimation technique, several video sequences are encoded. In this experiment, IPP sequence is used and number of frames is set to 50. Experimental results are tabulated at table 7. It is shown that bit rate increment is up to about 4%. Since the PSNR also increases, the resulting RD performance is very much closed with original one. The proposed algorithm reduces about 17% (on average) of computation time when full search motion estimation method is used.

| Sequence | QP | Δ $P_{snr}$ | Δ Bit% | Δ T% |
|---|---|---|---|---|
| Akiyo (QCIF) | 20 | +0.09 | +3.96 | 12.53 |
| | 28 | +0.12 | +2.94 | 6.66 |
| | 32 | +0.13 | +3.65 | 5.72 |
| Foreman (QCIF) | 20 | +0.07 | +2.86 | 20.66 |
| | 28 | +0.04 | +3.59 | 9.09 |
| | 32 | +0.08 | +3.50 | 6.62 |
| Mobile (QCIF) | 20 | -0.01 | +0.64 | 32.19 |
| | 28 | +0.11 | +2.52 | 24.42 |
| | 32 | +0.10 | +4.21 | 21.95 |
| Stefan (QCIF) | 20 | +0.02 | +1.48 | 24.80 |
| | 28 | +0.07 | +2.46 | 20.11 |
| | 32 | +0.08 | +2.57 | 15.78 |

Table 7. Experimental results with full search motion estimation

| Sequence | QP | Δ $P_{snr}$ | Δ Bit% | Δ T% |
|---|---|---|---|---|
| Akiyo (QCIF) | 20 | +0.02 | -0.91 | -4.11 |
| | 28 | +0.01 | -1.38 | -4.54 |
| | 32 | +0.05 | -1.47 | -4.02 |
| Foreman (QCIF) | 20 | +0.05 | -1.14 | -4.47 |
| | 28 | +0.07 | -0.77 | -4.61 |
| | 32 | +0.11 | -0.67 | -4.68 |
| Mobile (QCIF) | 20 | +0.22 | -0.29 | -5.86 |
| | 28 | +0.13 | -0.78 | -5.17 |
| | 32 | +0.06 | -1.02 | -5.02 |
| Stefan (CIF) | 20 | +0.33 | -0.52 | -5.59 |
| | 28 | +0.10 | -0.88 | -5.12 |
| | 32 | +0.11 | -1.23 | -4.92 |

Table 8. Comparison of proposed method with rate estimation method stated in (Tseng et al., 2006)

### 5.5 Comparison with other methods

In this experiment, the proposed method is compared with two different methods in terms of RD performance and complexity. Fast motion estimation technique described in (Chen et al., 2002) is used. Table 8 shows the comparison of our proposed method with rate estimation method defined in (Tseng et al., 2006). In this simulation, only intra 4x4 modes are used. RD performance of proposed method is better from method (Tseng et al., 2006). Positive value of Δ T% means complexity reduction and negative value means increment of complexity. It is shown that as compared with (Tseng et al., 2006), this algorithm reduces about 1% of bit rate and increases about 0.10 db PSNR with slight increment (about 4%) of computational time. Table 9 shows the RD performance as well as complexity reduction of this algorithm as compared with fast inter mode decision algorithm described in (Lim et al., 2003). IPP sequences are used in this comparison. Complexity reduction is about 14% (on average) for medium and high motion i.e. foreman, mobile and stefan sequences. It is also shown that the proposed method increases about 7% (on average) of computation of low motion sequence such as akiyo as compared with mode decision method stated in (Lim et al., 2003). RD performance is better for all types of sequences.

| Sequence | QP | Δ $P_{snr}$ | Δ Bit% | Δ T% |
|---|---|---|---|---|
| Akiyo (QCIF) | 20 | +0.05 | -0.24 | -10.71 |
| | 28 | +0.21 | -0.11 | -6.56 |
| | 32 | +0.15 | -0.67 | -4.16 |
| Foreman (QCIF) | 20 | +0.10 | -0.49 | 9.09 |
| | 28 | +0.11 | -0.95 | 7.93 |
| | 32 | +0.12 | -1.48 | 6.12 |
| Mobile (QCIF) | 20 | +0.03 | -0.39 | 31.53 |
| | 28 | +0.05 | -0.42 | 21.50 |
| | 32 | +0.04 | -0.84 | 14.28 |
| Stefan (CIF) | 20 | +0.08 | -0.35 | 19.60 |
| | 28 | +0.04 | -0.60 | 10.94 |
| | 32 | +0.09 | -1.03 | 8.34 |

Table 9. Comparison of proposed method with fast inter mode decision method stated in (Lim et al., 2003)

| QP | Akiyo (QCIF) | | Foreman (QCIF) | | Stefan(QCIF) | |
|---|---|---|---|---|---|---|
| | *ΔRate* % | *ΔPSNR* | *ΔRate* | *ΔPSNR* | *ΔRate* | *ΔPSNR* |
| 20 | 1.00 | -0.06 | 1.30 | 0 | 0.14 | -0.14 |
| 24 | 2.16 | -0.02 | 1.68 | +0.04 | 0.61 | -0.15 |
| 28 | 2.57 | +0.04 | 2.68 | +0.08 | 1.34 | -0.08 |
| 32 | 2.23 | -0.01 | 3.68 | +0.09 | 1.85 | -0.06 |
| 36 | 3.39 | 0 | 3.88 | +0.12 | 2.92 | -0.02 |
| 40 | 3.22 | -0.03 | 4.41 | +0.06 | 4.09 | +0.01 |

Table 10. Experimental results with CABAC entropy coding method

| QP | Akiyo (QCIF) | Foreman (QCIF) | Stefan(QCIF) |
|---|---|---|---|
| 20 | 32.20 | 40.58 | 46.25 |
| 24 | 27.78 | 39.13 | 43.42 |
| 28 | 23.53 | 25.45 | 37.68 |
| 32 | 22.45 | 25.00 | 35.48 |
| 36 | 15.22 | 20.41 | 29.82 |
| 40 | 11.36 | 17.02 | 24.53 |

Table 11. Percentage of complexity reduction with CABAC

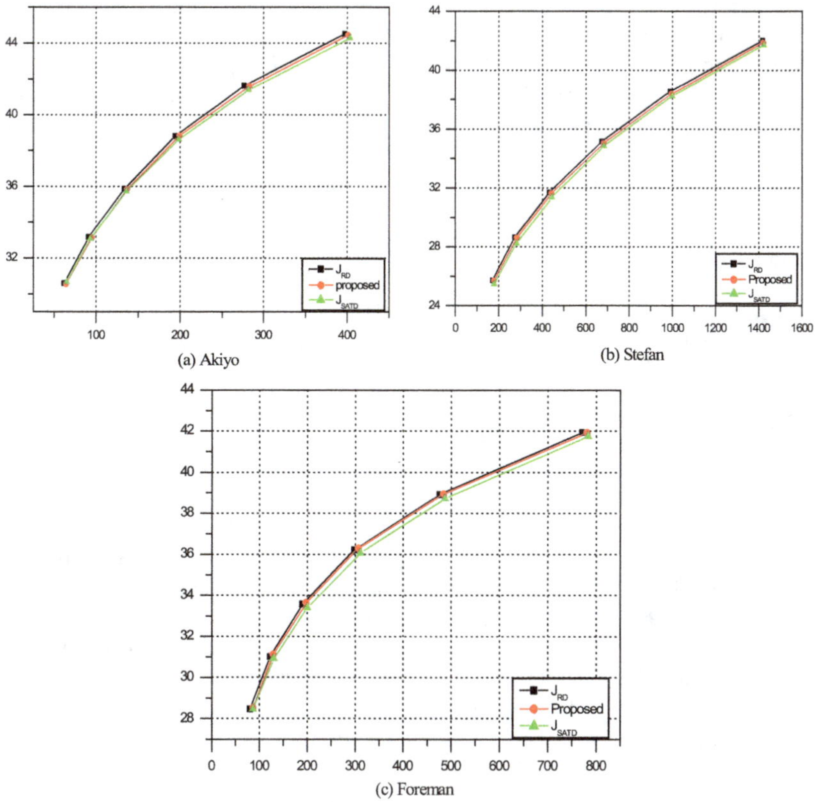


Fig. 15. RD performance with CABAC entropy coding method

### 5.6 Experiments with CABAC entropy coding method

In all of the above experiments CAVLC entropy coding method was used. Although the proposed algorithm is developed based on CAVLC, it is also suitable during mode decision of CABAC. This is because the proposed algorithm is used only for RD optimization. After selection of best mode, true entropy coding is used. To justify the performance of proposed rate estimation with CABAC entropy coding method, some video sequences are tested. IPP sequence is used in simulations and number of frames was set to 50. Table 10 shows the experimental results in terms of PSNR and bit rate. Table 11 shows the complexity reduction is also significant. The rate-distortion performance is given in Figure 15, which shows that the proposed algorithm is also suitable while CABAC entropy coding method is used. The proposed method is very close to RD optimized curves.

## 6. Conclusion

In this chapter, simple and fast bit rate estimation method for mode decision of H.264/AVC is proposed. This method is based on the VLC tables used in CAVLC entropy coding method. The experimental results verified that the proposed technique is suitable both for inter and intra mode decision of H.264/AVC. With the proposed scheme, entropy coding can be skipped during the mode decision process. The proposed technique reduces encoding time by 47 %, 34% and 32 % on average during intra frame, IPP sequences and IBPBPBP sequences respectively. The RD performance of this algorithm is better than both methods stated in reference (Tseng et al., 2006) and (Lim et al., 2003). The proposed method is also suitable for mode decision while CABAC entropy coding method is utilized.

## 7. Acknowledgement

The work described in this chapter was substantially supported by a GRF grant from Hong Kong SAR Government with project number of 9041251 (CityU 119207).

## 8. References

Chiang T. & Zhang Y. Q. (1997) A new rate control scheme using quadratic rate distortion model, *IEEE Trans. on Circuits and Systems for Video Technology*, vol. 7, No. 1, February 1997, pp. 246-250, ISSN 1051-8215

Coebera J. R. & Lei S. (1999). Rate control of DCT video coding for low-delay communication, *IEEE Trans. on Circuits and Systems for Video Technology*, vol. 9, No. 1, February 1999, pp. 172-185, ISSN 1051-8215

Chen Z.; Zhou P. & He Y. (2002) Fast Integer Pel and Fractional Pel Motion Estimation for JVT, *Joint Video Team (JVT) Docs*, JVT-F017, Dec. 2002.

Erol B.; Gallant M.; Cote G. & Kossentini F. (1998). The H.263+ video coding standard: complexity and performance, *Proceedings of IEEE Data Compression Conference*, pp. 259-268, Snowbird, Utah, March 1998.

Feng Pan F.; Lin X.; Rahardja S.; Lim K. P.; Li Z.G.; Wu D. & Wu S. (2005). Fast Mode Decision Algorithm for Intra-prediction in H.264/AVC Video Coding, *IEEE Trans. on Circuits and Systems for Video Technology*, vol. 15, no. 7, July 2005, pp. 813-822, ISSN 1051-8215

Han K. H. & Lee Y. L. (2005). Fast macroblock mode determination to reduce H.264 complexity, *IEICE Transactions on Fundamentals of Electronics, Communications and Computer Sciences*, vol. E88-A, No. 3, March 2005, pp. 800-804, ISSN 1745-1337

ITU-T Rec. (2002). Advanced Video Coding, ITU-T Rec. H.264/ISO/IEC 11496-10 Final Committee Draft, Documents JVT-E022, September 2002.

Iain E. G. Richardson (2003) *H.264 and MPEG-4 Video Compression – video coding for next generation multimedia*, John Wily & Sons Ltd, ISBN: 0-470-84837-5, West Sussex, England

Joint Video Team (JVT) (2002). Joint Video Specification ( ITU-T Rec. H.264/ISO/ISE 14496-10)- Joint Committee Draft, Doc. JVT-G050r1.doc, Dec. 2002.

Kim C.; Shih H.H. & Kuo C. C (2006). Fast H.264 Intra-prediction mode selection using joint spatial and transform domain features, *Journal of Visual Communication and Image Representation*, vol. 17, No. 2, April 2006, pp. 291-310, ISSN 1047-3203.

Lim K. P; Wu S.; Wu D. J; Rahardja S.; Lin X.; Pan F. & Li Z. G. (2003). Fast inter mode selection, *Joint Video Team (JVT) Docs*, JVT-I020, Sep. 2003.

Sullivan G. J. & Wiegand T. (1998). Rate-distortion optimization for video compression, *IEEE Signal Processing Magazine*, vol. 15, No. 6, November 1998, pp. 74-90, ISSN: 1053-5888

Sarwer M. G.; Po L. M. & Wu J. (2008) Fast Sum of Absolute Transformed Difference based 4x4 Intra Mode Decision of H.264/AVC Video Coding Standard, *Elsevier Journal of Signal Processing: Image Communications*, Vol. 23, Issue 8, September 2008, pp. 571-580, ISSN: 0923-5965.

Sarwer M. G. & Wu J. Q. M (2009) Region Based Searching for Early Terminated Motion Estimation Algorithm of H.264/AVC Video Coding Standard, *Proceedings of IEEE Canadian Conference on Electrical and Computer Engineering*, pp. 468-471. St John's, NL, May 2009

Topiwala. P.; Sullivan G.; Joch A. & Kossentini F. (2001). Performance evaluation of H.26L TML 8 vs. H.263++ and MPEG4, *Document VCEG-042, 15th Meeting, ITU-T Q.6/SG16*, Pattaya, Thailand, December 2001.

Tseng C. H.; Wang H.M. & Yang J. F. (2006), Enhanced Intra 4x4 Mode Decision for H.264/AVC Coders, *IEEE Trans. on Circuits and Systems for Video Technology*, vol. 16, no. 8, August 2006, pp. 1027-1032, ISSN 1051-8215

Weigand T.; Schwarz H.; Joch A.; Kossentini F. & Sullivan G. (2003). Rate-constrained coder control and comparison of video coding standards, *IEEE Trans. on Circuits and Systems for Video Technology*, vol. 13, No. 7, July 2003, pp. 688-703, ISSN 1051-8215

Wu D.; Pan F.; Lim K. P.; Wu S.; Li Z. G.;Lin X.; Rahardja S. & Ko C. C. (2005). Fast inter mode Decision in H.264/AVC Video Coding, *IEEE Trans. on Circuits and Systems for Video Technology*, vol. 15, No. 6, July 2005, pp. 953-958, ISSN 1051-8215

Yang C. L.; Po L. M. & Lam W. H. (2004). A fast H.264 Intra Prediction algorithm using Macroblock Properties, *Proceedings of IEEE International Conference on Image Processing*, pp. 461-464, Singapore, October 2004.

Yu K.; Yang J. F. &Sun M. T. (2006) Efficient rate-distortion estimation for H.264/AVC coders, *IEEE Trans. on Circuits and Systems for Video Technology*, vol. 16, no. 5, May 2006, pp. 600-611, ISSN 1051-8215

5

# On Cross-Media Correlation and its Applications

Wei-Ta Chu
*National Chung Cheng University*
*Taiwan*

## 1. Introduction

Multimedia researches integrate and manipulate different media to facilitate media management, browsing, or presentation such that the developed multimedia systems provide promising learning, entertainment, or information access functionalities. The essence of multimedia is that the processed media are often correlated. Cross-media correlation not only defines the uniqueness of a multimedia system, but also provides clues for efficient/effective processing.

Cross-media correlation comes from related properties between different modalities. Maintenance of these properties is often required to facilitate appropriate presentation and to convey correct information. For example, in a news video, the anchorperson's lip motion should temporally matches with the pronounced sound, or it would be very annoying for us to realize meanings of news stories (Chen, 2001). We call this requirement temporal synchronization, and we say that the anchorperson's lip motion has temporal correlation with the pronounced sound. Another common correlation lies on spatial relationship between different modalities. For example, it's very often that a web page contains text, images, animation, or even videos. How these media arranged on a page, i.e., layout, apparently affects whether information is correctly presented. Images should not occlude the text region, for example. This type of spatial correlation is automatically tackled by web browsers and is transparent to users.

As aforementioned, cross-media correlation apparently or subtly exists in various multimedia systems and plays important roles in many aspects. This article investigates four types of cross-correlations: temporal correlation, spatial correlation, content correlation, and social correlation. We will first give a few brief examples to introduce each type of correlation, and then demonstrate a main system that elaborately exploits one or more cross-media correlations to facilitate media management.

Among four types of correlations, temporal correlation and spatial correlation have been studied for years. For example, in audiovisual display and video compression, temporal synchronization guarantees correct presentation and processing, and different visual media should be placed at the right position to avoid misunderstanding. Moreover, some multimedia standards such as SMIL (Synchronized Multimedia Integration Language) are proposed to describe multimedia documents. In Section 2, we will describe a multimedia lecturing system that integrates tutor's speech, HTML-based lectures, and guided events to assist English learning.

One example for content correlation is the spreadsheet application. We have numerical data and the corresponding charts. If numerical values change, the corresponding chart changes accordingly. Although numerical data and charts present in different modalities, they convey the same meaning and thus have close content correlation. In Section 3, we will describe a video scene detection system that exploits content correlation between photos and videos taken in journeys. On the basis of video scenes, we propose novel photo summarization and video summarization methods, in which photo summarization is influenced by the correlated video segments, and video summarization is influenced by the characteristics of correlated photos.

Finally, we propose a new kind of cross-media correlation, i.e., social correlation, which emerges in recent years and facilitates multimedia content analysis from a new perspective. In Section 4, social relations between people are described as a network structure. We treat a movie as a small society, and explore the relationships between characters to facilitate movie video understanding.

## 2. Temporal Correlation and Spatial Correlation

### 2.1 Introduction

Among various corrleations between media, temporal and spatial correlatons have been studied for several decades. A simple example is slide presentation in Powerpoint. If there are animations to display objects, objects should be shown in correct temporal order to convey correct information. Another interesting example is automatic page turning or score following (Arzt et al., 2008). Music and text-based scores are temporally synchronized such that score pages can automatically change when the played music reaches the end of a page.

In addition to temporal order, objects should be located appropriately to prevent confusion. For objects at the same location or overlap, introduction of depth, or the so-called z-index, facilitates spatial description objects. Therefore, even Powerpoint, which is not thought as a complex multimedia application, needs careful consideration of temporal and spatial correlations between objects.

Recently, integration of various media into the same layout has been the most popular presentation. Synchronized multimedia integration language (SMIL) was proposed to enable authoring and interaction in audiovisual presentations. Through description by the markup language, we can specify media types, time information, spatial information, hyperlinks, and interactive functions for a multimedia document. Due to large-scale of applications and potential commercial benefits, many software developers propose multimedia document format to achieve vivid audiovisual presentations and enrich web-based browsing, such as Adobe's Flash and Microsoft's Silverlight.

Temporal and spatial correlations also present in one of the most important applications - video compression by MPEG and related coding standards. In these standards, audio and video are compressed separately, and correct decoding is achieved only if audio-video synchronization can be guaranteed. Temporal synchronization is especially important in coding schemes. Moreover, in the MPEG-4 standard, object-based coding is introduced and many coding tools such as sprite coding are proposed to describe spatial relationships among different objects.

In this section, we will introduce a multimedia lecturing system, which integrates text, images, audio, and animation to teach English as a second language. Correlations between different modalities would be discovered and manipulated to facilitate effective tutoring.

## 2.2 Web-based Synchronized Multimedia Lecturing System

The Web-based Synchronized Multimedia Lecturing system (WSML) aims to capture teaching activities and provides web-based lecturing, which is totally developed by dynamic HTML techniques and can be easily browsed via any webpage browser (Chu & Chen, 2005). Figure 1 show the system architecture composed of three main components: the WSML recorder, WSML document servers, and the WSML browser.

Lectures in the WSML system are all stored in the form of web pages. This characteristic facilitates tightly integration of distance learning and web browsing. To produce a WSML document, the WSML recorder retrieves HTML lectures prepared in advance, and records teacher's tutoring activities, such as teacher's speech and guided events on web pages. The guided events include cursor's trajectory, web page scrolling, highlighting, pen stroke, annotation, and hyperlink. These guided events animate still web pages, and provide vivid and practical tutoring activities on web pages.

In a WSML document, teacher's speech plays as foundation of the time axis, and all other guided events are associated to it by relative timestamps. For example, a scrolling event would occur at 1 minute and 23 seconds relative to the start of teacher's speech, and a highlight event would occur at 2 minute and 45 seconds. Therefore, temporal correlation exists between guided events and teacher's speech. In addition, it's obvious that spatial information of guided media is very important. For example, a pen stroke event should be displayed at the right place in a web page only if the coordinates of pen stroke pixels are appropriately stored. Similarly, the WSML recorder captures coordinates relative to the left-top corner of a web page. Cursor trajectory, highlight event, pen stroke, annotation, and scrolling event correlate to web pages with spatial information.

As shown in Figure 1, all guided events associated with temporal and spatial information are captured by the WSML recorder. At the client side, various media and their correlations should be integrated to present correct lecturing information. The WSML browser at the client side is a web browser equipped with dynamic HTML functionalities. It synchronizes various media and implements audiovisual presentations that were invoked by teachers.

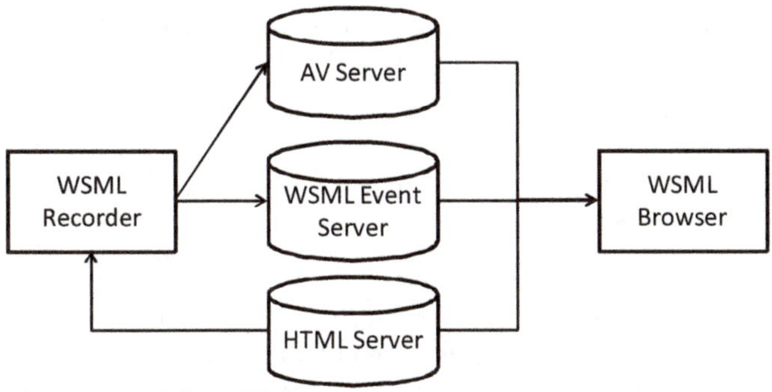


Fig. 1. System architecture of the WSML system.

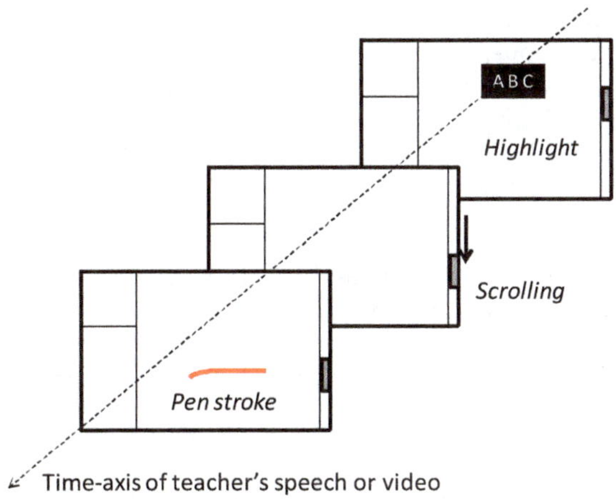


Fig. 2. Presentation scenario of the WSML browser.

Figure 2 shows the presentation scenario of the WSML browser. Along the time-axis of teacher's speech or video, various guided events specially designed for teaching English are displayed in appropriate temporal order and at appropriate positions. In this example, the highlight event is often used to indicate a new vocabulary. The scrolling event is the unique action of web-based lectures. The pen stroke event can be used to highlight a sentence, or to mark corrections on students' articles. In (Chen & Liu, 2009), the authors extend this function by visualized annotations that are commonly used by English teachers to correct students' composition homeworks. Animated visual annotations accompanied with the teacher's speech more accurately point out composition errors and show how to correct.

### 2.3 Explicit and Implicit Correlation

We can see various correlations exist between media in the WSML system. Nonetheless, according to whether the cross-media correlation can be easily captured or not, correlations in this system can be divided into two categories - explicit correlations and implicit correlations. Explicit correlations are able to be directly captured by the WSML recorder, such as position of the cursor, timestamp of a pen stroke, and the extent of scrolling. For example, the WSML recorder periodically stores the position of cursor, which can be implemented by dynamic HTML programming (Goodman, 2006). Actually, all spatial and temporal correlations of guided events described above can be explicitly captured.

On the other hand, some correlations are hidden between media and cannot be directly captured by the WSML recorder. In studying English, listening to teacher's reading and comparing it with text in lecture is an important process. Teacher's speech is related to text in web pages, but this relationship cannot be explicitly recorded. Therefore, we would like to develop a speech-text alignment module to discover correlations between two modalities.

Figure 3 shows the system flowchart of the speech-text alignment module. First, we apply a speech recognition module to recognize teacher's reading into text. Note that the recognition module not only transforms speech into text, but also stores timestamp of each recognized word. Through this process, aligning speech and text has been transformed into aligning two text sequences. However, recognized text is imperfect, and many words pronounced similarly would be erroneously recognized. Therefore, we further transform recognized words and text in lectures into phonetic sequences by the CMU pronunciation dictionary (CMU, 2009). Through this process, words with similar pronunciation are encoded as the same string. For example, both *through* and *threw* are converted to *"TH R UW"*, in which each term indicates a phoneme symbol.

Based on phonetic strings, we find the longest common subsequence (LCS) to determine the correspondence between recognized text and text in lectures. Due to variations of tense or plurality, words having the same meaning are not necessarily converted into exactly the same phonetic string. For example, the word *student* is converted to *"S T UW D AH N T"*, while the word *students* are converted to *"S T UW D AH N T S"*. Therefore, we calculate the edit distance between two phonetic strings, and claim them as matched strings if their distance is less than a threshold.

We apply a dynamic programming strategy to find the optimal LCS, which represents the best correspondence between two text sequences. The timestamps of the words matched with recognized words are then determined. For those words that are not aligned, we estimate their timestamps by interpolation or extrapolation. Finally, a fully timestamped sequence is obtained.

The proposed process discovers implicit temporal correlation between teacher's reading and text in lectures. With this correlation, a sentence can be especially highlighted when the teacher speaks it. It is very helpful for students with bad English listening comprehension.

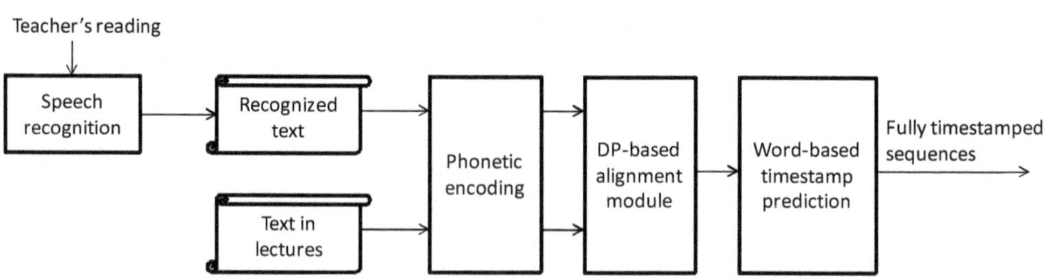


Fig. 3. System flowchart of the speech-text alignment module.

## 2.4 Evaluation

To evaluate the propose speech-text alignment process, one subjective experiment and one objective experiment are designed. In the subjective experiment that is similar to the investigation in (Steinmetz, 1996), we study how synchronization skews between highlighted sentences and teacher's reading affect human perception. We invited several males and females to evaluate sentence-based sync skews by giving scores from 1 to 5. Smaller score means higher degree of perceiving sync skew. The assessors were asked to see highlighted sentences and listen to corresponding speech, and then evaluate whether a sync error is perceived. In this work, the sentences with scores less than three are claimed to be out-of-sync.

Figure 4 that is by courtesy of (Chu & Chen, 2005) shows the relationships between human perception and sentence-based sync skews. The horizontal axis denotes the sync skews in milliseconds (ms), in which positive values mean sentences show after speech, and negative values mean sentences show before speech. The vertical axis denotes the percentage of assessors who are able to perceive sync errors. This figure can be divided into three regions: 1) The hardly-detected region ranges from -750 ms to +300 ms, in which few assessors can perceive sync errors. 2) The transient region ranges from +300 ms to +1000 ms and from -750 ms to -1350 ms. Synchronization skews in this region can be perceived by more than half of assessors, but they don't lead to misunderstanding. 3) The out-of-sync region spans beyond -1300 ms and +1000 ms. All assessors perceive sync errors, and this presentation largely annoys viewers and may cause misunderstanding.

From Figure 4, human perception is not symmetric when sentences are highlighted before or after the speech. Basically, humans have higher tolerance of speech-text sync skews when sentences are highlighted before start of the corresponding speech. This again confirms the non-uniformity nature of human perception.

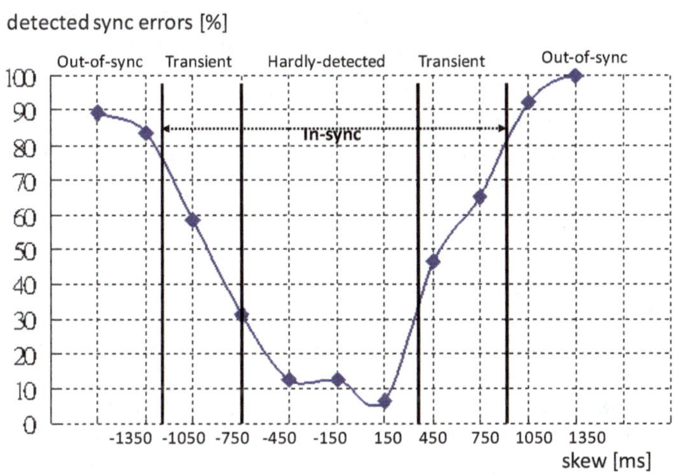


Fig. 4. Relationships between human perception and sync skews.

In the objective experiment, we measure the percentage of in-sync sentences under different speech recognition accuracy. From Figure 4, we define that sentences with sync skews in "hardly-detected" region or in "transient" region are in-sync. We adopt SPHINX speech recognition engine (Huang, 1993) in real implementation, and achieve different recognition accuracy in different teachers' speeches and in different documents. Because the recognition engine is not specially trained by any specific teacher, the recognition accuracy is generally not high. But fortunately, the proposed speech-text alignment process is still able to determine most of the correspondence based on partially correct text. In this experiment, 80% of sentences are in-sync when the recognition accuracy is 25%, i.e., only quarter of words are correctly recognized. All sentences can be correctly synchronized with speech when the recognition accuracy is higher than 40%. In summary, we effectively discover implicit temporal correlation between speech and text and facilitate teaching English as a second language.

## 3. Content Correlation

### 3.1 Introduction

Content correlation between different media or different data is also an important area of multimedia research. A straightforward example is content-based image retrieval. Given an image containing a specific scene or an object, we would like to find images with the same scene or object from image database or from the web. Generally these images have similar appearance or convey similar semantics. Extending from this study, multimedia indexing (Snoek & Worring, 2005), video concept detection (Snoek et al, 2007; Jiang et al, 2008), and video copy detection (Law-To et al., 2007) have been widely investigated in recent years.

Another perceptive of content correlation comes from spreadsheet applications. If we change numerical values, the corresponding chart changes dynamically. Numbers and charts present the same meanings but are in different presentations. In the WSML system described in the previous section, guided events are attached to the corresponding HTML pages. If the HTML lectures are removed, all corresponding guided events should be removed, too. Tight content correlations exist between different media.

In this section, we focus on media captured in journeys and find content correlations between images and videos to facilitate efficient media management, including video scene detection and video/photo summarization. We demonstrate the assist of cross-media correlation on multimedia content analysis.

### 3.2 Travel Media Analysis

There are at least two challenges in travel media analysis. First, there is no clear structure in travel media. Unlike scripted videos such as news and movies, videos captured in journeys just follow the travel schedule, and content in video may consist of anything people willing or unwilling to capture. Second, because amateur photographers don't have professional skills, the captured photos and videos often suffer from bad quality. The same objects in different photos or video segments may have significant appearance. Due to these characteristics, conventional image/video analysis techniques cannot be directly applied to travel media.

People often take both digital cameras and digital camcorders in journeys. Even with only one of these devices, digital cameras have been equipped with video capturing functions, and on the other hand, digital camcorders have the "photo mode" to facilitate taking high-resolution photos. Therefore, photos and videos in the same journey often have similar content, and the content correlation can be utilized to analyze travel media.

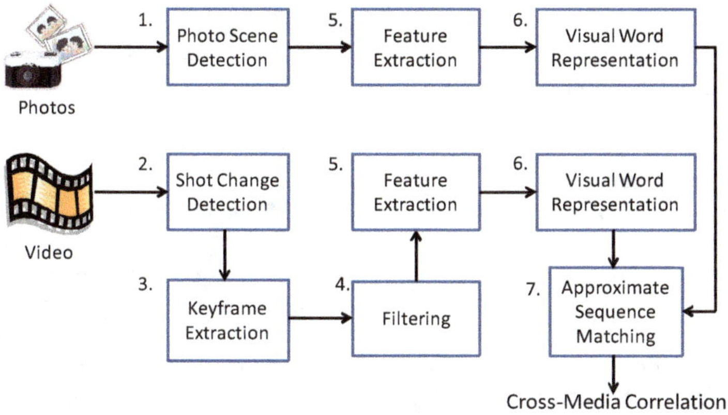


Fig. 5. Flowchart for finding cross-media correlation between photo and video.

### 3.3 Content Correlation Between Photos and Videos

We assume that travelers alternately take photos and videos when they visit each scenic spot. Along the travel schedule, photos and videos are captured in the same temporal order. Figure 5 shows the flowchart of finding cross-media correlation between a photo set and a video. Note that all video segments captured in the same journey are concatenated as a single video stream according to the temporal order.

- Photo Scene Detection

There are large time gaps between photos in different scenic spots because of transportation. We check time gaps between temporally adjacent photos, and claim a scene boundary exists between two photos if their time gap exceeds a dynamic threshold (Platt et al., 2003). The method proposed in (Platt et al., 2003) has been widely applied in photo clustering, and has been proven very effective. After this time-based clustering, photos taken at the same scenic spot (scene) are clustered together.

- Keyframe Extraction

For the video, we segment it into shots based on difference of HSV color histograms in consecutive video frames (Hanjalic, 2002). To efficiently represent each video shot, one or more keyframes are extracted. We adopt the method proposed in (Chasanis et al., 2007), which automatically determines the most appropriate number of keyframes based on an unsupervised global k-means algorithm (Likas et al, 2003). The global k-means algorithm is an incremental deterministic clustering algorithm that iteratively performs k-means clustering while increasing k by one at each step. The clustering process ends until the clustering results converge.

- Keyframe Filtering

Video shots with blurred content often convey less information, and would largely degrade the performance of correlation determination. To detect blurred keyframes, we check edge information in different resolutions (Tong et al, 2004). The video shots with blurred keyframes are then put aside from the following processes. After video shot filtering, fewer video shots (keyframes) are needed to be examined in the matching process. This filtering reduces influence of blurred content, which may cause false matching between keyframes and photos.

- Visual Word Representation

After the processes above, correlation between photos and videos is determined by matching photos and keyframes. Image matching is an age-old problem, and is widely conducted based on color and texture features. However, especially in travel media, the same place may have significantly different appearances, which may be caused by viewing angles, large camera motion, and overexposure/underexposure. On the other hand, landmarks or buildings with apparent structure are often important clues for image matching. Therefore, we need features that resist to luminance and viewpoint changes, and are able to effectively represent local structure.

We extract SIFT (Scale-Invariant Feature Transform) features (Lowe, 2004) from photos and keyframes. SIFT features from a set of training photos and keyframes are clustered by the k-means algorithm. Feature points belong to the same cluster are claimed to belong to the same *visual word* (Sivic & Zisserman, 2003). Before matching photos with keyframes, visual words in photos and keyframes are collected as visual word histograms. Based on this representation, the problem of matching two image sequences has been transformed into matching two sequences of visual word histograms.

Conceptually, each SIFT feature point represents texture information around a small image patch. After clustering, a visual word presents a concept, which may correspond to corner of building, tip of leaves, and so on. A visual word histogram presents what concepts compose an image. To discover cross-media correlation, we would like to find photos and keyframes that have similar concepts.

- Approximate Sequence Matching

To find the optimal matching between two sequences, we exploit the dynamic programming strategy to find the longest common subsequence (LCS) between them. Given two visual word histogram sequences, $X = \langle \boldsymbol{x}_1, \boldsymbol{x}_2, ..., \boldsymbol{x}_m \rangle$ and $Y = \langle \boldsymbol{y}_1, \boldsymbol{y}_2, ..., \boldsymbol{y}_n \rangle$, which correspond to photos and keyframes, respectively. Each item in these sequences is a visual word histogram, i.e., $\boldsymbol{x}_i = h[j]$, $0 \leq j \leq N-1$, where $N$ is the number of visual words. The LCS between two subsequences $X_m$ and $Y_n$ is described as follows.

$$LCS(X_m, Y_n) = \begin{cases} LCS(X_{m-1}, Y_{n-1}) + 1, & \text{if } x_m = y_n, \\ \max(LCS(X_{m-1}, Y_n), LCS(X_m, Y_{n-1})), & \text{otherwise}, \end{cases} \tag{1}$$

where $X_i$ denotes the $i$th prefix of $X$, i.e., $X_i = \langle \boldsymbol{x}_1, \boldsymbol{x}_2, ..., \boldsymbol{x}_i \rangle$, and $LCS(X_i, Y_j)$ denotes the length of the LCS between $X_i$ and $Y_j$. This recursive structure facilitates usage of the dynamic programming approach.

Based on visual word histograms, the equality in eqn. (1) occurs when the following criterion is met:

$$x_i = y_j \quad \text{if} \sum_{k=0}^{N-1} |(h_i(k) - h_j(k))| < \delta, \tag{2}$$

where $h_i$ and $h_j$ are the visual word histograms corresponding to the images $x_i$ and $y_j$. According to this measurement, if visual word distributions are similar between a keyframe and a photo, we claim that they are conceptually "common" and contain similar content.

### 3.4 Video Scene Detection

Figure 6 shows an illustrated example of video scene detection based on cross-media correlation. The double arrows indicate the determined correlations between photos and keyframes. If a video shot's keyframe matches the photo in the $i$th photo scene, this video shot is assigned as in $i$th video scene as well. For those video shots without any keyframe matched with photos, we apply interpolation and nearest neighbor processing to assign them (Chu et al., 2009).

Because photo scene detection is much easier than video scene detection, this method first solves an easier problem, finds the correlation between two problems, and then solves the harder problem by consulting with cross-media correlation. This idea brings a new perspective to conduct travel media analysis.

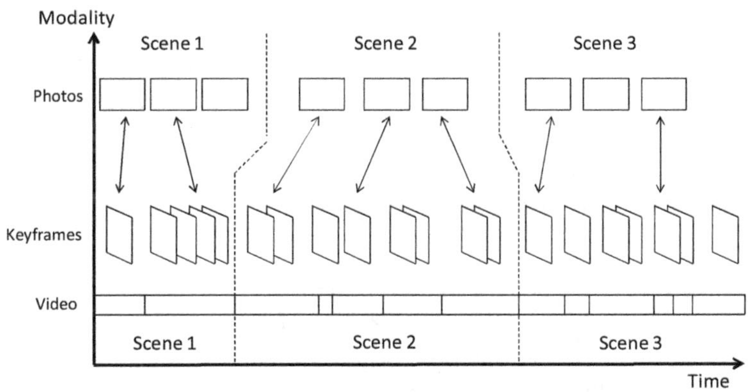


Fig. 6. Illustration of video scene detection using cross-media correlation.

### 3.5 Photo Summarization and Video Summarization

Correlation determined by the previous process suffices for scene boundary detection. However, to generate summaries, finer cross-media correlation is needed to define importance value of each photo and each keyframe. We call the correlation described above *global cross-media correlation*, which describes matching in terms of visual concepts. In this subsection, we need further analyze *local cross-media correlation* to find matching in terms of objects.

For photos and keyframes in the same scene, we perform finer matching between them by the SIFT matching algorithm (Lowe, 2004). For the photo $p_m$ and the keyframe $k_n$, we claim they contain the same object if the number of matched feature points exceeds a predefined threshold $\tau$. This threshold can be adjusted dynamically according to the requirements of users. Note that local cross-media correlation is determined based on SIFT features rather than visual word histograms. Visual word histograms describe global distribution of concepts (visual words), while feature points conveying local characteristics more appropriately describe whether two images have the same building or objects.

- Photo Summarization

The idea of defining each photo's importance comes from two perspectives. First, when a view or an object is both captured in photos and videos, the captured content must attract people more and is likely to be selected into summaries. The second factor is involved with considering characteristics of correlated videos to define photo's importance. When people take a closeup shot on an object, this object must attract people more. Therefore, a photo's importance is set higher if it matches with a keyframe that is between a zoom in action and a zoom out action, or is between a zoom in action and camera turning off. Two factors defining importance values can be mathematically expressed as follows.

Factor 1:
The first importance value of the photo $p_m$ is defined as

$$PT_{1,m} = \frac{I_{1,m}}{\max_{i=1,2,\ldots,M} I_{1,i}}, \tag{3}$$

where $M$ is the number of photos in this dataset. The value $I_{1,m}$ is calculated as

$$I_{1,m} = \begin{cases} L_1(h_{p_m}, h_{k_n}), & \text{if the photo } p_m \text{ matches with the keyframe } k_n, \\ 0, & \text{otherwise,} \end{cases}$$

where $h_{p_m}$ and $h_{k_n}$ are visual word histograms of the photo $p_m$ and the keyframe $k_n$, respectively. The value $L_1(\cdot,\cdot)$ denotes $L_1$-distance between two histograms.

Factor 2:
The second importance value of the photo $p_m$ is defined as

$$PT_{2,m} = \frac{I_{1,m} \times ZoomIn(p_m)}{\max_{i=1,2,\ldots,M} I_{1,i} \times ZoomIn(p_i)}, \tag{4}$$

where $ZoomIn(p_m) = 1$ if the keyframe $k_n$ that matches with $p_m$ locates between a zoom in action and a zoom out action, or between a zoom in action and camera turning off. The value $ZoomIn(p_m) = 0$, otherwise.

Two importance values are normalized and integrated to form the final importance value:

$$PT_m = \alpha \times PT_{1,m} + \beta \times PT_{2,m}. \tag{5}$$

Currently, the values $\alpha$ and $\beta$ are set as 1.

Users can set the desired number of photos in summaries. To ensure that the generated summary contains photos of all scenes (scenic spots), we first pick the most important photo in each scene to the summary. After that, we sort photos according to their corresponding importance values in descending order, and pick photos sequentially until the desired number is achieved.

According to the definitions above, only photos that are matched with keyframes have importance values larger than zero. If all photos with importance values larger than zero are picked but the desired number hasn't achieved, we define the importance value of a photo $p_i$ not picked yet by calculating the similarity between $p_i$ and its temporally closest photo $p_j$ that has nonzero importance value, i.e.,

$$T_i = L_1(h_{p_i}, h_{p_j}). \tag{6}$$

We sort the remaining photos according to the alternative importance values in descending order, and pick photos sequentially until the desired number is achieved.

- Video Summarization

Similar to photo summarization, we advocate that photo taking characteristics in a scene affect selection of important video segments. Two factors are also designed. The first factor is the same as that in photo summarization, i.e., video shots whose content also appears in photos are more important. Moreover, a video shot in which more keyframes match with photos is relatively more important. Two factors can be mathematically expressed as follows.

Factor 1:
The first importance value of a keyframe $k_m$ is defined as

$$KT_{1,m} = \frac{I_{1,m}}{\max_{i=1,2,\ldots,M} I_{1,i}}, \tag{7}$$

where $M$ is the number of keyframes in this dataset. The value $I_{1,m}$ is calculated as

$$I_{1,m} = \begin{cases} L_1(h_{k_m}, h_{p_n}), & \text{if the keyframe } k_m \text{ matches with the photo } p_n, \\ 0, & \text{otherwise,} \end{cases}$$

where $h_{k_m}$ and $h_{p_n}$ are visual word histograms of keyframe $k_m$ and the photo $p_n$, respectively.

Factor 2:
The second importance value of the keyframe $k_m$ is defined as

$$KT_{2,m} = \frac{I_{2,m}}{\max_{i=1,2,\ldots,M} I_{2,i}}, \tag{8}$$

where the value $I_{2,m}$ is defined as

$$I_{2,m} = \sum_{j=1}^{J} L_1(h_{k_j}, h_{p_{j^*}}). \tag{9}$$

This expression means there are $J$ keyframes in the shot containing $k_m$, and the notation $p_{j^*}$ denotes the photo matched with the keyframe $k_j$.

These two importance values are integrated to form the final importance value of $k_m$:

$$KT_m = \alpha \times KT_{1,m} + \beta \times KT_{2,m}. \tag{10}$$

Users can set the desired length of video summaries. To ensure that the generated summary contains video segments of all scenes (scenic spots), we first pick the most important keyframe of each scene. Assume that the keyframe $k_i$ is selected, we determine length and location of the video segment $S_i$ corresponding to $k_i$ as

$$S_i = \left( \frac{t(k_{i-1}) + t(k_i)}{2}, \frac{t(k_i) + t(k_{i+1})}{2} \right), \tag{11}$$

where $t(k_i)$ denotes the timestamp of the keyframe $k_i$, and $k_{i-1}$ and $k_{i+1}$ are two nearest keyframes that are before and after $k_i$, and with nonzero importance values. Two values in the parentheses respectively denote start time and end time of the segment $S_i$.

We pick keyframes and their corresponding video segments according to keyframe's importance values until the desired length is achieved. If all keyframes with nonzero importance values are picked but the desired length hasn't achieved, we utilize a method similar to that in eqn. (6) to define remaining keyframes' importance values, and pick appropriate number of keyframe accordingly.

### 3.6 Evaluation

We evaluate the proposed methods based on seven data sets. Each dataset includes a video clip and a set of photos, and there are totally 85 minutes of videos with 1084 keyframes and 423 photos. Photos are rescaled to smaller sizes due to the efficiency of feature points processing and visual word construction. Videos and photos are captured by different amateur photographers, with different capturing devices.

To measure video scene detection, we calculate purity value (Vinciarelli & Favre, 2007) by comparing detected video scenes and the ground truths. A purity value ranges from 0 to 1, and a larger purity value means that the detection result is closer to the ground truth. We averagely obtain a purity value of 0.95, which is very promising in scene detection, especially in the uncontrolled travel media.

To further show that the proposed method is more appropriate to travel videos, we compare it with the method proposed in (Chasanis et al, 2007). One of the major challenges in scene detection is the over-segmentation problem. We measure this effect in two methods and list the results in Table 1. In each cell of this table, the value $(m, n)$ denotes that a scene is segmented into $m$ and $n$ scenes, by the method in (Chasanis et al, 2007) and our method, respectively. For example, in the S2 column for Video 1, (4,1) means that the second scene in Video 1 is segmented into four scenes and one scene by the method in (Chasanis et al, 2007) and our approach, respectively. There are totally 6 scenes in Video 1, but it is segmented into 27 and 8 scenes by two methods. We see the effect of over-segmentation is severe in Chasanis's approach, and our approach works much better from this perspective.

To objectively demonstrate summarization results, we ask content owners to manually select subset of keyframes and photos as summarization ground truth. In generating video summaries or photo summaries, we set the number of keyframes or photos in manual summaries as the targeted number to be achieved. Summarization results are measured by precision values, i.e.,

$$\text{Precision} = \frac{\#\text{ correctly selected keyframes}}{\#\text{ selected keyframes}} \text{ and Precision} = \frac{\#\text{ correctly selected photos}}{\#\text{ selected photos}}. \tag{12}$$

Note that precision and recall rates are the same due to the selection policy.

| | S1 | S2 | S3 | S4 | S5 | S6 | Overall |
|---|---|---|---|---|---|---|---|
| Video 1 | (1,1) | (4,1) | (7,2) | (3,1) | (9,2) | (3,1) | (27,8) |
| Video 2 | (6,1) | (3,1) | (1,1) | (1,1) | | | (11,4) |
| Video 3 | (1,1) | (1,1) | (1,1) | (3,1) | (2,1) | | (8,5) |
| Video 4 | (1,1) | (2,2) | (1,1) | (5,2) | (1,1) | | (10,7) |
| Video 5 | (4,2) | (2,2) | (3,1) | | | | (9,5) |
| Video 6 | (3,1) | (2,1) | | | | | (5,2) |
| Video 7 | (5,1) | (2,2) | (2,2) | (1,1) | (3,2) | (1,1) | (14,9) |

Table 1. Over-segmentation situations in different videos.

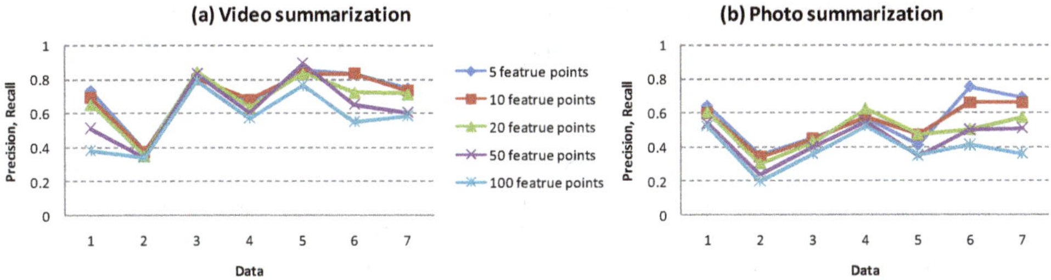


Fig. 7. Performance of (a) video summarization and (b) photo summarization.

Figure 7(a) shows precision/recall rates of video summarization under different matching thresholds $\tau$, while Figure 7(b) shows precision/recall rates of photo summarization. Generally, we see that using five or ten matched points as the threshold we can obtain better summarization results, i.e., looser thresholds draw slightly better performance. Summarization performance of the second dataset is especially worse for both video and photos. This reason is that photos and video in this dataset have less similar content, thus content correlation between them is weak. Except for the second dataset, the proposed methods overall achieves 80% of accuracy in video summarization and 60% of accuracy in photo summarization.

## 4. Social correlation

### 4.1 Introduction

In addition to the aforementioned correlations, we introduce a new type of cross-media correlation that hasn't been studied widely before. We can view objects or humans as instances of a modality. The appearance of this modality would be presented by sound, such as anchorperson and guest in radio broadcast programs, or would be presented by visual content, such as actors' faces in TV programs. How objects or humans interact embeds semantics, which facilitates multimedia content management and retrieval.

One of the earliest works about investigating social relationships between humans in multimedia content analysis was proposed in (Vinciarelli, 2007). For radio broadcastings, this work segments audio recordings into segments of different speakers, and utilizes characteristics of duration and interaction between speakers to recognize speaker's role as an anchorperson or a guest. Correlation between roles is conveyed by speaking duration and order. Another interesting work was proposed in (Rienks et al., 2006). By using features of speech behaviour, interaction, and topics in group meeting videos, they analyze the influence of each participant. With audiovisual features such as speaking length and motion activity, the work in (Hung et al., 2007) estimates the most dominant person in a group meeting. Also for meeting recordings, the work in (Garg et al., 2008) performs role recognition based on lexical information and social network analysis.

In this section, we exploit co-occurrence information of actors in movies to approach movie understanding. We treat a movie as a small society, and model social correlation between actors by a network called *RoleNet* (Weng et al., 2009). Based on this network, the leading roles are automatically determined and community structure of actors is discovered as well. With this information, we are able to develop an accurate story segmentation system.

## 4.2 RoleNet

A RoleNet is a weighted graph expressed by $G = \langle V, E, W \rangle$, where $V = \{v_1, v_2, ..., v_n\}$ represents a set of roles in a movie, $E = \{e_{ij} | \text{ if } v_i \text{ and } v_j \text{ have relationship}\}$, and the element $w_{ij}$ in $W$ represents strength of the relationship between $v_i$ and $v_j$. Relationship between roles is developed when they interact with each other. More often two roles appear in the same scenes, more chances they can interact, and closer relationship is built.

For a movie that consists of $m$ scenes and $n$ different roles, we can express the status of occurrence by a matrix $A = [a_{ij}]_{m \times n}$, where the element

$$a_{ij} = \begin{cases} 1, & \text{if the } j\text{th role appears in the } i\text{th scene,} \\ 0, & \text{otherwise.} \end{cases} \tag{13}$$

The $j$th column vector, $\boldsymbol{a}_j = (a_{1j}, a_{2j}, ..., a_{mj})$, of $A$ denotes the scenes where the $j$th role appeared. The co-occurrence of the $i$th role and the $j$th role is identified by

$$w_{ij} = \sum_{k=1}^{m} a_{ki} a_{kj} = \boldsymbol{a}_i^T \boldsymbol{a}_j, \text{ for } i \neq j. \tag{14}$$

The value of $w_{ij}$ is actually the inner product of $\boldsymbol{a}_i$ and $\boldsymbol{a}_j$. This measurement can be generalized to the whole matrix. The co-occurrence status between roles can be expressed by $W_{n \times n} = A^T A$, in which $w_{ij}$ is especially set as 0 when $i = j$.

The left side of Figure 8 shows the RoleNet of the movie "You've Got Mail," in which thickness of an edge represents weights on it. Relationships between roles seem to be complicated, and the goal of this work is to find the leading roles and associated communities.

## 4.3 Social-Based Analysis

- Leading Role Determination

There is a large gap between the impact of leading roles and that of supporting roles. Based on this observation, the problem of leading role determination can be mathematically expressed as follows.

$$\Gamma^* = \arg\max_{\Gamma}(\min\Theta_1 - \max\Theta_0), \tag{15}$$

where $\Theta_1 = \{c_i | \ell_i = 1\}$ and $\Theta_0 = \{c_i | \ell_i = 0\}$.

$\Gamma = \{\ell_i, i = 1, 2, ..., n\}$

$$\begin{cases} \ell_i = 1 & \text{if the } i\text{th role is assigned as a leading role,} \\ \ell_i = 0 & \text{otherwise,} \end{cases}$$

where $n$ is the number of roles, $\Gamma$ is a set of binary labels representing which roles are assigned as leading roles. The value $c_i$ is weighted degree centrality, which defines the importance value of the node $i$, and is calculated by

$$c_i = \sum_{j \neq i} w_{ij}. \tag{16}$$

The set $\Theta_1$ represents centrality values of the roles assigned to leading roles. The physical meaning of $(\min\Theta_1 - \max\Theta_0)$ is the difference of centrality values between the least important leading role and the most important supporting role. The result $\Gamma^*$ we want is the labels that cause the largest centrality difference.

Taking "You've Got Mail" as an example, we calculate the centrality value of each role, and then sort the centrality values in descending order, as shown in Figure 8(a) and Figure 8(b). Next, the differences of centrality values between two adjacent roles in Figure 8(b) are calculated. Figure 8(c) shows the centrality difference distribution, in which each point represents a boundary between two roles. Finally, we find the maximum point in the difference distribution, which represents the largest gap in centrality. In this example, the difference between the role no. 1 and the role no. 7 is maximal, and therefore the role no. 2 and role no. 1 are claimed as leading roles.

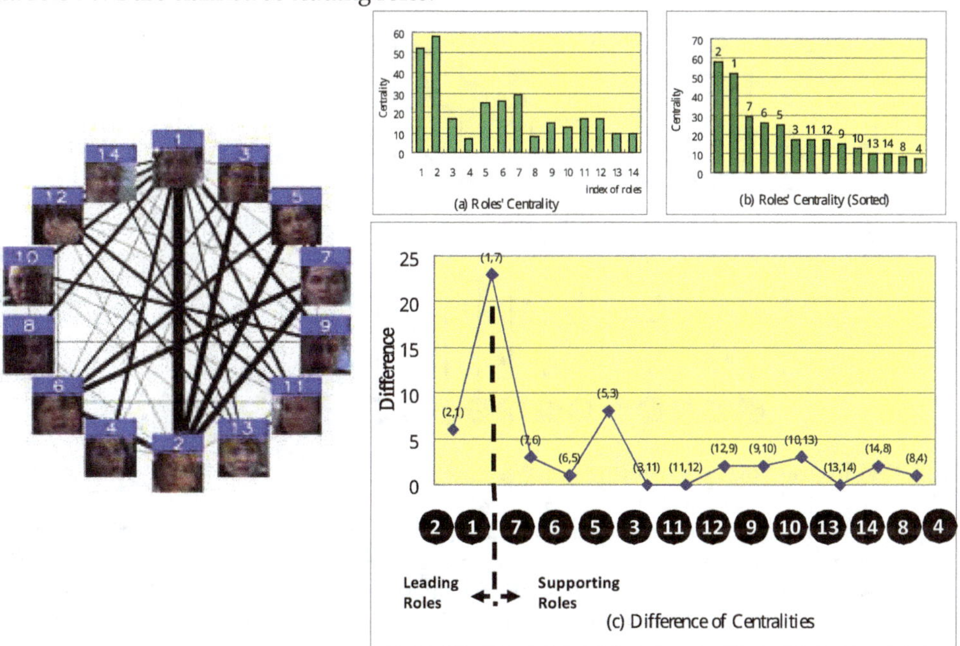


Fig. 8. Left: the RoleNet of "You've Got Mail"; Right: The process of leading role determination.

- Community Identification

After determining the leading roles, we devise a method to appropriately group certain roles into communities. Because leading roles may pass through several communities, it's not reasonable to assign them into any community. Therefore, we first remove leading roles and the edges linked to them from the RoleNet. Then, the following iterative algorithm is applied to the modified RoleNet. We use the value $t$ to index the community's evolution situation. The value $t$ is initialized as 0 in the beginning and increases by one when the community situation changes.

---

**Algorithm 1: Community Identification**

1. Initialize every individual node as a community. The set of community is denoted as $\Pi_t = \{T_1^t, T_2^t, ..., T_n^t\}$, $t$ = 0, if there are initially $n$ individual nodes. The size of the $p$th community in $\Pi_t$ is denotes as $|T_p^t|$, which is the number of nodes included in this community.
2. From the modified RoleNet, find the edge that has the largest weight, say the edge $e_{ij}$ between the node $v_i$ and the node $v_j$, $v_i \in T_p^t$ and $v_j \in T_q^t$, then
   - If $|T_p^t| \geq 1$ and $|T_q^t| = 1$, then $T_p^{t+1} = T_p^t \cup T_q^t$, $\Pi_{t+1} = \Pi_t - \{T_q^t\}$, and $t = t+1$.
   - If $|T_p^t| > 1$ and $|T_q^t| > 1$, then keep current community situation.
3. Remove the edge $e_{ij}$ from the modified RoleNet and go to Step 2 until all edges have been removed.

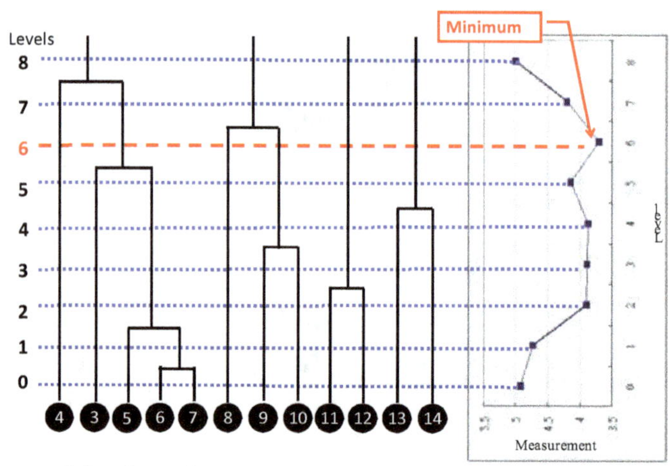


Fig. 9. Dendrogram of the clustering process.

The progress of this algorithm can be illustrated as a dendrogram, which describes how we cluster communities at each step. As shown in Figure 9, the roles no. 6 and no. 7 are first categorized together ($t$=1), then the role no. 5 is merged into this community at the second level ($t$=2). (We say "level" but not "iteration" because the community situation may not change at each iteration.) The same process can be iteratively applied until all nodes have been examined.

Each level in the dendrogram represents a case of community situation. Now the problem is to determine which level in the dendrogram is the best. We design a measurement to evaluate communities at different levels. For the level $t$, the measurement is defined as

$$AvgW_t = \frac{\sum w_{ij}}{\|\Pi_t\|}, \forall v_i \in T_p^t, v_j \in T_q^t, p \neq q, \tag{17}$$

where $\Pi_t$ denotes the community situation at the level $t$, and $\|\Pi_t\|$ denotes the number of communities in this case. The value $AvgW_t$ represents the average weight between different communities at level $t$. The right part of Figure 9 shows the measures at different levels.

In community identification, we prefer that roles in different communities are least related. Therefore, we pick the community case that causes the minimal $AvgW$. In Figure 9, the minimal $AvgW$ value occurs at the sixth level, in which six communities are found to include roles {4}, {3, 5, 6, 7}, {8}, {9, 10}, {11, 12}, and {13, 14}, respectively.

To our knowledge, there is no prior study to conduct movie understanding from social perspective. How characters interact affect us to understand a movie. By analyzing social correlation between roles, we not only can determine characters with high impacts, but also determine construct community structure. In the next subsection, we further demonstrate using social correlation to facilitate story segmentation.

### 4.4 Story Segmentation

- Scene Representation

We first define the representation of scenes. The major difference between the proposed representation and conventional ones is that we describe scenes by "the context of roles" rather than audiovisual features. Story segmentation is achieved by comparing the role's context in successive scenes.

Let $r(k)$ denote the identification of the $k$th character in a specific scene. The relationship between this role and others can be expressed by a "profile vector" $\boldsymbol{w}_{r(k)} = (w_{1r(k)}, w_{2r(k)}, ..., w_{nr(k)})$, which is the $r(k)$-th column vector of the matrix $W$. The vector $\boldsymbol{w}_{r(k)}$ denotes the closeness between the role no. $r(k)$ and others. It is normalized into a unit vector. For the $i$th scene, we collect the profile vectors of the roles appearing in this scene to form a matrix $CM_i = [\boldsymbol{w}_{r(1)}\boldsymbol{w}_{r(2)}...\boldsymbol{w}_{r(p)}]$. It is an $n$ by $p$ matrix if there are $p$ roles in this scene and there are totally $n$ roles in the movie. Similarly, the matrix $CM_j$ for the $j$th scene is denoted by $CM_j = [\boldsymbol{w}_{r(1)}\boldsymbol{w}_{r(2)}...\boldsymbol{w}_{r(q)}]$, if there are $q$ roles in this scene. Note that the vector $\boldsymbol{w}_{r(k)}$ in the $i$th scene and the vector $\boldsymbol{w}_{r(k)}$ in the $j$th scene would be different, i.e., the identifications of the $k$th characters in these two scenes are different. Using the notations of $\boldsymbol{w}^i_{r(k)}$ and $\boldsymbol{w}^j_{r(k)}$ is more precise but dazzles readers. Therefore, we use the simplified notation in the following description.

The context-based similarity between "the $s$th role in the $i$th scene" and "the $t$th role in the $j$th scene" is defined as the inner product of two corresponding profile vectors: $\boldsymbol{w}_{r(s)} \cdot \boldsymbol{w}_{r(t)} = \boldsymbol{w}^T_{r(s)}\boldsymbol{w}_{r(t)}$. By calculating the context-based similarities between every two roles in two successive scenes, the similarity between the $i$th scene and the $j$th scene can be expressed in a matrix form: $CM_{ij} = CM_i^T CM_j$. Finally, the context-based difference between the $i$th scene and the $j$th scene is defined as

$$d_{ij} = 1 - \frac{1}{pq} \sum_{s=1}^{p} \sum_{t=1}^{q} CM_{ij}(s,t), \tag{18}$$

which represents the average difference between pairs of roles in two different scenes. The value is between 0 and 1.

- Story Segmentation

Going through the whole movie, we can plot a "difference curve" that represents difference between adjacent scenes. Based on this curve, the goal of story segmentation is to find appropriate scene boundaries that represent changes of stories. We propose a story segmentation method called "storyshed," which is motivated by the watershed algorithm for image segmentation but is modified to meet the need of this task.

Denote the set of scene boundaries as $B = \{b_1, b_2, ..., b_{N-1}\}$, in which the element $b_i$ denotes the boundary between the $i$th and the ($i$+1)-th scenes, and $N$ is the total number of scenes. The proposed storyshed algorithm is to determine whether a scene boundary is a story boundary, based on the context-based difference between adjacent scenes. The context-based difference corresponding to $b_i$ is denoted by $d_i$. In the first step of the segmentation process, we first find the valleys and peaks from the difference curve by checking $d_i$. That is,

$$\begin{cases} b_i \in Y, & \text{if } d_i < d_{i-\alpha_1} \text{ and } d_i < d_{i+\alpha_2}, \\ b_i \in P, & \text{if } d_i > d_{i-\alpha_1} \text{ and } d_i > d_{i+\alpha_2}, \\ b_i \in OT, & \text{otherwise}, \end{cases} \tag{19}$$

$\alpha_1 = \min\{j | j \in A_1\}, \quad A_1 = \{k | (d_i - d_{i-k}) \neq 0, 1 \leq k \leq i-1\},$
$\alpha_2 = \min\{j | j \in A_2\}, \quad A_2 = \{k | (d_i - d_{i+k}) \neq 0, 1 \leq k \leq (N-1-i)\},$
where $2 \leq i \leq N-2$, $Y$ denotes the set of scene boundaries in valleys, $P$ denotes the set of boundaries in peaks, and the set $OT$ includes all other boundaries. Thus, $Y \cup P \cup OT = B$.

Initialize an empty set $SB$ that will store the story boundaries. For each valley $y_j$ in $Y$, find the nearest peaks to it. Let's denote the left peak of $y_j$ as $p_1$ and the right peak of $y_j$ as $p_2$, $p_1 \in P$ and $p_2 \in P$. Fill water into this valley until the height of the horizontal just floods $p_1$ or $p_2$. Without loss of generality, assume that $p_1$ is flooded first and the height of $p_1$ is $H$. Pick the scene boundaries $b_k$ between the peaks $p_1$ and $p_2$, for which the corresponding context-based difference $d_k$ is no less than $H$. Therefore, the set of story boundaries would be $SB = SB \cup \{b_k\}$.

The results reveal the boundaries that scenes around them have significantly different context information. However, the storyshed algorithm only considers local characteristics and may miss the ones that are indeed story boundaries. To consider the global characteristics, we take average of the context-based difference values of all peaks as a global threshold. If the difference value corresponding to a scene boundary is larger than this threshold, it's viewed as a story boundary. The global threshold is adaptively calculated according to the social relationships between roles in different movies.

Figure 10 shows an example of storyshed segmentation with the global threshold. Two valleys (solid black circles) in this example are at $b_{t+2}$ and $b_{t+6}$. The nearest peaks to $b_{t+2}$ are at $b_{t+1}$ and $b_{t+4}$, and that to $b_{t+6}$ are at $b_{t+4}$ and $b_{t+7}$. With the global threshold, the boundary $b_{t+5}$ is detected as a story boundary as well. Processing with this global threshold is the same as applying a constraint so that height of water is limited to be lower than the threshold.

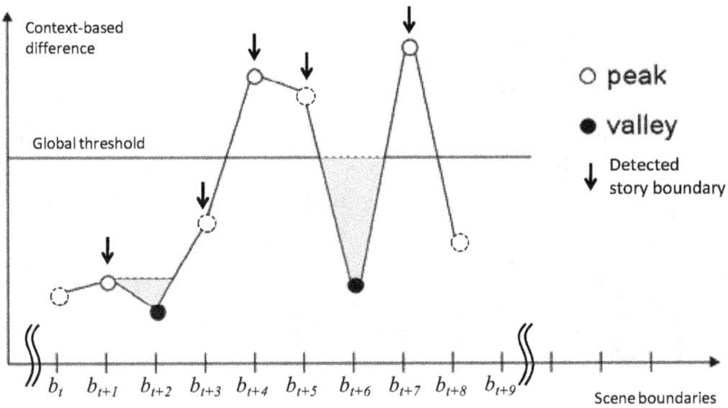


Fig. 10. An example of the storyshed segmentation method with a global threshold.

### 4.5 Evaluation

We use ten Hollywood movies and three TV shows to evaluate the proposed methods. Total length of evaluation data is over 21 hours, and 428 story segments are included. For each movie, we asked three persons to manually label leading roles. The ones that were labeled as the leading ones by all the three persons are treated as the ground truth. Table 2 shows performance of leading role determination. The numbers in each cell denote the indices of roles. Because the trend of appearance of leading roles is often apparent, the proposed method for leading role determination achieves very promising performance.

To evaluate story segmentation, the ground truths of story boundaries were also decided manually. We invited several subjects who were not familiar the goal and process of our work and knew nothing about the chapter information in advance. They were asked to examine every scene change boundary and decide whether it's a story boundary. We measure story segmentation performance in terms of purity value again (Vinciarelli & Favre, 2007). In addition, to show the superiority of utilizing social correlation in story segmentation, we compare our approach with a conventional tempo-based approach (Chen et al., 2004).

| MovieID | M1 | M2 | M3 | M4 | M5 | M6 | M7 |
|---|---|---|---|---|---|---|---|
| GT | 1 | 1, 2 | 1, 2, 6 | 1, 2 | 1 | 1 | 1 |
| Det. | 1 | 1, 2 | 1, 2, 6 | 1, 2 | 1 | 1 | 1 |
| MovieID | M8 | M9 | M10 | S1 | S2 | S3 | |
| GT | 1 | 1 | 1 | 1 | 1, 2, 4, 5, 6, 7 | 1, 2, 3, 4 | |
| Det. | 1 | 1 | 1 | 1 | 1, 2, 3, 4, 5, 6, 7, 9 | 1, 2, 3 | |

Table 2. Performance of leading role determination. GT: Ground Truth; Det.: Determined resuls.

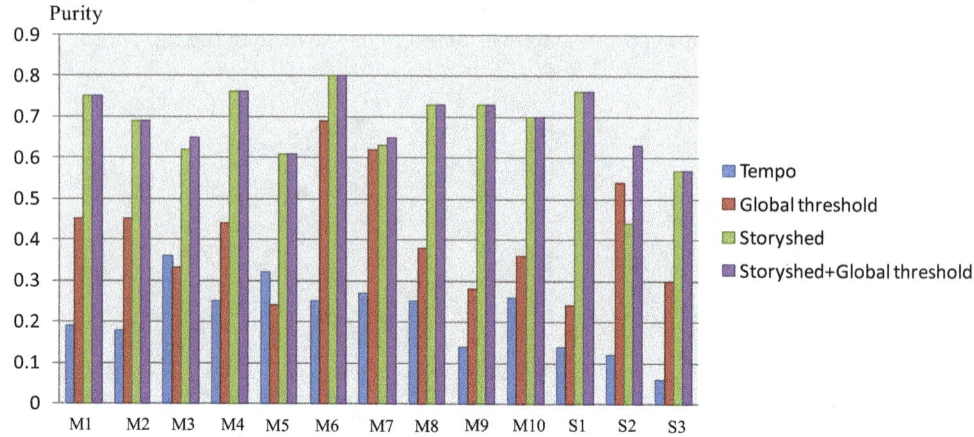


Fig. 11. Performance of story segmentation.

Figure 11 shows that the social-based approach works much better than the tempo-based one. Although the performance improvement varies in different movies, the storyshed algorithm has significantly better performance than thresholding. After combining storyshed with thresholding, the result is even slightly better than the storyshed algorithm, especially in M3, M7, and S2.

## 5. Conclusion

This article presents cross-media correlation and its applications in various multimedia systems. Four perspectives of correlations are investigated: temporal correlation, spatial correlation, content correlation, and social correlation. Regarding temporal and spatial correlations, we introduce a web-based multimedia lecturing system, in which various guided events have tight temporal correlation to teacher's speech, and have spatial correlation to HTML-based lectures. In addition, we design a speech-text alignment module to discover hidden correlation between teacher's reading and text in lectures. Elaborate usage of temporal and spatial correlation facilitates vivid multimedia lecturing for teaching English as a second language.

Regarding content correlation, a travel media analysis system is introduced to find correlation between photos and videos. The essential idea of this work is to solve a harder problem (video scene detection) by first solving an easier problem (photo scene detection) and then consulting with the correlation between two modalities. Besides, we argue that characteristics of photo taking can be exploited to conduct video summarization, and vice versa. We show that appropriately utilizing cross-media correlation facilitates effective multimedia content analysis.

Regarding social correlation, we analyze relationships between characters to determine leading roles and community structure. Community information makes us approach movie understanding and efficiently movie video management/retrieval. Evolution of social relationships is also studied to conduct story segmentation. We have demonstrated this approach more matches human's cognition and works better than conventional content-based segmentation methods.

Benefits of employing cross-media correlation in multimedia content analysis are evident. Although this article describes three practical applications, correlations are often specially extracted according to characteristics of different environments or applications. Systematic description and unified framework for cross-media correlation are needed to extend its applicable domain. Finally, this article introduces the new social correlation in multimedia content analysis. We wish to draw more attention on this issue; especially community websites and online video sharing have explosively grown in recent years.

## Acknowledgement

This work was partially supported by the National Science Council of the Republic of China under grants NSC 98-2221-E-194-056 and NSC 97-2221-E-194-050.

## 6. References

Arzt, A.; Widmer, G. & Dixon, S. (2008). Automatic Page Turning for Musicians via Real-Time Machine Listening. *Proceedings of European Conference on Artificial Intelligence.*

Chasanis, V.; Likas, A. & Galatsanos, N. (2007). Scene Detection in Videos Using Shot Clustering and Symbolic Sequence Segmentation. *Proceedings of IEEE International Conference on Multimedia Signal Processing*, pp. 187-190.

Chen, T. (2001). Audiovisual Speech Processing. *IEEE Signal Processing Magazine*, Vol. 18, No. 1, pp. 9-21.

Chen, H.-W.; Kuo, J.-H.; Chu, W.-T. & Wu, J.-L. Action Movies Segmentation and Summarization Based on Tempo Analysis. *Proceedings of the ACM SIGMM International Workshop on Multimedia Information Retrieval*, pp. 251-258.

Chen, H.-Y. & Liu, K.-Y. (2009). WMA : A Marking-Based Synchronized Multimedia Tutoring System for English Composition Studies. *IEEE Transactions on Multimedia*, Vol. 11, No. 2, pp. 324-332.

Chu, W.-T. & Chen, H.-Y. (2005). Towards Better Retrieval and Presentation by Exploring Cross-Media Correlations. *ACM Multimedia Systems Journal*, Vol. 10, No. 3, pp. 183-198.

Chu, W.-T.; Lin, C.-C. & Yu, J.-Y. (2009). Using Cross-Media Correlation for Scene Detection in Travel Videos. *Proceedings of ACM International Conference on Image and Video Retrieval.*

Carnegie Mellon University. (2009). CMU Pronouncing Dictionary. http://www.speech.cs.cmu.edu/cgi-bin/cmudict

Garg, N.P.; Favre, S.; Salamin, H.; Hakkani Tur, D. & Vinciarelli, A. (2008). Role Recognition for Meeting Participants: An Approach Based on Lexical Information and Social Network Analysis. *Proceedings of ACM Multimedia Conference*, pp. 693-696.

Goodman, D. (2006). *Dynamic HTML : The Definitive Reference*. O'Reilly Media, Inc.

Hanjalic, A. (2002). Shot-Boundary Detection : Unraveled or Resolved? *IEEE Transactions on Circuits and Systems for Video Technology*, Vol. 12, No. 2, pp. 90-105.

Huang, X.; Alleva, F.; Hon, H.W.; Hwang, M.Y. & Rosenfeld, R. (1993). The SPHINX II Speech Recognition System : An Overview. *Computer Speech and Language*, Vol. 2, No. 7, pp. 137-148.

Hung, H.; Jayagopi, D.; Yeo, C., Friendland, G., Ba, S., Ramchandran, J.; Mirghafori, N. & Gatica-Perez, D. (2007). Using Audio and Video Features to Classify The Most Dominant Person in A Group Meeting. *Proceedings of ACM Multimedia Conference*, pp. 835–838.

Jiang, Y.-G.; Yanagawa, A.; Chang, S.-F. & Ngo, C.-W. (2008). CU-VIREO374: Fusing Columbia374 and VIREO374 for Large Scale Semantic Concept Detection. *Columbia University ADVENT Technical Report* #223-2008-1.

Law-To, J.; Chen, L .; Joly, A.; Laptev, I.; Buisson, O.; Gouet-Brunet, V.; Boujemaa, N. & Stentiford, F. (2007). Video Copy Detection : A Comparative Study. *Proceedings of ACM International Conference on Image and Video Retrieval*, pp. 371-378.

Likas, A.; Vlassis, N. & Verbeek, J.J. (2003). The Global K-means Clustering Algorithm. *Pattern Recognition*, Vol. 36, pp. 451-461.

Lowe, D. (2004) Distinctive Image Features from Scale-Invariant Keypoints. *International Journal of Computer Vision*, Vol. 60, No. 2, pp. 91-110.

Platt, J.C.; Czerwinski, M. & Field, B.A. (2003). PhotoTOC: Automating Clustering for Browsing Personal Photographs. *Proceedings of IEEE Pacific Rim Conference on Multimedia*, pp. 6-10.

Rienks, R.; Zhang, D. & Post, W. (2006). Detection and Application of Influence Rankings in Small Group Meetings. *Proceedings of International Conference on Multimodal Interfaces*, pp. 257-264.

Sivic, J. & Zisserman, A. (2003). Video Google: A Text Retrieval Approach to Object Matching in Videos. *Proceedings of the International Conference on Computer Vision*, Vol. 2, pp. 1470-1477.

Snoek, C.G.M. & Worring, M. (2005). Multimodal Video Indexing: A Review of the State-of-the-art. *Multimedia Tools and Applications*, Vol. 25, No. 1, pp. 5-35.

Snoek, C.G.M.; Huurnink, B.; Hollink, L.; de Rijke, M.; Schreiber, G. & Worring, M. (2007). Adding Semantics to Detectors for Video Retrieval. *IEEE Transactions on Multimedia*, Vol. 9, No. 5, pp. 975-986.

Steinmetz, R. (1996). Human Perception of Jitter and Media Synchronization. *IEEE Journal on Selected Areas in Communications*, Vol. 14, No. 1, pp. 61-72.

Tong, H.; Li, M.; Zhang, H.-J. & Zhang, C. (2004). Blur Detection for Digital Images Using Wavelet Transform. *Proceedings of IEEE International Conference on Multimedia & Expo*, pp. 17-20.

Vinciarelli, A. (2007). Spearkers Role Recognition in Multiparty Audio Recordings Using Social Network Analysis and Duration Distribution Modeling. *IEEE Transactions on Multimedia*, Vol. 9, No. 6, pp. 1215-1226.

Vinciarelli, A. & Favre, S. (2007). Broadcast News Story Segmentation Using Social Network Analysis and Hidden Markov Models. *Proceedings of ACM Multimedia*, pp. 261-264.

Weng, C.-Y.; Chu, W.-T. & Wu, J.-L. (2009). RoleNet: Movie Analysis from the Perspective of Social Networks. *IEEE Transactions on Multimedia*, Vol. 11, No. 2, pp. 256-271.

# 6

# A Study on Garbage Collection Algorithm for Ubiquitous Real-Time System

Chang-Duk Jung, PhD; You-Keun Park, PhD
*Korea University*

Most parallel garbage collection algorithms are based on the *mark-and-collect* technique. a mark-and-collect technique an effective asynchronous marking algorithm. There are two basic marking techniques: coloring and stacking. The coloring technique is asynchronous but its time complexity is O(MN) where M and N are the total number of nodes in the list memory and the total number of active nodes, respectively. The stacking technique offers effective marking process having only O(N) time complexity but requires extra stack space which can be as large as the size of entire active nodes (N). A new parallel garbage collection algorithm in ubiquitous environment has been devised which takes advantage of the asynchronous processing of coloring algorithms and the time efficiency of stacking algorithms. The algorithm requires no synchronization between the collectors and the mutators. and its tome complexity is close to O(N) with a small fixed-size stack in ubiquitous real-time system.

**Key Words**: parallel garbage collection, real-tome, autonomous memory

## 1. Introduction

Recent interest in using artificial intelligence for time-critical ubiquitous real-time systems controlling physical devices such as dynamically unstable airplanes, nuclear reactors, and robots demands a large search space operating in the manner such that it *never runs out of space* [1] because these applications are required to create and to release large amounts of data continuously without interruption.

Lists are the fundamental data structure in artificial intelligence programs. List processing systems free the programmer from managing the memory storage. Instead, the list processing facility maintains a set of *free* memory cells (called nodes) and dynamically collects garbage memory nodes which are no longer accessible by the program into the set of free memory nodes. Thus, in time-critical real-time list systems, a *real-time garbage collection system* is a must.

With the emergence of multiple processor systems, parallel garbage collection algorithms have been proposed where more than one processor, called the collectors, exclusively collect garbage concurrently with the activity of other processors, called the mutators, which are dedicated only to the application processes [3, 2, 4]. The mutators proceed with the list processing activity while the collectors reclaim the garbage nodes concurrently. Thus, the mutator and the collector should operate independently of each other.

Recently, Shin [7] developed a parallel garbage collection algorithm using associative tags. His algorithm requires no synchronization between the collectors and the mutators. The algorithm is based on the *mark-and-collect* technique which consists of three phases.
In the *initializing phase*, every node except free nodes is initialized as a garbage node. Every reachable node is marked during the marking phase as in active node, starting form a set of root nodes. Nodes which remain as garbage nodes are reclaimed in the *reclaim phase*. The time complexity of Shin's marking process is O(N) and is does not require extra stack memory.
Although Shin's algorithm can be used for implementing a massively parallel garbage collection system, his algorithm requires associative tags which are expensive to construct.
we have developed a parallel garbage collection algorithm in ubiquitous real-time system which is linearly scalable and operates asynchronously; thus it is possible to construct a massively parallel garbage collection system for a large time-critical real-time system.
In section 2, we introduce general parallel garbage collection algorithms. We present a new parallel garbage collection algorithm suitable for implementing the autonomous memory in Section 3. In Section 4, The proof of correctness of the algorithm is given and the time complexity of the algorithm is presented in Section 5. Conclusions are drawn in section6.

## 2. Garbage Collection in Ubiquitous real-time system

There are two basic techniques for parallel garbage collection: copying [6] and mark-and-collect techniques[7, 5]
The copying technique employs the principle of *freezing* the memory at the instant in time at which the copying begins and preserving the list structure for the collectors.
There are two basic methods in the copying technique based on how the copying process is performed: duplication methods [8] and evacuating methods [6].
The duplication method is required to make a copy of a part or of the entire list memory before beginning the garbage collection precess. The mutator proceeds with the list processing activity while the collector reclaims the garbage nodes from the unchanging second copy of the list structure.
The evacuation method divides the available memory into two logical space: *newspace* and *oldspace*. A garbage collection cycle starts with a *flip*, in which newspace is converted to oldspace, and vice-versa. The mutator proceeds with the list processing activity in newspace while the collector copies (*evacuates*) all accessible nodes in oldspace into newspace by tracing them from a set of roof nodes. After completion of the evacuation precess, oldspace contains only garbage nodes and may be transferred to free nodes.
The copying garbage collection technique provides several advantages including the ability to reclaim circular structures and to compact the storage which reduces the storage fragmentation and improves locality of reference. The copying garbage collectors have been widely used in a virtual memory environment. However, this technique not only requires extra memory space which can be as large as the requires that list processing activity by the mutator be suspended while the mutator makes a copy of the list structures (duplication method) or the mutator be suspended while the collector must be tightly synchronized for a flip operation (evacuation method). Thus, the copying technique is not suitable for implementing a massively parallel garbage collection system.
Most parallel garbage collection algorithms are based on the mark-and-collect technique. The mark-and-collect technique requires tag bits. In general, a mark-and-collect algorithm

consists of there phases: initialization, marking, and collection, In the initialization phase, non-free nodes are initialized ad garbage nodes for the subsequent marking process. In the marking phase, all active nodes are marked b tracing form a set of root nodes, All the nodes that have been neither marked nor already declared as free nodes are transformed into free nodes in the collection phase. There are two basic methods for the mark-and-collect technique: coloring [7] methods and stacking [5] methods.

The coloring method starts by initializing all' non-free nodes as garbage nodes in the initialization phase. Marking process begins by marking all root nodes. Then, the collectior finds a marked node and marks all its immediate descendants. The procedure continues until there is no marked node with unmarked immediate descendants. Only nodes remaining in garbage status after the marking process are reclaimed in the collection phase. Since the mutator never changes the status of nodes to garbage status, this method does not require the suspension of the mutator. Thus, the coloring method can be used to implement a parallel garbage collection system. However, the time complexity off the marking process is O(MN) where M and N are the total number of nodes in the list memory and the total number of active nodes, respectively[1].

The stacking method offers efficient marking requiring only O(N) time at the expense of extra memory space for the stack which can be ad large as the size of the set of entire active nodes(N). Also, the access to the stack must be done through the critical section since the mutator and the collector both need to update the stack.
These algorithms are based on the following explicit or implicit assumptions.

1. The marking process is terminated before the mutator exhausts free nodes. Wadler presented sufficient conditions for this assumption in terms of the maximum rate at which free nodes are used, the maximum number of nodes in use at one time, and the total number of nodes in the system, which may be hard to determine. [1] However, in general, the average time needed for the creation of a list element is required to be greater than the average time interval between two consecutive instances of marking a node to guarantee proper termination of the marking process.

### 2.1 A set to root nodes for all active lists is provided for the collectors

In general, foot nodes are maintained by the mutator in special memory blocks such as internal registers or stack buffers. All accessible nodes, only those active nodes, are referencable via some paths from the nodes in these special memory blocks.
The requirement that the average time needed to create a list element be greater than the average time interval between two consentive instances of marking a node is particularly important because it limits the speed of the mutator relative to the speed of the collector. The most time-consuming process of the coloring method is the marking process, which is O(MN), because the worst time interval between two consecutive instances of marking a node is the tine required to search the whole memory. Shin introduced an algorithm using associative tags which provides a constant one-unit time for searching a marked node. [7] thus, the marking algorithm has time complexity O(N), which is optimal. However, it requires associative tags which are expensive.

## 3. Algorithm Model in Ubiquitous Real-time System

We present a marking algorithm whose time complexity is close to O(N) by combining the coloring and stacking methods. The algorithm is very similar to the Shin's algorithm[7].

Before proceeding with the algorithm statement, let's present the system model. In our system model, there is a collector for each memory block. The system maintains a separate set of rot nodes for each memory block which is an array of special pointers, ROOT(1), ROOT(2),....,ROOT(R). They contain the pointer to the root nodes of lists residing in the same memory block.

The system also maintains a separate free list for each memory block. There are two pointers to the free list: one to the head of the free list (F-HEAD) from which the mutator accesses the free list and the other to the tail of the free list (F-TALK) to which the collector appends free nodes. The advantage of this organization is that it gives better locality of reference; thus it minimizes the communication between collectors.

Identification of garbage nodes is achieved by marking all active nodes. However, when a mutator redirects an existing pointer which the collector has already marked to another active node which has not yet been marked, problems may occur. The conventional solution of these problems in to let the mutator mark the redirected node which has not yet been marked. This is one of the reasons that the conventional stacking method is required to maintain the backtracking pointers of more than one list which makes the stack size as big as the size of the set of entire active nodes. These problems are alleviated in the proposed system by maintaining a special list, called the *replaced node list* which contains the pointers of redirected nodes. Unlike a conventional list, the replaced node list is only accessible from the tail of the list. However, the first node of the list is always created at a fixed location. The system maintains a special record called R-POINT for the replaced node list. There are two fields in R-POINT and R-TAIL. The R-FLAG (value 1) indicates the recreation of the replaced node list; thus the first node will be created at the fixed location (R-NODE). A node of the replaced node list contains two fields: R-ROOT and R-PREV. R-ROOT contains the pointer of the redirected node. R-PREV contains the pointer of the previous replaced node except in the first node where the value is NIL.

There is a foxed-size small stack. The stack is organized as a last-in first-out circular queue. Thus, the stack maintains the most recent backtracking pointers up to the stack size(S).

The algorithm in ubiquitous real-time system is based on tagged memory. There are two tag bits. Thus, there are four possible states for a node, depending on the values of the tag bits () as followings:

1. (0,0) - F-state: The nodes in the F-state are free nodes (in the free list) which are available for the mutator to create a new list element.
2. (1,0) - G-state: The nodes in the G-state are garbage nodes. Nodes which are not free nodes (not in the F-state) are initialized as garbage nodes (the G-state). The nodes remaining in the G-state after the marking process are garbage nodes which can be transferred to the free list.
3. (1,0) - A-state: The nodes in the A-state are active nodes.
4. (1,1) - N-state: The nodes in the N-state are new nodes which are created during the current garbage collection cycle. A new node may or may not be a garbage node.

If a new node is create and released during the same garbage collection cycle, it is called a *floating* node. The algorithm collects floating nodes in the next garbage collection cycle. Thus, garbage nodes are guaranteed to be collected in two cycles.

The algorithm starts by setting the value of R-FLAG to 1 and then initializing all non-free nodes to garbage nodes (G-state) including the root nodes. After completion of the initialization, the marking process begins.
The nodes are traced starting from ROOT(i) for i = 1 to R. If the status of ROOT(i) is the G-state, the collector marks the nodes from ROOT(i) in a depth-first order. If any of its descendants nodes are in the G-state, is converts its state to the A-state. The algorithm uses the stack for storing backtracking pointers. Although the stack is small and fixed, the collector operates as if there is unlimited stack memory because the stack is organized as a last-in first-out circular queue. However, the stack maintains only the most recent backtracking pointers up to the size of the stack (S). After the stack is empty, the collector reexamines the states of the immediate descendants of ROOT(i). If any of them are still in the G-state, the collector retraces the list starting from ROOT(i).
This procedure is repeated until none of the immediate descendants of ROOT(i) is in the G-state, at which time the collector converts the state of ROOT(i) to the A-state and proceeds to the next ROOT(i). after the marking of the last ROOT(R), the collector traces the replaced node list backward from the tail (R-TAIL) using R-PRVE until the value of R-PREV is NIL. The collector marks the redirected nodes by tracing them from R-ROOT using the same procedures as above. The marking process terminates when the collector has examined all replaced nodes.

A: Initialization Phase in ubiquitous real-time system
Set R-FLAG to 1.
For i = 1 to M, of NODE(i) is not in the F-stage,
initialize it to the G-state.

**B: Marking Phase in ubiquitous real-time system**

**M1**: For all i = 1 to R, if ROOT(i) is in G-state,
let ROOT(i) be all parent node,

1. If LP = NIL of the state of NODE(LP) is cot G-state, go to step 3.
2. Push the parent node onto the stack and let NODE(LP) be the new parent node. Repeat step 1.
3. If RP = NIL or the state of NODE(LP) is not G-state, go to step 5.
4. Push the parent node onto the stank and let NODE(NODE(RP)) be the new parent node. Repeat step 1.
5. Mark (convert the modes from G-state to A-state) the parent node. Pop the stack. If the stack is empty, go to step 6. otherwise let the popped node be the new parent node. Repeat step 1.
6. Let ROOT(i) be a parent node. If (LP = NIL or NODE(LP) is not in G-state) and (RP = NIL or NODE(LP) is not in G-state), mark the ROOT(i); otherwise, repeat step 1.

**M2**: If R-FLAG = 1, skip the M2 procedure.
Let NODE(R-TALK) be a working node (R-N ODE) and NODE(R-ROOT) be a parent node.

1. If LP = NIL or the state of NODE(LP) is not G-state. go to step 3.
2. Push the parent node onto the stack and let NODE(LP) be a new parent node. Repeat step 1.
3. If RP = NIL of the state of NODE(RP) is not G-state, go to step 5.
4. Push the parent node onto the stack and let NODE(NODE(RP)) be a new parent node. Repeat step 1.
5. Mark (convert the nodes from G-state to A-state) the parent node. pop the stack. If the stack is empty, go to step 6, otherwise let the popped node be a new parent node. Repeat step 1.

6. Let NODE(R-ROOT) be a parent node. If (LP = NIL of NODE(LP) is not in G-state) and (RP = NIL or NODE(RP) is not in G-state), mark the NODE(R-ROOT), otherwise repeat step 1.
7. If R-PREV is not NIL, let NODE(R-PREV) be a working node (R-NODE). Let NODE (R-ROOT) be a parent node. Repeat step 1.

C: Collection Phase in ubiquitous real-time system

**C1**: *For all i = 1 to M, if the stare of NODE(i) is* G-state, append it to the free list after converting its state to F-state

**C2**: Set R-FLAG to 1.
The only function required in the mutator for garbage collection is to create the replaced node list whenever the mutator redirected a node which is still in the G-state to a node which is in the A-state.

1. If R-FLAG = 1, then reset it to 0 and create the first R-NODE at the special location, otherwise create an R-NODE at any location. Update the R-TAIL with the pointer of the newly created R-NODE.
2. If R-NODE is a frist node, move the NIL value to R-PREV, otherwise move R-TALK to R-PREV

3. Move the pointer to the replaced node to
R-ROOT

Fig. 2. Mutator Algorithm in ubiquitous real-time system

After completion of the marking process, nodes still remaining in G-state are garbage nodes. The collector converts these nodes to free nodes (F-state) and appends them to The tail of the free lost.

The only function required for the mutator related to garbage collection is the creation of the replaced node list. Whenever the mutator redirects a node which is still in G-state to a node which is in A-state, it creates an R-NODE and places the pointer of the redirected node into R-ROOT and updates R-POINT. However, if the value of R-FLAG is 1, the mutator resets R-FLAG to 0 and creates the first node at the fixed location (R-NODE).

The algorithms of the mutator and the collector are summarized in Figure 1 and Figure 2. The algorithm assumes that each node contains two pointers (LP and RP) to other nodes in the list structure. However, the algorithm can be modified easily to handle list structure having more than two pointers. NODE(LP) and NODE(RP) represent the child nodes pointed to by the pointers LP and RP of the parent node, respectively.

## 4. Correctness of the algorithm in ubiquitous real-time system

For brevity, we present a brief summary of the proof of correctness of the algorithm. To prove the correctness of the garbage collection algorithm, we need to show:

**C1. Invariance:** The active list structures should not be modified by the garbage colector

**C2. Termination:** The garbage collection processes terminate properly.

**C3. Validity:** No active nodes should be mistaken for garbage nodes.
The following theorems prove the correctness of the algorithm.

**Theorem 1:** The algorithm satisfies the Invariance condition.

**Proof:** The collector does not alter any pointer of lists except in the collection phase in which it only alters the pointer of inactive nodes (garbage nodes).

**Lemma 2:** The Initialization Phase terminates properly.
**Lemma 3:** The Collection Phase terminates properly.
**Proof:** The initialization and collection phases involve only the sequential scanning of the memory form top th bottom; they will terminate properly.

**Lemma 4:** The procedure M1 terminates properly.
**Proof:** after the initialization phase, all nodes are either in F-state, G-state, or N-state. The nodes in N-state are newly created nodes after the initialization process began. However, after the initialization process, neither the collector nor the mutator changes the state of

nodes to G-state. Thus, there are a fixed number of nodes in G-state. The procedure M1 converts the state of nodes from G-state to A-state; thus, it must terminate properly.

**Lemma 5:** The procedure M2 terminates properly.
**Proof:** The problem of redirecting nodes occurs only when the mutator redirects nodes which have not been marked to a node which already has been marked, Thus, after completion of the procedure M1, the redirecting of nodes will not cause a problem. Therefore, redirected nodes pointed to by R-NODE which is created after R-TAIL need not be examined. Since the collector traces the replaced node list backward from R-TAIL to the first R-NODE, it will terminate properly if the redirected lists are not expanded. After the completion of the procedure M1, all active nodes are either marked to A-state or in G-state. If the active node still is in G-state, it must be a member of a redirected list.
However, since there is only a finite number of nodes in G-state, the procedure M2 will terminate properly
**Theorem 6:** The marking phase terminates properly.
**Proof:** The Theorem is true by Lemma 4 and Lemma 5.

**Theorem 7:** The garbage collection processes terminate properly.
**Proof:** It follow from Lemma 2, Lemma 3, and Theorem6

**Theorem 8:** NO active nodes should be mistaken for garbage nodes.
**Proof:** The mutator only converts the state of nodes from F-state to N-state. The collector only initializes non-free nodes in the initialization phase. The active nodes in G-state must be marked by either the procedure M1 or M2. The collector only collects the nodes still remaining in G-state. Thus, no active nodes are mistaken for garbage nodes.

From the above theorems, We conclude that the algorithm is correct. However, the algorithm does not collect all garbage nodes in one cycle. Nodes created and released during the cycle(floating nodes) are collected in the next cycle. Thus, the algorithm guarantees that garbage nodes are collected within two cycles.

## 5. Time Complexity in the Ubiquitous Real-time System

The time complexity of the algorithm cam be estimated as follows. Assume that the distribution of the depth of lists is a normal distribution function with the mean μ and the variance. Since the time complexity of the initialization phase and the collection phase is O and the variance <IMG src=".\PIC9B.gif" width=13px height=16px >. Since the time complexity of the initialization phase and the collection phase is O an s n<SPAN STYLE='font-family:"바탕";font-size:13px;color:"#000000";line-height:20px;text-align:justify;'>The time complexity of the algorithm cam be estimated as follows. Assume that the distribution of the depth of lists is a normal distribution function with the mean  μ and the variance <IMG src=".\PIC9B.gif" width=13px height=16px >. Since the time complexity of the initialization phase and the collection phase is O and the variance <IMG src=".\PIC9B.gif"  width=13px  height=16px >. Since the time complexity of the initialization phase and the collection phase is O an s □ n&lt

where S is the size of the stack.

If we assume that the density function is normal distribution, then or by letting we have (1) where
Thus, the time complexity of the algorithm is worse than that of the stack algorithms by a factor of (2)
This is the typical time and space tradeoff. However, the time penalty (Equation 2) is considerably smaller than the spatial gain. If the stack size is, the time complexity of the algorithm is just 16% more than the optimum. If the stack size is, the time complexity of the algorithm is almost optimum (1.001 times of the optimum). The algorithm is not dependent on M or N; thus the time complexity of the algorithm is O(1).

| Algorithm | Stacking | Coloring | shin[7] | New Algorithm |
|---|---|---|---|---|
| Time | O(N) | O(MN) | O(N) | O(N) |
| Tag Bits | 1 | 2 | 2 | 2 |
| Assoc. Memory | no | no | no | no |
| Critical Section | stack | none | none | none |
| Extra Space | O(N) | none | none | O(1) |

Table 1. A performance comparison of marking algorithms for garbage collection.

This is a substantial improvement over stacking algorithms which require the stack space as big as the entire available memory (M) or coloring algorithms whose time complexity is O(MN).

## 6. Conclusions

We have presented a parallel garbage collection algorithm in ubiquitous real-time system which can be used for artificial intelligent systems for time-critical real-time applications. The algorithm takes advantage of the time efficiency of stacking algorithms and the space efficiency of coloring algorithms.
The algorithm requires no critical section and the time complexity of its marking process is close to O(N) with a small fixed-size stack. Thus, a massively parallel garbage collection system can be effectively constructed.
In this paper, we didn't discuss the case when a list is expanded form one memory bank to other memory bank for brevity. In this case, an address fault would occur and the collector needs to send the address of the children to other collectors. A receiving collector is required t create a temporary list similar to the replaced node list. At the end of the tracing of the replaced node list, the collector marks the active nodes whose roots are located in other memory blocks by tracing the temporary list.
To construct a massively parallel garbage collection system. we need to design a communication network to interconnect collectors. A communication system called a has been developed to interconnect multiple processors to from a massively parallel

computer at the Aerospace Technology Center of the allied-Signal Aerospace company [10]. The communication network exhibits a high degree of connectivity, modularity, extensibility, and scalability. The same module would be used for constructing a massively parallel garbage collection in ubiquitous real-time system.

## 7. Reference

[1] Richard Jones, "Garbage Collection", wiley and Sons, 2006

[2] Bill Venneers, " Java's Garbage collection Heap", Javaworld, August, 2005

[3] N.I.A Woodward, "Alternative approaches to multiprocessor garbage collection", Proc. Int. Conf. Parallel processing, 2004, pp. 205-210

[4] Amsaleg, P. Freerira,M. Fracklin and M. Shapiro, "Evaluating Garbage Collection for Large Persistent Stores", Proceedings of the 1995 OOPSLA Workshop on Object Database Behavior, Benchmarks, and Performance, Austin, Texas, October 2002.

[5] Y. Hibino, "A practical parallel garbage collection algorithm and its implementation", Proc. Proc. Annual Symp. on Computer Architecture, 2001, pp. 113-120

[6] S. G. Abraham and J. H. Patel, "Parallel Garbage Collection on A Virtual Memory System", Proc. Int'l Conf. Parallel Processing, 1987, pp. 243-246

[7] H. Shin, "A Boolean content addressable memory and its applications", Univ. of Texas, Austin, May 1986

[8] R. J. P. Ingria and M. Cohen, "LAMBDA release 3.0 Notes", LISP Machine Inc., Oct., 1986

[9] D. W. Clark and C. C. Green, "An empirical study of list structure in Lisp", comm. ACM 20, 2 (Feb. 1977), pp. 78-86

[10] You-Keun Park, et all, "Distributed Associative Processor" Proc. to ACM Computer Science Conference, Louisville, Kentucky, February, 1989

# 7

# Delay Difference between the Linear Traffic Model and the Polynomial Traffic Model

Woo-Young Ahn, Seon-Ha Lee and Gyeong-Seok Kim
*Faculty of Department of Civil & Environmental Engineering*
*Kongju National University*
*South Korea*

## 1. Introduction

In traffic-responsive signal control, a technique for interpreting the real-time detector data plays an important role in decision making process. The traditional Linear Traffic Model (LTM) is called a vertical queue traffic model and it is adopted widely in traffic signal control at signalized intersections. This model represents all vehicles have the same travel time before joining a queue. Thus, a queue is supposed to form vertically at the stop-line without occupying any space on the link. Due to the simplicity of this model, all vehicle motions are identical and unaffected by the signal display on their approach to the intersection. In the linear traffic model, the departure time of the leading vehicle is assumed to coincide with the start of the effective green time (Clayton, 1940; Webster & Cobbe; 1966; Allsop, 1970) and then departure times for the successive following vehicles are estimated in accordance with the saturation departure time at the stop-line. The delays and departure time estimates given by the vertical queue traffic models are not always realistic, because this model does not consider any braking motion until the stop-line. Namely, it is more focused on the queue delay rather than the geometric delay. The Robertson (1969) and TRANSYT (2004) uses vertical queue concepts in fixed-time signal optimization. Also, in traffic-responsive signal control, Miller (1963), Gartner (1983), and Heydecker (1990) use constant mean travel time from the detector to the stop-line. Traditional traffic theory focuses on modeling of queue discharge flow rates at signalized intersections with relatively little consideration of the corresponding queue discharge speed characteristics. This model uses a constant saturation flow rate and converts to an effective green time (Webster & Cobbe, 1966; Akcelick, 1981 & TRB, 2000).

In traffic-responsive signal control, the motion of each vehicle from the upstream detector to the downstream stop-line is needed for full interpretation of the detector output and for performance evaluation. It would be tedious and time consuming to describe the motion of each vehicle in detail at each time-step. Akcelick, et al (2002) describes the exponential queue discharge flow and speed models. In this paper, the concepts of kinematics in physics are applied to derive a Polynomial Traffic Model (PTM) at signalized intersections. The model developed in this paper requires one upstream detector, the position of detector is not an issue in this research. According to this model, arrival times and departure times of all detected vehicles at the stop-line, and also their delays are estimated on the basis of the on-line detector data. The model is developed to represent the individual vehicle motion in relation to the general car-following concept. Thus, it can be applied in the dynamic signal optimization at a microscopic level (Ahn, 2004).

This paper explores a microscopic traffic model based on the one dimensional Kinematic equations in physics. The motion of vehicles from the upstream detector to the downstream stop-line is formulated analytically as a function of the start of green time. The formulae are derived for two different vehicle groups: a motion of the leading vehicle is determined by the signal indication and then successive following vehicles are estimated using the behavior of the vehicles in front of them. A comparative evaluation in delay and sensitivity of delay difference between the LTM and PTM is presented. The results show that the delay estimate in the LTM model is always greater than or equal to the PTM; however, the sensitivity of delay in the PTM is greater than the LTM.

## 2. Kinematic equations in physics

Kinematics is the study of motion irrespective of the forces; it deals with the mathematical description of motion in terms of position, speed, acceleration (or braking) and time. If any three of those variables are known, then the fourth variable can be calculated by using Kinematic equations. According to these concepts, we can describe the motion of vehicles in the vicinity of signalized intersections. If a vehicle is moving, the speed $v$ is defined as the displacement of the vehicle divided by the time over which the displacement occurs. Furthermore, acceleration rate $a$ refers to the rate of change of speed over time, which is defined as the change of speed divided by the change of time. The acceleration is equal to the second derivative $x$ of with respect to time $t$:

$$a = \frac{dv}{dt} = \frac{d^2x}{dt^2} \tag{1}$$

The simplest case of translational motion assumes that the acceleration is constant, which means all vehicles are moving with maximum uniform acceleration rate. By using the Equation 1, the speed equation as a function of time, the position equation as a function of speed, and the position equation as a function of time are obtained as follows:

$$v_f = v_i + a(t_f - t_i) \tag{2}$$

$$x_f = x_i + \frac{v_f^2 - v_i^2}{2a} \tag{3}$$

$$x_f = x_i + v_i(t_f - t_i) + \frac{a}{2}(t_f - t_i)^2 \tag{4}$$

where $v_i$ is the initial speed, $v_f$ is the final speed, $x_i$ is the initial position, and $x_f$ is the final position.

## 3. Notation

The following notation will be used for the trajectory of the leading vehicle $n$ =1 and the following vehicles $n$ ($2 \le n \le N$), where $N$ is the serial number of the most recent detected vehicle at the position of detector. Let

| | |
|---|---|
| $a$ | be the acceleration rate ($a$ >0) |
| $b$ | be the braking rate ($b$ >0) |
| $v_0$ | be the free-flow speed |
| $t_g$ | be the start of green time (including the reaction time) |
| $v_g$ | be the speed of leading vehicle $n$ =1 at time $t_g$ |
| $X_g$ | be the position of leading vehicle $n$ =1 at time $t_g$ |
| $X_d$ | be the position of detector ($X_d \le 0$) |
| $X_s$ | be the position of stop-line ($X_s = 0$) |
| $\overline{X}_v$ | be the position at which any delayed vehicles can regain the free-flow speed ($\overline{X}_v = v_0^2 / 2a$) |
| $\overline{X}_b$ | be the maximum boundary of upstream ($\overline{X}_b = X_d - v_0^2 / 2b$) |
| $t_d^n$ | be the time at which the vehicle $n$ is detected at position $X_d$ |
| $v_d^n$ | be the speed of the vehicle $n$ at time which it detected at position $X_d$ |
| $X_b^n$ | be the position at which the vehicle $n$ starts to brake ($X_b^n = X_b^{n-1} - L$, where $L$ is the safety margin) |
| $t_b^n$ | be the time at which the vehicle $n$ starts to brake |
| $v_b^n$ | be the speed of the vehicle $n$ at position $X_b^n$ ($v_b^n = v_0$) |
| $t_a^n$ | be the time at which the vehicle $n$ starts to accelerate ($2 \le n \le N$) |
| $v_a^n$ | be the speed of the vehicle $n$ at time which the acceleration starts($2 \le n \le N$) |
| $X_a^n$ | be the position of vehicle $n$ starts to accelerate($2 \le n \le N$) |
| $X_q^n$ | be the position at which the vehicle $n$ stops completely after a full braking |
| $t_q^n$ | be the time at which the vehicle $n$ stops after a full braking at position $X_q^n$ |
| $X_v^n$ | be the position at which the vehicle $n$ regains the free-flow speed |
| $t_v^n$ | be the time at which the vehicle $n$ regains the free-flow speed at position $X_v^n$ |
| $t_s^n$ | be the time at which the vehicle $n$ crosses the stop-line $X_s$ |
| $v_s^n$ | be the speed of the vehicle $n$ at time which it crosses the stop-line $X_s$ |

## 4. Polynomial Traffic Model (PTM) development

This model assumes a constant acceleration rate and braking rate, no overtaking is allowed and no vehicle exceeds the free-flow speed. Here, the start of green time $t_g$ is defined as the beginning of the green time plus a reaction time $\tau$, Gipps (1981) used $\tau = 2/3$ seconds

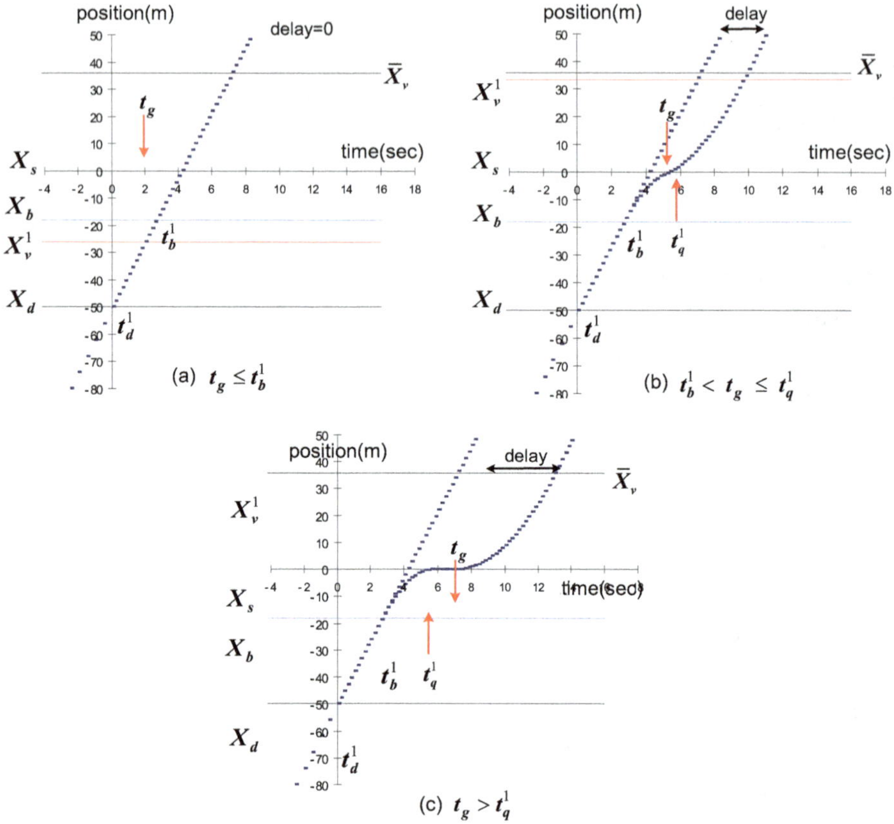


Fig. 1. Trajectory and delay for the leading vehicle in varying start of green time: Polynomial Traffic Model (PTM)

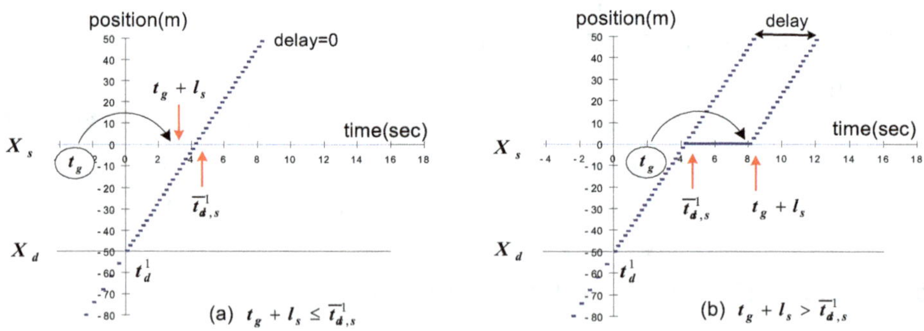


Fig. 2. Trajectory and delay for the leading vehicle in varying start of green time: Linear Traffic Model (LTM)

### 4.1 Trajectory of the leading vehicle

As can see in Figure 1, the motion of the leading vehicle is affected by the current signal indication. In respect of the start of green time $t_g$, the motion can be classified broadly into four regions: free-flow, braking (or braking and stopping), acceleration and free-flow. If current signal is green, the leading vehicle will cross the detector with free-flow speed and then reaches stop-line without experiencing any delays. However, if the signal is currently red, the vehicle from the detector can travel up to the braking position with free-flow speed, and on reaching that point the vehicle has to start to brake in order to stop safely at the stop-line. Meanwhile, if the signal changes to green, the vehicle will start to accelerate until it regains the free-flow speed; otherwise, the vehicle has to go through stopping until the next green starts. In this way, we can identify that the vehicle will pass the stop-line either at the free-flow speed or under. For the leading vehicle $n$ =1, three different trajectories are considered as follows:

If $t_g \le t_b^n$ : maintain free-flow speed (see Figure 1a)

If $t_b^n < t_g \le t_q^n$ : free-flow $\rightarrow$ braking $\rightarrow$ acceleration $\rightarrow$ free-flow (see Figure 1b)

If $t_g > t_q^n$ : free-flow $\rightarrow$ braking $\rightarrow$ stopping $\rightarrow$ acceleration $\rightarrow$ free-flow(see Figure 1c).

The motion of the leading vehicle from the detector position up to the braking position is unaffected by the current signal indication, thus it maintains free-flow speed. For the leading vehicle $n$ =1, the braking position $X_b^n$ , the braking time $t_b^n$ and the stopping time $t_q^n$ are calculated as follows:

$$X_b^n = -\frac{v_0^2}{2b},\ t_b^n = t_d^n - \frac{v_0}{2b} - \frac{X_d}{v_0} \text{ and}$$

$$t_q^n = t_b^n + \Delta t_b^n = t_d^n + \frac{v_0}{2b} - \frac{X_d}{v_0} \text{ (where } \Delta t_b^n = v_0 / b \text{)} \tag{5}$$

When the vehicle has reached its braking position, its further motion is determined by the current signal indication. There are three different trajectories to be considered with respect to the start of green time $t_g$ for the leading vehicle $n$ =1:

If $t_g \le t_b^n$ then

$$v_g = v_0,\ X_g = X_d + v_0(t_g - t_d^n),$$
$$t_v^n = t_g \text{ and } X_v^n = X_g \tag{6}$$

If $t_b^n < t_g \le t_q^n$ then

$$v_g = v_0 - b(t_g - t_b^n),\ X_g = X_b^n + v_0(t_g - t_b^n) - \frac{b}{2}(t_g - t_b^n)^2,$$

$$t_v^n = t_g + \frac{b}{a}(t_g - t_b^n) \text{ and } X_v^n = X_b^n + v_0(\frac{a+b}{a})(t_g - t_b^n) - (\frac{ab+b^2}{2a})(t_g - t_b^n)^2 \tag{7}$$

If $t_g$ starts after the vehicle has stopped ($t_g > t_q^n$) then

$$v_g = 0,\ X_g = 0,\ t_v^n = t_g + \frac{v_0}{a} \text{ and } X_v^n = \frac{v_0^2}{2a} \tag{8}$$

Finally, for the leading vehicle $n$ =1, the crossing time $t_s^n$ and its speed $v_s^n$ at the stop-line can be obtained by comparing the fixed position $X_s$ and the varying position $X_v^n$ :

If $X_v^n \le X_s$, which means that the vehicle is crossing the stop-line with free-flow speed, then

$$t_s^n = t_v^n - \frac{X_v^n}{v_0} \text{ and } v_s^n = v_0 \tag{9}$$

If $X_v^n > X_s$, which means that the vehicle is crossing the stop-line during the acceleration, then

$$v_s^n = \sqrt{v_g^2 - 2aX_g} \text{ and } t_s^n = t_g + \frac{\sqrt{v_g^2 - 2aX_g} - v_g}{a} \tag{10}$$

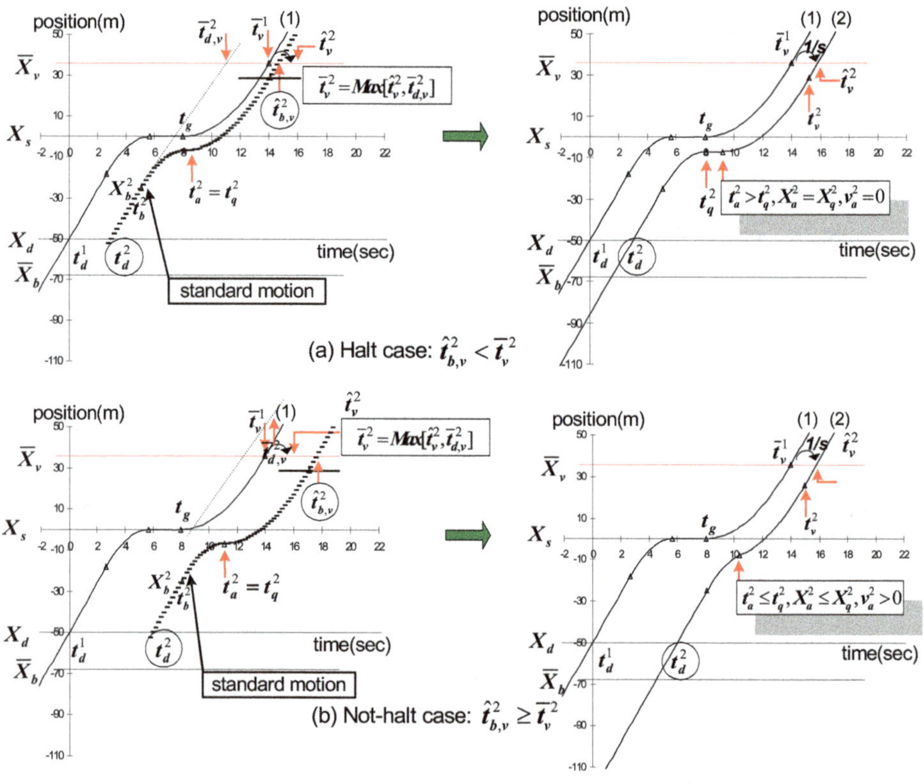


Fig. 3. A standard motion test for the following vehicles

## 4.2 Trajectory of the following vehicles

The variables estimated for the leading vehicle are used as parameters for the following vehicles trajectory in the following section. The basic concepts we use in the following calculations are the following vehicles cannot depart the downstream free-flow position $\overline{X}_v$ $\overline{X}_v$ with less than the minimum headways. Once we have characterised the full trajectory of the leading vehicle $n$ =1 as a function of the start of green time $t_g$, the trajectory of all successive following vehicles $n$ =2, 3, ... $N$ can be calculated directly based on the motion in front.

As can see in Fig 3, when the following vehicle $n$ =2 crosses the detector at time $t_d^n$, the first order of task is finding the possible departure time $\overline{t}_v^n = \text{Max}[\hat{t}_v^n, \overline{t}_{d,v}^n]$ at position $\overline{X}_v$, here $\hat{t}_v^n = \overline{t}_v^{n-1} + 1/s$ (where $s$ is a saturation flow) is the earliest departure time at position $\overline{X}_v$ and $\overline{t}_{d,v}^n = t_d^n + (\overline{X}_v - X_d)/v_0$ is the free-flow travel time from the detector to the position $\overline{X}_v$. By comparing variables $\hat{t}_v^n$ and $\overline{t}_{d,v}^n$, we can decide whether or not the following vehicle will be delayed. If $\overline{t}_{d,v}^n \geq \overline{t}_v^n$, the detected vehicle is identified as undelayed so it can reach the position $\overline{X}_v$ $\overline{X}_v$ from the detector with free-flow speed. Thus, it is not necessary to find acceleration variables. However, if $\overline{t}_{d,v}^n < \overline{t}_v^n$, the vehicle is identified as delayed, then we need standard motion test to find acceleration variables, in which we can test whether or not any stopped lost time due to a queue is involved. Here, the standard arrival time is the longest approach time from the braking position $X_b^n$ to the position $\overline{X}_v$ supposing that the vehicle has not stopped. The braking position is calculated by of adding minimum safe spacing $L$. The final information we are seeking for each following vehicle $n$ ($2 \leq n \leq N$) is its crossing time $t_s^n$, speed $v_s^n$ at stop-line $X_s$ and departure time $\overline{t}_v^n$ at position $\overline{X}_v$ : the time $t_s^n$ will be used to estimate the number of vehicles that can pass the stop-line if the green is extended by a certain control decision time, and $\overline{t}_v^n$ will be used to estimate its delays. In this analysis, the final information we are seeking for each following vehicle $n$ ($2 \leq n \leq N$) is its crossing time $t_s^n$, speed $v_s^n$ at stop-line $X_s$ and departure time $\overline{t}_v^n$ at position $\overline{X}_v$ : the time $t_s^n$ will be used to estimate the number of vehicles that can pass the stop-line if the green is extended by a certain control decision time, and $\overline{t}_v^n$ will be used to estimate its delays. The calculation algorithm for the following vehicles trajectory is as follows:

**Step 0: (Leading vehicle trajectory)**
Identify the leading vehicle trajectory $n$ =1 with respect to the current signal indication, and all identified variables are used as parameters in the following steps
$\Rightarrow$ if $N$ =1, stop processing (no following vehicles)

**Step 1: (Departure time at $\overline{X}_v$)**
Find the earliest departure time $\hat{t}_v^n$ and free-flow arrival time $\overline{t}_{d,v}^n$ at position $\overline{X}_v$, then the departure time will be $\overline{t}_v^n = \text{Max}[\hat{t}_v^n, \overline{t}_{d,v}^n]$, where $\hat{t}_v^n = \overline{t}_v^{n-1} + 1/s$ and $\overline{t}_{d,v}^n = t_d^n + (\overline{X}_v - X_d)/v_0$

**Step 2: (Motion definition for undelayed case or delayed case)**
Find the expected motion of the each following vehicle:
2-1) If $\overline{t}_{d,v}^n \geq \hat{t}_v^n$ which corresponds to undelayed motion, then standard motion test is not required

2-2) If $\overline{t}_{d,v}^{n} < \hat{t}_{v}^{n}$ which corresponds to delayed motion, then standard motion test is required

**Step 3: (Braking position and time)**
$X_b^n = X_b^{n-1} - L$ ($t_b^n$ is only possible to find when $X_b^n \geq \overline{X}_b$; otherwise, out of range)
From Step 2, if the motion is identified as an undelayed case and:
If ($X_b^n \geq \overline{X}_b$), then $t_b^n = t_d^n + (X_b^n - X_d)/v_0$,
Else, $t_b^n$ is unknown
⇒ **go to Step 4** to find the variable of crossing time to the stop-line.
From Step 2, if the motion is identified as a delayed case:
If $X_d \leq X_b^n < X_s$, then $t_b^n = t_d^n + (X_b^n - X_d)/v_0$
If $\overline{X}_b \leq X_b^n < X_d$, then $t_b^n = t_d^n - (v_0 - \sqrt{v_0^2 + 2b(X_b^n - X_d)})/b$
⇒ **go to Step 5** to find additional variables.

**Step 4: (Crossing time to the stop-line for undelayed vehicle)**
The crossing time $t_s^n$ at stop-line $X_s$ can be calculated by using a free-flow motion equation, that is $t_s^n = t_d^n + (X_s - X_d)/v_0$
⇒ if $n < N$, **go to Step 1**; otherwise, stop processing

**Step 5: (Standard motion test for delayed vehicle: halt case or not-hale case)**
The standard motion test is only necessary if the vehicle is identified as delayed and $X_b^n \geq \overline{X}_b$
From the braking position standard motion test is needed to find whether or not it will come to a halt
5-1) The standard motion arrival time, that is $\hat{t}_{b,v}^n = t_b^n + v_0(a+b)/2ab + (\overline{X}_v - X_b^n)/v_0$
5-2) Motion definition: halt-case or not-halt case
If $\hat{t}_{b,v}^n < \overline{t}_v^n$, the motion is identified as a halt-case, then the stopping is involved
If $\hat{t}_{b,v}^n \geq \overline{t}_v^n$, the motion is identified as a not-halt case, then the stopping is not involved

**Step 6: (Acceleration position, time and speed variables for delayed vehicle)**
6-1) For a halt-case, acceleration position is equal to the stopped position, then
$X_a^n = X_q^n$ (where $X_q^n = X_b^n + v_0^2/2b$), $v_a^n = 0$ and $t_a^n = \overline{t}_v^n - \dfrac{v_0}{2a} - \dfrac{(\overline{X}_v - X_a^n)}{v_0}$
6-2) For a not-halt case, acceleration starts meanwhile of braking, then
$t_a^n = t_b^n + \sqrt{\dfrac{(X_b^n - \overline{X}_v) + v_0(\overline{t}_v^n - t_b^n)}{(ab+b^2)/2a}}$, $X_a^n = X_b^n + v_0(t_a^n - t_b^n) - \dfrac{b}{2}(t_a^n - t_b^n)^2$ and $v_a^n = v_0 - b(t_a^n - t_b^n)$

**Step 7: (Position and time of regaining the free-flow speed for delayed vehicle)**
If $X_b^n \geq \overline{X}_b$, the time $t_v^n$ and the position $X_v^n$ can be calculated by using acceleration variables; otherwise, they can be calculated corresponding to the departure time $\overline{t}_v^n$ at $\overline{X}_v$

7-1) If ($X_b^n \geq \overline{X}_b$), $t_v^n = t_a^n + (v_0 - v_a^n)/a$ and $X_v^n = X_a^n + v_a^n(t_v^n - t_a^n) + \dfrac{a}{2}(t_v^n - t_a^n)^2$

7-2) If ($X_b^n < \overline{X}_b$) which is defined as a out of boundary case, then

$$t_v^n = t_d^n + \sqrt{\frac{2\left[(X_d - \bar{X}_v) + v_0(\bar{t}_v^n - t_d^n)\right]}{a}} \quad \text{and} \quad X_v^n = X_d + v_d^n(t_v^n - t_d^n) + \frac{a}{2}(t_v^n - t_d^n)^2$$

where the estimated speed of $v_d^n = v_0 - a(t_v^n - t_d^n)$

**Step 8: (Crossing time and speed to the stop-line for delayed vehicle)**

The departure time $t_s^n$ at the stop-line $X_s$ can be calculated by comparing position variables

8-1) If ( $X_b^n \geq \bar{X}_b$ ) and

If $X_v^n \leq X_s$, then $t_s^n = t_v^n - (X_v^n / v_0)$

If $X_v^n > X_s$, then $t_s^n = t_a^n + (v_s^n - v_a^n)/a$,

where $v_s^n = \sqrt{(v_a^n)^2 - 2aX_a^n}$

8-2) If ( $X_b^n < \bar{X}_b$ ) and

If $X_v^n \leq X_s$, then $t_s^n = t_v^n - (X_v^n / v_0)$

If $X_v^n > X_s$, then $t_s^n = t_v^n + (v_0 - v_s^n)/a$,

where $v_s^n = \sqrt{(v_d^n)^2 - 2aX_d}$

$\Rightarrow$ if $n < N$, **go to Step 1**; otherwise, stop processing.

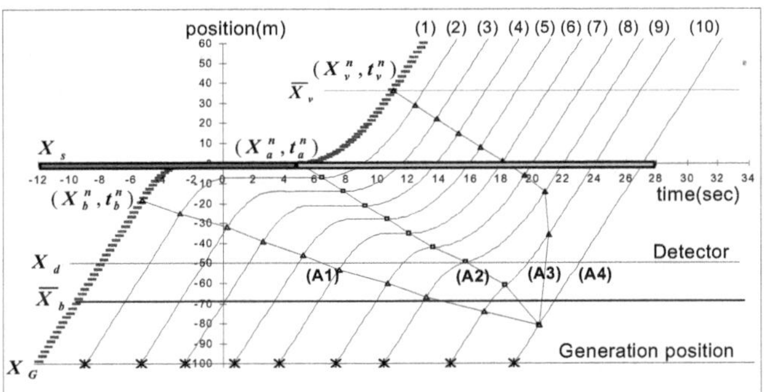


(a) PTM trajectory

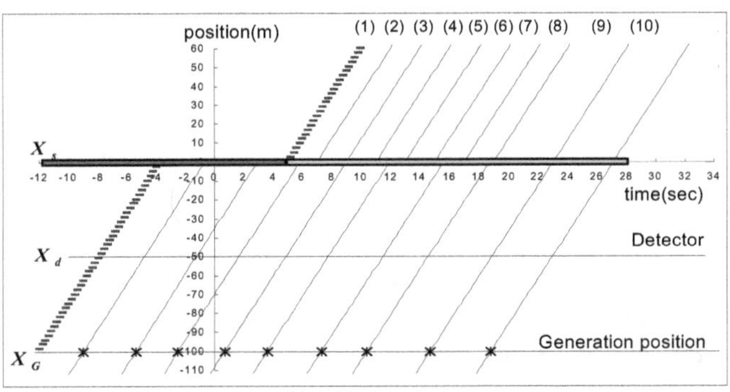


(b) LTM trajectory

Fig. 4. Trajectory of the following vehicles (PTM vs LTM)

As can see in Figure 4a, the PTM can provide plenty of information around the detector and the stop-line. There are four different sets of motions have been identified at the position of the detector during one green period. In respect of the start of green time, any detected vehicles until the time A1 have crossed the detector with free-flow speed, the times between A1 and A2 vehicles have crossed it while braking, the times between A2 and A3 vehicles have crossed it while accelerating, and any following vehicles after the time A4 will cross the detector with free-flow speed. Presumably, the time A4 is the queue (or delay) dissipation time of this stage. More detailed analysis is suggested by Ahn (2004).

## 5. Delay and sensitivity of delay

In this section, delay and sensitivity of delay difference between the LTM and the PTM is discussed in relations to varying start of green time $t_g$. The delay estimates in the LTM and the PTM differs around the time of green starts; the LTM delay is always greater than or equal to the PTM, but so long as there is a queue the delay estimates are identical; however, the maximum sensitivity of delay in the PTM traffic model is higher than that in the LTM.

### 5.1 Delay and sensitivity of delay for the leading vehicle

As can see in Figure 2, the delay in the LTM is identified as the time difference between the start of effective green time $t_g + l_s$ (where start lag $l_s = v_0 / 2a$) and its free-flow arrival time to the stop-line $\overline{t}_{d,s}^n = t_{d,s}^n - X_d / v_0$. The LTM delay for the leading vehicle $n$ =1 with respect to the time $t_g$ is expressed as $D_V^n(t_g)$, which are calculated as follows:

If ( $t_g + l_s \leq \overline{t}_{d,s}^n$ ) then

$$D_V^n(t_g) = 0 \tag{11}$$

If ( $t_g + l_s > \overline{t}_{d,s}^n$ ) then

$$D_V^n(t_g) = (t_g + l_s) - \overline{t}_{d,s}^n \tag{12}$$

If $t_g$ starts before the free-flow arrival time minus the start lag, no delay is incurred in LTM, and the resulting sensitivity is 0. However, from that time if $t_g$ is increased by an amount $\varepsilon$, delay is increased by an identical amount $\varepsilon$, so that the resulting sensitivity is 1. By differentiating the delay Equation (11 and 12) with respect to the time $t_g$, we can get the sensitivity of delay as follows:

$$D_V^{1\prime}(t_g) = \begin{cases} 0 & t_g \leq \overline{t}_{d,s}^n - l_s \\ 1 & t_g > \overline{t}_{d,s}^n - l_s \end{cases} \tag{13}$$

As seen in Figure 1, the delay for the PTM is calculated on the basis of the time $t_g$ in accordance with vehicular characteristic variables, such as, acceleration rate, braking rate and free-flow speed. The delay for the leading vehicle $n$ =1 with respect to the time $t_g$ is expressed as $D_K^n(t_g)$, which are calculated as follows:

If $t_g \le t_b^n$ then

$$D_K^n(t_g) = 0 \tag{14}$$

If $t_b^n < t_g \le t_q^n$ then

$$D_K^n(t_g) = (\overline{t}_b^{\,n} - \overline{t}_d^{\,n}) - \frac{(X_b^n - X_d)}{v_0} + \frac{(ab + b^2)}{2av_0}(t_g - \overline{t}_b^{\,n})^2 \tag{15}$$

If $t_g > t_q^n$ then

$$D_K^n(t_g) = (t_g - \overline{t}_d^{\,n}) + \frac{v_0}{2a} + \frac{X_d}{v_0} \tag{16}$$

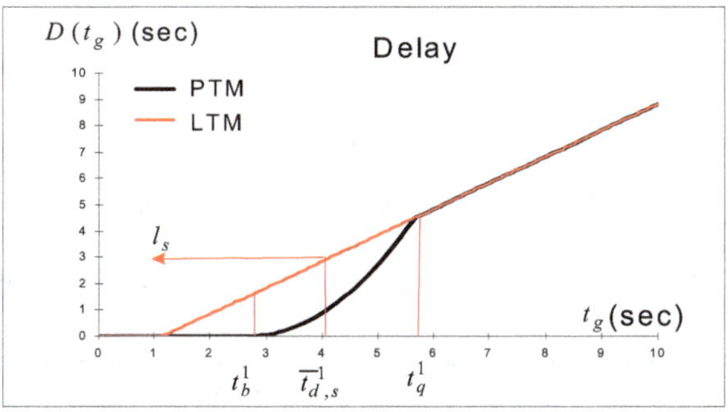


(a) Delay

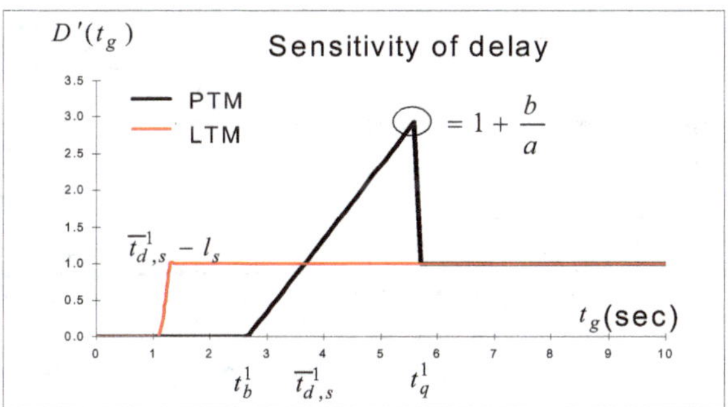


(b) Sensitivity of delay

Fig. 5. Delay and sensitivity of delay comparison for the leading vehicle

As can see in Figure 5, if $t_g$ starts before braking, no delay is incurred and the resulting sensitivity is 0. If $t_g$ starts between braking and stopping, the delay increases quadratically, and the resulting sensitivity increases linearly. Once the vehicle has stopped, if $t_g$ is increased by an amount $\varepsilon$, delay is increased by an identical amount $\varepsilon$, so that the resulting sensitivity is 1. By differentiating the delay Equations (14, 15 and 16) with respect to the varying time $t_g$, we can get the sensitivity of delay as follows:

If $t_g \le t_b^n$ then

$$D_K^{n\prime}(t_g) = 0 \tag{17}$$

If $t_b^n < t_g \le t_q^n$ then

$$D_K^{n\prime}(t_g) = \frac{(ab + b^2)}{av_0}(t_g - t_b^n) \tag{18}$$

If $t_g > t_q^n$ then

$$D_K^{n\prime}(t_g) = 1 \tag{19}$$

The maximum sensitivity of delay for the leading vehicle $n$ =1 in the LTM is always 1. In contrast, the maximum sensitivity of delay in the PTM is $1 + (b/a)$ that is obtained by differentiating the $t_v^n$ in Equation (7) that obtained when $t_g = t_q^1$.

### 5.2 Delay and sensitivity of delay for the following vehicles

In this section, the following results are based on the simulation. Two different cases of traffic are considered: a low density case and a high density case. In the present examples, the maximum number of vehicles that can be held in the queue with this given condition is 8-vehicle.

| | | vhicle $n$ = | | | | | | | |
|---|---|---|---|---|---|---|---|---|---|
| | | 1 | 2 | 3 | 4 | 5 | 6 | 7 | 8 |
| Low density $\alpha$ =0.5 $h_0$ =3.0 | $u$ | - | 0.613 | 0.321 | 0.824 | 0.569 | 0.851 | 0.312 | 0.67 |
| | $H$ | - | 3.97 | 5.27 | 3.38 | 4.12 | 3.32 | 5.33 | 3.79 |
| | $t_d^n$ | 0.0 | 4.0 | 9.3 | 12.7 | 16.8 | 20.1 | 25.4 | 29.2 |
| High density $\alpha$ =0.9 $h_0$ =2.0 | $u$ | - | 0.613 | 0.321 | 0.824 | 0.569 | 0.851 | 0.311 | 0.671 |
| | $H$ | - | 2.54 | 3.26 | 2.21 | 2.62 | 2.18 | 3.29 | 2.44 |
| | $t_d^n$ | 0.0 | 2.5 | 5.8 | 8.0 | 10.6 | 12.8 | 16.1 | 18.5 |

Table 1. Vehicle generation by using shifted exponential distribution of headways

In this The detector is located 50m away from the stop-line, and the minimum spacing of each following vehicle is $L$ =7m, saturation departure time is 1.8 sec/vehicle (2,000 veh/h) and two cases of vehicles are generated based on *shifted exponential distribution of headways*, which is given by

$$H = h_0 - \frac{1}{\alpha}\ln(u) \tag{20}$$

where

$u$ is the random value generation, in which variables are generated with equal probability between [0, 1]

$h_0$ is the minimum gap of following ( $h_0 \ge \tau + L/v_0$, where $\tau$ is 0.67sec)

$\alpha$ is the density parameter

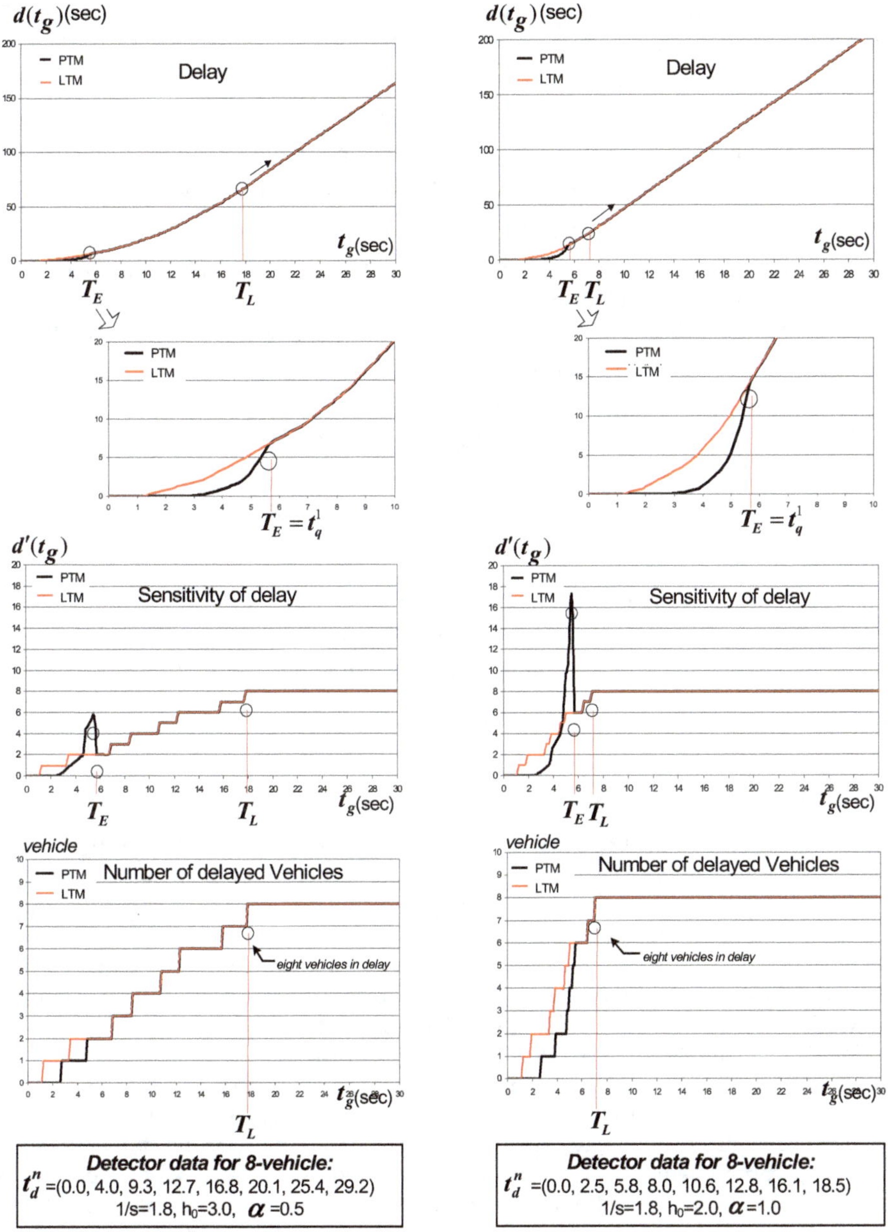


(a) Low density case (b) High density case

Fig. 6. Delay and sensitivity of delay comparison for the following vehicles

Using Equation (20), we can generate the vehicles without causing any headway violation. The detection time $t_d^n$ can be given by $t_d^n = t_d^{n-1} + H$ ( $n \geq 2$ ). Based on Table 1 data, the sensitivity of delay for 8-vehicle is tested with respect to the variations in the start of green time: in the range of $t_g$ = 0 ~ 30 sec and $t_g$ is incremented by 0.1 sec. As can see in Figure 6, let $T_E$ be the time at which the total delay of 8-vehicle for the PTM and the LTM become same, namely $T_E = t_q^1$, where $T_L$ is the time at which total delay becomes increasing linearly.

If $t_g$ starts before $T_L$, which means that all 8-vehicle have not delayed yet; in this range, we can suppose that some vehicles may go through the stop-line without experiencing any delay, thus the sensitivity fluctuates.

If $t_g$ starts after $T_L$, which means that all 8-vehicle have been delayed, the sensitivity of delay in this range with respect to $t_g$ is equal to the total number of delayed vehicles. The sensitivity of delay for the LTM is equal to the number of delayed vehicles in the time range. But it differs for the PTM, if $t_g$ starts before $T_E$, in some time range it shows a sensitivity higher than the total number of delayed vehicles. For the high density case simulation (see Figure 6b), the LTM delay is greater than or equal to the PTM delay. $T_E$ =5.7 sec and $T_L$ =7.1 sec. At time $t_g$ = 5.5 sec, the PTM shows a sensitivity of delay $D_K^{'}$ = 17.28, and the LTM shows $D_V^{'}$ = 6, which is equivalent to numbers of delayed vehicles. At this time, the sensitivity of delay for the PTM is about three times greater than for the LTM. At time $t_g$ = 7.1 sec, the sensitivity of delay for both models is equal to 8. From that time, we can see that all vehicles will experience some delay.

## 6. Conclusions

As explored in this paper, the delay estimated in the Linear Traffic Model (LTM) and the Polynomial Traffic Model (PTM) differs around the time of the green start, but so long as there is a queue the delay estimates from these models are identical. With respect to variations in the start of green time and provided that the braking rate exceeds the acceleration rate, the delay estimated in the LTM is always greater than or equal to the PTM traffic model; however, the maximum sensitivity of delay in the PTM is greater than that in the LTM. The PTM proposed in this paper has some attractions compared to the simpler LTM. The delay estimate in the PTM is on the basis of the vehicular characteristics, such as vehicle length, acceleration rate, braking rate and free-flow speed; however, the LTM takes adjusted time parameter of the start of effective green time. Thus, the delay estimated from the LTM is not realistic and always greater than or equal to the PTM. From these results, it is clear that the leading vehicle trajectory is the most important determinant for estimating the motion of vehicles at signalized intersections. Namely, the delay can be minimized in signal operation, if the start of green time begins before the vehicle starts to brake. The work described so far in this study is only at on early stage, in the sense that more work should be done for estimating the motion of vehicles in various intersection configurations.

## 7. References

Ahn, W-Y. (2004). Dynamic signal optimisation for isolated road junctions. Ph.D. thesis, University College London.

Akcelick, R. (1981). Traffic signals: Capacity and timing analysis. *Research Report ARR No. 123*. ARRB Transport research Ltd, Vwemont South Australia.

Akcelick, R. & Besley, M. (2002). Queue Discharge flow and speed models for signalised intersections. *Transport and Traffic Theory in the 21st Century*, theory, pp. 99-118.

Allsop, R.E. (1970). Optimisation techniques for reducing delay to traffic in signalised road junction. Ph.D. thesis, University College London.

Clayton, A.J.H. (1940). Road traffic calculation. *J. Inst. Civil Engineering*. 16 (7), pp. 247-284.

Gartner, N.H. (1983). OPAC: A demand-responsive strategy for traffic signal control. TRB, *Transportation Research Record 906*, pp. 75-84.

Gipps, P.G. (1981). A behavioural ca-following model for computer simulation. *Transportation Research*, 15(2), pp. 105-111.

Heydecker, B.G. (1990). A continuous-time formulation for traffic-responsive signal control. *Proceedings of the 11th International Symposium on Transportation and Traffic Theory*, Yokohama, pp. 599-618.

Miller, A. J. (1963). A computer system for traffic networks. *Proceedings of the Second International Symposium on the Theory of Road traffic Flow* (ed. Almond, J.), OECD, Paris, pp. 200-220.

Robertson, D.I. (1969). TRANSYT: A traffic network study tool. *RRL Report, LR253*.

TRANSYT (2000). A traffic network study, McTrans.

TRB (2000). Highway Capacity Manual. *Transportation Research Board*, National Research Council, Washington, D.C., U.S.A. (*HCM 2000*).

Webster, F.V. and Cobbe, B.M. (1966). *Traffic signals*. HMSO, London.

# 8

# Study on Data-driven Methods for Image and Video Understanding

Tatsuya Yamazaki
*National Institute of Information and Communications Technology*
*Japan*

## 1. Introduction

Owing to progress of broadband Internet communication infrastructure, people can enjoy multimedia services. Among the services, images and videos are making an appeal and people desire to find out what they want to see. But they do not always make a success of searching and it sometimes takes plenty of time to reach their targets. A solution is to attach information tags according to the image or video content. Since image and video submission into Internet is increasing day by day, manual tag attachment is almost impossible. Development of automatic tag attachment is an urgent theme for future Internet service.

Another imaging technology in the real world is environmental cameras. The environmental cameras mean the cameras set in the environment such as a ceiling or a street corner. One can easily imagine surveillance cameras as an example of the environmental cameras and sometimes they are considered to be identical. In this paper, I want to segregate them because the purpose of the environment cameras is not only to keep a watch on accidents or crimes but to understand peoples' situations and behaviours. Namely the surveillance cameras are a subset of the environmental cameras.

For both of the above cases, the key point is understanding image and video. It is one of the issues that have been discussed for a long time and related with the artificial intelligence technology. Therein image clustering and object extraction are most essential technologies.

Image clustering means to divide an image into several segmented regions in a way of unsupervised, which was used for object extraction (Meier & Ngan, 1998), image compression (Kunt, 1988), or image categorization. Since it is hard to say how many regions are included in an image in general, there are a few studies that estimated the number of regions. Usually the number of regions has been assumed to be known. As a previous research in which the number of region was estimated, Won and Derin (Won & Derin, 1992) proposed to use the Akaike Information Criterion to determine the number of regions. But these are model-based approaches, that is, how to select a suitable model is important.

Regarding with the environmental cameras, there have been previous works to extract moving object in order to capture human behaviours. Satake and Shakunaga (Satake & Shakunaga, 2004) proposed an appearance-based condensation tracker, which is composed of a condensation tracker and a sparse template matching method to detect the movement of people with a camera. The template-based condensation tracker is stabilized for tracking even in the case of object occlusion. Thonnat and Rota (Thonnat & Rota, 1999) used low-level image processing techniques to detect and track mobile objects. Their aim was rather to understand images, namely, to generate alarms automatically for operators when interesting scenarios had been recognized by the system. In both of the above works, they used only one camera. On the contrary, Matsuyama (Matsuyama, 1999) proposed a protocol for negotiation among multiple environmental cameras. Because of the protocol, they could synchronize several cameras in real time and grab the human behaviours more smoothly and more seamlessly.

As I described in the above paragraphs, automatic processing of image and video media should be deployed more in future Internet services for the information explosion era. Technically adaptation of processing based on the observed data, which is called data-driven, is necessary. Therefore, in this paper, data-driven image clustering and object detection methods are proposed.

## 2. Data-driven Image Clustering

In this section, a data-driven clustering algorithm for colour images is proposed based on a multi-dimensional histogram. A statistical model is introduced and the image data is assumed to be derived from a mixture of multi-variant distributions.

### 2.1 Multi-dimensional histogram

Although the R-G-B colour space is assumed to make a discussion simple, the proposed method can be applied to other colour spaces. The R-G-B colour image data is represented as $\mathbf{y}=(\mathbf{y}_1, \dots , \mathbf{y}_{Np})$, where $\mathbf{y}_i=(y_i^R, y_i^G, y_i^B)$ $(i=1, \dots , N_p)$ is the observed element at the $i$-th pixel. $N_p$ is the total number of pixels, $y_i^X$ is a scalar value observed on the $X$ plane at the $i$-th pixel, and $y_i^X$ is assumed to range from $G_{min}$ to $G_{max}$, where $X$ is $R$, $G$, or $B$.

The multi-dimensional histogram is formed easily. First, distribute the observed data into the R-G-B color space. Second, construct a complete set of nonoverlapping intervals, called bins, by dividing the cube ($[G_{min}, G_{max}]^3$) equally with a width $h$. Finally, count the number of elements in each bin. Fig. 1 shows a construction of a multi-dimensional histogram with $G_{min}$=0. The histogram width $h$ is an important parameter, and relates to the data distribution. When the data comes from a single density, several rules have been proposed to determine $h$. When the data are obtained a mixture of densities and the number of densities, $N_c$, is unknown, it is difficult to determine $h$. The multi-dimensional histogram of the colour image data deal with in this study corresponds to the latter case.

### 2.2 Data-driven clustering algorithm

It is assumed that there are a set of candidates for the histogram width, that is, $\{H=h_1, h_2, \dots , h_C\}$. Here, a novel algorithm is proposed to determine $h$ and $N_c$.

Step 1) Select a candidate $h_j$ $(j=1, \dots , C)$ from $H$. Construct a histogram with a width $h_j$. Select the bins that have at least one element in the histogram, and sort them in the order of the number of elements in each bin. The sorted bins are numbered in the order of the number of elements as $b_1^j, b_2^j, \dots, b_{nz}^j$, where $b_{nz}^j$ is the number of bins having at least one element. The $k$-th bin, $b_k^j$, has $n_k^j$ elements (Fig. 2).

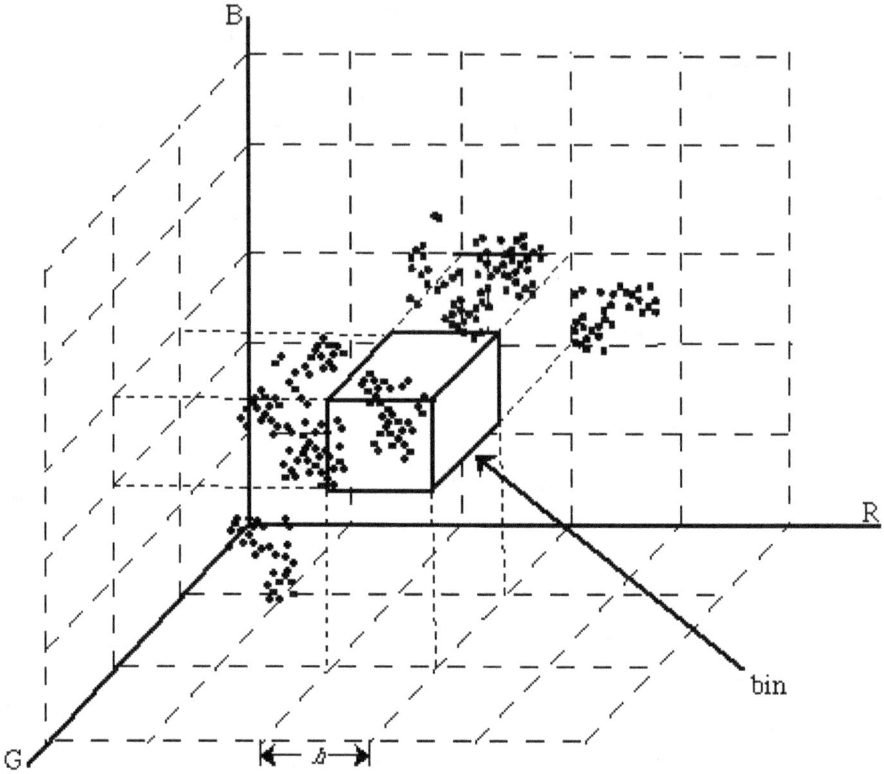


Fig. 1. Multi-dimensional histogram

Step 2) If $n_k^j < n_{cut}^j$, then $b_k^j$ is removed. $n_{cut}^j$ is a threshold calculated as

$$n_{cut} = \alpha_{h_j} \frac{b_{nz}}{N_p} \tag{1}$$

where $\alpha_{h_j}$ is a control parameter to be determined for each $h_j$ heuristically. $n_{cut}$ is the threshold that divides explicitly insignificant bins. Eventually $b_{cut}^j$ bins remain.

Step 3) Extract the top $b_{sig}^j$ bins as significant bins from $b_{cut}^j$ bins, where $b_{sig}^j$ is determined as follows.

$$b_{sig}^j = arg \max_{k=1,\ldots,b_{cut}^j} Cr_{sig}(k) \tag{2}$$

$$Cr_{sig}(k) = \sum_{l=1}^{k} \frac{\sum_{m=1}^{b_{cut}^j} n_m^j}{n_l^j} - \frac{b_{cut}^j}{k} \tag{3}$$

$Cr_{sig}(k)$ is a criterion to select significant bins that include as many elements as possible considering suppression of the number of selected bins.

Step 4) If $b_{sig}^j$ for every histogram-width candidate $h_j$ is calculated, then go to Step 5. Otherwise, go to Step 1 and pick up another candidate whose $b_{sig}^j$ has not been calculated.

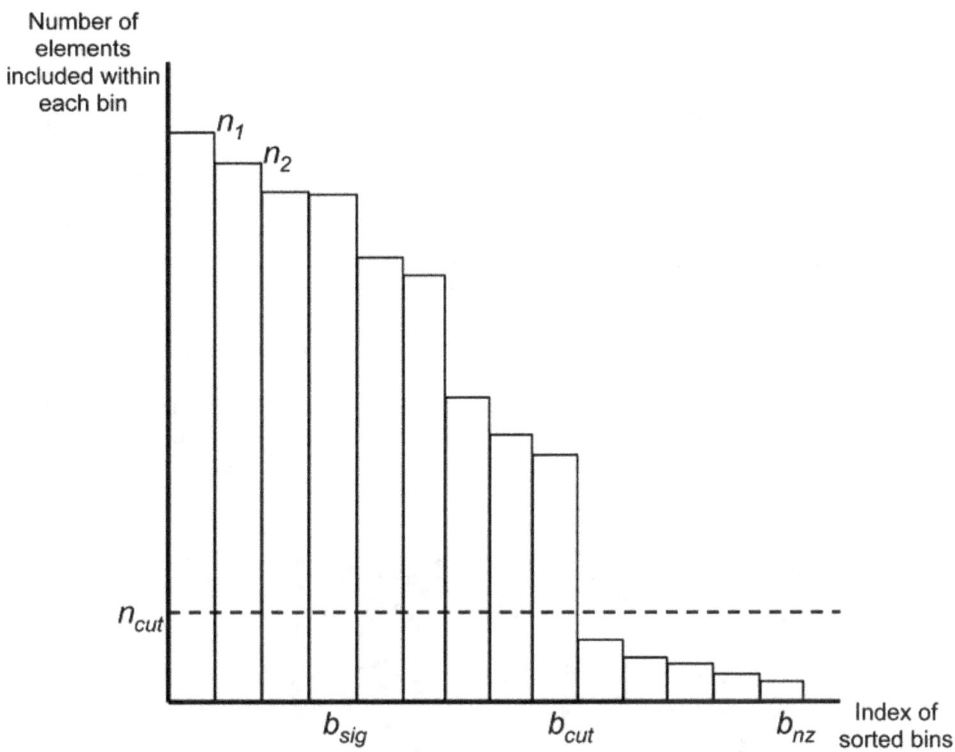


Fig. 2. Sorted frequency distribution of elements within each bin

Step 5) Calculate the optimal histogram width $h^*$ as

$$h^* = arg \max_{h_j \in H} \sum_{l=1}^{b_{sig}^j} n_l^j \tag{4}$$

where $b_{sig}^j$ corresponds to $h_j$, and $b_{sig}^j$ corresponding to $h^*$ is denoted as $b_{sig}^*$. Consequently $h^*$ is selected from $H$ as the optimal width from the perspective of extracting as many significant elements as possible to compute the distribution statistics.

The significant $b_{sig}^*$ bins are determined beforehand without considering the mutual relationships. Therefore, the adjacent bins that are supposed to belong to the same density must be merged to determine the final cluster count $N_c$. The clustering criterion is as follows. Calculate the average $(\mu_k^R, \mu_k^G, \mu_k^B)$ and the standard deviation $(\sigma_k^R, \sigma_k^G, \sigma_k^B)$ for the $k$-th bin ($k$=1, ..., $b_{sig}^*$).

Select any two bins, say $b_l$ and $b_m$, from $b_{sig}^*$ bins. If $|\mu_l^R - \mu_m^R| < \beta\overline{\sigma^R}$, $|\mu_l^G - \mu_m^G| < \beta\overline{\sigma^G}$ and $|\mu_l^B - \mu_m^B| < \beta\overline{\sigma^B}$, then the two bins belong to the same cluster, where $\overline{\sigma^X} = \sum_{i=1}^{b_{sig}^*} \sigma_i^X / b_{sig}^*$ for $X$=$R$, $G$, or, $B$ and $\beta$ is a parameter. Finally, cluster the $b_{sig}^*$ bins into $N_c$ clusters.

### 2.3 Proposed algorithm application to real data

The proposed algorithm was applied to real image data. Fig. 3 shows one of the original images, which is called the "Lady with a rose" image in this paper. The image size is 480 × 480. Although it is shown in grey scale, the original colour space is the RGB colour space. The histogram width candidates set used in the algorithm is $H$={4, 8, 16, 32}. The values of $\alpha_{hi}$ corresponding to each histogram width are $\alpha_4$ =1.0, $\alpha_8$=0.7, $\alpha_{16}$=0.35 and $\alpha_{32}$=0.05. In this experiment, $\beta$ is set to 0.0; this means that the merging process is skipped.
Applied the proposed algorithm, the histogram width was determined to be 32 and the number of clusters was 6 finally. These values were determined in a data-driven way.
Then, the statistics of each cluster were computed by the minimum distance method, and the conventional maximum likelihood method with the estimated statistics, under the normal distribution assumption, was performed to obtain the segmented image. The final result followed by the 3×3 mode filtering operation is shown in Fig. 4.

Fig. 3. Original image "Lady with a rose"

Fig. 4. Segmentation result of "Lady with a rose"

The final estimates of the means and the proportions are shown in Table 1.

| | Cluster 1 | Cluster 2 | Cluster 3 |
|---|---|---|---|
| R | 37.4 | 17.7 | 73.5 |
| G | 45.7 | 12.1 | 84.0 |
| B | 52.1 | 6.6 | 104.5 |
| Proportion | 0.282 | 0.166 | 0.172 |
| | Cluster 4 | Cluster 5 | Cluster 6 |
| R | 29.3 | 83.1 | 110.3 |
| G | 37.9 | 60.0 | 100.8 |
| B | 41.1 | 47.3 | 103.9 |
| Proportion | 0.132 | 0.157 | 0.091 |

Table 1. Final parameter estimates of the means and the proportions for "Lady with a rose"

## 3. Data-driven object detection

In the real world, cameras are becoming popular to detect and track moving objects not only for surveillance or security but also for digital signage or spoken dialogue systems. The background subtraction method, which can be used to detect objects moving in the foreground by determining the difference between the current frame and an image of the scene's static background, is still one of the useful methods to detect moving objects in video sequences. Although the background subtraction method is a simple and effective method to detect moving objects, it occasionally suffers from illumination changes and unexpected background changes such as shadow. To improve the original background subtraction method, we propose that knowledge application and data-driven parameter adaptation techniques be adopted.

### 3.1 Detection of People by Background Subtraction Method

In order to cope with the illumination changes, we adopt the normalized distance method. Here, a unit vector is defined as the projection onto the unit sphere of a vector whose elments are the intensity values of pixels in a target region. The normalized distance is defined as a distance between two unit vectors. Let $\boldsymbol{\tau}$ and $\boldsymbol{\beta}$ as vectors consiting of intensity values of pixels in an observed image and in a background image respectively. Then the distance $\boldsymbol{\delta}$ and normalized distance $\boldsymbol{\delta}'$ are shown as follows,

$$\boldsymbol{\delta} = |\boldsymbol{\tau} - \boldsymbol{\beta}| \tag{5}$$

$$\boldsymbol{\delta}' = \left|\frac{\boldsymbol{\tau}}{|\boldsymbol{\tau}|} - \frac{\boldsymbol{\beta}}{|\boldsymbol{\beta}|}\right| \tag{6}$$

Supposing that we process image frames during a period of $T_{int}$. We calculate $\boldsymbol{\delta}$ for each frame in $T_{int}$, then $Max(\boldsymbol{\delta})$, $Min(\boldsymbol{\delta})$, and $Ave(\boldsymbol{\delta})$ are calculated as maximum value, minimum value, and averaged value of $\boldsymbol{\delta}$. In the same way, $Max(\boldsymbol{\delta}')$ and $Min(\boldsymbol{\delta}')$ are calculated as maximum value and minimum value of the normalized distance $\boldsymbol{\delta}'$. Consequently, the following three discriminant functions are defined,

1. discriminant function for scene change
   $\max \boldsymbol{\delta} - \min \boldsymbol{\delta} > Th_{scene}$

2. discriminant function for background change
   $\text{Ave}\ \boldsymbol{\delta} > Th_{bs}$

3. discriminant function whether environment change or illumination change
   $\max\ \boldsymbol{\delta}' - \min\ \boldsymbol{\delta}' > Th_{ill}$

where $Th_{scene}$, $Th_{bs}$, and $Th_{ill}$ are thresholds to be determined.
Using these discriminant functions, whether there is a moving object detection or a background updating in $T_{int}$ can be judged as follows:

- If both (3) and (5) are true, there is a scene change by a moving object.
- If (3) is true and (5) is false, there is a scene change by an illumination change.
- If (3) is false and (4) is true, there is a background change.
- If both (3) and (4) are false, there is nothing. It is a normal background.

A challenging point in this method is adaptively setting the threshold value to differentiate foreground objects from the background image in spite of environmental changes.
To determine the threshold value, Wren et al. (Wren et al., 1997) modeled the background using a Gaussian distribution and estimated the parameters adaptively. Grimson et al. (Grimson et al., 1998) also set up parameters according to the statistical analysis of training samples of the background images. Stauffer and Grimson used a mixture model of Gaussian distributions of the images to cope with multimodal background distributions (Stauffer & Grimson, 1999).

### 3.2 Knowledge Application and Parameter Adaptation

We apply two techniques to the original background subtraction method in order to cope with unexpected moving objects and adaptive threshold parameter setting. Our aim is to detect and track people as moving objects. There are, however, other unexpected moving objects in the scene, such as an automatic door. To avoid detection of such an unexpected moving object, we introduce knowledge about special spots as the first technique. The positions of special spots are assumed to be known and masking is applied not to detect the unexpected moving object. This is a simple but effective technique.
To set the threshold values adaptively, we introduce a kind of steepest descent method as the second technique. The algorithm is depicted in Fig. 5.

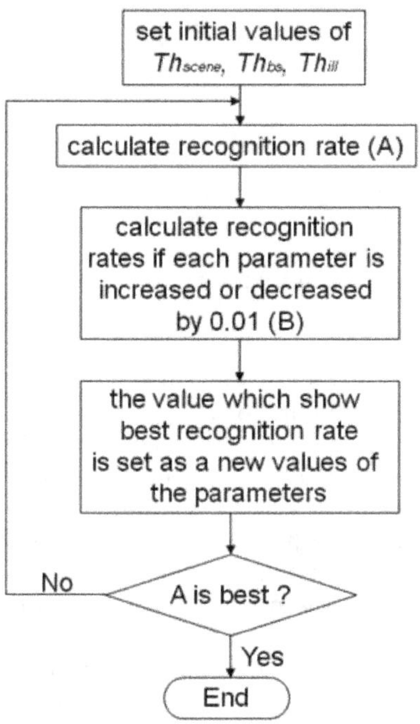


Fig. 5. Flowchart of threshold adaptation by steepest descent

In the first step of the algorithm shown in Fig. 5, initial values of $Th_{scene}$, $Th_{bs}$ and $Th_{ill}$ are set. Then the recognition rate $A$ with the current threshold values that are the same as the initial values at the very first stage of the algorithm. After the threshold values are increased or decreased by a small value, the new recognition rates $B$ are calculated. 0.01 is set as the small value in Fig. 5. $B$ is a set of the recognition rates because increasing and decreasing of each threshold value are tried. $A$ is compared with the best recognition rate in $B$. If $A$ is superior to the best recognition rate, the algorithm is terminated. Otherwise, the best threshold values that correspond to the best recognition rate are substituted to the current threshold values and the same steps are carried out.

### 3.3 Experimental results at the real world test bed

We constructed such a test bed in the entrance of our research laboratory. In the ceiling of the test bed, there are five cameras, and the area covered by the cameras is the meshed region in Fig. 6. The camera can take a 768 × 494 pixel image and has remote pan, tilt, and zoom functions.

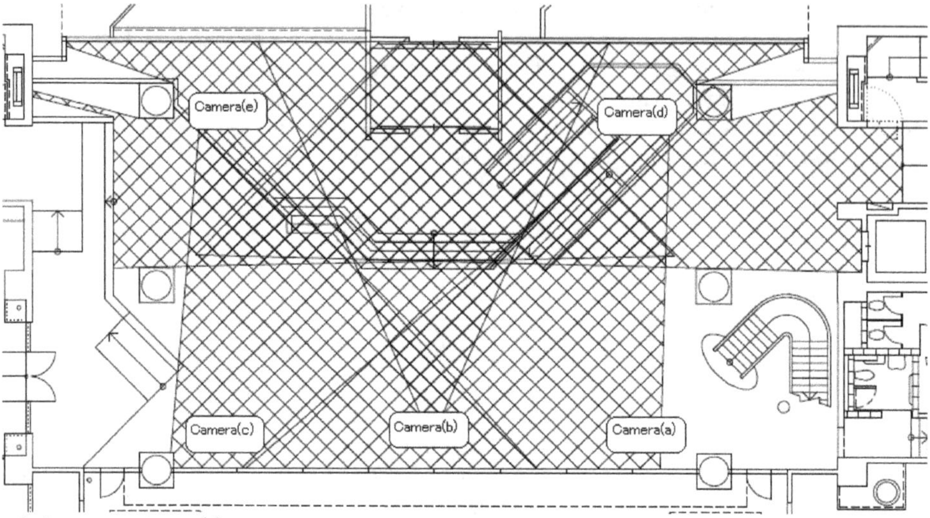


Fig. 6. Area monitored by cameras

In the test bed, we tried to detect moving objects using camera images and the background subtraction method. In the background subtraction method, first of all, we selected the initial image without any moving objects as the background image to be subtracted. Then, the difference between the current and the background images is calculated and pixels that have a difference larger than the threshold are registered as candidate pixels of an image of moving objects. This difference calculation is operated for each small image block of 80 × 60 pixels. The judgment described in the previous subsections is applied. The adjacent small image blocks of candidate pixels are merged into a larger image block. To track the moving objects, a two-dimensional histogram with hue and saturation values in an HSV color space is constructed to calculate the correspondence between objects in the current and previously captured images. When the difference between two images in the two-dimensional histogram is smaller, the probability that objects belong to the same object is higher.

We applied the above background subtraction method to a ten-second video captured in an actual situation. The number of frames captured from each camera was different because the time consumed for image compression was different.

Two experiments were carried out. The first experiment was moving object detection by the background subtraction method with knowledge application only. The second one was moving object detection by the background subtraction method with parameter adaptation as well as knowledge application. The first and the second are referred as Experiment I and Experiment II respectively. The applied knowledge is that the position of the automatic door is known.

In Experiment I, the threshold parameters were fixed as $Th_{scene}$=0.10, $Th_{bs}$=0.25 and $Th_{ill}$=0.05. One result of detecting a moving object is presented in Fig. 7. The people in the image should be recognized as moving objects, and rectangles are drawn as a result. Two larger rectangles (shown in red) are hand-made markings that indicate correct answers. Several smaller rectangles in the left larger rectangle (shown in yellow) indicate detected results obtained by the background subtraction method. In the right larger rectangle, no object was detected by the background subtraction method. We call the larger rectangles ground truth rectangles and the smaller rectangles are called detected rectangles.

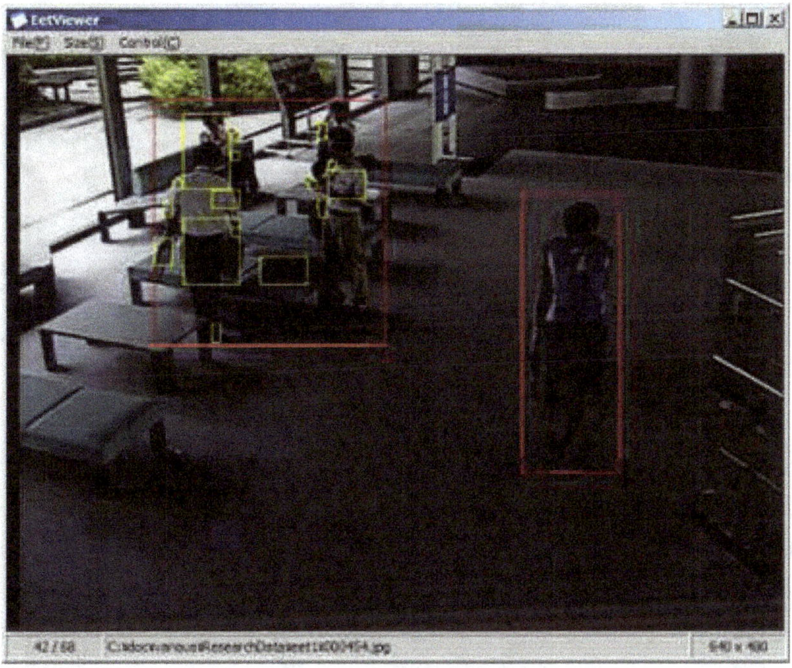

Fig. 7. Result of detecting moving objects in Experiment I

Although an identical match between ground truth and detected rectangles is desirable, detected rectangles are almost always included in or overlapped on ground truth rectangles. Here, we define two kinds of error: the type one error and the type two error. The type one error is that in which no detected rectangle is drawn where there was a ground truth rectangle. The type two error is that in which detected rectangles appeared where there was no ground truth rectangle. The total error rate can be calculated by averaging these two types of error. The rates of occurrence of two types of error and the total error rate are shown in Table 2 for cameras (a) - (e). The positions of the cameras are shown in Fig. 6.

| | Type one error rate (%) | Type two error rate (%) | Total error rate (%) |
|---|---|---|---|
| Camera(a) | 29.38 | 0.32 | 14.85 |
| Camera(b) | 54.35 | 27.94 | 41.15 |
| Camera(c) | 28.39 | 0.31 | 14.35 |
| Camera(d) | 10.23 | 16.19 | 13.21 |
| Camera(e) | 10.06 | 8.38 | 9.22 |

Table 2. Error rates with knowledge application and fixed parameters

Next, we applied threshold parameter adaptation presented in Fig. 5 as well as the knowledge application. This is Experiment II. The initial threshold parameters were set as $Th_{scene}$=0.10, $Th_{bs}$=0.25 and $Th_{ill}$=0.05. One moving object detection result with the parameter adaptation is presented in Fig. 8, that corresponds to Fig. 7. By comparing two images, it is found that the person in the right side was detected in Experiment II, who was missed in Experiment I. The rates of occurrence of two types of error and the total error rate are shown in Table 3.

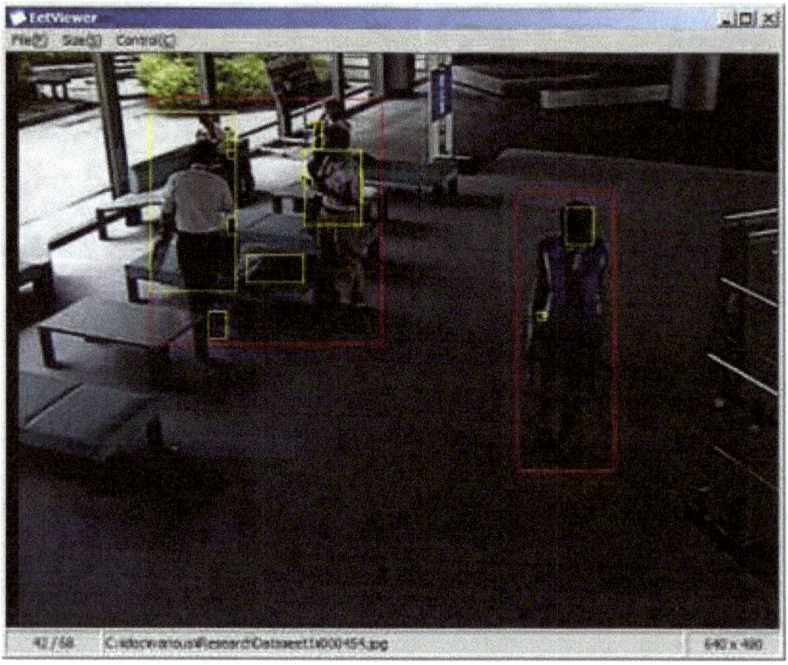

Fig. 8. Result of detecting moving objects in Experiment II

| | Type one error rate (%) | Type two error rate (%) | Total error rate (%) |
|---|---|---|---|
| Camera(a) | 14.69 | 0.27 | 7.48 |
| Camera(b) | 17.39 | 0.00 | 8.97 |
| Camera(c) | 19.36 | 1.97 | 10.67 |
| Camera(d) | 1.14 | 14.70 | 7.92 |
| Camera(e) | 10.06 | 0.08 | 5.07 |

Table 3. Error rates with knowledge application and parameter adaptation

Almost all error rates were improved. Especially improvement for camera (b) was splendid. It can be considered that the reason is owing to knowledge application. As the result of parameter adaptation, the final obtained parameters, $Th_{scene}$, $Th_{bs}$ and $Th_{ill}$, are shown in Table 4.

| | $Th_{scene}$ | $Th_{bs}$ | $Th_{ill}$ |
|---|---|---|---|
| Camera(a) | 0.10 | 0.21 | 0.04 |
| Camera(b) | 0.10 | 0.20 | 0.04 |
| Camera(c) | 0.10 | 0.21 | 0.04 |
| Camera(d) | 0.07 | 0.23 | 0.04 |
| Camera(e) | 0.12 | 0.26 | 0.04 |

Table 4. The final threshold parameters in Experiment II

## 4. Conclusion

Among multimedia, the roles of image and video media are becoming more important both in the cyber and real worlds. The cyber world means the information world structured by computer networks such as Internet. Videos and images are accumulated in the cyber world and the users are wandering to search for what they want. Also in the real world, cameras are becoming popular to collect the users' and environmental information. How to analyse these more efficiently is one of the issues to be solved urgently.

Image and video understanding has been studied and several approaches have been developed. In the parametric approaches, how to set the parameters is a challenging problem. In this paper, data-driven parameter adaptation was applied to image clustering and object extraction for still and video images. Although the experimental results were limited, definite improvement has been attained.

In the future, it is desired to extract contextual information from image and video media by applying image and video understanding techniques including the methods proposed in this paper. It must contribute to realize a personalized, adaptive, situation-aware service in a ubiquitous network society.

## 5. References

Meier, T. & Ngan, K.N. (1998). Automatic Segmentation of Moving Objects for Video Object Plane Generation. *IEEE Trans. on Circuits Syst., Video Technol.,* Vol. 8, No. 5, (Sept. 1998) pp. 525-538

Kunt, M. (1988). Progress in High Compression Image Coding. *Int. J. Pattern Recognition and Artificial Intelligence,* Vol. 2, No. 3, (1988) pp. 387-405

Won, C.S. & Derin, H. (1992). Unsupervised Segmentation of Noisy and Textured Images Using Markov Random Fields. *CVGIP: Graphical Models and Image Processing,* Vol. 54, No. 4, (July 1992) pp. 308-328

Satake, J. & Shakunaga, T. (2004). Multiple target tracking by appearance-based condensation tracker using structure information, *Proceedings of the 17th International Conference on Pattern Recognition (ICPR2004),* Vol.1ap, No. We-ii, pp. 537-540, 2004

Thonnat, M. & Rota, N. (1999). Image Understanding for Visual Surveillance Applications, *Proceedings of Third International Workshop on Cooperative Distributed Vision (CDV-WD'99),* No. 3, pp. 51-82, Nov. 2004

Matsuyama, T. (1999). Dynamic Memory: Architecture for Real Time Integration of Visual Perception, Camera Action, and Network Communication, *Proceedings of Third International Workshop on Cooperative Distributed Vision (CDV-WD'99)*, No. 1, pp. 1-30, Nov. 2004

Wren, C.; Azarbayejani, A.; Darrell, T. & Pentland, A. (1997). Real-time Tracking of the Human Body, *IEEE Trans. on Patt. Anal. and Machine Intell.*, Vol. 19, No.7, (1997) pp.780-785

Grimson, W.E.L.; Stauffer, C.; Romano, R. & Lee, L. (1998). Using adaptive tracking to classify and monitor activities in a site, *Proceedings of 1998 Conference on Computer Vision and Pattern Recognition (CVPR '98)*, pp. 22-29, 1998

Stauffer, C. & Grimson, W.E.L. (1999). Adaptive background mixture models for real-time tracking, *Proceedings of 1999 Conference on Computer Vision and Pattern Recognition (CVPR '99)*, pp. 246-252, 1999

# 9

# Using the Flow of Story for Automatic Video Skimming

Songhao Zhu[1] and Yuncai Liu[2]
[1]*play_tree@163.com*, [2]*whomliu@sjtu.edu.cn*
*Institute of Image Processing and Pattern Recognition,*
*Shanghai Jiao tong University*
*800, Don chuan Road, Shanghai 200240, China*

**Abstract:** In this chapter, we present a novel scheme to incorporate the flow of story to select salient scenarios for generating semantically meaningful skimming of continuously recorded video such as a movie. We obtain clues of a movie from scenario editing rules and movie production techniques, which are commonly adopted in the process of video making to express the flow of the movie explicitly. The generated skimming not only provides a bird view of the original video but also help viewers understand the overall story. Furthermore, different types of video skimming can be appropriately generated with respect to different user requirements. Experimental results show that the proposed scheme is a feasible solution for the management of video repository and online review services.

## 1. Introduction

Nowadays the huge amount of video material stored in multimedia repositories makes the browsing, retrieval and delivery of such content a very slow and usually difficult task. According to a report from the China Central Television Web site, the total click count for movie review services reaches almost 100 million per day. In other words, movie occupies up to 50% compared to other genres of review services. This is largely due to the fact that it will take a viewer at least several minutes to watch a film episode before he can understand what happens and why it happens in the episode. In such instance, it is desirable to quickly browse video content in limited bandwidth, which can be achieved by automatic video content skimming.

Video skimming is defined as a sequence of moving images that compactly present the content of a video without losing the main information [1]. According to different characteristics of video content, we can categorize videos into two genres: event-oriented videos and story-oriented videos. An event-oriented video, such as sports or news, has a predetermined structure, and viewers can obtain entertainment or information even by only watching a few interesting parts. However, a story-oriented video, e.g., a movie, has no explicit structure, and a viewer needs to watch the whole video if he wants to know the story. Therefore, the skimming of an event-based video aims to compactly provide entertainment or information to viewers, whereas that of a story-oriented video aims to render the impression of the content of entire video in a short period of time. Several techniques have been proposed to generate skimming for event-oriented videos by exploiting the well-known structures of videos. In [2-4], a highlight of a news video can be a collection of anchor shots, while that of a soccer video can be generated as a collection of goal shots [5-6]. However, issues related to the production of an abstraction of a story-oriented video have not yet been widely studied. One of the major challenges in generating skimming for a story-oriented video is that the cognitive process of viewers in perceiving the progress of a story while watching a video is not well understood. Most literatures [7-13] focus on the skimming production which presents the overall mood of the video, rather than help in perceiving the progress of the story. Sundaram *et al.* [14] first integrate viewers' comprehension of video contents into the generation of video skimming. More specifically, the video skimming is constructed by reducing scene duration, i.e., removing redundant shots and frames in scenes while preserving salient shots. To guide the reduction of scenes, a shot-utility function is utilized to model the degree of human understanding of a video shot with respect to its visual complexity and duration.

We propose a framework based on the progress of a story to perform the skimming of movie. As aforementioned, [14] solves the issue of video skimming at the scene level, while the proposed approach attempts to comprehend video contents from the progress and viewer's understanding of the overall story, which is realized as a sequence of scenarios and their relationships [15]. Considering that a scenario is usually captured by a scene, our approach can be considered as a higher level approach and a complement to Sundaram's scene-based scheme.

For the proposed framework based on the story progress, we first segment a video into shots based on the property of two-dimension histogram entropy of image pixels. Next, we generate semantically meaning scenarios by exploiting the spatio-temporal correlation among detected shots. Finally, we exploit general rules of special scenario and common techniques of movie production to grasp the flow of a story according to the degree of progress between scenarios to the overall story, which is evaluated in terms of the intensity of the interrelationships between scenarios.

To demonstrate the effectiveness of the proposed framework, we develop a video skimming system to conduct a set of comparison experiments using objective evaluation criteria, such as precision and recall. Furthermore, we also perform subjective tests to see the viewer's story understanding as well as to see the viewer's satisfaction. Results consistently show the advantages of the proposed framework. The basic idea of the proposed framework is shown in Figure 1.

The main contributions of the proposed framework are as follows.

- We propose a shot boundary detection approach by utilizing the property of two-dimension histogram entropy of image pixels;
- We generate scenarios of a video based on the spatio-temporal correlation between detected shots;
- We exploit clues about the progress of a story to implement the generation of video skimming.

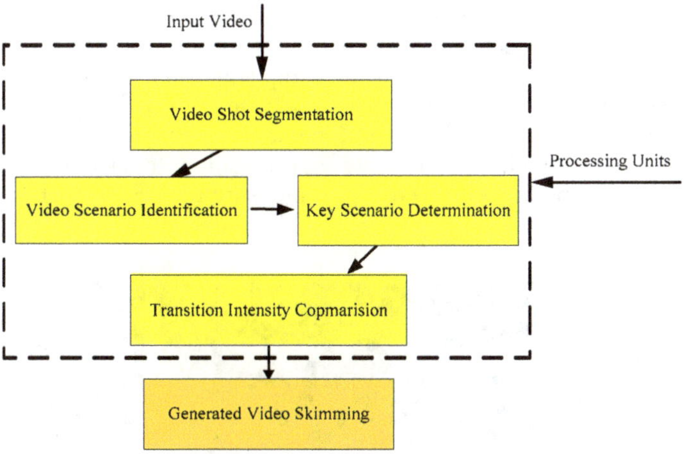


Fig. 1. Overview of the proposed framework.

The remainder of this chapter is organized as follows. In Sections 2 and 3, we introduce the process of temporal video segmentation and scenario detection, respectively. General rules of special scenario and common techniques of movie making are described in Section 4. Section 5 presents the story-oriented video skimming approach. Experimental results are provided in Section 6, followed by concluding remarks in Section 7.

## 2. Temporal Video Segmentation

In this section, we first depict the property of two-dimension entropy of image pixels, and then employ a progressive algorithm to detect shot boundaries.

### 2.1. Property of Two-Dimension Histogram Entropy

According to [16], two-dimensional histogram entropy of pixels can be used to describe the distribution of information of a grey-level image. Since the horizontal or vertical change of the gray value of pixels can not well represent the total characteristics of an image, we improve the construction of components of the two-dimensional histogram. More specifically, the gray value of pixel $x$ and the average gray value of pixels in its $3\times 3$ neighborhoods are replaced by the average gray value of pixels in its four neighborhoods $a^{x}{}_{1}$ and average gray value of other four pixels located in the corner of its $3\times 3$ neighborhoods $a^{x}{}_{2}$, respectively. The formulation of the two-dimensional histogram entropy of an image $I$ is:

$$\begin{cases} E = \sum_{i=0}^{L-1} \sum_{j=0}^{L-1} E_{ij}, \; E_{ij} = -N_{ij} * \ln N_{ij} \\ N_{ij} = H_{ij} / H, \qquad H = \sum_{i=0}^{L-1} \sum_{j=0}^{L-1} H_{ij} \end{cases} \tag{1}$$

where $H_{ij}$ presents the two-dimensional histogram of the two-dimensional channel $(i, j)$, and $L$ is set at 256 for gray pixel. Here, $i$ and $j$ represents $a^{x}_{1}$ and $a^{x}_{2}$, respectively.
Figure 2 lists some examples to show the relationship between the information contained in image and corresponding value of two-dimensional histogram entropy.
Based on our daily observation and movie editorial techniques, the information contained in images will usually change when there exists shot transition. In such instance, the issue of the detection of shot boundaries can be resolved by using the property of two-dimensional histogram entropy.

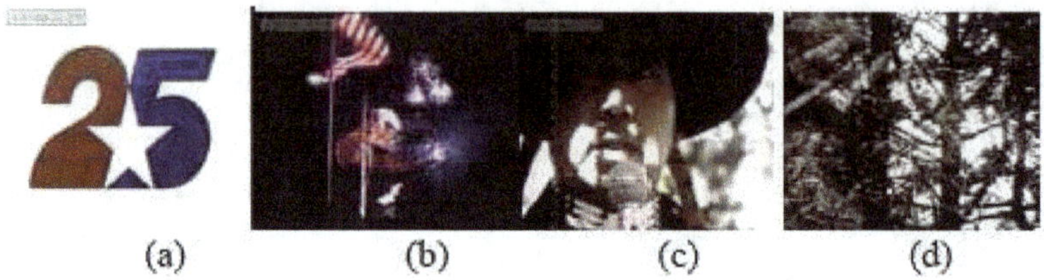


Fig. 2. Examples of image with more information having bigger two-dimension histogram entropy value.

### 2.2. Shot Boundary Detection

Our shot boundary detection algorithm consists of two levels: one is the coarse identification of candidate segmentation boundaries and the other is the refinement processing of candidate segmentation boundaries. One of the advantages of this progressive scheme is that it can speed up the overall processing with reduced number of video frames and effectively detect the gradual transitions (such as fade in/out, dissolve and wipe).

#### 2.2.1. Coarse Boundary Identification

To coarsely identify candidate boundaries, we first perform temporal subsampling of the input video. In this chapter, the sub-sample rate is typically set to be 10 frames per second. Then, image space of each frame $f$ in the temporally sub-sampled sequence is divided into five regions as shown in Figure 3 due to the following fact. In most cases, the difference between images can be determined according to the information of region ①.

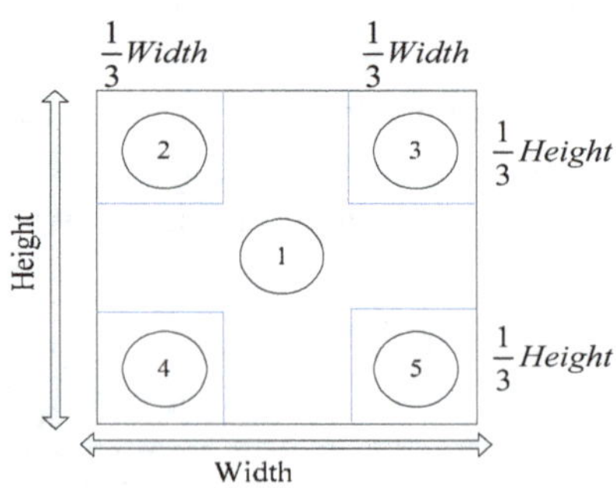


Fig. 3. Selected region for coarse candidate boundaries.

We now perform the coarse identification for candidate boundaries on the extracted main-image sequences in temporally sub-sampled sequence. Given the sequence of two-dimensional entropy difference between successive main-images, a set of candidate boundaries can be detected by appropriate thresholding. Instead of the global thresholding scheme in [17], we make use of the local thresholding approach presented by [18].

### 2.2.2. Exact location Determination

For those coarse candidate boundaries from the sub-sampled sequence, it is necessary to identify their exact locations at original temporal resolution. If the temporal sub-sampling rate is $N$ (here $N$=6) and the frame number of candidate boundary is $m$, the precise position of shot transition will then fall into the localized neighbor region $r$ centered on the candidate boundary $m$ which contains frames from number $m*N-2*N$ to $m*N+2*N$. That is, the exact position of shot transition $k$ is achieved by picking a minimum valley within the neighbor region. The overall coarse-to-fine refinement procedure under a certain sub-sample rate is shown in Figure 4.

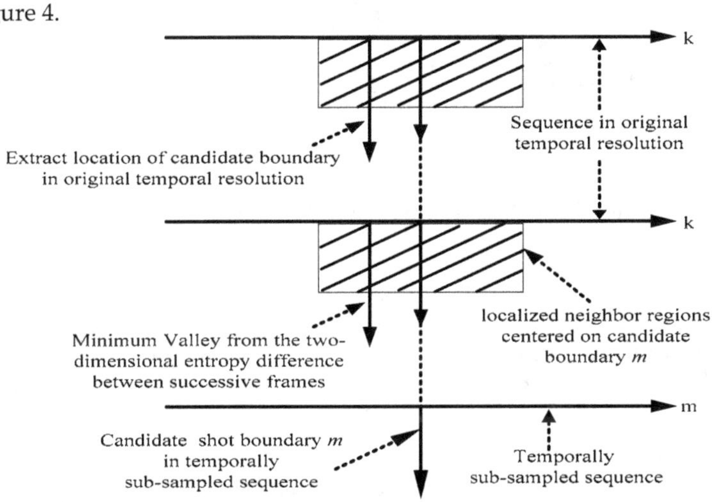


Fig. 4. Overview of the coarse-to-fine refinement procedure.

### 2.3. Shot Transition Verification

Since coarse candidate boundaries are detected using increased inter-frame difference in sub-sampling sequence, false detections maybe generated in the set of candidate boundary. Therefore, it is indispensable to perform verification of each identified shot transition frame $k$.

To robustly verify detected shot boundaries with respect to various transitions and special effects, we present a novel method to evaluate the similarity of visual content of frames within a local neighbor region $r$ as shown in Figure 5 (a). More specifically, suppose the size of $r$ is $2*N+1$. Then, feature set of left and right neighbor region, $F_L$ and $F_R$, are:

$$\begin{cases} F_L = [F_{k-2*N}, \ldots\ldots, F_{k-1}] \\ F_R = [F_{k+1}, \ldots\ldots, F_{k+2*N}] \end{cases} \qquad (2)$$

where $F_i$ is a 5-dimension vector of 2-dimension entropy extracted from five regions as shown in Figure 3.

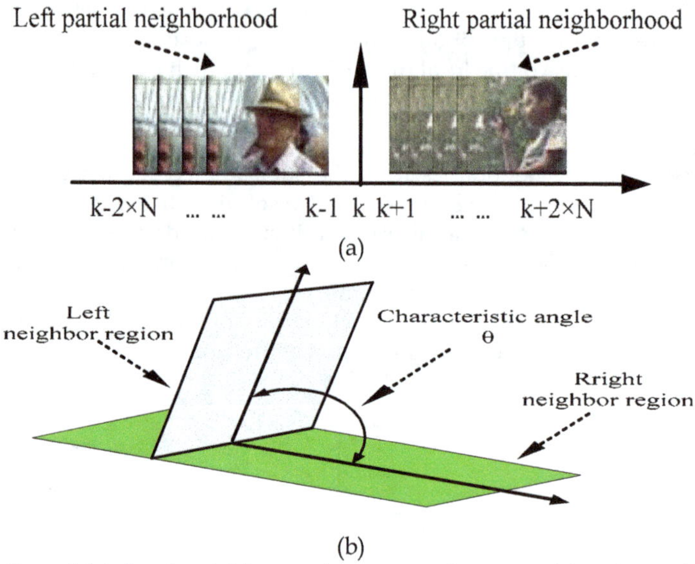


Fig. 5. Illustration of (a): local neighbor region centered on transition frame k and (b): Characteristic angle.

Principal component analysis is then utilized to preserve sub-images with more information for later computation of characteristic angle. $P_L$ and $P_R$ are corresponding orthonormal matrices of $F_L$ and $F_R$ by preserving $n$ eigenvectors corresponding to first $n$ largest eigenvalues. Next, singular value decomposition is performed on $P_L{}^T P_R$ to obtain the characteristic angles $\theta$ as in Figure 5 (b):

$$\begin{cases} \theta = \arccos(\delta) = \arccos\left[\max\left(\delta_1, \delta_2, ..., \delta_n\right)\right] \\ U^{-1}\left(P_L^T P_R\right)\left(V^T\right)^{-1} = \Sigma = Diag\left(\delta_1, \delta_2, ..., \delta_n\right) \end{cases} \tag{3}$$

Finally, any detected shot transition frame is considered as actual one only if its characteristic angles $\theta$ is bigger than a predefined threshold. Figure 6 shows two examples of shot detection results.

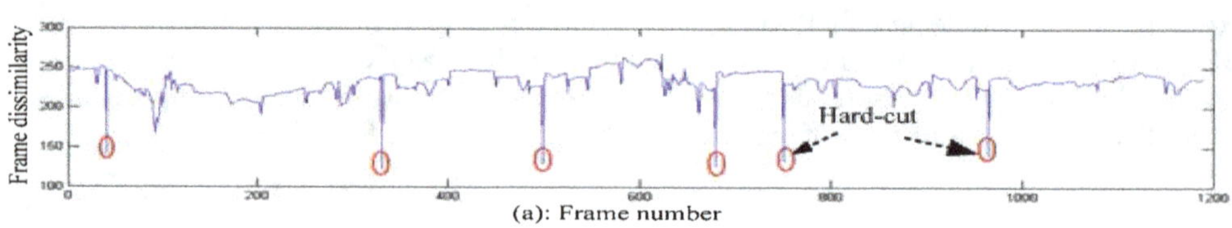

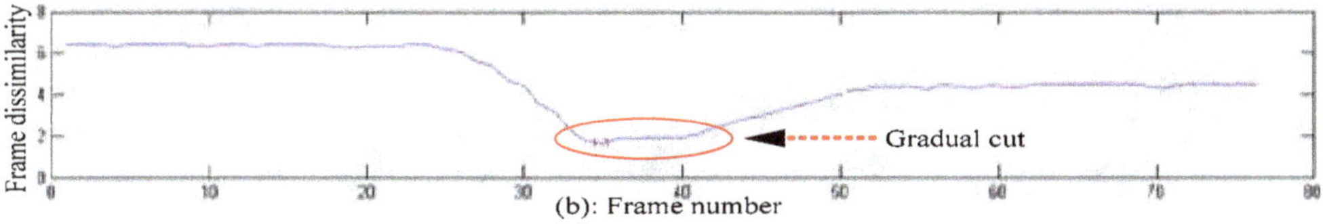


Fig. 6. Shot detection results for (a): abrupt transition and (b): gradual transition.

### 2.4. Key Frames Extraction within Shots

Representing the content of a video shot concisely is a necessary step for various video processing. In this chapter, a two-pass algorithm is used to complete the task of the selection of key-frames. Given a shot $Sh=\{f_1, f_2, \ldots\ldots, f_U\}$ with $U$ frames, the process of key-frames choosing is then described as follows.

- First, $f_1$ is chosen as the first key-frame into the:

$$KFS = \{Kf_1\} = \{Kf_N\} = \{f_1\},\ N = 1 \tag{4}$$

where $N$ is the total number of key-frame.

- For each frame $f_m$ behind the current key-frame $Kf_N$, the value of two-dimension histogram intersection between $f_m$ and each key-frame from $KFS=\{Kf_1, Kf_2, \ldots\ldots, Kf_N\}$ is then computed:

$$\begin{cases} FraSim(f_m, Kf_n) = \sum_{i=0}^{L\text{-}1}\sum_{j=0}^{L\text{-}1}\min(H_{ij}^{f_m}, H_{ij}^{Kf_n}) \\ FraSim(f_m, KFS) = \{FraSim(f_m, Kf_n)\}\ 1 \le n \le N \end{cases} \tag{5}$$

If values in $FraSim(f_m, KFS)$ are all greater than a pre-fixed threshold decided using the method in [17], then $f_m$ is absorbed into the key-frame set $KFS$ as a new key-frame:

$$KFS = \{Kf_1, Kf_2, \ldots\ldots, Kf_N, f_m\} = \{Kf_1, Kf_2, \ldots\ldots, Kf_N, Kf_{N+1}\} \tag{6}$$

Figure 7 shows some examples of key frame extraction from different shots, where the most left image in each row is the detected shot followed by its key frame(s).

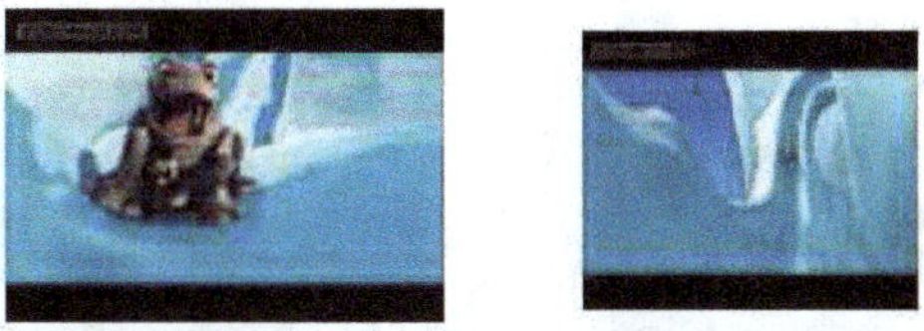

(a)

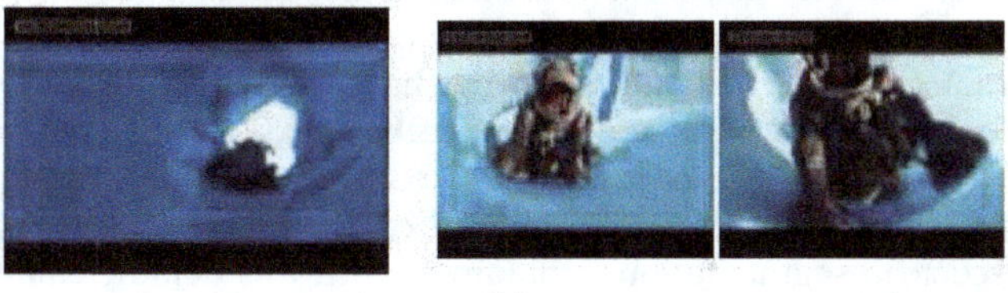

(b)

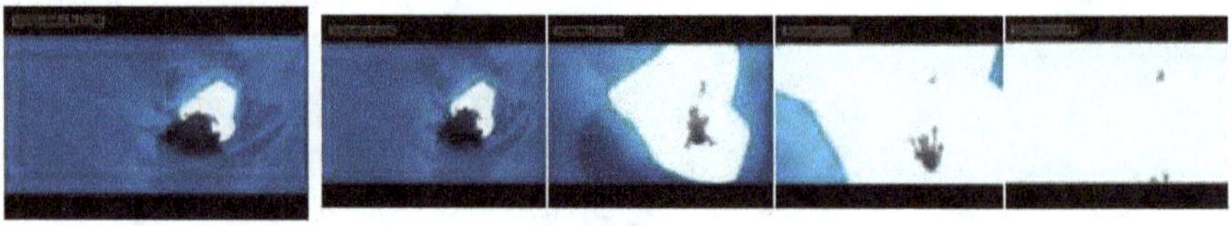

(c)

Fig. 7. Examples of key frame extraction with respect to visual content.

## 3. Scenario Boundary Detection

In this section, using the detected shots we construct a spatial correlation chain within certain temporal constraint, and then determine scenario boundary with the constructed spatio-temporal correlation chain.

### 3.1. Temporal Constraint Analysis

To avoid under-segmentation or over-segmentation of scenarios, we introduce the concept of temporal constraint similar to [20]. However, compared to [20], both the form and goal are different. Specifically, if the temporal spam between shots exceeds certain constraint, then they will not be grouped into the same scenario although their visual content is similar. For example, two shots in Figure 8 (a) are from different scenarios of movie 'X Man III' although there exists certain similarity between these two shots in the visual aspect. Two shots in Figure 8 (b) are another group of comparison shots, where the image information in terms of human understanding is also fully different.

(a) (b)

Fig. 8. Illustration the importance of temporal constraint. (a) and (b) are two groups of comparison shots both from different scenarios though they share certain visual information.

Temporal constraint (analysis window) depicts the largest number of shots contained in a scenario, which means only shots falling into the analysis window and satisfying spatial correlation can then be grouped into the same scenario.

The choice of the size of analysis window needs to be seriously considered due to its great impact on final video skimming. On the one hand, if this value is too large, shots from different scenarios may be clustered into the same one. That is, too large size will bring about the under-segmentation of scenario. On the other hand, if this value is too small, shots belonging to the same scenario may have different scenario labels. In this case, the issue of the over-segmentation of scenario will occur. Therefore, the size of analysis window is set to be fifty as default based on the heuristic rule. Final experimental results demonstrate that the best accuracy of scenario segmentation is obtained with this default value compared with other values.

### 3.2. Scenario boundary Identification

To accurately segment scenario, besides the information of visual aspect, the factor of temporal aspect is also taken into account. Different scenarios are obtained by the following passes.

(1) The similarity between two key frames $p$ and $q$ from different shots is measured by the Euclidean distance:

$$S_f(p,q) = \sqrt{\sum_{i \in allbins} \left( \left| F_p^i \right| - \left| F_q^i \right| \right)^2} \tag{7}$$

where $F_p^i$ denotes the $i^{th}$ two dimension entropy of frames $p$.

(2) The measurement of the dissimilarity between shot $m$ with $M$ key frames and shot $n$ with $N$ key frames is the average distance across all the possible pairs of key frames in each shot:

$$S_{shot}^{m,n} = \frac{\sum_{i \in M} \sum_{j \in N} S_f(i,j)}{M * N} \tag{8}$$

(3) Within one given analysis window $Tw$, the shot similarities between all pairs of shots are computed by:

$$S_{scenario}^{T_w} = S_{shot}^{m,n}, \ m \in T_w, \ n \in T_w \tag{9}$$

(4) For the current shot $c$ within $Tw$, all the subsequent shots sharing similar visual content ($f_1, f_2 \ldots f_{s-1}$ and $f_s$) are:

$$S_{shot}^{c,k} < T_{scenario}, \ c < k \le T_w \tag{10}$$

where $T_{scenario}$ is the threshold. Furthermore, shot $f_s$ is chosen as the current shot $c$ for next processing.

(5) For shots between $f_{s-1}$ and $f_s$, similar shots ($r_1, r_2 \ldots r_{t-1}$ and $r_t$) between shot $f_s$ and $T_w$ are located by:

$$S_{shot}^{c,k} < T_{scenario}, f_{s-1} < c < f_s, f_s < k \le T_w \tag{11}$$

Furthermore, shot $r_t$ is also chosen as the current shot $c$ for further processing.

(6) Repeat step 4 or / and 5 until the end of $T_w$, and there exists two types of scenario boundary. One is if the iterative process stops at step 4, then shot $f_s$ is the current scenario boundary and shot $f_s + 1$ is the beginning shot for the next scenario. The other is if the iterative process stops at step 5, then shot $r_t$ is the current scenario boundary and shot $r_t$ +1 is the beginning shot for the next scenario.

Figure 9 shows an example of the scenario boundary detection procedure for one testing video: interview video. Shot $f_0$ is first chosen as the current shot $c$, and shots $f_1$, $f_2$, $f_3$, and $f_4$ are visually similar shots according to inequality (7). Next, shot $f_4$ is selected as the current shot $c$, and shots $r_1$, $r_2$ and $r_3$ are visually similar shots satisfying inequality (8). Then, shot $r_3$ becomes the current shot $c$ with respect to the scheme of scenario identification. Since there are no more shots meeting the conditions of inequality (8), shot $r_3$ is the last shot for current scenario X, and the procedure of the boundary detection for scenario X ends. That is, scenario X is composed of all of the shots from shot $f_0$ to shot $r_3$.

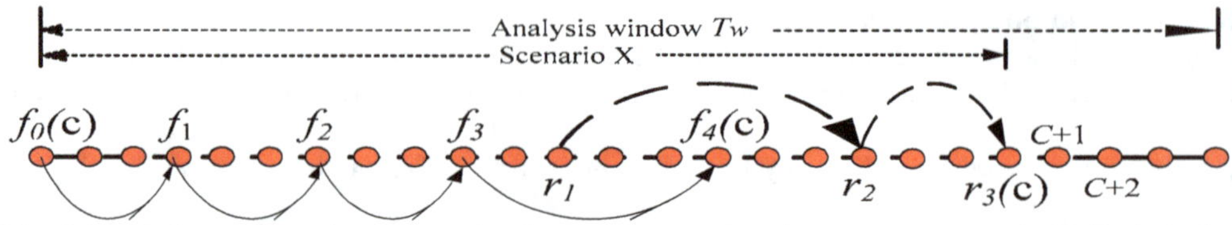


Fig. 9. Procedure of spatio-temporal coherence clustering for current scenario X. Red circles denotes shots within one given analysis *Tw*. Shots ($f_0$, $f_1$, $f_2$, $f_3$, $f_4$, and $f_s$) linked by solid line are similar ones generated by inequality (8). Shots ($r_1$, $r_2$, *r*and $r_3$) linked by dotted line are similar ones satisfying inequality (9). Scenario X is composed of all of the shots from shot $f_0$ to shot $r_3$.

### 3.3. Key Frames Extraction within Scenarios

Just like the purpose of extracting key frames from a video shot, the main content of a video scenario can also be concisely represented by corresponding key frames. Key frames of a scenario are chosen from the key frames of each shot within the scenario using the same method as discussed in subsection 2.4.

## 4. Scenario editing rules and movie making techniques

To construct a skimming for story-oriented videos (such as movies), it is necessary for viewers to grasp the flow of the story from scenario editing rules. According to [21], these rules can effectively describe the semantics of a scenario and so are commonly utilized in the movie production process. Moreover, story progress can be obtained from movie making techniques that are frequently adopted in movie making procedure to articulate a story. Next, we will explore the form of movie from these rules and techniques to introduce common types of key scenario and metrics of the story progress.

Based on our observation and the scenario editing rules, there exist several types of scenarios named key scenarios. These key scenarios often present vital information and hence always attract viewers' attention:

1) Dialog scenario: see Figure 10 (a); 2) Suspense scenario: see (b); 3) Action scenario: see (c).

(a) Dialog scenario

(b) Suspense scenario

(c) Action scenario

Fig. 10. Examples of different types of scenarios.

In [22], a film consisting of scenarios is regarded as a system and the flow of a film is depicted as the interrelationships between key scenarios. Generally, the interrelationship between scenarios is often captured by different types of transitions including temporal transition, spatial transition and rhythmic transition. From the point of view of film editing techniques and human understanding, the more a story progress between scenarios, the more the transition intensity is. Therefore, the intensity of scenario transition is considered as an important metric for evaluating the flow of a film as well as an important basic for the production of video skimming.

## 5. Video Skimming Approach

This section details the proposed story-oriented video skimming approach, which aims to enable viewers to grasp main content of original video by watching the generated short skimming. Thus, final video skimming should comprise those pairs of video segments with more contributes to the flow of a story. At the same time, the total duration of selected segments should satisfy the user-defined target duration.

The structure of this section is organized as follows. Related symbols are first introduced. Next, key scenarios are identified using visual and audio features. Then, an Intensity of Flow (IoF) function is defined to depict the transition intensity between key scenarios to the whole story. Finally, a Story Structure Tree (SST) is adopted to describe the interrelationship between scenarios in a story-oriented video, and the proposed skimming approach in subsequent sections is described with the SST.

### 5.1. Related Symbols

Table 1 lists the symbols used in the proposed story-oriented video skimming approach.

| Symbol | Meaning |
|---|---|
| $V$ | A story-oriented video |
| $Sh_i$ | *i-th* shot in $V$ |
| $Ks_j$ | *j-th* key scenario in $V$ |
| $ShKs(Sh_i,Ks_j)$ | *i-th* shot of *j-th* key scenario in $V$ |
| $N(Sh_i,Ks_j,Kf_s)$ | Number of characters of *s-th* key frame of *i-th* shot from *j-th* key scenario in $V$ |
| $TI(Ks_i, Ks_j)$ | Transition intensity between key scenario *i* and *j* |

Table 1. Related symbols.

### 5.2. Key Scenarios Identification

According to the discussion is Section 4, a story-oriented video is composed of a sequence of scenarios including key scenarios as shown in Figure 10 and remaining scenarios. Recall that our purpose in this chapter is to achieve a highly compact skimming of a long video. Therefore, finally generated skimming contains only key scenarios while omitting remaining scenarios. Next, we will detail the process of key scenarios identification.

Based on our observation and scenario editing rules, typical characteristics of three kinds of key scenarios discussed in Section 4 are described as below.

- Dialogue scenario: faces with similar spatial position and similar size, a sequence of shots with low activity intensity, and strong similarity between shots.
- Action scenario: a set of shots with short duration, and intensive activity or audio energy.
- Suspense scenario: a set of shots with low average intensity distribution, a long period of low audio energy, and low activity intensity followed by a sudden change either in sound track or in activity intensity or both.

Next, features from different fields are first introduced and then heuristic rules are proposed to determine these three key scenarios.

#### 5.2.1. Audio Features Selection

In order to achieve the accuracy of the scenario classification, audio information is an important and necessary clue. Because feature extraction is very important for audio content analysis, the extracted features should capture the temporal and spectral structure of different audio classes from each scenario talked above. Here, following features are selected to complete the task of audio clip classification, such as zero-crossing rate, energy envelope, spectrum flux, band periodicity, mel-frequency cepstral coefficients, spectral power, and linear prediction based cepstral coefficients.

Furthermore, in our experiment, all audio clips are divided into non-overlapping sub-clips. A sub-clip is of one second duration and is further divided into forty twenty-five millisecond-long frames, and short-time energy envelope entropy. The classification is performed based on these one-second sub-clips.

- **Zero-crossing Rate**. Zero-crossing rate is a simple measure of the audio signal frequency content. The *N*-length short-time zero-crossing rate of the $n^{th}$ audio frame $s(n)$ is defined as:

$$ZCR(n) = \frac{1}{N} * \sum_{t=n-N+1}^{n} \frac{|\operatorname{sgn}\{s(t)\} - \operatorname{sgn}\{s(t-1)\}|}{2} w(n-t) \tag{12}$$

where $w(n)$ is a rectangular window, and

$$\operatorname{sgn}[s(n)] = \begin{cases} 1 & s(n) \geq 0 \\ -1 & s(n) < 0 \end{cases} \tag{13}$$

- **Energy Envelope.** Energy envelope is used to calculate the global temporal information. It can be computed in following way: third order Butterworth low-pass filtering of the analytical signal root mean square amplitude of each audio frame:

$$EE(n) = \sqrt{\frac{1}{N} \sum_{t=1}^{N} [s_t(n)]^2} \tag{14}$$

where $N$ is the number of sample points in the $n^{th}$ audio frame.

- **Spectrum Flux**. Spectrum flux is defined as the two-norm of the frame-to-frame spectrum amplitude difference vector:

$$SF(n) = \left\| \left|M_f(n)\right| - \left|M_f(n+1)\right| \right\| \tag{15}$$

where $|M_f(n)|$ is the magnitude of the FFT of the $n^{th}$ frame at frequency value $f$. Both magnitude vectors are normalized in energy. Spectrum flux is a measure of spectral change between the adjacent two frames.

- **Band periodicity**. Band periodicity describes the property of each sub-band. In this chapter, we consider four sub-bands including 500~1000Hz, 1000~2000Hz, 2000~3000Hz, and 3000~4000Hz respectively. The periodicity property can be represented by the maximum local peak of the normalized correlation function.
- **Mel-Frequency Cepstral Coefficients (MFCCs)**. It has been proved that the mel-frequency cepstrum is a useful and highly effective feature in modeling the subjective pitch and frequency content of audio signals. The MFCCs are computed from fast Fourier transformation:

$$\begin{cases} MFCC(n) = \sqrt{\dfrac{2}{J}} \displaystyle\sum_{j=1}^{J} \left\{ \left(\log S_j\right) \times \cos\left[ t\left(j-0.5\right)\dfrac{\pi}{J} \right] \right\} \\ t = 1, 2, \ldots\ldots, T \end{cases} \tag{16}$$

where the parameter $J$ denotes the number of band-pass filters, and the parameter $T$ means the order of the cepstrum. In our scheme, $J$ and $T$ are set to be 24 and 12 respectively, namely the 24 band-pass filters and 12-order MFCCs are used.

- **Spectral Power**. Spectral power of each audio frame is computed with a Hanning window $h(n)$ :

$$h(n) = \sqrt{\frac{2}{3}} \times [1 - \cos(2\pi \frac{n}{N})] \tag{17}$$

The spectral power of the $n^{th}$ audio frame $s(n)$ is:

$$SP(k) = 10\log_{10}\left[ \frac{1}{N} \left\| \sum_{n=0}^{N-1} s(n)H(n)\exp(-j2\pi\frac{nk}{N}) \right\|^2 \right] \tag{18}$$

- **Linear prediction based cepstral coefficients (LPCCs)**. LPCCs are utilized to represent the timbre information of the voice components. The basic idea behind linear predictive analysis is that an audio frame can be approximated as a linear combination of past audio frames. By minimizing the sum of the squared differences over a finite interval between the actual audio frames and the linear predictive ones, a unique set of predictor coefficients can be determined.

### 5.2.2. Audio signal Classification

After removing silent clips, audio clips are classified into two categories firstly, i.e. speech and non-speech, based on the information of zero-crossing rate, energy envelope, and spectrum flux. Then, speech clips are classified into emotional voice and common voice based on the spectrum flux, band periodicity, mel-frequency cepstral coefficients, and non-speech clips are classified into special sound and music based on the spectral power, and Linear prediction based cepstral coefficients. Finally, special sound is further classified into several classes, including gunshot, explosion, scream, beating, crashing of glass, and rubbing of tires using hidden markov models (HMM). Figure 11 illustrates the classification scheme.

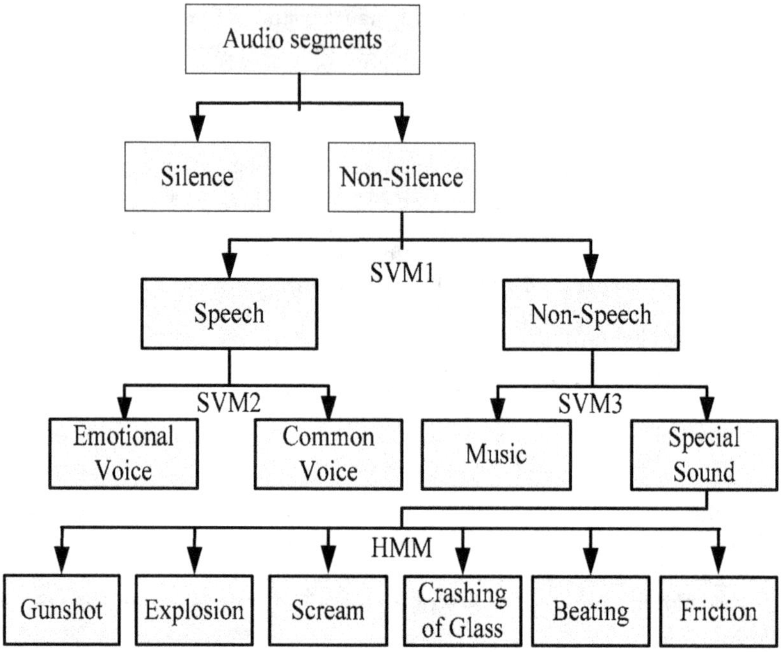


Fig. 11. Audio Classification scheme.

For support vector machines-based classification, features are first combined to construct a feature vector. Then, the mean and standard deviation of these feature vectors over all forty audio frames are calculated, and these statistics compose another feature vector. Finally, this new feature vector is normalized by its standard deviation of training data. The normalized feature vector is considered as the final representation of one-second audio signal.

The information of timbre and rhythm is utilized in the generative model for recognition, namely hidden markov models. Timbre allows one to tell the difference between sounds at the same loudness made by different objects. Each kind of timbre is denoted by one state of HMM, and represented with the Gaussian mixture density. Here, rhythm is adopted to represent the change pattern of timbres, and is denoted by transition and duration parameters in HMM.

### 5.2.3. Visual Features Selection

- **Face Information**. The occurrence of face is a salient feature in video, as it means the present of human in the scene. The size of a face is also a hint for the role of the person, i.e., a large face denotes that this person is in the center of attention. In the experiment, we use the face detection algorithm proposed by Li et al. [23] which performs reasonably good for faces with different scales in the video. As a result of the face feature extraction process, we obtain the position and size of each detected face, and the number of hits.

- **Illumination Intensity**. Reference [24] indicates "the amount and distribution of light in relation to shadow and darkness and the relative tonal value of the scene is a primary visual means of setting mood." The amount of light in scene *Sc(k)*, here, is described as the average illumination intensity:

$$\begin{cases} II(k) = \dfrac{\sum_i ShAvgInt(i) \times ShLen(i)}{N(k)} \\ ShAvgInt(i) = \dfrac{\sum_j KfInt(j)}{N(i)} \end{cases} \tag{19}$$

where *ShAvgInt(i)* is the average illumination intensity of the entire key frames in the $i^{th}$ shot, *ShLen(i)* is the length of the $i^{th}$ shot in terms of frames, and *N(k)* is the total number of frames within the $k^{th}$ scene. Furthermore, *KfInt(j)* is the illumination intensity of the $j^{th}$ key frames in the $i^{th}$ shot, and *N(i)* is the total number of frames within the $i^{th}$ shot.

- **Activity Intensity**. The activity intensity indicates the tempo in video. For example, in conversational scenario, the activity intensity is relatively low. On the other hand, in action scenario, the activity intensity is relatively high. The activity intensity of the $k^{th}$ scene is:

$$AI(k) = \frac{1}{N_k - 1}\sum_{l=1}^{N_{k-1}} \min\left[\sum_{i=0}^{i=L-1}\sum_{j=0}^{j=L-1}\left(H_{ij}^{l}, H_{ij}^{l+1}\right)\right] \tag{20}$$

- **Average Duration**. Similar to activity intensity, average duration in terms of frames is another measurement of the video tempo and is computed as follows:

$$AD(k) = \frac{1}{N_k}\sum_{l=1}^{N_k} ShLen(l) \tag{21}$$

### 5.2.4. Dialogue Scenario Determination

- **Dialogue Scenario Determination.** To locate the dialogue scenarios, we first adopt the information of face to detect shot sequence with alternately recurring visual contents, which include similar size, similar position and same number. Figure 12 shows an example of dialogue-like scenario.

Fig. 12. A dialogue-like scene detected using face information.

Given these dialogue-like scenes, we exploit their corresponding audio information to further make sure they are actual conversation contents. Specifically, we should differentiate speech signals from music and other sounds. Here, a simple classification method is utilized to complete the task of discrimination using zero-crossing rate, energy envelope, and spectrum flux as shown in Figure 11.

- **Emotional Dialogue Scenario Determination.** Among many dialogues, emotional conversations often attract viewers' attention and effect upon the flow of story. To discriminate the emotional contents from common ones, two acoustic features including average pitch frequency and temporal intensity variations are used. The first feature is estimated by 12-order linear prediction based cepstral coefficients, and the second one is represented by the variance of spectral power levels over all forty signal segments within one-second audio sub-clip.

### 5.2.5. Active Scenario Discrimination

- **Active Scenario Discrimination.** Similar to dialogue scenario, active scenario is another conceptually meaningful story content. Among active scenarios, gunfight scenario, beating scenario, and chasing scenario are often the most interesting events and can instantly attract viewers' attention in films. Therefore, based on the recognition of active scenario by integrating audio-visual signatures, three specific and distinct events are identified one-by-one.

According to the characteristics of active scenario as talked above; these scenes with average duration less than twenty-five frames and average activity intensity are identified as active scenarios.

Among active scenarios, gunfight, beating and chasing events are three important types and mostly the climaxes in feature films. Next, we will detect these important active scenarios using their unique audio-visual signatures.

- **Gunfight Scenario Discrimination.** Gunfire, explosion, and bleeding are the most typical visual features of gunfight scenarios as shown in Figure 13.

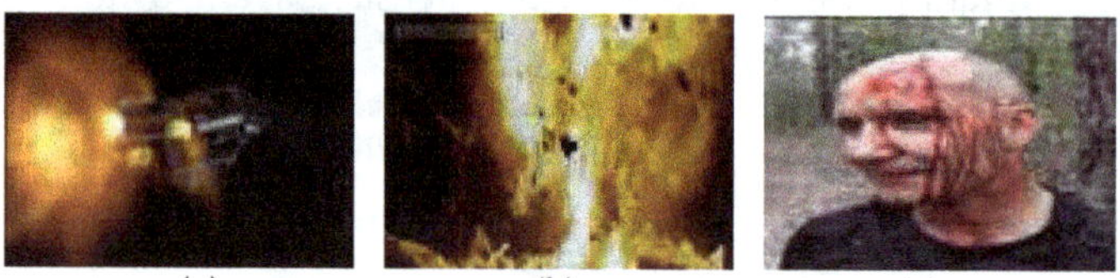

(a) (b) (c)

Fig. 13. The most typical visual features of gunfight scenario including (a) gunfire; (b) explosion; (c) bleeding.

Compared to gunfire cases, flames from an explosion show longer duration and cover wider areas. However, flames from an explosion and gunfire both have dominant yellow, orange and/or red color histogram. Hence, a predefined color table containing a certain range of color values is adopted to identify the gunfight-like scenario.

Since some violent actions, such as beating, gunshot and explosion can result in bleeding, bleeding is considered as another violence-related visual feature of gunfight event. We detect bloody color pixels using simple pixel-matching with the predefined color table.

Since other events may have similar visual features as gunfire, explosion and bleeding, the audio information provides a supplement to the detection of gunfight scenario. A distinct feature of gunfight scenarios is the unique sound track. Specifically, given the audio track for successive gunfight-like shots, we discriminate its class based on a hidden markov model. The likelihood ratio between the input audio track and the defined sound classes is calculated to determine which class the associated sound belongs to as shown in Figure 11.

- **Beating or Chasing Scenario Identification.** In general, beating or chasing events are inherently accompanied by unique sound (e.g., beating, rubbing of tires, etc.). In particular, for active scenario, we identify its specific class (beating or chasing) based on the likelihood ratio between its audio track and the given sound classes as shown in Figure 11.

### 5.2.6. Suspense Scenario Detection

- **Suspense Scenario Detection**. Suspense scenarios are often the most events and instantly attract a viewer's attention in horror and detective genres. According to the unique characteristics of suspense scenario as talked about in the introduction of Section five, a scenario can be declared as a suspense scenario if following criterions are satisfied simultaneously:

**(1)**. Average illumination intensity is less than 50;
**(2)**. There exist shots with audio energy envelope change suddenly from 5 to over 50;
or / both
There exist shots with activity energy change instantly from 5 to over 100.

## 5.3. Scenario Transition Form

As aforementioned, there exist three forms of scenario transition: temporal transition, spatial transition and rhythmic transition. Next, we formulate each of them.

- Generally speaking, viewers can understand the temporal transition with respect to the different number of characters appearing in two scenarios *k(i)* and *k(j)* with respect to the change of number of face:

$$TT(k_i,k_j)=\left|\sum_{s=1}^{S}C(s,m,k_i)-\sum_{t=1}^{T}C(t,n,k_j)\right| \tag{22}$$

where $S(m,k_i)$ is the last shot of *k(i)* and $S(n,k_j)$ the first shot *k(j)*. Temporal transition between two scenarios is discriminated f the following inequality is true:

$$TT(k_i,k_j)>\frac{1}{S+T}\left[\sum_{s=1}^{S}C(s,m,k_i)+\sum_{t=1}^{T}C(t,n,k_j)\right] \tag{23}$$

where *S* and *T* are the number of key frames in $S(m,k_i)$ and $S(n,k_j)$, respectively.

- Spatial transition depicts the change of positions in successive scenarios for the same characters, which can be determined in terms of the change color information of background regions. The background regions are obtained by excluding the face region of each character, which is feasible due to most characters are shown in close-up views in a film. The intensity of spatial transition between two scenarios *k(i)* and *k(j)* is formulated as below:

$$\begin{aligned}ST(k_i,k_j) = &\left|\frac{1}{S'}\sum_{s=1}^{S'}RA(s)-\frac{1}{T'}\sum_{t=1}^{T'}RA(t)\right|+\left|\frac{1}{S'}\sum_{s=1}^{S'}GA(s)-\frac{1}{T'}\sum_{t=1}^{T'}GA(t)\right|\\&+\left|\frac{1}{S'}\sum_{s=1}^{S'}BA(s)-\frac{1}{T'}\sum_{t=1}^{T'}BA(t)\right|+\left|\frac{1}{S'}\sum_{s=1}^{S'}LA(s)-\frac{1}{T'}\sum_{t=1}^{T'}LA(t)\right|\end{aligned} \tag{24}$$

where *RA(s)*, *GA(s)*, *BA(s)*, and *LA(s)* are average red, green, blue, and luminance values in the background of the $s^{th}$ *key* frame, respectively. *S′* and *T′* are the number of key frames in

$S(m,ki)$ and $S(n,kj)$ for the same character, respectively. There exists spatial transition between $k(i)$ with the last shot $S(m,ki)$ and $k(j)$ with the first shot $S(n,kj)$ when the following inequality holds:

$$ST(k_i, k_j) > \frac{1}{2}\left|\frac{1}{S'}\sum_{s=1}^{S'} RA(s) + \frac{1}{T'}\sum_{t=1}^{T'} RA(t)\right| + \frac{1}{2}\left|\frac{1}{S'}\sum_{s=1}^{S'} RA(s) + \frac{1}{T'}\sum_{t=1}^{T'} RA(t)\right| + \frac{1}{2}\left|\frac{1}{S'}\sum_{s=1}^{S'} GA(s) + \frac{1}{T'}\sum_{t=1}^{T'} GA(t)\right| + \frac{1}{2}\left|\frac{1}{S'}\sum_{s=1}^{S'} LA(s) + \frac{1}{T'}\sum_{t=1}^{T'} LA(t)\right| \quad (25)$$

- Rhythmic transition in terms of duration is adopted to represent the tense or clam atmosphere. The intensity of rhythmic transition between scenarios $k(i)$ with the number of $M$ shots and $k(j)$ with the number of $N$ shots is computed using following equation:

$$RT(k_i, k_j) = \left|\frac{1}{M}\sum_{m=1}^{M} S(m, ki) - \frac{1}{N}\sum_{n=1}^{N} S(n, kj)\right| \quad (26)$$

There can be declared as the rhythmic transition if the condition in following inequality is true

$$RT(k_i, k_j) > 2\left|\frac{1}{M}\sum_{m=1}^{M} S(m, ki) + \frac{1}{N}\sum_{n=1}^{N} S(n, kj)\right| \quad (27)$$

### 5.4. Scenario Transition Intensity

As aforementioned, the intensity of the flow between two scenarios to the whole story is formulated as the Intensity of Flow (IoF) function. At the same time, according to the discussion in Section 4, the flow of a story consists of various aspects, such as temporal transition, spatial transition, and rhythmic transition, and each metric is normalized between 0 and 1. Therefore, the form of IoF function between scenarios $k(i)$ and $k(j)$ is the weighted sum of these three metrics as expressed in Equation (16):

$$IoF(k_i, k_j) = \alpha * TT_n(k_i, k_j) + \beta * ST_n(k_i, k_j) + \gamma * RT_n(k_i, k_j) \quad (28)$$

where $TT_n(k_i,k_j)$, $ST_n(k_i,k_j)$, and $RT_n(k_i,k_j)$ are the corresponding normalization form of $TT(k_i,k_j)$, $ST(k_i,k_j)$, and $RT(k_i,k_j)$, respectively. $a+\beta+\gamma=1$.

### 5.5. Video Skimming Approach

After calculating all pairs of transition intensity of a story-oriented video and given a user-defined target length, the next step for us is to choose the pairs of scenarios with the maximum total IoF value among all possible candidate scenarios.

Many approaches can be used to create video skimming based on the values of intensity of flow among detected key scenarios. We have developed a straightforward scenario-based approach to generate skimming, which does not require complex heuristic rules. Skimming segments of scenario around key frames are selected according to the given skimming duration. The process of skimming segment selection is illustrated in Figure 14.

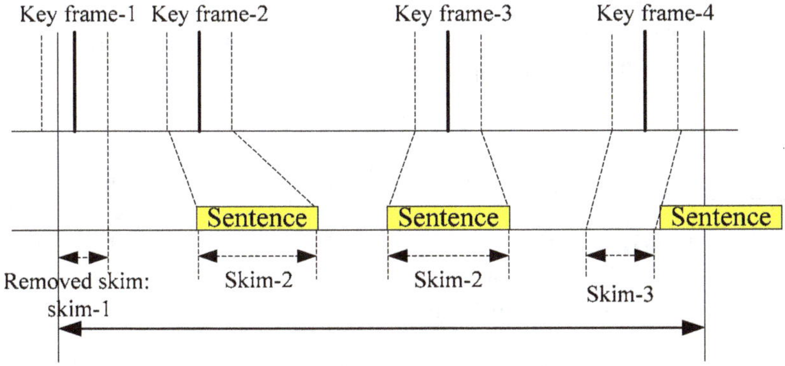


Fig. 14. Video skimming approach.

One crucial element in generating video skimming is the integrity of sentence. It must be uncomfortable for viewers to hear an interrupted sentence while watching a video skimming. Therefore, for the purpose of making a video skimming smoother, we should avoid splitting the speech within a sentence into several parts. In this case, it is indispensable to identify sentence boundary precisely for video skimming. In this chapter, sentence boundary identification comprises following steps.

- Discriminating pause segments from non-pause ones using audio energy and zero-crossing rate.
- Smoothing results with respect to the minimum pause duration and the minimum speech duration.
- Determining sentence boundary by longer pause duration.

Besides IoF value, scenario boundary, sentence boundary and key-frames, only four simple rules are used to create video skimming, as shown in Figure 14. The process of video skimming should comply with several criteria described as follows.

- Given a user-defined target length, pairs of key scenarios with the maximum total IoF value among all possible candidate scenarios are chosen to create video skimming.
- Any video skimming segment should not be less than one second due to the following two aspects. On the one hand, any segment no more than one second is too short to convey message. On the other hand, too short skimming segment may bring annoying impact on human understanding on video content.
- The length of each scenario skimming segment is proportional to the number of key frames in the scenario. Specifically, the default duration of any skimming segment centered on key frame is set to be one second.
- If a skimming segment is beyond the scenario boundary, it will be removed like skim-1 in Figure 14.
- The skimming segment boundaries should be adjusted appropriately in terms of the speech sentence boundaries to prevent from splitting a speech sentence into several parts. Here, the adjustment includes two aspects. One is aligning to the sentence's boundary like skim-2 in Figure 14; the other is evading the sentence's boundary like skim-3 in Figure 14.

Figure 15 shows examples of the story-oriented video skimming. Figure 15 (a) is a graph of the transition intensity among key scenarios of a story-oriented video. The durations of each scenario skimming *ks1, ks2, ks3,* and *ks4* are 5 seconds, 10 seconds, 15 seconds, and 10 seconds, respectively. The skimming with the target durations of 7 seconds and 10 seconds are shown in Figure 15 (b) and (c), respectively.

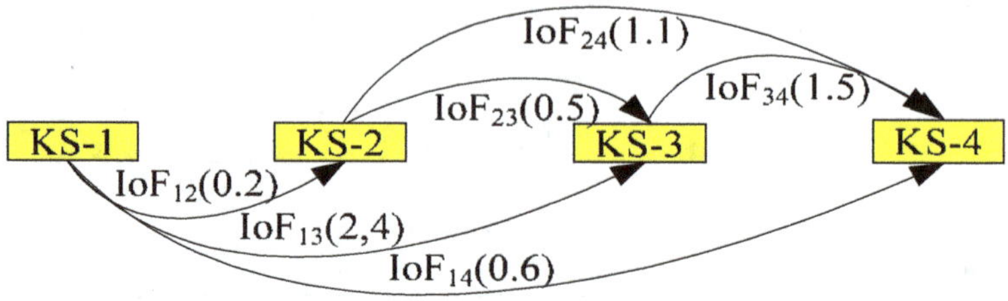


(a): Intensity of flow of a video.

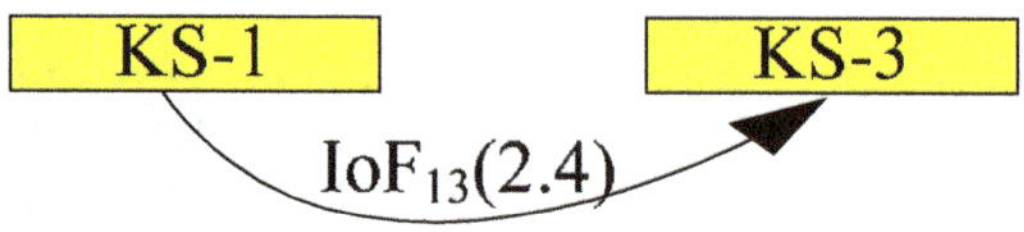


(b): A skimming with target length of 7 seconds.

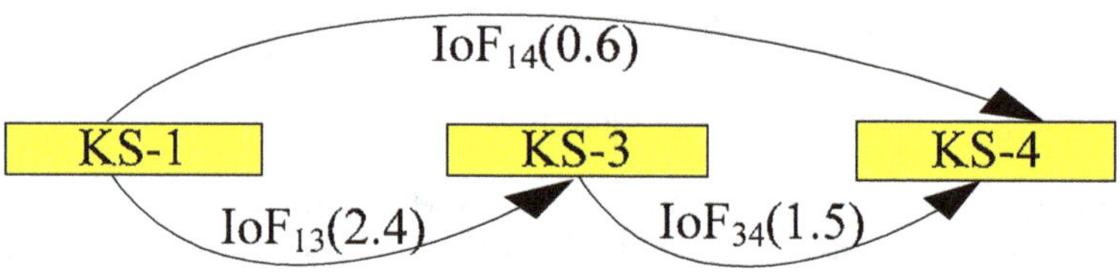


(c): A skimming with target length of 10 seconds.

Fig. 15. Examples of the skimming of a story-oriented video.

## 6. Experimental Results

In this section, we will discuss some implementation issues in practical application and evaluate our approach on various genres of films with existing state-of-the-art methods.

### 6.1. Experimental Settings

Totally seven full-length movies in MPEG-1 format are selected to evaluate the performance of the proposed algorithm. Each video track is analyzed at 25 frames per second with a resolution of 320×240, while the sound track is processed at the sampling rate of 22 kHz with mono-channel, 16-bit precision. As shown in Table 2, the data set consists of various types of contents, which would demonstrate that the proposed algorithm can work on different kinds of movies. All the experiments are performed on an Intel Pentium IV 3.0 GHz machine and 1G memory computer running Windows XP.

| No. | Name | Genre | Length (hh:mm:ss) |
|---|---|---|---|
| 1 | Mission Impossible III | Bodyguard | 1:55:23 |
| 2 | X Man III | Action | 1:44:03 |
| 3 | Walk in the Clouds | Family | 1:42:14 |
| 4 | The Girl Next Door | Love | 1:48:10 |
| 5 | The Ring | Horror | 1:53:43 |
| 6 | The Sound Of Music | Musical | 2:54:33 |
| 7 | N Death on the Nile | Detective | 2:11:50 |

Table 2. Summary of the testing dataset.

### 6.2. Experiment I: Scenario Boundary Detection

The performance of scenario boundary detection (SBD) is important for video skimming because the proposed video skimming scheme is based on the scenarios. In order to evaluate the effectiveness of the proposed SBD approach, we compare it with the SBD approach proposed by Rasheed *et al.* [25] and Zhao *et al.* [26].

To get the ground truth of scenarios, ten graduate students are invited to watch the movies and then give their own scene boundaries. The ground truth used for the experiments is the intersection of their segmentation. Generally speaking, there is no such a clear boundary between two adjacent scenes in movies due to film editing effects. Therefore, the most commonly used criterion, Hanjalic's evaluation [19] is here used to match the ground truth with the detected ones: if the detected scene boundary is within four shots from the boundary detected manually, this boundary is counted as a correct boundary.

We use 'Precision', 'Recall' and 'F1-Score' to evaluate the performance of those techniques. The values of recall and precision are in the range of [0, 1]. The higher recalls indicate a higher capacity of detecting correct shots, while the higher precisions indicate a higher capacity of avoiding false matches.

| No. | Proposed | | [25] | | [26] | |
|---|---|---|---|---|---|---|
| | Pre | Re | Pre | Re | Pre | Re |
| 1 | 0.755 | 0.809 | 0.641 | 0.695 | 0.712 | 0.763 |
| 2 | 0.741 | 0.814 | 0.572 | 0.609 | 0.676 | 0.638 |
| 3 | 0.813 | 0.849 | 0.713 | 0.737 | 0.708 | 0.718 |
| 4 | 0.835 | 0.878 | 0.687 | 0.623 | 0.722 | 0.693 |
| 5 | 0.814 | 0.839 | 0.706 | 0.723 | 0.683 | 0.706 |
| 6 | 0.843 | 0.862 | 0.734 | 0.713 | 0.714 | 0.704 |
| 7 | 0.834 | 0.857 | 0.753 | 0.741 | 0.727 | 0.707 |

Table 3. Comparison of Scenario Boundary Detection (Pre: Precision, Re: Recall).

The results are given in Table 3. From Table 3, it can be seen that average F1-Score of the proposed approach, Backward Shot Coherence method and the Normalized Cuts method are 0.824, 0.688, and 0.704 respectively. That is, the proposed approach exhibits a gain 19.7% and 16.9% of the average F1-Score compared with the method in [25, 26] respectively. The reason why the proposed approach gains a large improvement in all the evaluating measures is based on following two phases. On the one hand, the temporal constraint is integrated into the spatial coherence clustering in the procedure of scene segmentation. On the other hand, the process of forward and backward clustering also helps to improve the performance.

(a)

(b)

Fig. 16. Example of scenario detection. (a): Ground truth scenes and (b): detected scenes of the movie 'X Man III'.

Figure 16 shows the detail scene detection results of the movie 'X Man III'. The upper row indicates the ground truth scenes represented by alternating black / white stripes, and the bottom row is the detected results using the proposed scheme.

### 6.3. Experiment II: Key Scenario Identification

Since the proposed video skimming scheme is based on the flow of story between key scenarios, the detection precise of key scenarios have an important impact on final video skimming. Like the method used in providing the ground truth of scenario boundary, ten volunteers are invited to manually label key scenario.

Table 4 lists experimental results of the identification of key scenarios. As seen in Table 4, the average F1-Score is 0.855, which clearly demonstrate that the proposed scheme can detect and classify video scene into categories. That is to say, the selected features for describing scene content and the way of deciding scene type are satisfactory.

| | | |
|---|---|---|
| Conversation scene | Precision | 0.897 |
| | Recall | 0.863 |
| | F1 | 0.880 |
| Suspense scene | Precision | 0.863 |
| | Recall | 0.843 |
| | F1 | 0.853 |
| Action scene | Precision | 0.846 |
| | Recall | 0.824 |
| | F1 | 0.835 |

Table 4. Experimental results of Key Scenario Identification.

Figure 17 shows some examples of different types of scenario transitions.

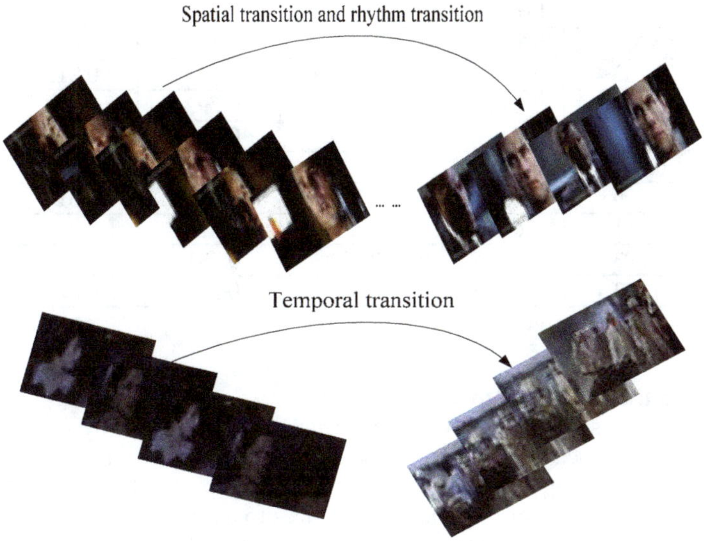


Fig. 17. Examples of scenario transition.

### 6.4. Experiment III: Video Skimming

Generally speaking, a good video skimming should be as short and as information as possible. However, it is difficult to achieve the two objectives at the same time. In this chapter, three criteria are adopted to evaluate the algorithm performance.

For a good video skimming, the first criterion is required to correctly select essential segments for viewers to grasp the clue of the flow of a story. We set the first criterion as informativeness including coverage and conciseness, where *coverage* means a skimming should include all the important segments of a story and *conciseness* means a skimming should comprise only the necessary segments. The second criterion is required to maintain the validity of interrelationships between segments. We set the second criterion as *coherence*, which denotes each segment of a skimming should be interrelated with others with respect to the whole story. Besides, *satisfaction* of the video skimming is also an important criterion. The last criterion appraises not only the smoothness of an image sequence, but also the integrality of speech sentence. Consequently, we will carry out two different experiments according to above discussed three criteria.

#### 6.4.1. Verifying the First Criteria

This experiment aims to measure the precision and recall of each skimming compared to the manually produced ground truth by evaluating the coverage and conciseness of the proposed approach.

Table 5 shows the experimental results of precision and recall for each skimming with three different lengths (5, 10, 20 minutes). From this table, we can see that the overall average precision are 80.3%, 82.6%, and 84.2% for video skimming with the duration of 5, 10, and 20 minutes, respectively. The overall average recall are 80.8%, 82.9%, and 84.3% for video skimming with the duration of 5, 10, and 20 minutes, respectively. These numbers indicate that the proposed skimming scheme is effective in generating highly compact skimming.

| No. | Precision | | | Recall | | |
|---|---|---|---|---|---|---|
| | 5 M. | 10 M. | 20 M. | 5 M. | 10 M. | 20 M. |
| 1 | 0.753 | 0.793 | 0.812 | 0.773 | 0.812 | 0.829 |
| 2 | 0.784 | 0.806 | 0.821 | 0.792 | 0.813 | 0.817 |
| 3 | 0.812 | 0.832 | 0.852 | 0.833 | 0.846 | 0.853 |
| 4 | 0.836 | 0.848 | 0.863 | 0.827 | 0.846 | 0.864 |
| 5 | 0.805 | 0.827 | 0.843 | 0.826 | 0.819 | 0.832 |
| 6 | 0.841 | 0.856 | 0.872 | 0.824 | 0.843 | 0.862 |
| 7 | 0.793 | 0.817 | 0.834 | 0.781 | 0.826 | 0.841 |
| Avg. | 0.803 | 0.826 | 0.842 | 0.808 | 0.829 | 0.843 |

Table 5. Results of informativeness. (M.: minute).

### 6.4.2. Evaluating the last two Criteria

We perform subject tests to measure the *coherence* and *satisfaction* by evaluating viewers' satisfaction and preference over skimming sequences with different duration. Twenty volunteered subjects, including 11 males and 9 females, are invited to participate in the experiment. They are required to specify their preferences to each skimming sequence according to a list of prepared questions, where the measurement of preference is categorized into three following levels: "bad", "neutral" and "good".

To achieve precise scores, the subjects should be kept innocent of the video content before they view the video skimming. The subjects view the video skimming sequences of 5, 10, and 20 minutes and the original video in turn, and they are required to give a score to the test sequence when he/she finishes viewing a skimming sequence. To be fair, the subjects are given the chance to modify the scores assigned to the skimming sequences any time during the review process, because they would understand the video content in more details with the passage of time. With the scores assigned by subjects, corresponding average scores are then calculated, which reflect the viewers' satisfactory degree to different video skimming sequences.

| L | Q1 | | | Q2 | | | Q3 | | |
|---|---|---|---|---|---|---|---|---|---|
| | B | N | G | B | N | G | B | N | G |
| 5 | 5 | 20 | 75 | 5 | 12 | 83 | 6 | 14 | 80 |
| 10 | 3 | 13 | 84 | 2 | 8 | 90 | 2 | 10 | 88 |
| 20 | 0 | 10 | 90 | 0 | 9 | 91 | 0 | 9 | 91 |

Table 6. Performance Evaluation of Video Skimming (L.: length, B: Bad, N: Neutral, G: Good).

The experimental results of the subject preference of video skimming are list in Table 6. From this table, we can see that the produced skimming sequences show good performance in terms of viewers' satisfaction and preference. The units of later fine columns are '%'. The prepared issues are list as follows.

- Q1: Do you think that scenario segments in the skimming are mutually coherent?
- Q2: Do you think that scenario segments in such duration are all appropriate?
- Q3: Do you think that the meaning of speech sentence in each scenario segment is unambiguous?

## 7. Conclusions

Automatic video skimming is a powerful tool for video browsing and retrieval. In this chapter, we present a new approach for story-oriented videos. The proposed framework automatically generates video skimming that help viewers grasp the main content within a given duration, which is achieved by exploring the clues about human understanding of a story according to general scenario writing rules and editorial techniques. After the process of the detection of scenario boundaries and the identification of key scenarios, a video skimming is produced by selecting the maximum total Intensity of Flow value among all possible candidate scenarios satisfying the given target duration.

Experiments reveal that our framework obtains good performance for all the criteria of a story-oriented video skimming: informativeness, coherence, and satisfaction. The overall average precision and recall are both over 80% compared to the manually generated ground-truth. Furthermore, the subjective tests show that viewers can achieve high satisfaction and preference over the skimming sequences. We believe that these experimental results indicate our scheme is a feasible solution for the management of video repository and online review service.

## Acknowledgement

This work is supported by the National High-Tech Research and development Project of China (973) under Grant No. 2006CB303103, and also supported by the National High-Tech Research and development Project of China (863) under Grant No.2009AA01Z330 and the National Natural Science Foundation of China under Grant No. 60833009.

## 8. References

[1] Pfeiffer, S., Lienhart, R., Fischer, S., and Effelsberg, W. Abstracting digital movies automatically. Int. J. Visual Communication and Image Representation, 7(4) (1996) 345–353.

[2] Hanjalic, A., Kakes, G., Lagendijk, R. L., and Biemond, J. Indexing and retrieval of broadcast news programs using Dancers. SPIE J. Electronic Imaging, 10(4) (2001) 871–882.

[3] Kim, J., Hyun S., Kang K., Kim M., Kim J., and Kim H. Summarization of News Video and Its Description for Content-based Access. Int. J. of Imaging Systems and Technology, 13(5) (2003) 267-274.

[4] Lie. W., and Lai, C. News Video Summarization Based on Spatial and Motion Feature Analysis. (PCM 2004).

[5] Babaguchi, N., Kawai, Y., and Kitahashi, T. Event based indexing of broadcasted sports video by intermodal collaboration. IEEE Trans. Multimedia, 4(1) (2002) 68–75.

[6] Chen, C., Wang, J., and Wang, J. Efficient News Video Querying and Browsing Based on Distributed News Video Servers IEEE Trans. Multimedia, 8(2) (2006) 257-269.

[7] Yeung, M, and Yeo, B. Video visualization for compact presentation and fast browsing of pictorial content. IEEE Trans. Circuits System and Video Technology, 7(5) (1997) 771–785.

[8] Hanjalic, A., and Zhang, H. An integrated scheme for automated video abstraction based on unsupervised cluster validity analysis. IEEE Trans. Circuits System and Video Technology, 9(8) (1999) 1280–1289.
[9] Ma, Y., Lu, L., Zhang, H., and Li, M. A user attention model for video summarization. (ACM MM 2002).
[10] Lee, S., and Hayes, M. An application for interactive video abstraction. (ICASSP 2004).
[11] Ma, Y., Lu, L., Zhang, H. Video Snapshot: A Bird View of Video Sequence. (MMM 2005).
[12] Valdés, V., and Martínez, J. On Video Abstraction Systems' Architectures and Modeling. (SAMT 2008).
[13] Luo, H., Gao, Y., Xue, X., Peng, J., and Fan, J. Incorporating feature hierarchy and boosting to achieve more effective classifier training and concept-oriented video summarization and skimming. ACM Trans. Multimedia Computing, Communications and Applications, 4(1) (2008) 1-25.
[14] Sundaram, H., and Chang, S Computable scenes and structures in films. IEEE Trans. Multimedia, 4(4) (2002) 482–491.
[15] Bordwell, D., and Thompson, K. Film Art: An Introduction. Technology report, McGraw-Hill Companies, 1996.
[16] Abutableb, A. Automatic thresholding of gray-level pictures using two-dimensional entropies. J. Computer Vision, Graphics, Image Processing, 47(1) (1989) 22 - 32.
[17] Smoliar, S., and Zhang, H. Content-based video indexing and retrieval. IEEE Mage. Multimedia, 1(2) (1994) 62–72.
[18] Yeo, B., and Liu, B. Rapid scene analysis on compressed videos. IEEE Trans. Circuits and Systems for Video Technology, 5(6) (1995) 533–544.
[19] Hanjalic, A., Lagendijk, R., and Biemond, J. Automated high-level movie segmentation for advanced video-retrieval systems. IEEE Trans. Circuits System and Video Technology, 9(4) (1999): 580–588.
[20] Bouthemy, P., Garcia, C., Ronfard, R., Tziritas, G., Veneau, E., and Zugaj, D. Scene Segmentation and Image Feature Extraction for Video Indexing and Retrieval. (VIIS 1999).
[21] Arai, H. Fundamental Techniques for Scenario Writing. Da-Bo Munhwa, 1987.
[22] Bordwell, D., and Thompson, K. Film Art: An Introduction. McGraw-Hill Companies. 1996.
[23] Chaisorn, L., Chua, T., and Lee, C. The segmentation of news video into story units. (ICME 2002).
[24] Aner, A., and Kender, J. Video summaries through mosaic-based shot and scene clustering. (ECCV, 2002).
[25] Rasheed, Z., and Shah, M. Scene detection in Hollywood movies and TV shows. (CVPR 2003).
[26] Zhao, Y., Wang, T., Wang, P., Hu, W., Du, Y., Zhang, Y., and Xu, G. Scene Segmentation and Categorization Using NCuts. (CVPR 2007).

# 10

# Software Applications for Visualization Territory with Web3D-VRML and Graphic Libraries

Eduardo Martínez Cámara, Emilio Jiménez Macías, Julio Blanco Fernández, Félix Sanz Adán, Mercedes Pérez de la Parte and Jacinto Santamaría

*University of La Rioja*

*Spain*

## 1. Introduction

In the last ten years, the increasing power of computers and graphics cards has stimulated developers and users to deepen Virtual Reality (Huang & Lin, 1999; Kreuseler, 2000; Bernhardt et al., 2002). One of its natural applications of interest for the academic and the industrial communities is the Terrain Visualization Systems (TVS) (Lin et al., 1999; Luebke et al., 2003; Ellul & Haklay, 2006). In this field, two-dimensional representations have been completely superseded since three-dimensional (3D) visualization is closer to reality as well as easier to interpret. Furthermore, it allows the user to interact realistically with the environment (Hirtz et al., 1999; Kersting & Döllner, 2002).

Nowadays, there exist lots of issues to bear in mind on designing a TVS: various Web3D technologies to represent the Digital Terrain Elevation Models (DTEM), several ways to provide the TVS with sufficient realism, many graphic libraries both private and open-source projects, different applications to enable the user to interact with the system, etc. For example, some recent works can been reviewed about the use of non-proprietary available Web3D technologies (Web3D Consortium, 2006), specifically VRML, X3D and Java3D (Fairbairn & Parsley, 1997; Huang & Lin, 2002; Hay, 2003; Geroimenko & Chen, 2005; Hirtz et al., 2006). The creation of a DTEM can be referred for instance in (Ayeni, 1982; Longley et al., 2001; Fencík et al., 2005). There exist also several databases that can be used as starting point (GTOPO30, 2006; ETOPO2v2, 2006; Gittings, 1996). It is necessary to operate with these databases to extract a grid according to the necessities of realism and fast screen refresh required for this type of application. Furthermore, a correct structure and nomenclature for this grid must be carried out, in order to facilitate and to expedite its management. Another important aspect is the inclusion of texture-mapping in the model to give realism to the visualization (Heckberts, 1986; Guedes et al., 1997; Döllner et al., 2000). The applied textures are the terrain orthophotographs, which are previously treated -to readjust them according to the coordinates of the VRML environment-, partitioned -with the appropriate size for the different elements that constitute the DTEM- or properly structured in order to improve the interactive visualization of massive textured terrain datasets if needed. Regarding the VRML viewers that can be used to represent the DTEM, some well-known samples are DeepView™ , CASUSPresenter™ , WorldView™ , BS Contact, Viewpoint Media Player, Emma 3D (Emma3D, 2006; g3DGMV, 2006; Universal 3D Format, 2006). Once 3D navigation system is developed, some interaction tools can be added using VRML Script and Java (Moore et al., 1999).

As it can be seen, there are several developments all over the world and very recent semantics in 3D visualization, so it is necessary to make an special effort in generating surveys and standards (Duke et al., 2005). In this chapter, we wish to contribute to clarify the process of development of a TVS in real time by providing a guide through the issues previously commented and illustrating the stages with practical examples. We explain the pros and cons of some of the different currently available options, offering criteria for an appropriate development. We come out of our experience in the Renewable Energy Research Group of La Rioja (Spain) to illustrate this guide. In order to overcome the limitations given by Web3D technologies in general, and VRML in particular, a specific graphic engine developed with open source graphic libraries is shown. Some programs - used to rename the terrain textures according to general VRML structures - and small applets, as interaction tools between the user and the 3D scene, have been implemented in a virtual TVS of La Rioja (one of the 17 autonomous regions in Spain, with a surface of about 5000 $Km^2$). They are used to clarify and exemplify some issues throughout the chapter.

The chapter is organized as follows. First, the basic characteristics of a TVS will be briefly commented in Section 2. The Web3D-VRML technologies are introduced in Section 3 where their strong and weak points are shown. Section 4 is devoted to explore the VRML viewers and some tips to create the DTEM and to endow the TVS with interactivity are provided. The development of the graphic engine, and its libraries, which present the 3D geometry of the scene, are discussed in Section 5. Finally, Section 6 concludes the chapter and refers to future work.

## 2. Terrain Visualization

The spatial distribution of the terrestrial surface is a continuous function, but for a digital storage and representation of these values it is necessary to reduce the infinite number of points to a finite and manageable number, so that the surface can be represented by a series of discrete values (GeoInformation, 2002) (surface discretization). For this purpose, Digital Terrain Models (DTM) and DTEM are used.

A DTM is a numeric data structure that represents the spatial distribution of a quantitative and continuous variable. These variables may be height, slope, contour and orientation, as well as any other data applicable specifically to the terrain and the characteristics of any given point. A DTEM is a numeric data structure that represents the height of the surface of the terrain. By definition it can be seen that a DTEM is a particular type of DTM (Kumler, 1994).

DTEM are usually stored in two digital formats: a) as a map of heights, that is, a two-dimensional matrix in which each quadrant represents the corresponding height of each point; b) by means of chromatic representation of the heights, that is, an image either in shades of grey or in colours, where they depend on the specific height of each point defined. In general, dark colours are assigned to areas with low heights, and light colours are assigned to areas of high heights.

Fig. 1. Creation of a 3D terrain model from a DTEM and an orthophotograph

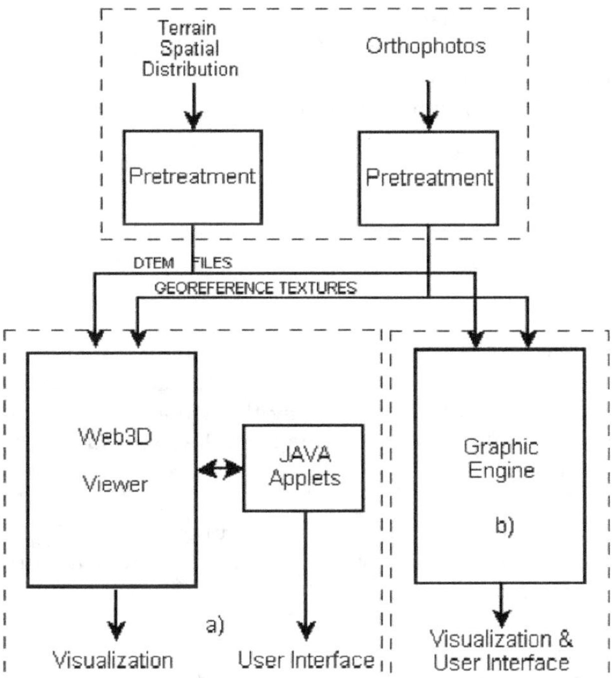


Fig. 2. Virtual Terrain Visualization Systems: a) with Web3D viewers b) with graphic engine

Obviously both formats are similar, but the main problem with this second storing method is the colour scaling assigned to the true terrain height. Starting from this point and taking any of the DTEM available on the market as a reference, it is possible to develop an own 3D DTEM. For this purpose, a polygonal surface can be created, where the vertexes agree with the coordinates taken from the appropriate DTEM (Lindstrom & Pascucci, 2001).

The next step is to achieve that this 3D model has a realistic appearance; that is to say, that it allows the user to perceive more details of any height of one given point with respect to any other one. To achieve this objective, we can think about the possibility of incorporating a specific model texture. The quickest method for achieving this realistic aspect is by using orthophotographs of the terrain.

An orthophotograph is a digitally corrected photographic presentation that represents an orthogonal projection of an object, generated from real oblique photographs. Thus, in an orthophotograph, actual horizontal measurements can be taken, the same way in which they can be taken from a map. Incorporating these corrected photographs to a DTM, an acceptable realistic representation can be obtained (see Figure 1). Figure 2 shows a diagram with the elements involved in a TVS development.

First, the orthophotos and the terrain spatial distribution data must be pre-treated, and the results are the data input to the graphic engine (case a) or to the Web3D viewer (case b). In this latter case, it can be seen that it is necessary to use Java applets, independent of the visualization, which provide the system with the capability of interaction with the user. In this chapter, Section 4 is devoted to the basic steps for a TVS implementation based on VRML, whereas Section 5 deals with a development based on a graphic engine.

## 3. Web3D Technologies

One of the possible ways to implement a TVS consists in using Web3D technologies. The use of any of the available Web3D technologies permits to develop a 3D environment that can be shared on Internet.

The term 'Web3D' (Web3D Consortium, 2006) refers to any programming language, protocol, archive format or technology that may be used for creating or presenting interactive 3D environments on Internet. Among these languages, used to program virtual reality, VRML (Virtual Reality Modelling Language), Java3D and X3D (Extensible 3D) are open standards.

There are also a large number of proprietary-level solutions that satisfy the specific needs of the customers, generally aimed at electronic trade and entertainment purposes, such as Cult 3D, Pulse 3D, ViewPoint, etc.

However, to use an open standard presents important advantages. For instance, the specifications and documentation are well known, and there are all kinds of applications that support these standards. Next paragraphs briefly analyse the available standards, their main characteristics, and their advantages and disadvantages.

### 3.1 VRML

VRML is an archive format that permits the creation of interactive 3D objects and environments. The standard VRML was created and developed by the VRML Consortium, in principle a non-profit-making organization exclusively aimed at the development and promotion of VRML as a standard 3D system on Internet. VRML appeared in 1994 as the first officially recognized technology for the creation, distribution and representation of 3D elements on Internet by the ISO (International Standards Organization). VRML was designed to cover the following basic requirements (Bell et al., 1995):

(i) To make possible the development of programs to create, publish, and maintain VRML archives, as well as programs that can import and export VRML and other 3D graphic formats.

(ii) To provide the capacity to use, combine, and re-use 3D objects in the same VRML environment.

(iii) To incorporate the capacity to create new types of objects that has not been defined as part of VRML.

(iv) To provide the possibility of being used in a wide variety of systems available on the market.

(v) To emphasize the importance of interactive functioning in a wide variety of existing applications.

(vi) To allow the creation of 3D environments at any scale or size.

VRML is a hierarchic language of marks that uses *nodes, events* and *fields* to model static or dynamic virtual realities:

- *Nodes* are used to represent particular instances of the 54 primitives of the language. Instances are defined with a collection of *fields* that contain values of the basic attributes of the primitive form.
- *Fields* are attributes that define the behaviour of the primitive forms. There are special *fields* (EventIn and EventOut) that allow the sending and reception of events to other *fields*. With these special *fields* and the command ROUTE, the flow of *events* can be controlled, directing the effect of one action among other multiple objects in order to animate a scene or simply to pass information to any of these objects.

### 3.2 X3D

X3D is an open standard XML (eXtensible Markup Language), a 3D archive format that permits the creation and transmission of 3D data between different applications, especially web applications.

Its principal characteristics are:

(i) X3D is integrated in XML; this represents a basic step to achieve a correct integration in:
   - Web services.
   - Distributed networks.
   - Multiplatform systems and transference of archive and data among applications.

(ii) X3D is modular; this allows the creation of a lighter 3D kernel, adjusted to the needs of developers.
(iii) X3D is extensible; this allows adding components to provide more functions, in order to satisfy the market demands.
(iv) X3D is shaped; this means that different appropriate extension groups can be chosen according to the specific needs of each application.
(v) X3D is compatible with VRML; this implies that the development, the content and the base of VRML97 is maintained.

X3D, instead of being limited to a single static wide specification - as in VRML that requires total adoption to achieve compatibility with X3D - has been designed with an structure based on components that give support for the creation of different profiles, which can be individually used. These components can be independently extended or modified, adding new levels or new components with new characteristics.

Thanks to this structure, the advances in X3D specification are faster and the development of one area does not delay the evolution of the global specification.

### 3.3 Java3D

Java3D™ API is a set of classes to create applications and applets with 3D elements (Sowizral et al., 1998). It offers to developers the possibility of managing 3D complex geometries. The main advantage that this application programming interface (API) presents against other 3D programming environments is that it allows the creation of 3D graphic applications, independently of the type of system. It forms part of API JavaMedia. Therefore, it can make use of the versatility of Java language, and it can support a great number of formats, including VRML, CAD, etc.

Java3D has a set of high class interfaces and libraries, which make good use of the high speed on graphic loading of many graphic cards. The calls to Java3D methods are converted into Open GL or Direct 3D functions. Though either conceptually or officially Java3D form part of API JMF, it has libraries that are installed independently of JMF. Despite Java3D does not directly support each possible 3D necessity, it permits a compatible implementation with Java code; in other cases, VRML loaders are available. They translate files from this format to appropriate objects of Java3D, which are visualized by means of an applet.

Java3D provides a high-level programming interface based on the object-oriented paradigm. This fact implies some advantages such as to obtain a more powerful, faster, and simpler development of applications.

The programming of 3D applications is based on 'scene graph models', which connect separated models with a tree-like structure, including geometric data, attributes, and visualization information. These graphs give a global description of the scene, also known as 'virtual universe' (Sowizral & Deering, 1999). This permits us to focus on geometric objects instead of on the low level triangles existing in the scene.

### 3.4 Comparisons

X3D takes the work carried out by VRML97 and it tackles matters that have not been specifically treated so far. From the VRML basis taken as premise, X3D provides more flexibility than VRML. The main change is the total rewriting of the specifications in three different chapters, regarding: abstract concepts, file formats, and ways to access to the programming language. Other modifications provide a greater precision in illumination and event models and they also rename some fields in order to constitute a solider standard.

The most important changes are:

- (i) Expansion of the graphic capacities.
- (ii) A revised and unified model of programming of applications.
- (iii) Multiple files coding to describe the same abstract model, including XML.
- (iv) Modular structure that permits ranges of adoption levels and support for the different kinds of market.
- (v) Expansion of the specification structure.

The X3D scene graphics, the core of any X3D application, are identical to the VRML97 scene graphics. The original design of VRML graphic structure and its node types are based on already existing technology for interactive graphics. The changes initially introduced in X3D aimed at incorporating the advances in commercial hardware by means of the introduction of new nodes and types of fields for data. Later, a single unified API was developed for X3D; this means an important difference from VRML97, which had a scripting internal API apart from the external API. The X3D unified API simplifies and solves many of the problems found in VRML97, as the result of a more robust implementation.

X3D supports multiple codification archives, such as VRML97 and XML, or compressed binary (being developed at present). It uses a modular structure that provides greater extensibility and flexibility. The great majority of these applications neither need the full power of X3D nor the support for all its platforms and its functionalities defined in the specification. One of the ad- vantages of X3D is that it is organized in components that can be used for the implementation of a defined platform or specific market. For that purpose, X3D includes the concept of profiles. They are a predefined collection of components generally used in certain applications and platforms, or in scenarios like the geometric interchange between design tools. Unlike VRML97, which requires total support from the implementation, X3D allows a support for each particular need. The mechanism of X3D components also permits the companies to implement their own extensions following a rigorous set of rules.

Furthermore, X3D specification has been restructured in order to allow a greater flexibility in the life cycle of this standard, which is adjusted to its own evolution. The standard X3D is divided into three different specifications that permit ISO to achieve the adaptations of the concrete parts of the specification and their distribution in time.

One of the main differences between VRML/X3D and Java3D, at a conceptual level, is that Java3D is defined as a low-level 3D-scene programming language. This means that the creation of 3D objects in Java3D does not only require the 3D element building, but also the definition of all the aspects related to the visualization and control of the environment capabilities. For example, for the creation of the simplest scenes, the Java3D code is notably larger than the necessary code in VRML/X3D. On the other hand, the control of the different elements in the system is more powerful and natural in Java3D. This does not mean that it is not possible to control a 'virtual universe' in VRML to include user interaction, but that it is more complex. VRML has been the favourite of most Web 3D GIS researchers for over fifteen years because it is cheap, it can provide middle-quality interactive visualization, and it has high compatibility with Java applets (Zhu et al., 2003). However, recently a growing number of engineers in the graphics and design communities are using Java3D technology (Huang, 2003; Java 3D, 2007). Because of its control power, it may be interesting to use Java3D as a VRML/X3D viewer in a TVS (Lukas & Bailey, 2002; Jin et al., 2005). It is only necessary to use some of the VRML/X3D loaders developed for Java3D. At present, the Web3D Consortium is developing under GNU LGPL (Lesser General Public License), Xj3D as a tool - completely written in Java - to show VRML and X3D contents.

The main advantages of using Java3D as a VRML/X3D viewer is its execution capability in different platforms and the fact that the final user is released of installing specific VRML/X3D plug-ins for the browser. In contrast, it must be considered the loss of speed and performance when using by Java3D vs. other VRML/X3D viewers developed in C/C++ (Burns & Wellings, 2001) and vs. viewers that directly use Direct 3D or OpenGL (Mason et al., 1999). Whichever viewer used, it must be taken into account that it is necessary to choose between internal or external programming within the VRML/X3D code. This choice is subject to the VRML/X3D implementation specification chosen by the programmer of the VRML/X3D viewer. For instance, at the level of External Authoring Interface (EAI) implementation, some VRML viewers, like CosmoPlayerTM, are based on Sun's Microsystem Java Virtual Machine, and others, like BS Contact, are based on the version of Microsoft.

## 4. Use of VRML for the Implementation of a TVS

### 4.1 Selection of the VRML Viewer

The first decision to make in a TVS implementation is to choose a VRML viewer, which must be capable of supporting and managing the great amount of data to visualize with a satisfactory performance. It is important to be very clear about this issue in order to achieve the best possible results according to the needs of the specific application to develop. In the list of Web3D viewers available on the market at present, we can specially remark, among others, those represented in Table 1.

Regarding their technological characteristics, we can distinguish between those viewers based on the use of a VRML/X3D plug-in in the browser - first column in Table 1 - and those viewers that use Java applets - second column in Table 1 -. Furthermore, we can find different non-standard format solutions that use their own technologies and file formats to store virtual environments. Although these non-standard format solutions can be better adjusted to the specific needs of a particular application at a given moment, they lack the advantage to work on an open standard that is universally recognized. So, they are subject to the decisions of the company proprietary of that format and solution. However, the use of a system based on an open standard allows us to port our own virtual environment to other different developments that also support the standard.

| VRML/X3D | | Non-Standard Format |
|---|---|---|
| Plug-in | Java | |
| CosmoPlayer | AppletXj3D | Exel |
| Cortona | WireFusion | ViewPoint Media Player |
| BS Contact | 3DzzD | Adobe Atmosphere |
| Octaga | BS Contact J | Deep View |
| Flux | Shout 3D | Emma 3D |
| FreeWRL | Blaxxun Contact3D | Cult 3D |
| OpenVRML | | |
| Venues | | |
| OpenWorlds | | |

Table 1. Web3D viewers

For instance, Viewpoint Media Player uses a file format based on XML, and includes the interaction capability through the use of scripting - continuous lines of interpreted commands -. Scripting vs. VRML presents a similar capability to interact directly with the environment in terms of execution time. On communicating with the Viewpoint Media Player plug-in from an HTML page, the possibility of using either JavaScript or Flash may be taken into consideration. Adobe Atmosphere and Deep ViewT M (Deep View, 2006) are different applications mainly used by Adobe to give to its PDF documents the possibility to include 3D contents.

Adobe stopped the development of Adobe Atmosphere in December 2004, and presently it uses the Deep View technology developed by HighHemisphere. In this case, Universal 3D (U3D) file format is used (Universal 3D Format, 2006). Emma 3D (Emma3D, 2006) is an open source development based on Ogre3D graphic engine and uses an archive format similar to VRML. Cult3D allows the visualization of models imported directly from 3D Studio and other formats, as well as basic animation and interaction with the scene. For example, if we use CosmoPlayer™ as a viewer, we must take into account that it is old software; that implies that it cannot make good use of the graphic capabilities of new 3D graphic cards, and it make mainly the rendering by using software instead of hardware.

On the other hand, if we use Xj3D, as well as any other viewer based on applets, we must remember that we use a viewer running in Java. Therefore, we must have the Java Virtual Machine (JVM) from Sun Microsystem installed and, according to the particular viewer, we may also need the Java3D library. In this case, to use the Java3D library allows us to accede to the graphic capabilities of 3D graphics cards available nowadays. However, using JVM involves certain declines in the performance of the application, since it is an interpreted programming language (Barr et al., 2005) - or semi-interpreted language because a pre-compilation is carried out at bytecode level -. In the Table 2, a comparison can be observed about the loss of performance and speed of Java3D - pure Java (with 3D) in Table 2 - against other VRML/X3D developed in C/C++ and directly using Direct 3D or OpenGL - C++ (with 3D) in Table 2 -.

| Elements Used | Comparison with C++ |
|---|---|
| C++ (no 3D) | 0% |
| Pure Java (no 3D) | 54% |
| Mixed Java/C++ (no 3D) | 22.5% |
| C++ (with 3D) | 0% |
| Pure Java (with 3D) | 92.4% |
| Mixed Java/C++ (with 3D) | 32% |

Table 2. Comparison of performances between Java and C++ (Marner, 2002)

Another important aspect on choosing a viewer is to know on which platforms it can run (see Table 3), and then, which is the possible range of users having access to the application. Let us recall here that a viewer developed in Java is multiplatform and requires the JVM of Sun Microsystem.

As commented in the first Section of this chapter, our research group has developed a virtual TVS of La Rioja that will be used to illustrate the different stages of the process of development. In the decision-making process of choosing a viewer, the use of proprietary solutions was discarded in order to make good use of the advantages of an open standard such as VRML.

As previously shown, VRML viewers can be classified into two main groups according to the technology employed: those that make use of JVM and those that incorporate plug-ins for the browser by means of ActiveX. The principal disadvantage that the former group presents against the latter one -applications compiled at machine-code level- is the loss of performance and speed (Wellings, 2004). This is the reason for discarding the use of any VRML viewer developed in Java; in general the specific needs of a TVS demands mainly high performance in refresh rates of the visualization (frames per second - FPS) and in memory use.

Finally, once the capability of the remaining viewers to execute our developed particular application was tested, we decided to use the Bitmanagement Software viewer (Bitmanagement, 2006) (BS Contact). At present, Bitmanagement Software and Octaga develop the leading viewers for the visualization of Web3D VRML/X3D technologies. The other viewers are a step behind as regards performance and updating on the development of new standards such as X3D (Bitmanagement, 2006).

| VRML Viewer | Windows | Pocket PC | Linux | Mac OS |
|---|---|---|---|---|
| BS Contact | X | X | - | - |
| Cortona | X | - | - | X |
| Octaga | X | - | X | - |
| Flux | X | - | - | - |
| FreeWRL | - | - | X | X |
| CosmoPlayer | X | - | - | - |
| OpenVRML | X | - | X | X |
| Venues | X | - | - | - |
| OpenWorlds | X | - | - | - |

Table 3. Summary of the running capability in different platforms

### 4.2 3D Model Creation

Once the different available Web3D technologies have been analysed and one has been selected, as well as the necessary Web3D viewer, we have to determine the specific needs of the system that we want to implement. In this stage, the first step to develop the 3D TVS is to prepare a DTEM. In order to use this model, it is necessary to obtain the terrain heights corresponding to each pair of coordinates (X, Y) in the specific area that is to be visualized.

Nowadays, there is the possibility of knowing free the height of any point on Earth with a resolution of approximately 1 kilometre. This is possible thanks to files such as GTOPO30 (Global Topographic Data horizontal grid spacing of 30 arc seconds) which provides a global digital elevation model of the U.S.

Geological Survey's Center (USGS) for Earth Resources Observation and Science (EROS) (GTOPO30, 2006). Without any doubt this is a highly useful tool, but they do not reach the desired precision for our TVS of La Rioja; so it was necessary to resort to other local databases with higher resolution. In this case, as a starting point for the generation of the DTEM, a database with a 5-metre spatial resolution was used. This database is in dBASE format and occupies several Gigabytes. In order to work with it, it was necessary to create a program that allowed consulting automatically through coordinates X and Y, represented in Universal Transverse Mercator projection (UTM) (Longley et al., 2001).

So, it was possible to sequence the process of generation of the grid on the terrain. For this purpose, a program using PERL was created, which permitted covering the whole area, a total surface of more than 5.000 $Km^2$, and extracting the corresponding height coordinates. Although the program worked correctly, the consulting process was too slow since the different databases used were not correctly indexed. In order to solve this problem we had to resort to a program in C++ Builder that makes the automation of the indexation of the different databases. Subsequently, another specific application was necessary to choose the step of the grid and the area from where the data would be extracted. In the code in Figure

3, it can be seen how the Borland Data Base Engine (BDBE) is used to accede to the databases by means of the use of TTable (named as Table1 in the code).

Thus, a dynamic access to the databases and to their different index archives -previously generated is achieved, which accelerates the search of heights in UTM coordinates. This piece of program shows a nested loop that accedes to the databases, which contain the terrain elevation data. Inside this loop, another nested loop allows obtaining the grid desired. The horizontal and vertical grid steps are defined by the user as input parameters of a C++ Graphical User Interface (GUI).

```
for(int j=initrow;j<=endrow;j++){
  ...
   for(int i-initcolumn;i<-endcolumn;i++){
  ...
        DB="Xy"+IntToStr(numdb); //Name of the Database
  ...
        for (int h=U;h<ypoints;h++){
      ...
             for (int k=0;k<xpoints;k++){
                   Table1->TableName=DB;
                   Table1->IndexName="UTMXY";  //Name of the file
      //of indexation
                   Table1->Open();  //Database open
                   ...
                   Table1->SetKey();  //Activation of the search
      //by key
                   Table1->FieldByName("UTMX")->AsString = utmx;
      //Set of the UTMX parameter for the search
                   Table1->FieldByName("UTMY")->AsString - utmy;
      //Set of the UTMY parameter for the search
                   if(Table1->GotoKey()){ //Test of existence of
      // some element with these UTM coordinates
                       utmz=Table1->FieldByName("UTMZ")-
      >Text+"\n"; //Obtaining of the corresponding height
                   }else{
                       utmz="0\n"; //If there is no existence then
      //set 0
                   }
                   Table1->Close(); //Database close
             ...
             }
      ...
      }
  ...
  }
```

Fig. 3. DTEM Creation code

Once we obtained the height of each one of the desired coordinates, the following step is to classify the resulting information into an appropriate structure for its subsequent treating and processing. In our exemplary application, it can be noted in Figure 6 that the region of La Rioja (Spain) was divided into different Zones with the aim of facilitating dynamic up-loading and down-loading according to the relative position of the observer/user. It was decided to build a dot-matrix structure totally adaptable to the step of the grid terrain at any moment for each zone.

From this point, different tests must be carried out to adjust the size of the grid step to the specific needs of each application. In our TVS of La Rioja, we are concerned with a terrain visualization application in which a flight at a determined height is simulated; then an excessive precision is not required, as it is not going to provide anything visually important for the observer (Ayeni, 1982).

So finally, a compromise was reached for obtaining satisfactory resolution fidelity, a required level of detail, and an admissible visualization refresh rate (the previously mentioned FPS): the value of 100 meters grid step was selected. This value is more than sufficient to maintain an acceptable realism in a topographic environment, and even provides a fluid navigation.

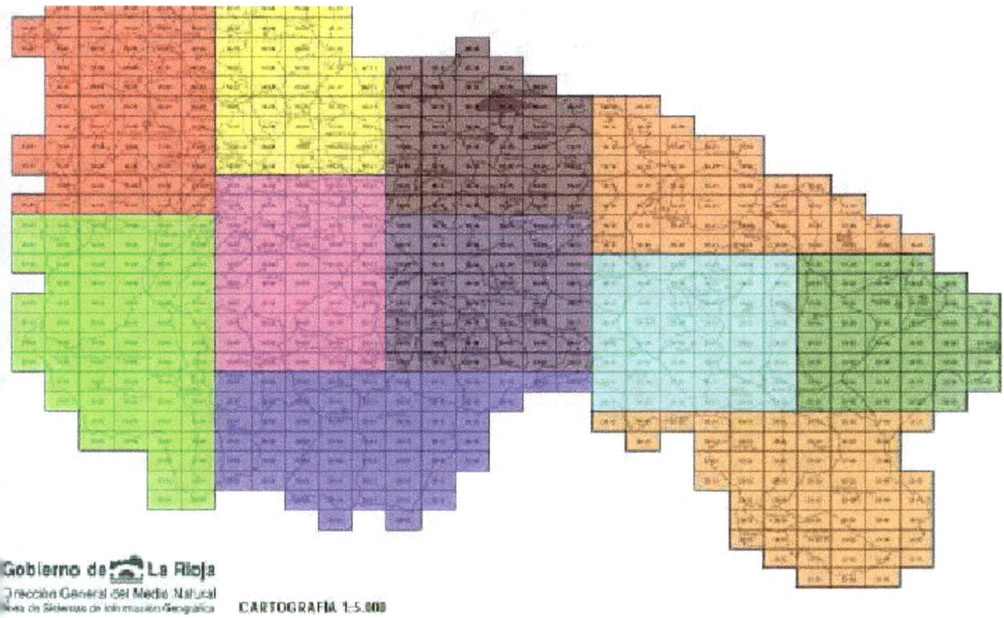


Fig. 4. Division in zones of the surface to be visualized (116x75 Km). Each colour represents a different zone

### 4.3 Texture Treatment

The next step to achieve a realistic TVS is to map textures on the DTEM by means of orthophotographs obtained from aerial photographs (Höhle, 1996; Ewiak & Kaczynski, 2006). Moreover, some treatments must be applied to the orthophotographs before mapping them, in order to optimise the implementation. For example, in our TVS of La Rioja, the orthophotos were obtained from the Autonomous Government of La Rioja, in JPG format, covering 10 Km$^2$ of surface everyone. When carrying out a simulation of a VRML environment, it is necessary that the model files and texture files are not excessively large.

That is the reason why each scene is stored in dot-matrix file, which cover an extension of only 1 Km$^2$. Therefore, the texture/orthophotographs have to be divided into partitions. A specific C++ program was employed to obtain these partitions. This application allows the user to define on the orthophotos some parameters, such as their origin and destination directories, their new names once they are partitioned and new size. It considers their original size in case of being necessary to use data from some of them.

Another treatment required is to adjust the optimum resolution of the textures for its further visualization during the simulation. In order to find this optimum resolution, some tests were carried out from 0.5 m/pixel up to 4.0 m/pixel. Finally, it was proved that using resolutions lower than 2 m/pixel does not really provide a more realistic scene, due to the texture treatment that the different viewers carry out. Furthermore, to use high resolution textures implies that the files are heavier, more work for the viewers, and a lower visualization refresh rate (FPS). With all these issues in mind, we opted for 2 m/pixel as an appropriate texture resolution for our particular application.

Another important aspect in order to accelerate the simulation is the inclusion of levels of detail (Blow, 2000; Luebke et al., 2003), so that it is possible to lighten the viewer load without losing realism or quality for the observer user. The level of detail was established with the use of different resolution textures depending on the distance from the observer to them.

(i) From 0 to 1,500 metres: 2 m/pixel resolution.

(ii) From 1,500 to 5,000 metres: 4 m/pixel resolution.

(iii) From 5,000 metres to eye-sight reach: without texture and only the net-meshing is observed.

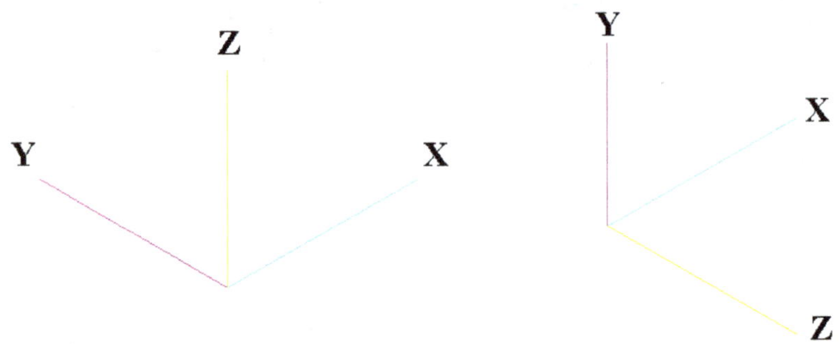


Fig. 5. Orthophotograph reference system

Another noteworthy treatment of the orthophotographs is their reference coordinates. The orthophotographs are represented in UTM (see Figure 5a) and they have to be adjusted to the coordinate system used in the VRML simulation (see Figure 5b). For that reason, it is necessary to make a 180° clockwise turn of the orthophotographs with a software application (for instance, it is sufficient to use any photo-editor application). In this way, orthophotograph UTM coordinate system and VRML environment system fit one another perfectly. Once the texture files are prepared, the graphic engine or the web3D viewer can read them for a realistic visualization.

### 4.4 Tools for implementing the user interaction

What provide VRML with the capability of implementing the user interaction is the JavaScript Code (usually denominated VRMLScript) and the Java code. On the one hand writing VRMLScript code requires the incorporation of different interaction elements within the VRML virtual scene; on the other hand it is possible to interact with the scene from some external applets with Java code.

Thus, the programmer is completely free to create his own user interface with Java libraries and to connect with the virtual scene with the EAI library (Gosling et al., 1996; Yu et al., 2005; Sowizral & Deering, 2005).

For the use of VRMLScript or Java, it is necessary to resort to VRML package libraries (see Figure 7): whilst VRMLScript needs the vrml.node and vrml.field packages, when using Java applets, vrml.external library is required. Let us focus on the use of applets to connect with VRML scenes by means of EAI library. The following elements are examples that may be taken into account in order to pro-vide a TVS with interactivity; in fact, they were used in the TVS of La Rioja (see Figure 6):

(i) HTML file: in the own HTML page, the reference to the VRML file and to the applet must be included. The reference to the VRML files is made with the label '<embed src="scene.wrl"...>' and the applets are usually inserted using the label '<applet width="150" height="40" code="joystick.class">'.

(ii) Applets: they present their usual generic code, but they must also include the necessary code to communicate with the VRML scene. This communication is achieved with the creation of an instance in the Browser class. By means of these instances, we can accede to the VRML scene and control it.

(iii) References to the nodes: in order to read certain information from the VRML scene or to control certain parameters, it is necessary to make reference to a specific node that contains this information or parameters. To achieve this, the getNode 'Node node1 = browser.getNode ("Control-Position")' is used. This way, we can make reference to a specific node that has been previously defined in the scene by means of the key-word 'DEF'.

(iv) Reading/Writing of the VRML scene: Once a specific node is referenced, their fields can be acceded with the functions getEventIn(String) and getEventOut(String): 'Orientation = (EventOutSFRotation) node1.getEventOut ("orientation changed");'. The use of these functions is limited to access to the fields defined as eventOut and exposedField. Once the reference to the field is created, its value can be read by means of getValue(): 'orientation = Orientation.getValue();' or it can be written with the function SetValue(): 'avatarSize.setValue(size);'.

(v) Receiving VRML scene events: In the case of needing to receive events produced by the scene, we must implement in our applet the interface EventOutObserver: 'public class compass extends Applet implements EventOutObserver'. The next step in the definition of the applet is to overwrite the callback method, which will reply each event produced in the scene: 'public void callback(EventOut eventout, double d, Object obj)'.

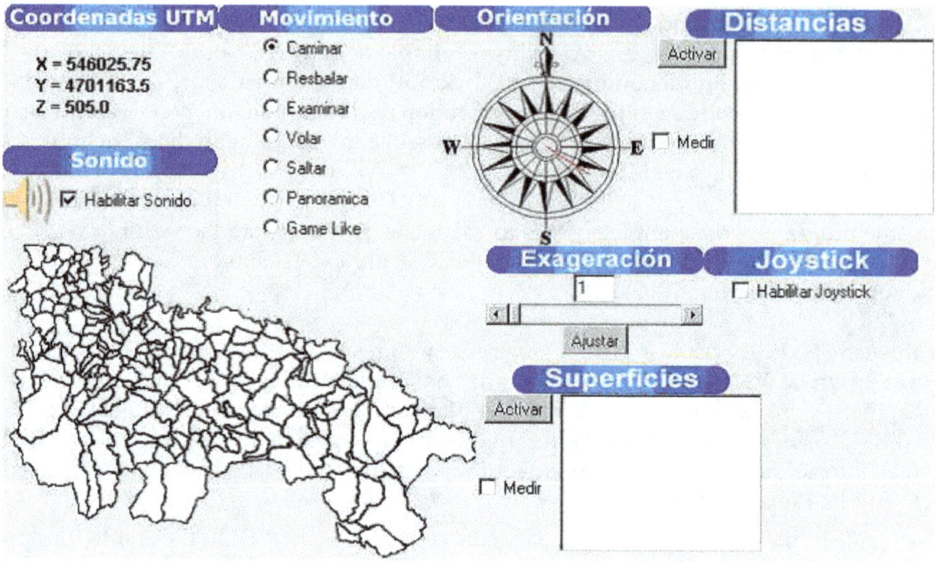


Fig. 6. External applets for interaction with the user

In Figure 6, the different applets that have been developed for our exemplary application are shown:

(i) UTM Coordinates: this applet shows at any time the position of the user in UTM coordinates.

(ii) Orientation: with this element, the user can know the angle from where he is watching.

(iii) Movement: this panel permits to change rapidly the way we move in the 3D scene (walking, sliding, inspecting, flying, jumping, panoramic view, Game-like view).

(iv) Sound: this application allows to activate or deactivate the background sound.

(v) Distances: with this applet, the zenith view and measure distances in two or three dimensions can be activated.

(vi) Surfaces: the option to measure the surface defined with a series of points pointed out in the scene can be used.

(vii) Exaggeration: this applet permits to increase the height, exaggerating it in order to watch the size of the different heights increased.

(viii) Joystick: it allows activating or deactivating the navigation or the scene control by means of a Joystick added to the computer.

(ix) Map: this applet includes a map of the terrain and shows us at any moment the position and orientation of the user. Besides, it permits us to move directly to any point on the map simply by clicking on it.

```
import vrml.external.Browser; //Importation of VRML libraries
import vrml.external.Node;
...
public class brujula extends Applet
    implements EventOutObserver, Runnable
{
    ...
    //Applet initialisation
    public void run()
    {
        if(browser == null)
        {
            //Reference to the VRML viewer
            for(; browser == null; browser = Browser.getBrowser(this))
                try
                {
                    Thread.currentThread();
                    Thread.sleep(5L);
                }
                catch(InterruptedException ex) { }

            ...
            //Reference to the node of position control
            Node node1 = browser.getNode("PositioonControl");
            //Reading of the output events of the orientation changes
            Orientation =
(EventOutSFRotation)node1.getEventOut("orientation_changed");
            //Definition of this applet to answer to the events
            Orientation.advise(this, null);
            ...
        }
    }
...
    //Answer of the output events generated by the VRML viewer and
    //associated to this applet
    public void callback(EventOut eventout, double d, Object obj)
    {
      //Reading of the present orientation value
      orientation = Orientation.getValue();
      //Orientation treatment
      ...
    }
```

Fig. 7. Basic structure for interconnection between an applet and the VRML scene

## 5. Graphic Engine for a TVS

### 5.1 Open Source Libraries for 3D Visualization

An alternative solution to the Web3D viewers for the TVS performance is to develop a program known as graphic engine. It executes graphic routines by calling methods from specialized libraries, like Open inventor TM, Coin3D, or OpenSceneGraph, among others. Let us focus on this latter mentioned library to explain some of their common characteristics. OpenSceneGraph (OSG) (OpenSceneGraph, 2006) is a recently-developed graphic library which incorporates the different primitive basic concepts of OpenGL (Mason et al., 1999). This library uses the programming language C++, because it is independent of the platform and open source. Among the possible uses of this library we find simulations, scientific visualizations, virtual engineering and game development.

OpenSceneGraph uses scene graph techniques to contain all the information regarding the scene generated. A scene graph is a data structure that permits the creation of a scene hierarchic structure, keeping the father-son connections among the different elements. For example, variations of position and orientation in the father node affect son nodes; thus, an arm robot with several joints can be created, with each piece dependent on the previous one, and simply applying movement to the initial piece; the rest of the dependent pieces will automatically move according to the defined structure.

Another important father-son relationship exploited by the scene graph techniques is the possibility of defining enveloping volumes, which gather close elements. Thus, during the process of rejection of the elements that will be represented on screen, it is not necessary to analyze the children of a node father already rejected.

Although the library is still under development at present, it is being employed by different users in research and commercial applications. There are even other open source developments, which extend and give support to the capabilities of OpenSceneGraph, such as OpenProducer (OpenProducer, 2006) or VT Jugger (VR Juggler, 2006), for instance. OpenProducer is a library that permits the treatment of different current representation systems and interaction devices.

Although there is other libraries providing this support, OpenProducer offer the advantage of being an open source development and it allows working with the OpenScreneGraph library. VR Juggler is a technology that supplies necessary tools for the development of virtual reality applications. It constitutes a virtual platform for the development of applications that are applicable to nearly all the virtual reality systems.

## 5.2 Graphic Engine Development

Once the graphic library is selected, the graphic engine consults the 3D model; so, it must be optimized for satisfactorily fast terrain visualization. At software level, the way to deal with this matter is to maintain at any time a similar amount of information (textures and DTM), which allows a fluid data management.

For this purpose, let us resort to a dynamic up-loading and down-loading of the scene according to the position and direction of the user at each moment. This process is carried out with a database that paginates the different scene areas and allows us to decide which parts are necessary to bear in mind at each moment (see Figure 8). At a theoretical level, the database limit is not defined, but in practice, the larger the size, the less performance, and the dynamic up-loading and down-loading are affected. That is the reason why a database restructuring was carried out in our TVS of La Rioja, regarding communities and provinces.

The restructuring consists in searching for a way to limit the database size to the specific needs at each moment according to the zone where the user goes. In this way, it was possible to maintain a more or less constant loading process with a reasonable order for a desktop PC with the following minimum characteristics: Pentium 4 1,7 GHz, 80 GB ATA 100 Hard-Drive, 512 Mb DDRAM, Ati Rage 128 Pro II. In order to achieve this, we can set several levels of texture resolution with a PagedLOD node. So, according to the distance between the observer view-point and the model, the appropriate level will be visualized. The PagedLOD node (see Figure 9) is a variant of the LOD node, but it also allows the up-loading and down-loading of the memory of the scene elements. Then, the scene graph that the system has to manage during the rendering process is smaller.

```
osgDB::DatabasePager* databasePager = osgDB::Registry::instance()-
>getOrCreateDatabasePager();
databasePager->registerPagedLODs(root);
sceneView->getCullVisitor()->setDatabaseRequestHandler(databasePager);
```

Fig. 8. Activation of the dynamic up-load and down-load system

```
PagedLOD {
      DataVariance DYNAMIC
      nodeMask 0xffffffff
      cullingActive TRUE
      Center 488500 4.694e+006 0
      Radius -1
      RangeMode DISTANCE_FROM_EYE_POINT
      RangeList 3 {
        5000 15000
        1000 5000
        0 1000
      }
      NumChildrenThatCannotBeExpired 0
      FileNameList 3 {
        f29c1_C.ive
        f29c1_B.ive
        f29c1_A.ive
      }
      num_children 0
    }
```

Fig. 9. PagedLOD node of a scene element

The rendering in OpenSceneGraph is divided into three stages. The first stage is the Update Process, in which changes in the scene graph regarding execution time are made. The second stage is the Cull Process, in which the list of scene elements that will be rendered in the next stage is set. Finally, the Draw Process is the last stage. With this structure, and the ranges for rendering appropriately chosen for each level, constant refresh rates from 20 to 30 FPS were achieved, even during the loading of the application (see Figure 10).

On the other hand it is important, although not strictly necessary, to generate the whole geometry of the scene in the binary format of OpenSceneGraph. This binary format (IVE) facilitates the initial process of scene loading, so the waiting time that users spend in loading the application is reduced.

Fig. 10. Screen capture of the application at an initial moment and FPS

```
class MyKeyboardMouseCallback : public Producer::KeyboardMouseCallback
{
public:
    MyKeyboardMouseCallback(osgUtil::SceneView* sceneView) :
        Producer::KeyboardMouseCallback(),
        _mx(0.0f),_my(0.0f),_mbutton(0),
        _done(false),
        _trackBall(new Producer::Trackball),
        _sceneView(sceneView)

    {
      ...
    }
      ...

    osg::Matrixd getViewMatrix()
    {
      ...
      // Utilization of the IntersectVisitor
      osgUtil::IntersectVisitor iv;
      // Creation and initialisation of the row with present and next
      // positions
      osg::ref_ptr<osg::LineSegment> segNormal = new osg::LineSegment;
      segNormal->set(fp,lfp);
      // Addition of the row to the IntersectVisitor
      iv.addLineSegment(segNormal.get());
      // Launch of the Visitor on the scene
      _sceneView->getSceneData()->accept(iv);
      // Verification of collision detection and consequent actuation
        if (iv.hits())
        {
        ...
        }
      ...
      return osg::Matrixd( trackBall->getMatrix().ptr());
    }
...
};
```

Fig. 11. Terrain collision detection

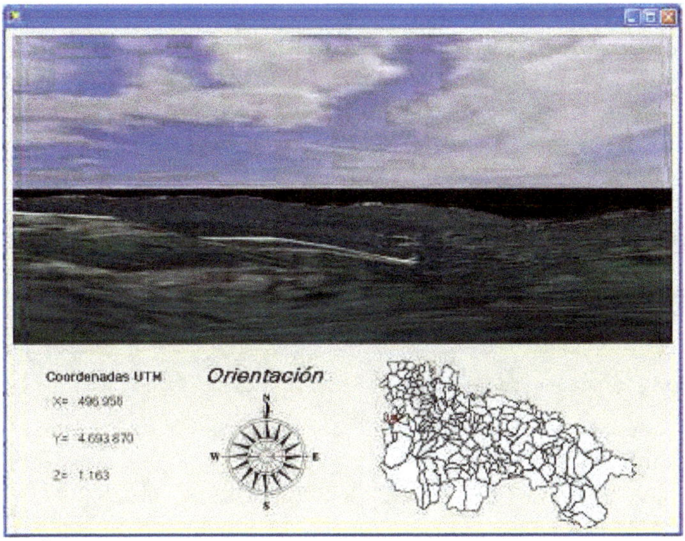


Fig. 12. User interface

### 5.3 User Interaction Tools

One of the most important aspects in a graphic application of a TVS is to provide the user with an easy and friendly navigation. For this purpose, user interaction is usually implemented by means of the mouse, so the cursor can be moved over the scene on screen.

Therefore, it is required to endow the application with the capability of receiving and responding to the mouse events happened on the scene. This can be achieved by creating a new class from the class 'Producer::KeyboardMouseCallback' and implementing the appropriate methods to define the interaction between this object and the rest of the objects in the environment.

For example, in a TVS, the user must always be above ground level, and, generally, at a determined height. Then, it is necessary to use a collision detection system, which prevents the user from going through the ground as he moves over the scene. For this purpose we used a specifically designed visitor in OpenSceneGraph: 'IntersectVisitor'. The visitor is a design patter of performance, which permits to define the operations that will be applied to the elements of a heterogeneous structure of objects.

A design pattern in programming is just the structure or the core of the solution of a common problem of software development. In this case it is an algorithm that allows determining whether a certain segment/line intersects any point of the geometry of the object that accepts the visitor. In the code in Figure 11, the results of the operations executed by IntersectVisitor are sent and accepted by the object that stores the geometries of the scene 'sceneView → getSceneData()→ accept(iv)'. In the code in Figure 11, the results of the operations executed by IntersectVisitor are sent and accepted by the object that stores the geometries of the scene 'sceneView→ getSceneData()→ accept(iv)'.

Apart from facilitating 3D visualization of the scene, it is also necessary to create a user-friendly interface (see Figure 12). With this interface, the user can interact in a simple way, and it provides him with the capability to control or to obtain information from the scene. In Figure 13, the screen refresh loop in C++ that has been used in our TVS is shown. The observer position can be obtained and presented on screen at any moment by means of the last two sentences in C++ code shown in Figure 13.

## 6. CONCLUSIONS AND FUTURE WORK

In this chapter we have set out the main steps to be followed for the development of an application for terrain visualization.

```
    while( renderSurface->isRealized()&& !kbmcb->done() )
    {
     // set up the frame stamp for current frame to record the current
     // time and frame
     // number so that animtion code can advance correctly
        osg::ref_ptr<osg::FrameStamp> frameStamp = new
osg::FrameStamp;
        frameStamp->setReferenceTime(osg::Timer::instance()-
>delta_s(start_tick,osg::Timer::instance()->tick()));
        frameStamp->setFrameNumber(frameNum++);
     // pass frame stamp to the SceneView so that the update, cull and
     // draw traversals all use the same FrameStamp
        sceneView->setFrameStamp(frameStamp.get());
     // pass any keyboard mouse events onto the local keyboard mouse
     // callback.
       kbm->update( *kbmcb );
     // set the view
        sceneView->setViewMatrix(kbmcb->getViewMatrix());
     // update the viewport dimensions, incase the window has been
     // resized.
        sceneView->setViewport(0,0,renderSurface-
>getWindowWidth(),renderSurface->getWindowHeight());
      // do the update traversal the scene graph - such as updating
      // animations
        sceneView->update();
      // do the cull traversal, collect all objects in the view
      // frustum into a sorted
      // set of rendering bins
        sceneView->cull();
      // draw the rendering bins.
        sceneView->draw();
      // Swap Buffers
            renderSurface->swapBuffers();
      // Reading of the present position value
       sceneView->getViewMatrixAsLookAt(eye, center, up, 0.0f);
      // Observer position updating
       refresCoord(eye, center, up);
     }
```

Fig. 13. C++ code for the screen refresh loop

First, the basic characteristics of a TVS and a diagram of the development process have been presented. Then, a brief study of the different applicable Web3D technologies (VRML, X3D, or Java3D) has been included. With this base, the different necessary steps to realize a TVS based on VRML have been detailed, from the choice of the viewer to the incorporation of external tools in Java for the interaction with the user. Aspects such as DTEM creation and the inclusion of photorealistic textures to the model have been also explained.

From the aforementioned, it can be deduced that the use of VRML for the creation of terrain visualization is viable, but always at the expense of depending on an external element that takes over the scene visualisation, on which neither real control exists, nor its code is known, nor its program can be modified. In order to overcome these limitations, the development of a specific graphic engine by means of the use of open source libraries has been proposed. To achieve this aim, several available open source graphic libraries and their basic functioning characteristics have been analysed.

Finally, the steps followed in the implementation of a TVS by means of OSG library have been detailed. Several tips and codes are also involved in this chapter to illustrate some stages in the development process. One of the potential capabilities of the developed system, which may be implemented in the future, is to include different 3D geometries, with the final purpose of facilitating aspects such as management, distribution and planning of the terrain, as a further onward step in geographical information systems (Longley et al., 2001). One practical example may be the inclusion of tracing of roads in the design stage (see Figure 14).

The starting point would be the road design maps, in this particular case, or any other element on which one may be working (canalisation, electricity posts and lines, railways and other forms of communication networks, etc.). From these graphic maps a previous treatment should be carried out, with any of the 3D design tools that exist on the market (3D Studio, Mayer, Blender, etc).

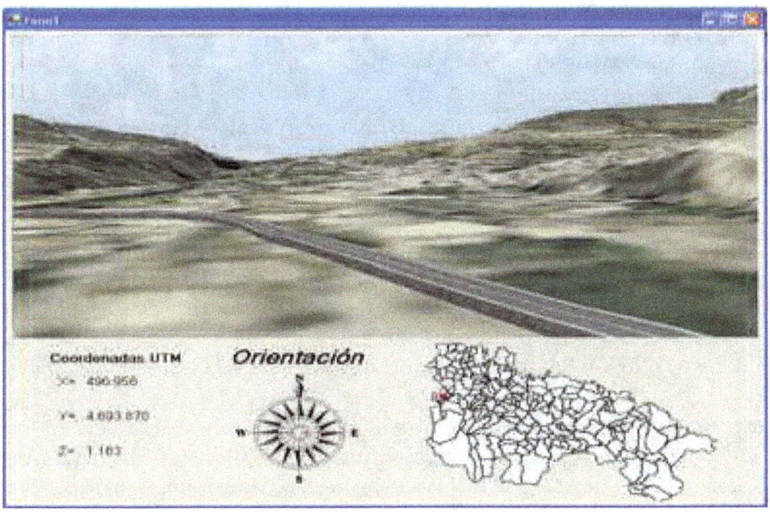


Fig. 14. Example of the incorporation of external geometries

## 7. Acknowledgements

To the Autonomous Government of La Rioja, Ministry of Tourism, Natural Environment and Terrain Policy, for making available to us digital orthophotographs and terrain digital models, which enabled us to develop this simulation.

To GER (Grupo Eólicas Riojanas) for the partial financing of this project and for the interest shown in applying simulation in its own specific field of activity.

## 8. References

Ayeni, O.O. (1982). Optimum sampling for digital terrain models: a trend towards automation, *Photogrammetric Engineering & Remote Sensing*, 48, 11, 1687–1694.

Barr R.; Haas Z.J. & Van Renesse R. (2005). JiST: an efficient approach to simulation using virtual machines. *Software – Practice and Experience*, 35, 6, 540–576.

Bell G.; Parisi A. & Pesce M. (1995). *The Virtual Reality Modeling Language: Version 1.0 Specification,* Technical Report.

Bernardin T.; Cowgill E.; Gold R.; Hamann B.; Kreylos O. & Schmitt A. (2006). Interactive mapping on 3-D terrain models. *Geomistry Geophysics Geosystems*, 7, 10.

Bernhardt Saini-Eidukata B.; Schwerta D.P. & Slator B.M. (2002). Geology explorer: virtual geologic mapping and interpretation. *Computers & Geoscience*, 28, 10, 1167–1176.

Bishop J. & Horspool N. (2004). Developing Principles of GUI Programming Using Views, *In Proceedings of SIGCSE'04*, pp. 373–377, Norfolk (VA-USA), March.

Bitmanagement Software. http://www.bitmanagement.de/ [26 July 2006].

Blow J. (2000). Terrain rendering at high levels of detail, *In Proceedings of Games Developers Conferences*, San Jose (CA-USA).

Bradley J. (1999). An Efficient Modularized Database Structure for a High-resolution Column-gridded Mars Global Terrain Database. *Software- Practice and Experience*, 29, 5, 437–456.

Burns A. & Wellings A.J. (2003). *Real-time systems and programming languages*, Addison-Wesley, isbn 0201729881.

Burrows A.L. & England D. (2002). Java 3D, 3D graphical environments and behaviour. *Software-Practice and Experience*, 32, 4, 359–376.

Deep View. http://www.righthemisphere.com/company/links/solutions/Adobe/index pdf.htm [25 July 2006].

Döllner J.; Baumman K. & Hinrichs K. (2000). Texturing techniques for terrain visualization, *In Proceedings of Conference on Visualization'00*, pp. 227–234, Los Alamitos (CA-USA.

Duke D.J.; Brodlie K.W.; Duce D.A. & Herman I. (2005). Do You See What I Mean?. *IEEE Computer Graphics and Applications*, 25, 3, 6–9.

Ellul C. & Haklay M. (2006). Requirements for Topology in 3D GIS. *Transactions in GIS*, 10, 2, 157–175.

Emma3D. http://www.emma3d.org/ [25 July 2006].

ETOPO2v2 DEM. http://www.ngdc.noaa.gov/mgg/fliers/06mgg01.html [26 August 2006].

Ewiak I. & Kaczynski R. (2006). True ortho-sat vs. aerial. *GEO: connexion*, 5, 5.

Fairbairn D. & Parsley S. (1997). The Use of VRML for cartographic presentation. *Computers & Geoscience*, 23, 4, 475–481.

Fencík R.; Vajsáblová M & Vaníková E. (2005). Comparison of interpolating methods of creation of DEM, *In Proceedings of 16th Cartographic conference*, pp. 77–87, Brno (Czech Republic).

g3DGMV. 3D Graphical Map Viewer. http://g3dgmv.sourceforge.net [13 July 2006].

GeoInformation Technologies Group, 2002. Digital elevation models and digital terrain models. Swiss Federal Institute of Technology, Zurich, Switzerland. http://www.geoit.ethz.ch/education/presentations/dem dtm/ [08 August 2006].

Geroimenko V. & Chen C. (2005). *Visualizing Information Using SVG and X3D, XML-based technologies for the XML-based Web*, Springer-Verlag, isbn 1852337907.

Gittings B.M.; 1996. Digital Elevation Data Catalogue. http://www.geo.ed.ac.uk/home/ded.html [04 January 2007].

Gosling J.; Joy B. & Steele G. (1996). *The Java Language Specification*, Addison-Wesley, isbn 0201634554.

GTOPO30 DEM. http://edc.usgs.gov/products/elevation/gtopo30/gtopo30.html [26 August 2006].

Guedes L.C.; Gattass M. & Carvalho P.C.P. (1997). Real-time rendering of phototextured terrain height fields, *In Proceedings of SIBGRAPI 97*, pp. 18-25, Campos de Jordao (SP-Brazil).

Guillen A.; Meunier C.H.; Renaud X. & Repusseau P.H. (2001). New Internet tools to manage geological and geophysical data. *Computers & Geoscience*, 27, 5, 563–575.

Hay R.J. (2003). Visualisation and Presentation of Three Dimensional Geoscience Information, *In Proceedings of 21st International Cartographic Conference*, Durban (South Africa).

Heckbert P.S. (1986). Survey of Texture Mapping. *IEEE Computer Graphics & Applications*, 6, 11, m-y, 56–67.

Hirtz P.; Hoffmann H. & Nuesch D. (1999). Interactive 3D landscape visualization: improved realism through the use of remote sensing data and geoinformation, *In Proceedings of Computer Graphics International*, pp. 101-108, Cannmore (Alberta-Canada).

Hirtz P.; Hoffmann H. & Nuesch D. (2006). Evaluating X3D for use in software visualization, *In Proceedings of ACM symposium on Software visualization*, pp. 161-162, Brighton (United Kingdom).

Höhle J. (1996). Experiences with the production of digital orthophotos. *Photogrammetric Engineering and Remote Sensing*, 62, 10, 1189–1194.

Huang B. (2003). Web-based dynamic and interactive environmental visualization. *Computers, Environment and Urban Systems*, 27, 6, 623–636.

Huang B. & Lin H. (1999). GeoVR: a web-based tool for virtual reality presentation from 2D GIS data. *Computers & Geoscience*, 25, 10, 1167–1175.

Huang B. & Lin H. (2002). A Java/CGI approach to developing a geographic virtual reality toolkit on the Internet. *Computers & Geoscience*, 28, 1, 13–19.

Java 3D Applications. http://www.j3d.org/sites.html [24 January 2007].

Jin B.; Bian F.; Zuo X.; Wang F., 2005 Study on visualization of virtual city model based on Internet. Geo-Spatial Information Science ; 8(2):115–121.

Kersting O. & Döllner J. (2002). Interactive 3D visualization of vector data in GIS, *In Proceedings of tenth ACM international symposium on Advances in geographic information systems*, pp. 107–112, McLean (VA-USA).

Kreuseler M., 2000. Visualization of geographically related multidimensional data in virtual 3D scenes. Computers & Geoscience; 26(1): 101–108.

Kumler M.P., 1994. An Intensive Comparison of Triangulated Irregular Networks (TINs) and Digital Elevation Models (DEMs). Cartographica; 31(2):1–99.

Lindstrom P. & Pascucci V. (2001). Visualization of large terrains made easy, In Proceedings of IEEE Visualization, pp. 363-371, Piscataway (NJ-USA).

Lin H.; Gong J.; Wang F., 1999. Web-based three-dimensional geo-referenced visualization. Computers & Geoscience; 25(10): 1177–1185.

Longley P.A.; Goodchild M.F.; Maguire D.J. & Rhind D.W. (2001). *Geographic Information Systems and Science*, Wiley, isbn 0471892750.

Luebke D.P. et al. (2002). *Level of Detail for 3D Graphics: Application and Theory. Terrain Level of detail*, Morgan Kaufmann, isbn 1-55860-838-9.

Lukas S. & Bailey M. (2002). FlySanDiego: A Web-aware 3D interactive regional information system, *In Proceedings of SPIE - The International Society for Optical Engineering*, pp. 368–378, San Diego (CA-USA).

Marner J. (2002). *Evaluating Java for Game Development*, Technical report.

Marschallingera R.; Johnson S.E., 2001. Presenting 3-D models of geological materials on the World Wide Web. Computers & Geoscience; 26(1): 467–476.

Mason W and others, 1999. OpenGL programming guide. Addison-Wesley. Moore K., Dykes J., Wood J., 1999. Using Java to interact with geo-referenced VRML within a virtual field course. Computers & Geosciences ; 25(10):1125–1136.

OpenProducer. Introducing OpenProducer. http://www.andesengineering.com/Producer [26 August 2006].

OpenSceneGraph. http://www.openscenegraph.org [26 August 2006].

Sowizral H.A.; Deering M.F., 1999. The Java 3D API and virtual reality. IEEE Computer Graphics and Applications ; 19(3):12–15.

Sowizral H.A.; Deering M.F., 2005. Virtual university three-dimension query system based on VRML and java technology. Computer Engineering; 31(6):173–175.

Sowizral H.; Rushforth K.; Deering M., 1998. *The Java 3D API Specification*. Addison-Wesley.

Universal 3D Format. http://www.intel.com/technology/systems/u3d/ [25 July 2006].

VR Juggler: About the Juggler Suite of Tools. http://www.vrjuggler.org/about.php [26 August 2006].

VR Juggler: The Programmer's Guide. http://www.vrjuggler.org [26 August 2006].

Web3D Consortium - Open standards for real-time 3D communication. http://www.web3d.org/ [22 July 2006].

Wellings A.J., 2004. Concurrent and real-time programming in Java. Wiley. Wu Q., Xu H., 2003. An approach to computer modeling and visualization of geological faults in 3D. Computers & Geoscience; 29(4): 503–509.

Yu C.; Wu M. & Wu H. (2005). Combining Java with VRML worlds for web- based collaborative virtual environment, *In Proceedings of IEEE Networking, Sensing and Control, Tucson*, pp. 299–304, Arizona (USA).

Zhu C.; Tan E.C. & Chan K.Y. (2003). 3D Terrain visualization for Web GIS, *In Proceedings of Map Asia*, Kuala Lumpur (Malaysia).

# 11

# An Interactive Fire Animation on a Mobile Environment

DongGyu Park, SangHyuk Woo, MiRiNa Jo
*Dept. of Information and Communications Engineering, Changwon National University, Changwon City, 641-773, GyeongNam, Korea*

DoHoon Lee
*School of Computer Science and Engineering, Pusan National University, 609-735, Pusan City, Korea*

## 1. Introduction

One of the most difficult problems for computer graphics system is the physics based fluid simulations. Accurately rendering fire, smoke, and water is a challenging problem due to various subtle ways in which the fluid mechanics interact with this complex participating medium. Fluid mechanics is used as the standard mathematical framework on which these simulations are based. There is a consensus among scientists that the Navier-Stokes equations are a very good fluid flow model. Thousands of articles and books are published in many areas to compute Navier-Stokes equations with numerical methods.
Also, many fluid solvers have been proposed to compute the Navier-Stokes equation in realtime. However, the complexity of fluid formation, dynamics, and light interaction make fire and smoke simulation and rendering difficult in realtime. In an interactive fire and smoke simulation, users would like to look around and pass through them. Also, simulated fire and smoke should be realistically illuminated by light and in its own light.
The recent rapid increase in speed and programmability of graphic processors has enabled us to use graphic processing units (GPU) for more than just rendering fluids. In addition, the GPU implementation of variety for physically-based simulation outperforms implementations that perform all computations on the CPU.
In computer games, fluid-like animation, including fire and smoke animation, are commonly used for augmenting realistic scenes. As the gaming industry produces new games on mobile platforms, realistic-looking fluid simulation has become more and more important. Also, the development of mobile hardware enables us to run various application software, including interactive 2D or 3D games on mobile handsets. Although fire and smoke simulations are widely used on personal computer platforms, interactive physically-based simulation of fluids still has many problems on mobile platform. We have established effective physically-based fire and smoke simulation techniques in a mobile 3D environment.

Figure 1 shows some snapshots of our fire and smoke animation based on physically-based modeling and billboard layout in a mobile environment. The simulations are adopted on our mobile 3D game "Rupee Story," which is a first-person adventure game. The motion of the game characters is controlled by the arrow keypad, and we can shoot using the "OK" key on the keypad. Also we can control the camera while playing the game.

Fig. 1. Snapshots of fire and smoke animation in a mobile environment.

Our fire simulation and its applications are implemented on a WIPI (Wireless Internet Platform for Interoperability), which is the standard mobile platform in Korea. Based on the WIPI platform, there are several extended platforms for mobile 3D contents, such as NF3D, M3D and G3D. Most of the mobile 3D platforms are based on the OpenGL-ES (Embedded System) Engine. Therefore, all of our implementations are based on the NF3D platform.

## 2. Previous Works

In this section, we present an overview of the previous techniques for fluid simulation and rendering. Modeling and animating fluids have captured the attention of many graphics researchers. However, no one has created general fluid models that are physically realistic and computationally efficient for real-time animation. Fluid simulation is a useful building block that is the starting point to simulating a variety of natural phenomena. One of the most popularly reviewed examples of computer-generated fire appears in the movie Star Trek II : The Wrath of Khan(Paramount, 1982).

Fournier and Reeves first introduced particle systems to models and rendered fuzzy objects such as fire, where the particles are motion-blurred in order to avoid temporal aliasing or strobing(Reeves, 1983; Shinya & Fournier, 1992).

A number of simulation-based methods for generating realistic fluid animation have been proposed. These techniques use computational nodes that are either fixed in space (Eulerian) or that move with the fluid (Lagrangian). Stam introduced a semi-Lagrangian technique for velocity advection coupled with a projection method for enforcing mass conserving. While this approach is unconditionally stable, it suffers from mass dissipation and excessive numerical damping, especially of the vortices that are so interesting in fluid flows(Stam, 1999).
In "Visual Simulation of Smoke" Fedkiw et al. combat this using a relatively new technique from the Computational Fluid Dynamics literature called vorticity confinement and higher order interpolation. In Computational Fluid Dynamics, the vorticities are detected and receive augmenting forces(Fedkiew et al, 2001). Foster and Fedkiw interpolated this into a water solver and added a level set-augmented by using marker particles to counter mass loss-for high quality surface tracking(Foster & Fedkiew, 2001).
Selle et al. proposed a hybrid method between the grid based method and particle method for enhancing vorticity confinement, which produces a good turbulent flow(Selle et al, 2005). They implemented large rolling explosion effects and smoke explosion using a grid and large vortex particles.

## 3. Stam's Stable Navier-Stokes Solver

The incompressible Navier-Stokes equations can be written as

$$\frac{\partial \mathrm{u}}{\partial t} = -(\mathrm{u}\cdot\nabla)\mathrm{u} - \frac{1}{\rho}\nabla p + \nu\nabla^2\mathrm{u} + \mathrm{f}\,. \quad (1)$$

$$\nabla\cdot\mathrm{u} = 0\,. \quad (2)$$

with velocity u=(u, v, w), pressure p, constant fluid density ρ, kinematic viscosity, where f represents external forces that act on the fluid. Buoyancy, vorticity confinement, and gravity forces are good examples of external forces. Equation (1) is the momentum equation and equation (2) is the continuity equation. Equation (1) represents acceleration due to advection, pressure, diffusion, and external forces, respectively. Adding vorticity confinement and buoyancy as external forces produces a good appearance of turbulent flow Selle et al, 2005).
Stam described a stable numerical technique for interactive simulation of fluid motion(Stam 1999). Our fluid simulation solver is based on Stam's algorithm, which is stable and prevents numerical dissipation. Stam's stable fluid simulation solver is based on the Helmholtz-Hodge decomposition theorem(Stam 1999; Stam 2000, Stam 2002). The theorem states that any vector field w can uniquely be decomposed into the form:

$$w = u + \nabla q \quad (3)$$

where u has zero divergence. Here, u and q is a scalar field. Equation (3) means that any vector field is the sum of the mass conserving field and a gradient field. The equation can be reduced to a Poisson equation for scalar field q.
There are several kinds of fluids like water, smoke, cloud, fire, and mud. We implemented smoke and fire effects on our mobile games. The smoke and fire simulation can be easily

simulated on a billboard, because they can be easily simulated on regular grids. Also, they can be simulated using the same simulation equation, the fire equation.

### 3.1 Fire Equation

Generally, fire consists of the following components: fuel (F), heat (H), oxygen (O) and inert gas (G). If the fuel is hot enough and there is sufficient oxygen, then the fuel will react with oxygen. We assume that there always will be enough oxygen to react with the fuel gas, which simplifies the combustion computation. Using them up, they create heat and waste. These burning procedures are simplified when interacting with three arrays. The rate of reaction depends on the concentration of the reactants and temperature; in addition, the initial value of the fuel and heat are controlled by the game story. If we want to grow or shrink a fire, we can control it by providing much fuel and heat.

The next step is the convection step; here, we have some heat sources, which causes convection. The temperature can be converted into convection forces. There are several constants, such as an energy barrier, a rate constant, a max rate, and exothermicness, which controls various aspects of the reaction.

### 3.2 Coloring the Fire and Smoke

The last step is rendering. Fire has heat sources which emit light. The hotter the gas, the more energy is given off. Slightly hot gas gives off a mostly long wavelength light (infra red). As the temperature increases, it begins to give off light of shorter wavelengths: the colors are red, green (yellow), blue, and white.

The colors of the flame change, depending on its heat sources and chemical reactions. In our simulation, we implemented the gradient class to simulate various heat sources. The temperature of the fire determines the color of the flame. The fire color gradients are useful for determining various kinds of gaseous phenomena.

Figure 2 shows that various colors are implemented on our gradient class. Compared to Figure 2(a), we can see that Figure 2(b) creates smoke effects using gradient color and temperature.

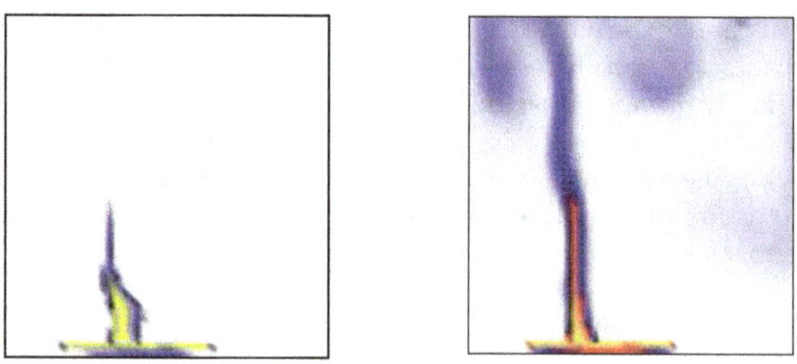

(a) (b)

Fig. 2. Simulations of various chemical reaction of fire based on different gradient color. Here we can see that different colors are assigned to the core of the flame.

## 4. Stable Fluid Simulation on Billboards

A 3D volume rendering is widely used for realistic fire animation, but it requires much time and many resources. Therefore, the technique is not adequate for interactive games, including mobile games. Also, our technique is simulated on mobile platforms, which cannot support high resolution LCD screens. Currently, most mobile phones use 320x240 resolution LCD screens. One of the major constraints of a mobile handset is its small display device. But from the viewpoint of fluid simulation, fluid solvers do not need many grids. Hence we can save many system resources.

Two dimensional animated texture maps have been used to create the effect of the upward movement of burning gas, but such models are effective only when viewed from a specific direction. Orienting the polygon based on the view direction is called billboarding, and the polygon is called a billboard(Reeves 1983;Parent 2002)

As the view changes, the orientation of the polygon changes. Our billboard technique is combined with alpha texturing and fire animation. Figure 3 shows a billboard tree modelling on our Mobile 3D Environment.

Fig. 3. Billboard Tree modeling on Mobile Environment

Figure 4 shows the fluid animation of our billboard technique in a mobile environment. The fluid is simulated on 64x64 grid billboard. The fluids are simulated on offscreen memory and the simulated images are mapped on a screen billboard.

The red color shows the velocity field and the black and white color shows the density field. As you can see, the velocity field and density fields are changed by external forces. The external forces are added by user interactions. Also, we can see that as the view changes, the orientation of the polygon changes.

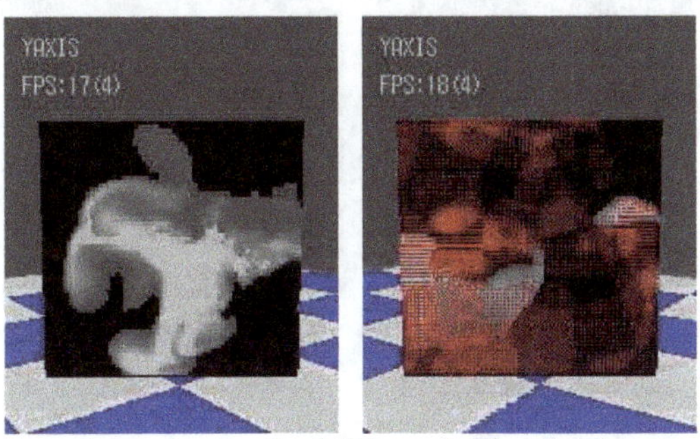


Fig. 4. Simulation of fire and smoke on the billboard. The fluid animation is simulated on a 64x64 grid billboard.

## 5. Alpha Blending with Background

In image based modeling, including in the billboard animation area, alpha blending is widely used for realistic looking effects with billboards and backgrounds. We used NF3D's sprite attributes for alpha blending.

Figure 5 shows the alpha blending effects of fire. Figure 5(a) is an alpha blended fire (alpha with 0.5), while Figure 5(b) does not have an alpha blended billboard (alpha with 0.0). If we apply the same alpha value on the billboard, we cannot get realistic-looking fire (see Fig 5(a)). Therefore, we can specify different alpha values to specific billboard colors (Fig 5(c)). In fire simulation, the core part of the flame emits strong lights and it has a small alpha value, while outer part the flame has a large alpha value.

We can get realistic-looking fire from billboarding and alpha blending.

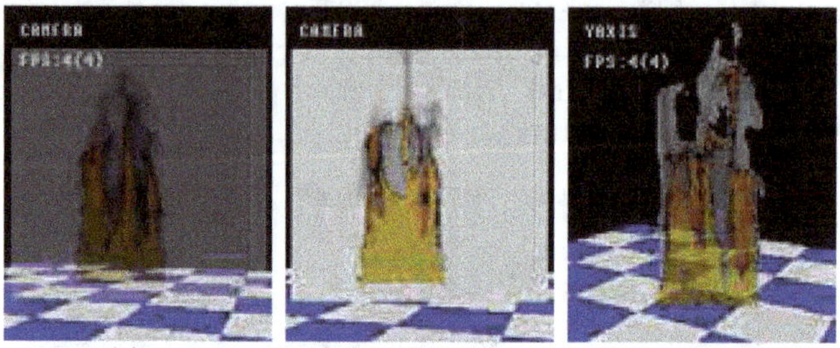

(a) (b) (c)

Fig. 5. (a) Alpha blended billboard with fire simulation, while (b) does not have an alpha blended fire with background. In figure (c), the original white background colors are erased by alpha blending.

## 6. Realtime Interaction with Game Characters

In computer games, interaction with characters in realtime is a very important issue. If fire and smoke animations are implemented without user interaction, they will look fake. Figure 6 shows fire animation under convection and buoyancy force. Notice that the fire's flames are moving only in an upward direction in Figure 6(a). Figure 6(b) shows the fire animation when additional external forces(like wind) are applied. In Fig 5(b), we applied external force on its left side.

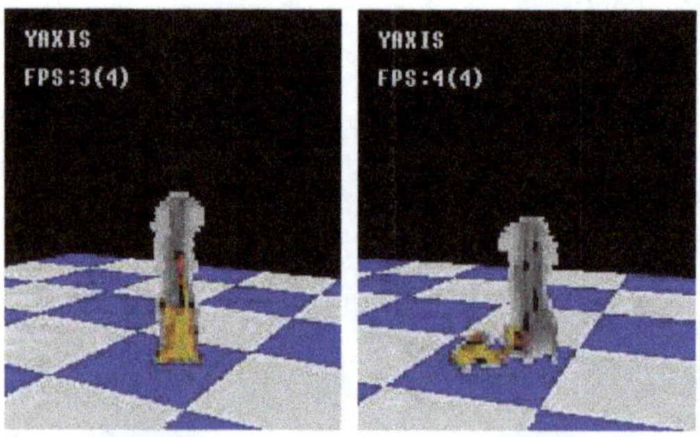


(a) (b)

Fig. 6. (a) Fire animation under convection and buoyancy forces. (b) Fire animation with additional external force on its left side.

Figure 7 shows some snapshots of our mobile game "Rupee Story." As the game character approaches the fire, additional forces are applied on the fire. Therefore, it is influenced by the game character. The technique makes realistic looking fire animation in a mobile environment.

Fig. 7. The interactions are applied on our mobile 3D game "Rupee Story." As the game character is approaching the fire, the fire is influenced by the game character.

## 7. Performances

When simulating a fluid, the number of grid cell and the simulation time have a big trade-off. As can be seen from the results in Figure 8, the frame rate rapidly deteriorates when the simulation grid size increases.

Although a larger grid size would create a more detailed simulation, grid sizes larger than 96x96 are not adequate for interactive games on our 1024 Kb heap memory emulator. As you can see in Figure 8, less than 14 FPS animation is not a feasible frame rate for games.

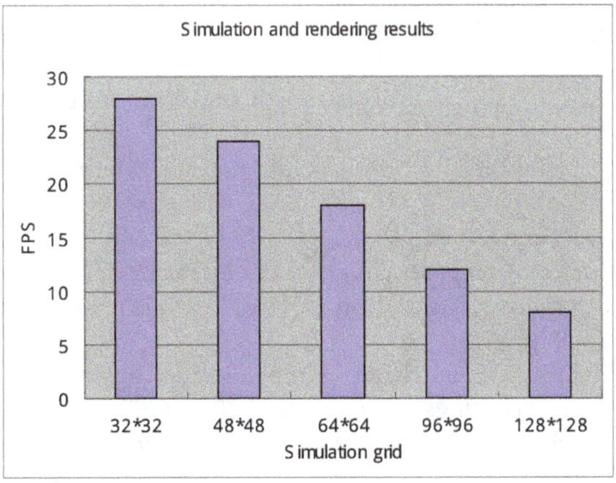


Fig. 8. Frame rates for a different implementation (on a 1024 Kb heap size).

## 8. Conclusions and Future Works

Physics based fluid simulations are very important but are difficult to implement for mobile platforms. We have presented a plausible physically based model for animating and rendering fire and smoke on a mobile platform. Our fire and smoke animation was also implemented on the mobile 3D game, "Rupee Story." We demonstrated that this model could be used to produce realistic looking fire and smoke animation and plausible realtime interaction for mobile games.

Currently, Korean mobile standard forums are trying to create a mobile 3D standard API(Application Programming Interface). We are also attempting to develop more realistic fluid effects on new mobile 3D platforms.

We are also trying to implement water and ocean effects on mobile platforms, which are more difficult to render and must be implemented with level-set methods. The level-set methods are very effective methods for tracking fluid surfaces, but they require many system resources.

Also, we must implement more controls for fluid simulation, including defining the fire skeleton, and detaching flames.

## 9. References

Paramount: Star Trek II: The Wrath of Khan(film), June (1982)

Parent, R: *Computer Animation algorithms and technique,* Morgan Kaufmann, San Francisco (2002)

Stam. J.: Stable Fluids, *Proceedings of SIGGRAPH 99,* Los Angeles, (1999) 121-128

Harris, M. J.: Real-Time Cloud Simulation and Rendering, Ph. D Dissertation, University of North Carolina at Chapel Hill, (2003)

Reeves, W. T.: Particle Systems. A Technique for Modeling a Class of Fuzzy Objects, *Proceedings of SIGGRAPH 83,* (1983) 359-376

Shinya, M. and Fournier, M.: Stochastic Motion – Motion Under the Influence of Wind, *Proceedings of Eurographics 92,* (1992) 119-128.

Fedkiw, R., Stam, J., Jensen, H.: Visual Simulation of Smoke, *Proceedings of SIGGRAPH 2001,* (2001) 23-30.

Foster, N. and Fedkiw, R.: Practical Animation of Liquids, *Proceedings of SIGGRAPH 2001,* (2001) 15-22.

Selle, S., Rasmussen, N., Fedkiw, R.: A Vortex Particle Method for Smoke, Water and Explosions, *Proceedings of SIGGRAPH 2005,* (2005) 910-914.

Nguyen, D. Q., Fedkiw, R., Jensen, H. W.: Physically Based Modeling and Animation of Fire, *International Conf. on Computer Graphics and Interactive Techniques,* (2002) 721-728.

Melek, Z., Keyser, J.: Interactive Simulation of Fire, Technical Report 2002-7-1, Texas A&M University, (2002)

Carlson, M., Mucha P. J., Turk. G.,: Rigid Fluid: Animating the Interplay Between Rigid Bodies and Fluid, *Procedings of SIGGRAPH 2004,* (2004) 377-384.

Stam, J.:Interacting with Smoke and Fire in Real-time, *Communications of the ACM,* Vol. 43, Issue 7, (2000) 76-83.

Stam, J.: A Simple Fluid Solver based on the FFT, *Journal of Graphics Tools,* Vol. 6, Number 2, (2002) 43-52.

# 12

# Error Resilient Video Coding Techniques Based on the Minimization of End-to-End Distortions

Wen-Nung Lie[1] and Zhi-Wei Gao[2]
[1]*National Chung Cheng University, Chia-Yi, Taiwan*
[2]*TECO Group Research Institute, Taipei, Taiwan*

## 1. Introduction

Due to successful development of video compression techniques, the huge amount of redundancies contained in raw videos can be removed effectively. This makes it possible to transmit videos over bandwidth-limited channels. The applications can be video conferencing, distance learning, streaming videos on Internet and mobile phones, digital high quality TV, ..., etc.

Generally speaking, redundancies in videos can be categorized into different types: spatial, temporal and statistical redundancies. Operations of discrete cosine transform (DCT) and quantization are used to remove the spatial redundancy and motion estimation and compensation (ME/MC) are used to remove the temporal redundancy. Entropy coder is, on the other hand, for removing the last type of redundancy.

However, highly compressed videos are often fragile to noises. Once compressed video bit streams encounter any kinds of errors in transmission, the quality of the reconstructed videos at decoder side degrades seriously. The reason is that error propagation in spatial or temporal direction occurs when the decoder decodes erroneous bit streams to reconstruct videos. In order to enhance the quality of the decoded videos at decoder side, two common techniques are often adopted: one is to generate robust compressed video bit streams at encoder side, known as the "error resilience"; the other is to conceal errors in the reconstructed videos at decoder side, known as the "error concealment". Both techniques are capable of substantially improving the quality of the decoded videos in error-prone transmission environments.

This chapter will focus on the issue of error resilient video coding. The main concept of error resilient coding is to increase the robustness of the compressed videos at the expense of extra bit rates; that is, inserting redundancies important to video error recovery. The coding efficiency (i.e., PSNR/bit-rate) unavoidably lowered down, whereas a lower PSNR degradation at decoder side can be achieved in case of severe channel errors. Researchers often faced a problem of how to schedule the overall bit resources such that error resiliency capability can be maximized.

Among the algorithms developed for video error resiliency, end-to-end distortion, which measures the difference between the raw video data and that finally obtained before display at decoder side (possibly with channel errors and according error concealment), was recently popularly adopted as the criterion for optimization (minimization). Here, in this book chapter, we first propose an algorithm of error-resilient motion estimation and mode decision by considering end-to-end distortions for H.264/AVC standard. Then, this algorithm is extended for the enhancement of H.264-based multi-hypothesis coding (MHC) at a given hypothesis-weighting vector, which was traditionally proposed with its good rate-distortion performance in noise-prone channels. Finally, based on the availability of motion vectors, an adaptive hypothesis-weighting algorithm is proposed to make error resiliency adaptive to video contents, frame by frame.

## 2. Modelling of end-to-end distortions

End-to-end distortion, the distortion between the raw data and the one reconstructed at decoder side (possibly incurred with channel errors), has been adopted as an optimized criterion in applications such as intra/inter mode decision (Chang et al., 2005; Cote & Kosentini, 1999; Leontaris & Cosman, 2004; Zhan et al., 2000) and motion estimation (ME) (Harmanci & Tekal, 2005; Wiegand et al., 2000; Yang & Rose, 2005). We first model the end-to-end distortions to include (He et al, 2002): source distortion $D_s$, incurred by $n_q$, and channel distortion $D_c$, incurred by $n_c$. Here, $n_q$ is related to the quantization noise and $n_c$ to the incompleteness of error concealment and motion compensation (or, error propagation). A pictorial illustration of our model is depicted in Fig.1, where the subscript $n$ is the frame index, $f_n$ represents the original video signal, $\hat{f}_n$ represents the encoded video (i.e., decoded video without errors), and $\tilde{f}_n$ represents the video reconstructed at the decoder side in presence of channel noise $n_c$.

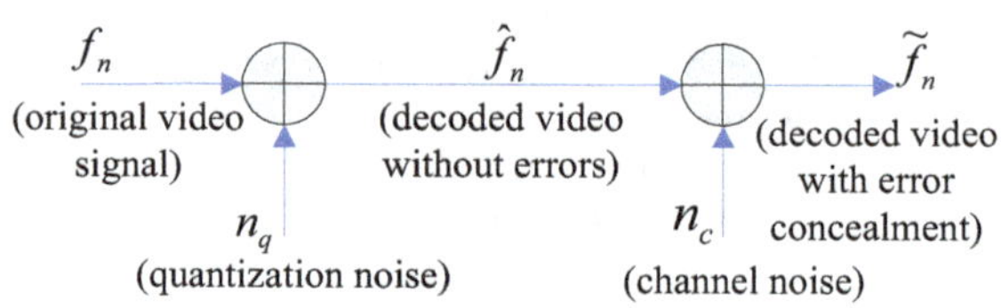


Fig. 1. The modelling of end-to-end distortion.

Via the above model, it is ready to observe that the end-to-end distortion $D_{end\text{-}to\text{-}end}$ can be formulated as

$$\begin{aligned} D_{end-to-end} &= E\{(f_n - \tilde{f}_n)^2\} \\ &\cong E\{(f_n - \hat{f}_n)^2 + (\hat{f}_n - \tilde{f}_n)^2\} = D_s + D_c \end{aligned} \tag{1}$$

where $D_s = E\{(f_n - \hat{f}_n)^2\}$ and $D_c = E\{(\hat{f}_n - \tilde{f}_n)^2\}$. (2)

Obviously, a cross product term is ignored in deriving Eq.(1). This model was first verified on the H.263 test platform (He et al., 2002) and then proved to have an averaged deviation of only 0.863% on H.264/AVC platform (Lie et al, 2006). Based on this fact, $D_{end\text{-}to\text{-}end}$ can then be reduced by minimizing $D_s$ and $D_c$ separately.

However, reducing $D_s$ may conflict with reducing $D_c$ at a specified constant bit-rate (since a lower $D_s$ causes a higher source bit-rate and hence, a lower channel bit-rate and larger $D_c$). Therefore, the original problem of minimizing end-to-end distortions becomes a typical problem of multi-objective optimization.

## 3. Minimizing end-to-end distortions for error resilient motion estimation (ERME)

One criterion to optimize the error resiliency of the transmitted videos in error-prone environments is to consider the end-to-end distortions under a given bit rate budget. The difficulty in estimating end-to-end distotions is mainly on knowing well the effect of error propagation caused by the loss of motion vectors (MVs) and the strategy of error concealment at decoder. Generally, the applicable methods up to now can be roughly categorized into simulation-based and model-based.

For simulation-based methods, a set of error patterns are generated according to channel conditions (e.g., signal-to-noise ratio (SNR), bit error rate (BER), or packet loss rate (PLR)) and coding parameters, such as period of resynchronization, intra-refreshing rate, etc., are tuned accordingly to minimize the end-to-end distortions. The drawback of the simulation-based approaches is the high computing load, which makes them only suitable for off-line video streaming applications (e.g., video transcoding (Reyes et al., 2000; Xia et al., 2004). On the other hand, for model-fitting approaches (He et al., 2002; Stuhlmuller, et al., 2000; Eisenberg et al., 2006), effects of error propagation are described in terms of mathematical models. Model parameters are then determined in accordance with the video contents by collecting a small set of training data. Hence, evaluation of coding parameters becomes a process of model interpolation, which would reduce the computational complexity substantially.

To suppress error propagation without sacrificing much coding efficiency, methods of searching MVs in criteria other than the traditional least SAD (sum of absolute difference) have ever been proposed. For example, Wiegand et al. (2000) adopted the end-to-end distortion as the optimizing criterion in searching MVs. This kind of algorithms could be classified as the Error Resilient Motion Estimation (ERME). However, their method generates/simulates the error patterns and analyzes the possible error propagation by constructing trees whose sizes will grow substantially for a large GOP (group of picture) size. This restricts their practical applications, in views of both memory requirements and computing loads. We need an effective but simple procedure to estimate the end-to-end distortions during the computationally intensive ME process.

An alternative method in estimating end-to-end distortions, well known as the ROPE (Recursive Optimal Per-pixel Estimate) (Zhan et al, 2000), was developed for intra/inter mode decision of each coded frame. They differently modeled error propagation caused by lost MVs by exploiting a statistical approach. Following that, the ROPE algorithm was applied to motion estimation (Yang & Rose, 2005; Harmanci & Tekal, 2005) for increasing the performance in error resiliency. Essentially, the end-to-end distortions are decomposed into three sources: error propagation, error concealment, and quantization. To estimate the quantization errors, a series of processes like DCT/IDCT, quantization and inverse quantization, should be performed for each candidate under evaluation. This causes no problems in mode decision where only two modes (intra/inter) are considered, but certainly incurs prohibitively high computational loads for motion estimation (Yang & Rose, 2005) (normally over one thousand of MV candidates).

Extending the prior concept and avoiding the high computational complexity in estimating the end-to-end distortions, a new optimization algorithm is proposed for ERME in this chapter. The new optimizing criterion of our proposed algorithm consists of two conflicting objective functions; specifically, one of them relates to the enhancement of error resiliency and the other to the increase of coding efficiency. Hence, finding a MV that minimizes this criterion becomes a problem known as the multi-objective optimization (Ringuest, 1992). In this situation, a solution that minimizes all objective functions simultaneously does not always exist when the objective functions conflict with each other. Instead, a constrained optimization method can be developed to find a solution that compromises among these conflicting objective functions. Applying this concept, MVs thus found is capable of compromising between error resiliency and coding efficiency. Moreover, since the computing procedure of our proposed algorithm does not include the terms relating to the quantization errors, the computational complexity is not as high as that of Yang & Rose (2005).

To derive error resilient MVs, the channel distortion $D_c$ should be modelled first. The search criterion is defined below:

$$(\Delta x^*, \Delta y^*) = \arg \min_{(\Delta x, \Delta y) \in S} \left\{ \sum_{i=1}^{B} E\left\{ \left( \hat{f}_n^i(\Delta x, \Delta y) - \tilde{f}_n^i(\Delta x, \Delta y) \right)^2 \right\} \right\} \tag{3}$$

where the subscript $n$ is the frame index, $\Delta x$ and $\Delta y$ are the horizontal and vertical components of the MV, $S$ is the feasible set for motion vectors, $B$ is the number of pixels in a block, both $\hat{f}_n^i(\Delta x, \Delta y)$ and $\tilde{f}_n^i(\Delta x, \Delta y)$ represent the $i^{\text{th}}$ pixel of a block motion-compensated by using MV= $(\Delta x, \Delta y)$, and $E\{.\}$ is the expectation operator. Note that $\hat{f}_n^i(\Delta x, \Delta y)$ represents the pixel value correctly decoded, wheras $\tilde{f}_n^i(\Delta x, \Delta y)$ is the pixel value obtained by considering erroneous reconstruction.

Equation (3) is actually not suitable for practical applications since a series of DCT/IDCT and quantization processes is required in computing $\hat{f}_n^i(\Delta x, \Delta y)$ and $\tilde{f}_n^i(\Delta x, \Delta y)$. Approximation of computations is necessary to make it mathematically tractable. Here, Eq.(3) is modified by changing the squared term into an absolute term:

$$(\Delta x^*, \Delta y^*) = \arg \min_{(\Delta x, \Delta y) \in S} \left\{ \sum_{i=1}^{B} E\left\{ \left| \hat{f}_n^i(\Delta x, \Delta y) - \tilde{f}_n^i(\Delta x, \Delta y) \right| \right\} \right\} \tag{4}$$

Based on the inequality $E\{|\hat{x}-\tilde{x}|\} \geq |E\{\hat{x}-\tilde{x}\}|$, Eq.(5) will hold.

$$\begin{aligned}
&\min_{(\Delta x,\Delta y)\in S}\left\{\sum_{i=1}^{B} E\left\{\left|\hat{f}_n^{\,i}(\Delta x,\Delta y)-\tilde{f}_n^{\,i}(\Delta x,\Delta y)\right|\right\}\right\} \\
&\geq \min_{(\Delta x,\Delta y)\in S}\left\{\sum_{i=1}^{B}\left|E\left\{\hat{f}_n^{\,i}(\Delta x,\Delta y)-\tilde{f}_n^{\,i}(\Delta x,\Delta y)\right\}\right|\right\} \\
&= \min_{(\Delta x,\Delta y)\in S}\left\{\sum_{i=1}^{B}\left|\hat{f}_n^{\,i}(\Delta x,\Delta y)-E\left\{\tilde{f}_n^{\,i}(\Delta x,\Delta y)\right\}\right|\right\}
\end{aligned} \tag{5}$$

Note that the first term in summation is considered to be deterministic with respect to the $E\{.\}$ operator, due to its independence from the channel conditions. The term $E\left\{\tilde{f}_n^{\,i}(\Delta x,\Delta y)\right\}$ in Eq.(5) can be easily estimated by (Zhan et al., 2000):

$$E\left\{\tilde{f}_n^{\,i}(\Delta x,\Delta y)\right\} = (1-p_e)\left(E\left\{\tilde{f}_{n-\alpha}^{\,j}\right\}+r_n^i(\Delta x,\Delta y)\right)+p_e\cdot E\left\{\tilde{f}_{n-1}^{\,i}\right\} \tag{6}$$

where $p_e$ is the error probability of a considered pixel, $r_n^i(\Delta x,\Delta y)$ is the residual produced after motion prediction (with MV= $(\Delta x,\Delta y)$ ), $E\left\{\tilde{f}_{n-\alpha}^{\,j}\right\}$ is the pixel value compensated from the $j^{th}$ pixel (pointed to by MV= $(\Delta x,\Delta y)$ ) of the $(n\text{-}\alpha)^{th}$ frame, $\alpha$ is a positive number (accounting for the long-term memory prediction in H.264/AVC), and $E\left\{\tilde{f}_{n-1}^{\,i}\right\}$ is the pixel value recovered by adopting zero-motion as the scheme of error concealment.

According to the coding principle, $\hat{f}_n^{\,i}(\Delta x,\Delta y)$ can be expressed as:

$$\hat{f}_n^{\,i}(\Delta x,\Delta y)=\hat{f}_{n-\alpha}^{\,j}+r_n^i(\Delta x,\Delta y), \tag{7}$$

where $\hat{f}_{n-\alpha}^{\,j}$ is the pixel value motion-compensated from the $j$-th pixel of the $(n\text{-}\alpha)^{th}$ frame. Substituting Eqs.(6) and (7) into Eq.(5), we change the optimization problem in Eq. (4) to become:

$$\begin{aligned}
&(\Delta x^*,\Delta y^*) \\
&= \arg\min_{(\Delta x,\Delta y)\in S}\left\{\sum_{i=1}^{B}\left|\begin{array}{l}\left(\hat{f}_{n-\alpha}^{\,j}+r_n^i(\Delta x,\Delta y)\right)-p_e E\left\{\tilde{f}_{n-1}^{\,i}\right\} \\ -(1-p_e)\left(E\left\{\tilde{f}_{n-\alpha}^{\,j}\right\}+r_n^i(\Delta x,\Delta y)\right)\end{array}\right|\right\}
\end{aligned} \tag{8}$$

Equation (8) is actually not a good criterion, due to its prohibitively high complexity in computing $r_n^i(\Delta x,\Delta y)$. To yield $r_n^i(\Delta x,\Delta y)$, the processes of DCT, quantization, and IDCT need to be performed for each MV candidate $(\Delta x,\Delta y)$. This is also the reason why algorithms provided in Yang & Rose (2005) and Harmanci & Tekal (2005) are impractical in view of computing complexity. Equation (8) can be rewritten to be

$$(\Delta x^*, \Delta y^*) = \arg\min_{(\Delta x,\Delta y)\in S}\left\{\sum_{i=1}^{B}\left|\begin{array}{l}(\hat{f}_{n-\alpha}^{j}) - \left((1-p_e)\cdot E\{\tilde{f}_{n-\alpha}^{j}\} + p_e\cdot E\{\tilde{f}_{n-1}^{i}\}\right) \\ + (p_e \cdot r_n^i(\Delta x, \Delta y))\end{array}\right|\right\} \tag{9}$$

Considering that $r_n^i(\Delta x, \Delta y)$ is the prediction residual (expectedly smaller than the pixel reconstructions $\hat{f}_{n-\alpha}^{j}$, $E\{\tilde{f}_{n-\alpha}^{j}\}$, and $E\{\tilde{f}_{n-1}^{i}\}$ and $p_e < 1 - p_e < 1.0$ (for $p_e < 0.5$), the term $p_e \cdot r_n^i(\Delta x, \Delta y)$ can be ignored, with respect to the other three terms, reducing Eq.(9) into Eq.(10):

$$(\Delta x^*, \Delta y^*) = \arg\min_{(\Delta x,\Delta y)\in S}\left\{\sum_{i=1}^{B}\left|(\hat{f}_{n-\alpha}^{j}) - \left((1-p_e)\cdot E\{\tilde{f}_{n-\alpha}^{j}\} + p_e\cdot E\{\tilde{f}_{n-1}^{i}\}\right)\right|\right\} \tag{10}$$

Note that, the ignorance of $p_e \cdot r_n^i(\Delta x, \Delta y)$ eases the computation of channel distortions significantly. In Eq.(10), the first term $\hat{f}_{n-\alpha}^{j}$ is readily available when encoding the $n^{\text{th}}$ frame, while the second term (also called the first moment of $\tilde{f}_{n-\alpha}^{j}$) can be derived by using the technique proposed in Zhan et al. (2000). According to Eq.(6), the first moment of $\tilde{f}_n^i$ (i.e., $E\{\tilde{f}_n^i\}$) can be recursively updated after its motion vector $(\Delta x, \Delta y)^*$ and residual $r_n^i$ are figured out. This guarantees the availability of $E\{\tilde{f}_{n-\alpha}^{j}\}$ and $E\{\tilde{f}_{n-1}^{i}\}$ on evaluating Eq.(10) for the $n^{\text{th}}$ frame. Clearly, the extra computations required in computing Eq.(10) come from the updating of $E\{\tilde{f}_n^i\}$.

The quantity to be optimized in Eq.(10) approximates the channel distortion described in Eq.(3). Hence, we can have a constraint on the source distortion $D_s$ when optimizing the channel distortion $D_c$. That is,

$$\begin{array}{l}\min_{(\Delta x,\Delta y)\in S}\left\{\sum_{i=1}^{B}\left|(\hat{f}_{n-\alpha}^{j}) - \left((1-p_e)\cdot E\{\tilde{f}_{n-\alpha}^{j}\} + p_e\cdot E\{\tilde{f}_{n-1}^{i}\}\right)\right|\right\} \\ \text{subject to} \quad D_s^{\min} < \sum_{i=1}^{B}\left\{(f_n^i - \hat{f}_n^i)^2\right\} \le \sigma_1^2\end{array} \tag{11}$$

where $D_s^{\min}$ is the achievable lower bound when considering to optimize $D_s$ only and $\sigma_1^2$ is a selected threshold. It is known that constraining the source distortion is equivalent to limiting the quantization noise, i.e., keeping the quantization parameter (QP) below a value. Accordingly, the motion-prediction residues should be kept low to control the resulting bit rate to a targeted value (since a small QP will increase the bit rate). Hence, we change the above inequality condition to

$$\gamma^{\min} < \sum_{i=1}^{B} \left( f_n^i - \hat{f}_{n-\alpha}^{j(w,\alpha)} \right)^2 \leq Thd1 \tag{12}$$

where $(w,\alpha)$ stands for a MV candidate $w$ that refers to the $(n\text{-}\alpha)^{th}$ frame, $j(w,\alpha)$ represents the pixel $j$ pointed to by $w$ in frame-$(n\text{-}\alpha)$, $f_n^i - \hat{f}_{n-\alpha}^{j(w,\alpha)}$ is the motion-prediction residue for pixel $i$ of the frame $n$, $\gamma^{\min}$ represents the smallest residual power that can be achievable, and *Thd1* is a selected threshold. This change of constraint obviously eases the evaluation process significantly since the computation of $\hat{f}_{n-\alpha}^{j(w,\alpha)}$ is in no need of IDCT for a given $(w,\alpha)$, while the computation of $\hat{f}_n^i$ requires $r_n^i$ (Eq.(7)), which needs DCT, quantization, and IDCT for each MV candidate $(w,\alpha)$.

Replacing the constraint of Eq.(11) with the inequality in Eq.(12), we have the following constrained optimization problem:

$$\underset{(w,\alpha)}{Min}\left\{EP_{(w,\alpha)}\right\} \qquad \text{subject to} \quad CR_{(w,\alpha)} \leq Thd1 \tag{13}$$

where

$$EP_{(w,\alpha)} = \sum_{i=1}^{B} \left| \hat{f}_{n-\alpha}^{j(w,\alpha)} - \left( (1-p_e) \cdot E\left\{ \tilde{f}_{n-\alpha}^{j(w,\alpha)} \right\} + p_e \cdot E\left\{ \tilde{f}_{n-1}^{i} \right\} \right) \right| \tag{14}$$

$$CR_{(w,\alpha)} = \sum_{i=1}^{B} \left( f_n^i - \hat{f}_{n-\alpha}^{j(w,\alpha)} \right)^2 \tag{15}$$

In another viewpoint, $EP_{(w,\alpha)}$ measures the level of error propagation caused by channel distortion and $CR_{(w,\alpha)}$ reflects the power of the motion-prediction residuals relating to source distortion, for a given $(w,\alpha)$. By adjusting *Thd1*, different levels of compromise between $EP_{(w,\alpha)}$ and $CR_{(w,\alpha)}$ can be achieved.

Traditionally, the optimal solution of Eq.(13) can be found via a full or a fast search on all possible $(w,\alpha)$'s. Note that our algorithm would not change the nature of full/fast search in the traditional ME process, but to provide a more proper criterion in selecting MVs that are expected to achieve better compromise between error resiliency and coding efficiency.

## 4. Minimizing end-to-end distortions for error resilient mode decision (ERMD)

In comparison with H.263 and MPEG-1/2/4 standards, mode decision (MD) for both intra and inter-coded frames (here, we only focus on the inter-coding case due to its close relation to the ME topic) is one of the most distinctive and evolving features that make significant progress in coding efficiency. Essentially, a MB is divided into sub-blocks of variable sizes (e.g., 16×16, 16×8, 8×16, 8×8, 4×8, 8×4, and 4×4 pixels), each of which is associated with an estimated MV (via the ERME method previously discussed). A cost is then measured with each combination (or, called a mode) of block partition for a MB. Mode decision is thus to determine a partition, together with the estimation of associated MVs, that minimizes a selected cost function for each MB. The traditional cost function in H.264/AVC is based on the so-called SATD (Sum of Absolute Transform Difference). It is shown (Stuhlmuller et al., 2000) that for error-free transmission, mode selection in a Lagrangian rate-distortion framework is capable of enhancing the coding efficiency effectively.

Essentially, different goals would require different optimizing criterion or cost functions. It is straightforward to motivate us that both ME and MD based on modified criteria would enhance error resiliency for error-prone transmission.

In H.264/AVC, the cost (i.e., SATD) defined for Lagrangian optimization framework is related to the residuals after motion compensation, or, the difference between the motion-predicted MB and the original data. Instead of that, the end-to-end distortion defined in Eq. (1) is incorporated into the algorithm of Lagrangian optimization. More precisely, after finding MVs for each mode candidate by using the ERME algorithm, the following optimization problem is to be solved:

$$\min_{m \in \mathbf{M}} D_s(m) + D_c(m) + \lambda R(m) , \tag{16}$$

where $\mathbf{M}$ is the set of mode candidates $m$'s allowable in H.264/AVC, $D_s$ and $D_c$ represent the source and channel distortion as defined in Eq.(1), $R$ is the bit rate needed to encode a MB given $m$, and $\lambda$ is a Lagrangian multiplier.

$D_s$ can be computed directly from the original data and the reconstructed data at local decoder. To evaluate $D_c$, cases of inter- and intra-coded MBs are to be separately discussed.

For intra-coded MBs, channel distortion $D_{C,i}^{I}$ totally results from incompleteness of error concealment. Equation (17) below formulates this observation:

$$D_{C,i}^{I,n} = p_e \cdot E\left\{\left(\hat{f}_n^i - \tilde{f}_{n-1}^i\right)^2\right\} \tag{17}$$

where $i$ is the pixel index in an MB, $n$ is the frame index, $p_e$ is the error probability relating to the transmission environment, and $E\{.\}$ is the expectation operator. Equation (17) can be further arranged to yield Eq.(18):

$$\begin{aligned} D_{C,i}^{I,n} &= p_e \cdot E\left\{\left(\hat{f}_n^i - \hat{f}_{n-1}^i + \hat{f}_{n-1}^i - \tilde{f}_{n-1}^i\right)^2\right\} \\ &\le p_e \cdot E\left\{\left(\left|\hat{f}_n^i - \hat{f}_{n-1}^i\right| + \left|\hat{f}_{n-1}^i - \tilde{f}_{n-1}^i\right|\right)^2\right\} \\ &\le p_e \cdot E\left\{\left(\hat{f}_n^i - \hat{f}_{n-1}^i\right)^2\right\} + 2p_e \cdot E\left\{\left|\hat{f}_n^i - \hat{f}_{n-1}^i\right|\left|\hat{f}_{n-1}^i - \tilde{f}_{n-1}^i\right|\right\} \\ &\quad + p_e \cdot E\left\{\left(\hat{f}_{n-1}^i - \tilde{f}_{n-1}^i\right)^2\right\} \end{aligned} \tag{18}$$

Note that $\left|\hat{f}_n^i - \hat{f}_{n-1}^i\right|$ stands for the frame difference after encoding, which is independent of the channel condition (hence, deterministic with respect to the $E\{.\}$ operator). Hence, Eq. (18) is reduced to

$$\begin{aligned} D_{C,i}^{I,n} &\le p_e \cdot \left(\hat{f}_n^i - \hat{f}_{n-1}^i\right)^2 + 2p_e \cdot \left|\hat{f}_n^i - \hat{f}_{n-1}^i\right| \cdot \left|\hat{f}_{n-1}^i - E\left\{\tilde{f}_{n-1}^i\right\}\right| + p_e \cdot E\left\{\left(\hat{f}_{n-1}^i - \tilde{f}_{n-1}^i\right)^2\right\} \\ &= p_e \cdot \left(\hat{f}_n^i - \hat{f}_{n-1}^i\right)^2 + 2p_e \cdot \left|\hat{f}_n^i - \hat{f}_{n-1}^i\right| \cdot \left|\hat{f}_{n-1}^i - E\left\{\tilde{f}_{n-1}^i\right\}\right| + p_e \cdot D_{C,i}^{n-1} \end{aligned}, \tag{19}$$

where $D_{C,i}^{n-1}$ represents channel distortion of the pixel $i$ in frame ($n$-1).

For inter-coded MBs, distortions resulting from error propagation should be taken into consideration. First, let us consider the case in which MVs and residuals $\hat{e}_n^i$ are received correctly. In this case, the decoded pixel $\tilde{f}_n^i$ will be

$$\tilde{f}_n^i = \hat{e}_n^i + \tilde{f}_{n-\alpha}^k, \tag{20}$$

where $\tilde{f}_{n-\alpha}^k$ stands for the pixel value compensated from the $k$-th pixel of frame $n$-$a$. If errors occur, the error concealment procedure will replace the erroneous MB $\tilde{f}_n^i$ with $\tilde{f}_{n-1}^i$ (zero-motion recovery is assumed). Combining this observation with Eq.(20), channel distortion of a pixel $i$ in an inter-coded MB can be formulated as

$$D_{C,i}^{P,n} = p_e \cdot E\left\{\left(\hat{f}_n^i - \tilde{f}_{n-1}^i\right)^2\right\} + (1-p_e) \cdot E\left\{\left[\hat{f}_n^i - \left(\hat{e}_n^i + \tilde{f}_{n-\alpha}^k\right)\right]^2\right\}. \tag{21}$$

Similar to the treatment of the term in Eq. (17), Eq. (21) can be arranged to yield

$$\begin{aligned} D_{C,i}^{P,n} &\le p_e \cdot E\left\{\left(\hat{f}_n^i - \hat{f}_{n-1}^i\right)^2\right\} + 2p_e \cdot \left|\hat{f}_n^i - \hat{f}_{n-1}^i\right| \cdot \left|\hat{f}_{n-1}^i - E\left\{\tilde{f}_{n-1}^i\right\}\right| \\ &\quad + p_e \cdot E\left\{\left(\hat{f}_{n-1}^i - \tilde{f}_{n-1}^i\right)^2\right\} + (1-p_e) \cdot E\left\{\left(\hat{f}_{n-\alpha}^k - \tilde{f}_{n-\alpha}^k\right)^2\right\} \\ &= p_e \cdot \left(\hat{f}_n^i - \hat{f}_{n-1}^i\right)^2 + 2p_e \cdot \left|\hat{f}_n^i - \hat{f}_{n-1}^i\right| \cdot \left|\hat{f}_{n-1}^i - E\left\{\tilde{f}_{n-1}^i\right\}\right| + p_e \cdot D_{C,i}^{n-1} + (1-p_e) \cdot D_{C,k}^{n-\alpha} \end{aligned} \tag{22}$$

where $D_{C,k}^{n-\alpha}$ stands for the channel distortion of the $k$-th pixel in frame ($n$-$a$).

Based on Eqs. (19) and (22), we are able to estimate the channel distortion term in Eq. (16) for each considered mode $m$. When applying Eq. (19) and (22), it is necessary to estimate $E\left\{\tilde{f}_{n-1}^i\right\}$, $D_{C,i}^{n-1}$, and $D_{C,k}^{n-\alpha}$. The technique in Zhan et al. (2000) can be used to recursively calculate $E\left\{\tilde{f}_{n-\alpha}^i\right\}$, $\alpha = 1,2,3,\cdots$. A general formula to evaluate $E\left\{\tilde{f}_n^i\right\}$, in case of intra-coded MBs, is given in Eq. (23), whereas Eq. (24) is adopted in case of inter-coded MBs.

$$E\left\{\tilde{f}_n^i\right\} = (1-p_e) \cdot \hat{f}_n^i + p_e \cdot E\left\{\tilde{f}_{n-1}^i\right\} \tag{23}$$

$$E\left\{\tilde{f}_n^i\right\} = (1-p_e)\cdot\left(\hat{e}_n^i + E\left\{\tilde{f}_{n-\alpha}^k\right\}\right) + p_e \cdot E\left\{\tilde{f}_{n-1}^i\right\} \tag{24}$$

For $n$=0, we set $E\left\{\tilde{f}_0^i\right\} = \hat{f}_0^i$, i.e., no channel errors are assumed. On the other hand, the term $D_{C,i}^{n-1}$, and $D_{C,k}^{n-\alpha}$ are available when processing frame $n$, they are computed by using Eq. (19) and Eq. (22), depending on the encoding type (I or P) of the MB considered.

## 5. Multi-hypothesis coding based on minimization of end-to-end distortions

The so-called Multi-Hypothesis Coding (MHC) was proposed to find out more than one motion compensated MB, called hypothesis, from different reference frames and combine these hypotheses via weighting coefficients to form a predicted MB. It is verified (Sullivan, 1993; Flierl et al., 1998; Flierl et al., 2000) that by choosing the number of hypotheses and the weighting coefficients, the multi-hypothesis technique improves coding efficiency further when compared with the single hypothesis technique. Theoretical discussions about the rate-distortion performance of the multi-hypothesis technique can be found in literature (Flierl et al., 2002; Girod, 2000).

Error resiliency property of the multi-hypothesis coding technique has also been discussed (Lin & Wang, 2002; Kung et al., 2006), where the effect of temporal error propagation after burst errors is modeled. Specifically, in Kung et al. (2006), the proposed model is applied at encoder to decide determine the hypothesis-weighting to minimize propagation errors. However, their model restricted to a single burst error, which is not feasible in practical situation.

In this chapter, we try to apply the technique of end-to-end distortion optimization for multi-hypothesis video coding to further enhance the robustness of the transmitted video. The application is two folds: 1) finding error resilient MVs for a given set of hypothesis-weighting coefficients, similarly as in Section 3, and 2) adapting hypothesis-weighting coefficients to video contents. Both the above two techniques (ERME for a given hypothesis-weighting vector and adaptive hypothesis-weighting) can be integrated for further enhancing the error resiliency of the transmitted videos.

Rate-distortion theorem tells us that minimization of $D_S$ can be alternatively achieved by minimizing the power of the residual signal. In case of multi-hypothesis coding technique, it is the power of the signal $f - \boldsymbol{h}^T\hat{\boldsymbol{c}}$ that needs to be minimized, where $\hat{\boldsymbol{c}}$ is a column vector composed of $N$ hypotheses, and $\boldsymbol{h}$ is an $N \times 1$ weighting vector. For the channel distortion $D_C$, it is formulated similarly as in Section 3. Hence, finding MVs that minimize the end-to-end distortions for a given $\boldsymbol{h}$ can be conducted similarly as in Section 3.

In this case, error resilient motion estimation for MHC can be formulated as finding :

$$(\mathbf{\Delta x}^*, \mathbf{\Delta y}^*) = \arg\min_{(\mathbf{\Delta x},\mathbf{\Delta y})\in S}\left\{\sum_{i=1}^{P} E\left\{\left(\hat{f}_n^i(\mathbf{\Delta x},\mathbf{\Delta y}) - \tilde{f}_n^i(\mathbf{\Delta x},\mathbf{\Delta y})\right)^2\right\}\right\}, \tag{25}$$

where $\mathbf{\Delta x}$ and $\mathbf{\Delta y}$ denote the vectors of x and y components, respectively, of MVs for producing hypotheses (hence, the dimension of $\mathbf{\Delta x}$ and $\mathbf{\Delta y}$ equals the number of hypotheses, *N*), *i* is the pixel position index, **S** is the feasible region where MVs is evaluated and *p* is the number of pixels in a MB. Notice the similarity between Eq.(3) and Eq.(25). The only difference comes from the fact that $\hat{f}_n$ and $\tilde{f}_n$ are now function of $N$ MVs, i.e., $(\mathbf{\Delta x},\mathbf{\Delta y})_{N\times 2}$, for multi-hypothesis coding.

We will not waste space to derive similar formulas as Eqs.(4)~(6) for ERME of MHC, but go directly to the one similar to Eq.(7). In accordance with the principle of MHC, it implies

$$\hat{f}_n^{\,i}(\mathbf{\Delta x},\mathbf{\Delta y}) = \sum_{k=1}^{N} h_k \hat{f}_{n-k}^{\,i,j}(\Delta x_k,\Delta y_k) + \hat{r}_n^{\,i}(\mathbf{\Delta x},\mathbf{\Delta y})\,, \tag{26}$$

where $h_k$ represents the weighting coefficient applicable to the *k*-th hypothesis, $\hat{f}_{n-k}^{\,i,j}(\Delta x_k,\Delta y_k)$ is the hypothesis obtained by using the MV whose *x*- and *y*-components are $(\Delta x_k,\Delta y_k)$ from the prediction frame with time index $n-k$, and $\hat{r}_n^{\,i}(\mathbf{\Delta x},\mathbf{\Delta y})$ is the quantized residual (prediction error). It is assumed that different hypotheses come from different frames. By assuming that each lost or corrupted MB is recovered via zero-motion replacement from the previous frame, $E\{\tilde{f}_n(\mathbf{\Delta x},\mathbf{\Delta y})\}$ (similarly as in Eq. (4)), with the knowledge of the error probability $p_e$, can be estimated below (Sun & Reibman, 2001):

$$E\left\{\tilde{f}_n^{\,i}(\mathbf{\Delta x},\mathbf{\Delta y})\right\} = (1-p_e)\left\{\left(\sum_{k=1}^{N} h_k E\left\{\tilde{f}_{n-k}^{\,i,j}(\Delta x_k,\Delta y_k)\right\}\right) + \hat{r}_n^{\,i}(\mathbf{\Delta x},\mathbf{\Delta y})\right\} + p_e \cdot E\left\{\tilde{f}_{n-1}^{\,i}\right\} \tag{27}$$

It should be noted that in Eq. (27), even current residual data is correctively received, the hypothesis prediction source may be erroneous due to error propagation and incompleteness of error concealment. Substituting Eq. (26) and Eq. (27) into Eq (25), we get

$$(\mathbf{\Delta x}^*,\mathbf{\Delta y}^*) = \arg\min_{(\mathbf{\Delta x},\mathbf{\Delta y})\in \mathbf{S}} \left\{ \sum_{i=1}^{p} \left| \begin{array}{l} \sum_{k=1}^{N} h_k \hat{f}_{n-k}^{\,i,j}(\Delta x_k,\Delta y_k) + \hat{r}_n^{\,i}(\mathbf{\Delta x},\mathbf{\Delta y}) - p_e E\left\{\tilde{f}_{n-1}^{\,i}\right\} \\ -(1-p_e)\left(\sum_{k=1}^{N} h_k E\left\{\tilde{f}_{n-k}^{\,i,j}(\Delta x_k,\Delta y_k)\right\} + \hat{r}_n^{\,i}(\mathbf{\Delta x},\mathbf{\Delta y})\right) \end{array} \right| \right\} \tag{28}$$

Again, based on the triangular inequality $|A+B| \le |A| + |B|$ and the fact that all $h_k$'s sum to 1.0, we change Eq. (28) to:

$$(\mathbf{\Delta x}^*,\mathbf{\Delta y}^*) = \arg\min_{(\mathbf{\Delta x},\mathbf{\Delta y})\in \mathbf{S}} \left\{ \sum_{i=1}^{p} \left( \sum_{k=1}^{N} h_k \left| \left( \begin{array}{l} \hat{f}_{n-k}^{\,i,j}(\Delta x_k,\Delta y_k) + \hat{r}_n^{\,i}(\mathbf{\Delta x},\mathbf{\Delta y}) \\ -(1-p_e)\left(E\left\{\tilde{f}_{n-k}^{\,i,j}(\Delta x_k,\Delta y_k)\right\} + \hat{r}_n^{\,i}(\mathbf{\Delta x},\mathbf{\Delta y})\right) - p_e E\left\{\tilde{f}_{n-1}^{\,i}\right\} \end{array} \right) \right| \right) \right\} \tag{29}$$

Note that MV's obtained from Eq. (29) will be sub-optimal with respect to that obtained from Eq. (28) due to a higher end-to-end distortion. However, this arrangement reduces the computing complexity since it divides the original optimization problem into $N$ sub-problems which can be solved individually.

Similarly as in Section 3, considering that the error probability $p_e$ is commonly less than 0.2 and that the magnitude of $r_n^i(\mathbf{\Delta x}, \mathbf{\Delta y})$ is usually smaller than the hypothesis signal $\hat{f}_{n-k}^{i,j}(\Delta x_k, \Delta y_k)$, we ignore the term $p_e \hat{r}_n^i(\mathbf{\Delta x}, \mathbf{\Delta y})$ and rearrange Eq. (29) to be:

$$(\mathbf{\Delta x}^*, \mathbf{\Delta y}^*) = \arg \min_{(\mathbf{\Delta x},\ \mathbf{\Delta y}) \in \mathbf{S}} \left\{ \sum_{i=1}^{p} \left[ \sum_{k=1}^{N} h_k \left| \left( \hat{f}_{n-k}^{i,j}(\Delta x_k, \Delta y_k) - (1-p_e) E\left\{ \tilde{f}_{n-k}^{i,j}(\Delta x_k, \Delta y_k) \right\} - p_e E\left\{ \tilde{f}_{n-1}^{i} \right\} \right) \right| \right] \right\} \tag{30}$$

Expressing the power (variance) of the prediction residual signals in MHC as:

$$\sigma_n^2(\mathbf{\Delta x}, \mathbf{\Delta y}) = \sum_{i=1}^{p} \left( f_n^i - \sum_{k=1}^{N} h_k \hat{f}_{n-k}^{i,j}(\Delta x_k, \Delta y_k) \right)^2, \tag{31}$$

the following constrained optimization problem is formulated to better compromise between coding efficiency and error resiliency:

$$\min_{(\mathbf{\Delta x},\ \mathbf{\Delta y}) \in \mathbf{S}} \left\{ \sum_{i=1}^{p} \left[ \sum_{k=1}^{N} h_k \left| \left( \hat{f}_{n-k}^{i,j}(\Delta x_k, \Delta y_k) - (1-p_e) E\left\{ \tilde{f}_{n-k}^{i,j}(\Delta x_k, \Delta y_k) \right\} - p_e E\left\{ \tilde{f}_{n-1}^{i} \right\} \right) \right| \right] \right\} \tag{32}$$

$$\text{Subject to}: \ \sigma_n^2(\mathbf{\Delta x}, \mathbf{\Delta y}) = \sum_{i=1}^{p} \left( f_n^i - \sum_{k=1}^{N} h_k \hat{f}_{n-k}^{i,j}(\Delta x_k, \Delta y_k) \right)^2 < T$$

Obviously, the threshold $T$ determines the tradeoff between coding efficiency and error resiliency. It is not straightforward enough to see from Eq. (32) how the $T$ impacts upon finding error resilient MV for each hypothesis. For more clarity, Eq. (31) is re-written as:

$$\sigma_n^2(\mathbf{\Delta x}, \mathbf{\Delta y}) = \sum_{i=1}^{p} \left[ \begin{array}{l} \sum_{k=1}^{N} h_k^2 \left( f_n^i - \hat{f}_{n-k}^{i,j} \right)^2 \\ \quad + 2 \sum_{k=1,\ k \neq q,}^{N} \sum_{q=1}^{N} h_k h_q \left( f_n^i - \hat{f}_{n-k}^{i,j}(\Delta x_k, \Delta y_k) \right) \left( f_n^i - \hat{f}_{n-q}^{i,j}(\Delta x_q, \Delta y_q) \right) \end{array} \right]. \tag{33}$$

Define

$$\delta_k^2(\Delta x_k, \Delta y_k) \equiv \sum \left( f_n^i - \hat{f}_{n-k}^{i,j}(\Delta x_k, \Delta y_k) \right)^2 \tag{34}$$

which represents the autocorrelation (or, variance) of the motion residual signal and is always lager than the cross-correlation term (a Gaussian residual signal of zero-mean is assumed). Therefore, for a given hypothesis number $k$ and for each $q=1\sim N$, $q\neq k$, the following inequality will hold,

$$h_k^2\delta_k^2 \geq \sum_{i=1}^{p}\left[h_k h_q\left(f_n^i-\hat{f}_{n-k}^{i,j}(\Delta x_k,\Delta y_k)\right)\left(f_n^i-\hat{f}_{n-q}^{i,j}(\Delta x_q,\Delta y_q)\right)\right] \tag{35}$$

Hence, $\sigma_n^2(\mathbf{\Delta x},\mathbf{\Delta y})$ in Eq. (33) can be expressed in terms of $\delta_k^2(\Delta x_k,\Delta y_k)'s, k=1\sim N$:

$$\sigma_n^2(\mathbf{\Delta x},\mathbf{\Delta y}) \leq \sum_{k=1}^{N} h_k^2\delta_k^2 + 2\sum_{k=1}^{N} h_k^2(N-k)\delta_k^2 = \sum_{k=1}^{N} h_k^2\delta_k^2(1+2N-2k) \tag{36}$$

Hence, a constraint $T$ on $\sigma_n^2(\mathbf{\Delta x},\mathbf{\Delta y})$ can be decomposed into separate constraints $T_k's$ on $\delta_k^2(\Delta x_k,\Delta y_k)'s, k=1\sim N$. In other words, there exists a mapping between ($T_1$, $T_2$, ...$T_N$) and $T$ via

$$T=\sum_{k=1}^{N} h_k^2 T_k(1+2N-2k), \tag{37}$$

which is similar to Eq. (36). We can specify the value of the total threshold $T$ indirectly via individual $T_k's$ to tradeoff between coding efficiency and error resiliency separately for each hypothesis. That is, we divide the original constrained optimization problem into $N$ sub-problem, which is much simpler.

The proposed error resilient motion estimation algorithm for a given weighting vector $\boldsymbol{h}$ is now summarized as follows. First, set a constraint $\delta_k^2(\Delta x_k,\Delta y_k)\leq T_k$ for each reference frame $f_{n-k}$ for motion estimation and then choose among the MVs, which satisfy the above constraint, the one that minimizes

$$\sum_{i=1}^{p}\left|\left(\hat{f}_{n-k}^{i,j}(\Delta x_k,\Delta y_k)-(1-p_e)E\left\{\tilde{f}_{n-k}^{i,j}(\Delta x_k,\Delta y_k)\right\}-p_e E\left\{\tilde{f}_{n-1}^{i}\right\}\right)\right| \tag{38}$$

The above procedure is performed for each hypothesis $k$, $k$= 1~$N$. Finally, generate the motion prediction residual by subtracting the weighted hypothesis $\sum_{k=1}^{N} h_k\hat{f}_{n-k}^{i,j}(\Delta x_k,\Delta y_k)$ from the original video data.

## 6. Adaptive multi-hypothesis coding

In Section 5, error resilient motion estimation for a given set of hypothesis-weighting coefficients $\boldsymbol{h}$ is discussed. That is, $\boldsymbol{h}$ remains constant along the whole video. Now, in this section, we explore the advantage of varying the weighting coefficients $\boldsymbol{h}$, frame by frame, to further enhance error resiliency of the transmitted videos, according to the channel packet loss rate and video contents.

Before illustrating how to estimate the optimal $\boldsymbol{h}$ for error-prone video transmission, the power of the channel distortion signal is derived similarly as in Section 5:

$$\begin{aligned}\sigma^2_{\tilde{n}\tilde{n}} &= \sum_{i=1}^{p} E\left\{\left(\hat{f}_n^i - \tilde{f}_n^i\right)^2\right\} \\ &= \sum_{i=1}^{p}\left(p_e \cdot E\left\{\left(\hat{f}_n^i - \tilde{f}_{n-1}^i\right)^2\right\} + (1-p_e)\cdot E\left\{\left[\hat{f}_n^i - \left(\hat{r}_n^i + \sum_{k=1}^{N} h_k \tilde{f}_{n-k}^{i,j}\right)\right]^2\right\}\right)\end{aligned} \tag{39}$$

The $i^{\text{th}}$ term in summation can be reformulated as follows.

$$\begin{aligned}& p_e \cdot E\left\{\left(\hat{f}_n^i + \hat{f}_{n-1}^i - \hat{f}_{n-1}^i - \tilde{f}_{n-1}^i\right)^2\right\} + (1-p_e)\cdot E\left\{\left[\sum_{k=1}^{N} h_k \hat{f}_{n-k}^{i,j} - \sum_{k=1}^{N} h_k \tilde{f}_{n-k}^{i,j}\right]^2\right\} \\ &= p_e \cdot E\left\{\left(\hat{f}_n^i - \hat{f}_{n-1}^i\right)^2\right\} + p_e \cdot E\left\{\left(\hat{f}_{n-1}^i - \tilde{f}_{n-1}^i\right)^2\right\} + 2p_e \cdot E\left\{\left(\hat{f}_n^i - \hat{f}_{n-1}^i\right)\left(\hat{f}_{n-1}^i - \tilde{f}_{n-1}^i\right)\right\} \\ &\quad + (1-p_e)\cdot E\left\{\left[\sum_{k=1}^{N} h_k \hat{f}_{n-k}^{i,j} - \sum_{k=1}^{N} h_k \tilde{f}_{n-k}^{i,j}\right]^2\right\} \\ &= p_e \cdot \left(\hat{f}_n^i - \hat{f}_{n-1}^i\right)^2 + p_e \cdot E\left\{\left(\hat{f}_{n-1}^i - \tilde{f}_{n-1}^i\right)^2\right\} + 2p_e \cdot \left(\hat{f}_n^i - \hat{f}_{n-1}^i\right)\left(\hat{f}_{n-1}^i - E\left\{\tilde{f}_{n-1}^i\right\}\right) \\ &\quad + (1-p_e)\cdot E\left\{\left[\sum_{k=1}^{N} h_k \hat{f}_{n-k}^{i,j} - \sum_{k=1}^{N} h_k \tilde{f}_{n-k}^{i,j}\right]^2\right\}\end{aligned} \tag{40}$$

It is further assumed that $\left(\hat{f}_{n-k}^i - \tilde{f}_{n-k}^i\right)$ and $\left(\hat{f}_{n-q}^i - \tilde{f}_{n-q}^i\right)$, $k \neq q$, are independent. Then, the channel distortion power in Eq.(39) can be approximated as:

$$\sigma^2_{\tilde{n}\tilde{n}} \cong \sum_{i=1}^{p}\left(\begin{aligned}& p_e \cdot \left(\hat{f}_n^i - \hat{f}_{n-1}^i\right)^2 + p_e \cdot E\left\{\left(\hat{f}_{n-1}^i - \tilde{f}_{n-1}^i\right)^2\right\} + 2p_e \cdot \left(\hat{f}_n^i - \hat{f}_{n-1}^i\right)\left(\hat{f}_{n-1}^i - E\left\{\tilde{f}_{n-1}^i\right\}\right) \\ &\quad + (1-p_e)\cdot \sum_{k=1}^{N} h_k^2 E\left\{\left(\hat{f}_{n-k}^{i,j} - \tilde{f}_{n-k}^{i,j}\right)^2\right\}\end{aligned}\right) \tag{41}$$

Some notes about Eq. (41) are emphasized below. First, for given MVs, the first moment $E\left\{\tilde{f}_{n-1}^i\right\}$ can be estimated by using Eq. (27). Secondly, Eq. (41) is a recursive formula, meaning that the channel distortion power of the previous $N$ frames, i.e., $E\left\{\left(\hat{f}_{n-k}^i - \tilde{f}_{n-k}^i\right)^2\right\}$, $k = 1 \sim N$, are used in estimating the channel distortion power of the current frame. Finally, if a strategy other than zero-motion is adopted for error concealment, the first two terms in Eq. (41) will change accordingly and may result in a lower channel distortion power. However, discussions about finding proper concealment strategies that are able to minimize channel distortion power are beyond the scope of this chapter.

The last term in Eq. (41) reveals that it is possible to find one combination of $h_k$'s such that the channel distortion power is minimized. This problem can be formulated as follows:

$$\begin{aligned} &\text{minimize} \quad \left(\tfrac{1}{2}\right) \boldsymbol{h}^T \mathbf{D} \boldsymbol{h} \\ &\text{subject to} \quad \mathbf{1}^T \boldsymbol{h} = 1 \quad \text{and} \quad \boldsymbol{h} \succeq 0 \end{aligned} \tag{42}$$

where **D** is an $N \times N$ diagonal matrix whose elements on diagonal, denoted as $\sigma^2_{\tilde{n}_k \tilde{n}_k}$, is

$$\sum_{b=1}^{M} \sum_{i=1}^{p} E\left\{ \left( \hat{f}^{b,i,j}_{n-k} - \tilde{f}^{b,i,j}_{n-k} \right)^2 \right\}, \tag{43}$$

where $b$ is the MB index and $M$ is the total number of MBs in a video frame.

The problem in Eq. (43) is a convex optimization problem and the Karush-Kuhn-Tucker (KKT) conditions can be applied to find a solution of Eq. (42). Here, we consider the case of $N = 3$ for better understanding:

$$\begin{bmatrix} \sigma^2_{\tilde{n}_1\tilde{n}_1} & 0 & 0 \\ 0 & \sigma^2_{\tilde{n}_2\tilde{n}_2} & 0 \\ 0 & 0 & \sigma^2_{\tilde{n}_3\tilde{n}_3} \end{bmatrix} \begin{bmatrix} h_1 \\ h_2 \\ h_3 \end{bmatrix} + v \begin{bmatrix} 1 \\ 1 \\ 1 \end{bmatrix} = \begin{bmatrix} 0 \\ 0 \\ 0 \end{bmatrix}, \tag{44}$$

where $v$ is a Lagrange multipliers. Equation (44) is used to estimate the optimal value of $h_k$, $k = 1\sim3$, with a constraint of $h_1 + h_2 + h_3 = 1.0$.

$$h_k = \frac{\sigma^2_{\tilde{n}_i\tilde{n}_i} \sigma^2_{\tilde{n}_l\tilde{n}_l}}{\sigma^2_{\tilde{n}_1\tilde{n}_1}\sigma^2_{\tilde{n}_2\tilde{n}_2} + \sigma^2_{\tilde{n}_1\tilde{n}_1}\sigma^2_{\tilde{n}_3\tilde{n}_3} + \sigma^2_{\tilde{n}_2\tilde{n}_2}\sigma^2_{\tilde{n}_3\tilde{n}_3}}, \quad \text{for } i \neq k \neq l \tag{45}$$

Note that the determination of optimal $\boldsymbol{h}$ is based on the availability of MVs for all the MBs in a frame. That is, multi-hypothesis motion estimation based on the conventional algorithm is performed first, then Eq. (45) (as well as other related formula) is used to figure out the optimal hypothesis-weighting coefficients $\boldsymbol{h}^*$, and finally these $N$ hypotheses are combined to estimate the prediction. By the way, the overhead for transmitting $\boldsymbol{h}$ information is less and can be ignored.

## 7. Experimental results

### 7.1 Experiments for ERME and ERMD

The proposed ERME and ERMD algorithms are implemented on H.264/AVC test model JM 9.3 with rate control being enabled to meet channel bandwidth constraint. The number of reference frame and the search range for motion estimation are 3 and ±16 pixels, respectively. There are a total of 100 CIF frames for each test sequence. The performance of the proposed ERME algorithm is verified first by encoding the first frame as I picture and the rest as P pictures without intra-coded MBs therein. To evaluate the proposed ERME algorithm, mode decision for MBs in P pictures is purposely disabled, that is, only the block size of 16x16 pixels is considered. The setting of the threshold *Thd1* in Eq. (13) needs to be explained further. Theoretically, by adjusting *Thd1*, one can explore the trading behaviours between error resiliency and coding efficiency of MVs. For the purpose of analysis, let $Thd1 = \alpha \cdot \hat{\sigma}^2$ , where $\alpha$ is a pre-set constant and $\hat{\sigma}^2$ is derived via dynamic MB analysis.

For better understanding, we let $\hat{\sigma}^2$ be equal to $\gamma^{\min}$ (previously stated in Eq. (12)), the smallest residual energy that can be achievable via conventional motion estimation process. Henceforth, $\alpha$ is selected to be larger than 1. It follows that a larger $\alpha$ implies a larger sacrifice on matching optimality (in a metric of square errors), or, the coding efficiency. Note that *Thd1* is dynamically varied on the MB base to account for the variation in video contents.

Figure 2 illustrates the PSNR performance at varying $\alpha$ and transmission bit rates. Curves marked with "alpha_*x*" represent the results obtained by setting $\alpha$ to *x*, e.g., "alpha_10" means $\alpha = 10$ . On the other hand, curves annotated with "alpha_*" represent the results obtained by using conventional ME method (i.e., no consideration on error resiliency). It is assumed that each transmitted packet contains a slice which is composed of a row of consecutive MBs. When errors occur during transmission, the method of zero motion is adopted for error concealment at receiver, i.e., the damaged MB is replaced with that at the same location in the previous frame. Different error patterns for each packet loss rate (5% or 15%) are simulated to obtain an ensemble average PSNR of the reconstructed video.

From the figures, it is observed that with an increasing $\alpha$ , the coding efficiency decrease (i.e., less PSNR at a given bit rate) as expected when PSNRs are measured at encoder's local decoder (i.e., error-free scenario, (a)(b)). This is reasonable since the number of MV candidates satisfying the constraint in Eq. (12) is increased and all of them lead to residual energy larger than $\gamma^{\min}$ . The sacrificed coding efficiency would lead to a gain on error resiliency, if the PSNRs are measured at receiver's decoder (i.e., error-prone scenario, (c)(d)). Take the curve of $\alpha = 2$ and $\alpha = 6$ for comparison, there exists a crossing point where the average PSNR for $\alpha = 6$ becomes better than that for $\alpha = 2$ . However, this is not the similar case (no distinct crossing point exists) between $\alpha = 10$ and $\alpha = 20$ .

It is observed from Fig, 3(a) that the anchor's face encounters severe distortion due to the lack of error resiliency for conventional ME algorithms. On the other hand, distortions of the anchor's face in (b) and (c) are much less than that in (a) of Fig. 3, due to the enhancement of error resiliency for increasing $\alpha$ . However, increasing quantization errors in other areas (e.g., words in the background) may lower down the total PSNR performance. This situation becomes clearer when $D_s$ dominates $D_c$ (e.g., $\alpha = 20$ not shown here).

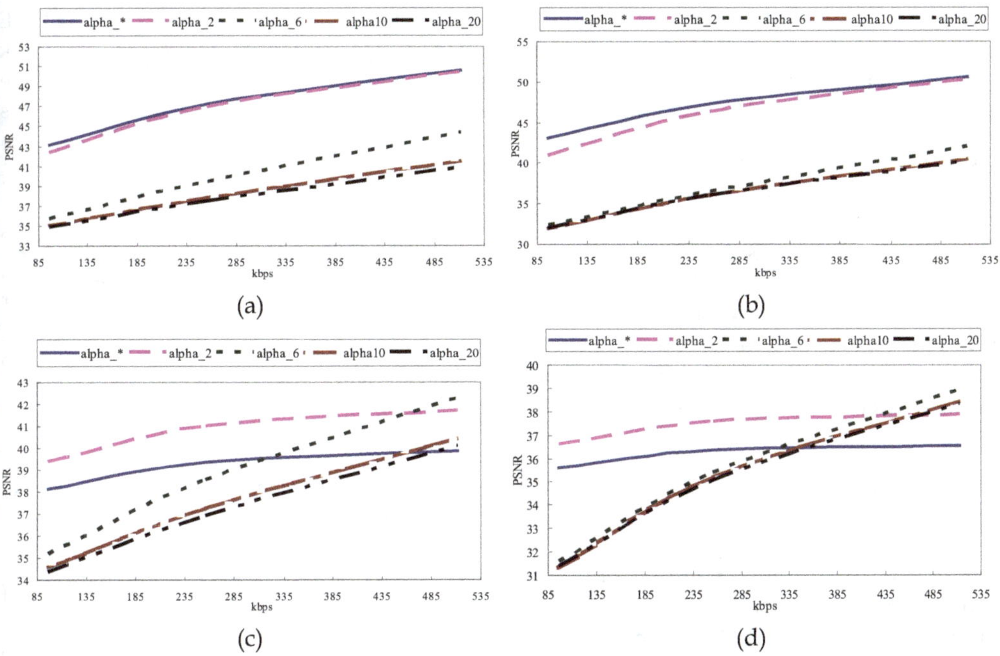


Fig. 2. Illustration of compromising error resiliency with coding efficiency of the proposed ERME algorithm. (a)(b) Reconstructed "Akiyo"at local decoder. (c)(d) Reconstructed "Akiyo"at decoder. The packet loss rate is (a)(c) 5% and (b)(d) 15%, respectively.

(a) Traditional ME (b) $\alpha = 2$ (c) $\alpha = 10$

Fig. 3. Visual quality at varying α, showing different compromises between $D_s$ and $D_c$. The bit rate is 256 kbps and the packet loss rate is 5%.

Another experiment of compromising error resiliency with coding efficiency is conducted for the video "Foreman" (with high motion), which is also not shown here. In comparison with the experiments for "Akiyo" (Fig. 2), the PSNR crossing point is advanced to a lower bit rate for high motion videos. We can temporarily come to a conclusion that $\alpha$ can be chosen smaller (e.g., 2) for static videos while larger (e.g., $\geq 6$) for high motion videos.

Remind that the choice of $\hat{\sigma}^2 = \gamma^{\min}$ is only for comparison purpose. Practically, $\hat{\sigma}^2$ should be derived by a fast and simple analysis for each MB, e.g., by summing the square of the temporal difference with respect to the previous frame. This method is certainly computationally cheaper and makes the threshold *Thd1* MB-adaptive.

Next, rate-distortion performance of our proposed ERME+ERMD algorithm is illustrated. We relax the allowable modes to include $16\times16$, $8\times16$, $16\times8$, $8\times8$, and intra $16\times16$. Notice that since we focus on finding MVs which can improve robustness to transmission errors of the compressed videos, the methods for compressing I-pictures here conforms to that recommended in the H.264/AVC standard. The integration of both techniques means that for each mode in $\mathbf{M}$, except the intra $16\times16$, the ERME algorithm is first applied to find the respective MVs, then the ERMD algorithm, with embodiment in term of Eq. (16), is applied to select the optimal mode among $\mathbf{M}$. In the following experiments, a value of $\alpha = 2$ is selected for ERME algorithm.

In Fig. 4, rate-distortion performances of several variational methods are compared. Three test sequences are chosen to represent typical videos of high motion (e.g., "Stefan"), moderate motion (e.g., "Foreman"), and static (e.g., "Akiyo") contents. In these figures, curves annotated with "MEO-MDO" represent the proposed "ERME+ERMD" algorithm, those annotated with "MEN-MDO" represent "ME+ERMD" algorithm, and curves annotated with "MEN-MDN" represent the traditional "ME+MD" algorithm adopted in H.264/JVC JM 9.3 model. For packet loss rate of 5% and 15%, the proposed ERME+ERMD improves error resiliency of the compressed video significantly (by 1~7 dB). These experiments also verify that ME+ERMD algorithm is not sufficient to support transmission robustness. The ERME algorithm is promising to provide additional support to complement this deficiency.

In Table 1, statistics of coding modes finally chosen by conventional H.264/AVC and the proposed ERME+ERMD algorithm are listed, which are obtained after gathering the related information for three different video sequences under different bit rates and a given 5% packet loss rate. It is observed that although ERME is able to prevent compressed videos from temporal error propagation, which has been verified in Fig. 2, the most efficient mode to prevent error propagation is "intra". The percentage is higher for higher bit rates. This behavior is reasonable since the additional bit rate will gain more benfits from intra-coding than from finer quantization.

### 7.2 Experiments for MHC

The multi-hypothesis coding algorithm is also implemented based on the H.264 video coding standard. Also, the first frame is coded as I frame and the rest are coded as P frames without any intra-coded blocks in them. It is assumed that a packet contains of a row of MBs.

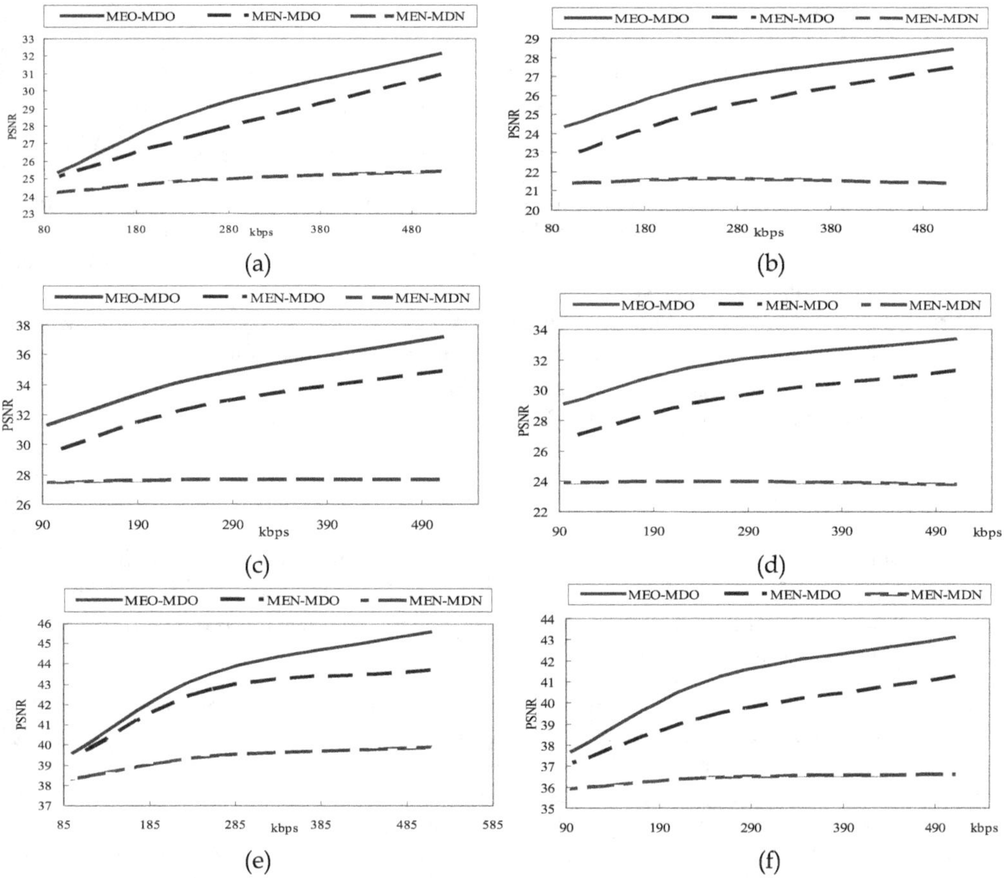


Fig. 4. Rate-distortion performances of reconstructed video at decoder for ERME+ERMD (MEO-MDO), ME+ERMD (MEN-MDO), and ME+MD (MEN-MDN) methods. (a)(b) "Stefan", (c)(d) "Forman", (e)(f) "Akiyo". (a)(c)(e) : PLR=5%, (b)(d)(f): PLR=15%.

| Bit rate = 128kbs, Packet loss rate = 5% | | | | | | |
|---|---|---|---|---|---|---|
| Modes | Foreman` | | Stefan | | Mobile | |
| | H.264 (%) | Proposed (%) | H.264 (%) | Proposed (%) | H.264 (%) | Proposed (%) |
| 16x16 | 47.6 | 22.3 | 52.3 | 22.1 | 54.1 | 31.9 |
| 16x8 | 20.5 | 3.4 | 19.1 | 1.8 | 23.2 | 6.2 |
| 8x16 | 24.0 | 3.0 | 15.9 | 2.3 | 22.3 | 8.6 |
| 8x8 | 0 | 0 | 0 | 0 | 0 | 0 |
| Intra | 7.9 | 71.3 | 12.7 | 73.8 | 0.4 | 53.3 |

Table 1. Statistics of coding modes chosen by H.264 and the proposed ERME+ERMD.

First, the performance of the proposed error resilient motion estimation algorithm for MHC is evaluated. According to Eq. (38), we have decomposed the multi-hypothesis problem into $N$ single-hypothesis problem. Let the threshold $T_k$ for each hypothesis be in a form of $x \cdot \delta_k$, where $\delta_k$ is the energy of the prediction errors based on the MV (i.e., $\Delta x_k$ and $\Delta y_k$) obtained by using the conventional motion estimation algorithm and $x$ is a scale factor.

Obviously, for each hypothesis, the threshold $T_k$ is capable of adapting to video contents block-wise rather than frame-wised. On the other hand, adjustment of $x$ makes us able to control the degree of compromise between coding efficiency and error resiliency. It is also easy to observe that the larger scaling factor $x$ is chosen, the larger source distortion $D_s$ is incurred, i.e., the more coding efficiency is sacrificed. Note that the above-mentioned way of getting $\delta_k$ is only for comparison purpose. One more practical method is to let $\delta_k$ be the energy of the residuals obtained via zero-motion compensation. Note that zero-motion compensation (or direct frame-difference) incurs less computational load and is hence more feasible.

In Figs. 5 and 6, rate-distortion performances in both the error-free and error-prone transmission environments between the proposed error resilient motion estimation and the conventional H.264 motion estimation techniques, are compared. The curves with "alpha_$x$" represent the results obtained by varying $x$ in $T_k = x \cdot \delta_k$ to account for different levels of tradeoffs between coding efficiency and error resiliency. The curve marked with "alpha_*" represents the conventional ME algorithm.

From the figures, it is observed that in error-free environments, the proposed algorithm always results in a poorer performance than the conventional ME algorithm. This situation is even worse when $x$ is increased (thus $T_k$ is increased). It is observed that with packet losses, our proposed algorithm improves videos quality at higher bit rates. A larger $T_k$ will result in a better error resiliency (up to 1 dB). At low bit rates, since the coding efficiency is quite sacrificed, the gain in error resiliency is not enough to overcome the former loss. It is also observed that similar performances are obtained for different weighting coefficients $\boldsymbol{h}$.

Next, the performance of our adaptive multi-hypothesis coding technique is to be evaluated. The number of hypotheses is 3 and the quantization parameter (QP) remains fixed during encoding a video. The packet loss rate is set to 5% and PSNR is measured between the reconstructed frames at local decoder and the reconstructed frames at receiver's decoder. Since the accuracy of the estimated channel distortion power is essential to the determination of the hypothesis-weighting coefficients to improve error resiliency, the accuracy of Eq. (41) is evaluated first. In experiments not shown here, the average difference between the estimated (via Eq.(41)) and the measured PSNRs for the high-motion video STEFAN is no more than 3.16 %.

Figure 7 relates to the experiment results of adaptive multi-hypothesis coding based on Eqs. (42) and (45). Notice that now MVs for each MB are obtained by using the conventional motion estimation algorithm. The two-state Gilbert channel as described in Zorzi et al. (1997) is used to simulate error conditions of packet error rate = 10% and average packet-error-burst length = 18.

In Fig. 7, the curves marked with "Adaptive" represent our proposed algorithm and curves marked with "Fixed" represent the conventional algorithm (i.e., constant and even weighting coefficients). From the figure, it is observed that our proposed algorithm really enhances the error resiliency of the multi-hypothesis video coding technique by up to 1 dB.

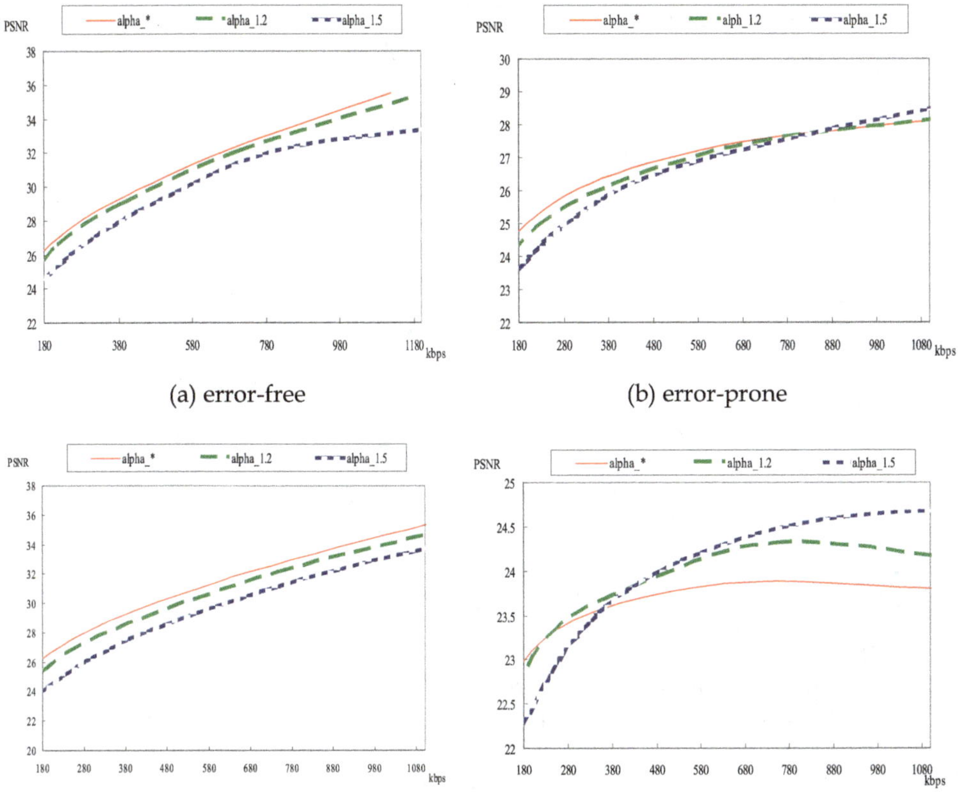


(a) error-free (b) error-prone

(c) error-free (d) error-prone

Fig. 5. Rate-distortion performance comparison with hypothesis-weighting coefficients (1/3, 1/3, 1/3) along the whole video "STEFAN". The packet loss rate for (a)(b) and (c)(d) is 5% and 15%, respectively.

## 8. Conclusion

In this chapter, error resilient coding techniques considering end-to-end distortions for videos transmitted on error-prone channels are discussed. The main concept of the algorithms is to decompose end-to-end distortions into two parts: source distortion relating to coding efficiency and channel distortion relating, on the other hand, to error resiliency. Most often, these two objectives are intrinsically mutual conflicting under a target bit rate. Hence it needs to make a proper compromise between them.

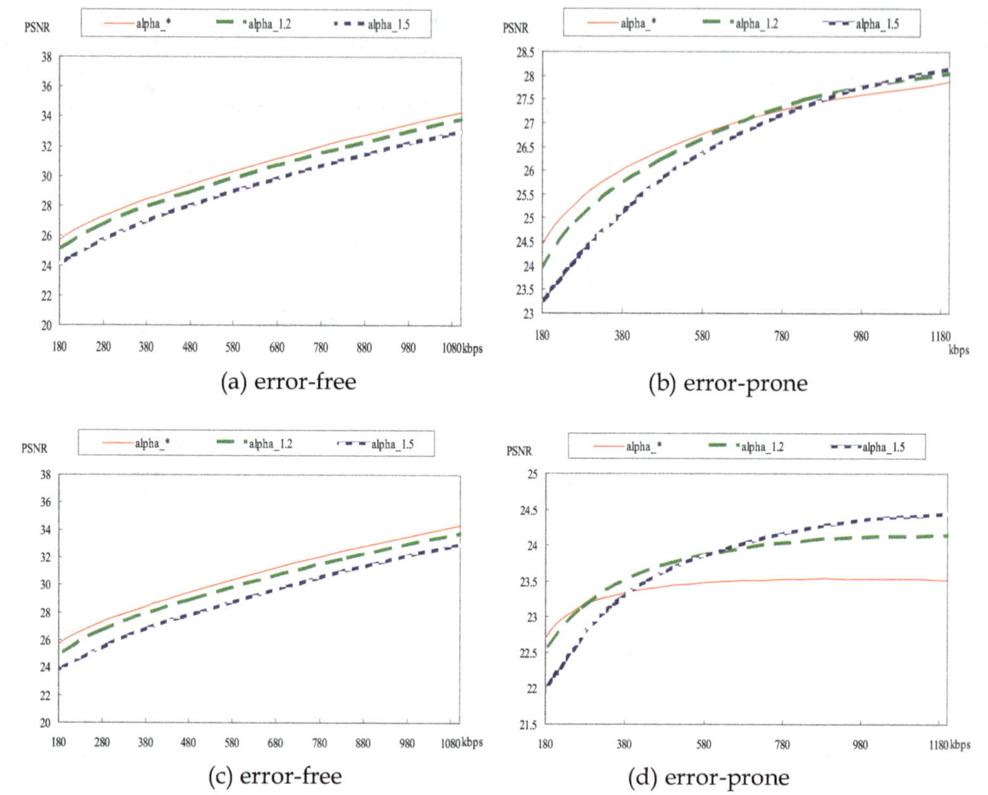


Fig. 6. Rate-distortion performance comparison with hypothesis-weighting coefficients (0.7, 0.2, 0.1) along the whole video "STEFAN". The packet loss rate for (a)(b) and (c)(d) is 5% and 15%, respectively.

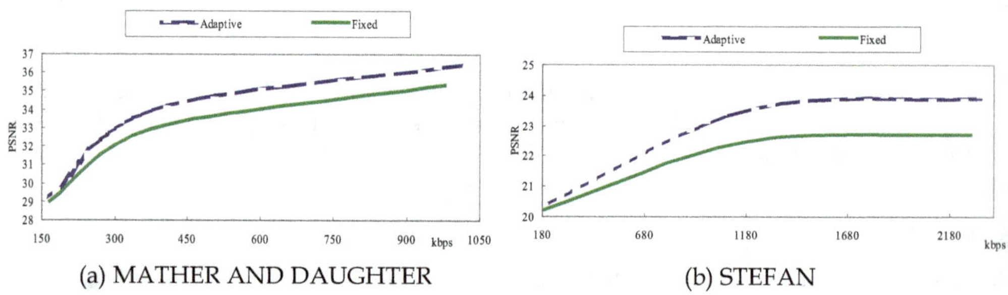


Fig. 7. Performance of the adaptive multi-hypothesis coding technique. The average packet-error-burst length is 18 and the packet-error-rate is 10 %.

In accordanc with the above concept, we propose ERME algorithms for both traditional H.264/AVC and multi-hypothesis coding architectures to suppress the temporal error propagation effectively with relatively low computational overhead. The similar concept is also applied to inter mode selection of H.264/AVC and to adaptive multi-hypothesis coding by finding out the relationship between the end-to-end distortions and the coding parameters, e.g., coding modes or hypothesis weighting coefficients before solving the optimization problem. Experiment results verify the accuracy of the proposed end-to-end distortion model in respective area.

The performance of the ERME algorithm is sunstantially affected by the constraint that controls different degrees of compromise between coding efficiency and error resiliency. How to set the constraint more accurately is a quite important issue that needs to be investigated further. Besides, integrating the ERME and adaptive hypothesis-weighting algorithms for further enhancement of error resiliency is not done yet. Note that the premise of the ERME is a given weighting $\boldsymbol{h}$, while adaptive hypothesis-weighting relies on the availability of MVs, seemingly a chicken-and-egg problem. A possible way is to compute the optimal $\boldsymbol{h}$ for frame $t$+1 based on the MVs of frame $t$ by assuming that consecutive frames have strong similarity on MVs or channel distortion power, thought it might be violated due to large motion or scene change.

## 9. References


Boyd, Stephen & Vandenberghe, Lieven (2004). *Convex Optimization*, Cambridge University Press.

Chang, Pao-Chi; Lee, Tien-Hsu; Chen, Jhin-Bin & Tsai, Ming-Kuang (2005). Encoder-originated error resilient schemes for H.264 video coding. *Proceedings of 18th IPPR Conference on Computer Vision, Graphics and Image Processing,* pp. 406–412, Aug. 2005.

Cote, G. & Kossentini, F. (1999). Optimal intra coding of blocks for robust video communication over the Internet. *Signal Processing: Image Commu.*, Sep.1999,pp. 25-34.

Eisenberg, Yiftach; Zhai, Fan; Papppas, Thrasyvoulos N.; Berry, Randall & Katsaggelos, Aggelos K. (2006). VAPOR: Variance-aware per-pixel optimal resource allocation. *IEEE Trans. on Image Processing*, Vol. 15, No 2, Feb. 2006, pp. 289-200.

Flierl, M.; Wiegand, T. & Girod, B. (2000). A Video Codec Incorporating Block-Based Multi-Hypothesis Motion-Compensated Prediction. *Proceedings of the SPIE Conference on Visual Communications and Image Processing,* Vol. 4067, pp. 238-249, June 2000.

Flierl, Markus; Wiegand, Thomsa & Girod, Bernd (1998). A locally optimal design algorithm for block-based multi-hypothesis motion-compensated prediction. *Proceedings of IEEE Conf. On Data Compression*, pp. 239-248, March 1998.

Flierl, Markus; Wiegand, Thomas & Girod, Bernd (2002). Rate-constrained multihypotheis prediction for motion-compensation video compression. *IEEE Trans. on Circuits and Systems for Video Technology*, Vol. 12, No. 11, Nov. 2002, pp. 957-969.

Girod, Bernd (2000). Efficiency analysis of multihypothesis motion-compensated prediction for video coding. *IEEE Trans. on Image Processing*, Vol. 9, No. 2, Feb. 2000, pp.173-183.

Harmanci, Oztan & Tekal, A. Murat (2005). Stochastic frame buffers for rate distortion optimized loss resilient video communications. *Proceedings of IEEE Int'l Conf. Image Processing,* Vol. 1, pp. 789-792, Sep. 2005.

He, Zhihai; Cai, Jianfei & Chen, Chang Wen (2002). Joint source channel rate-distortion analysis for adaptive mode selection and rate control in wireless video coding. *IEEE Trans. on Circuits and Systems for Video Technology,* Vol.12, No.6, Jun. 2002, pp. 511-523.

Kung, Wei-Ying; Kim, Chang-Su & Kuo, C. –C. Jay (2006) Analysis of multi-hypothesis motion compensation prediction for robust video transmission. *IEEE Trans. on Circuits and Systems for Video Technology,* Vol. 16, No. 1, Jan. 2006, pp. 146-153.

Leontaris, A. & Cosman, P.C. (2004). Video compression for lossy packet networks with mode switching and a dual-frame buffer. *IEEE Trans. on Image Processing,* Vol. 13, July 2004, pp. 885-897.

Lie, Wen-Nung; Gao, Zhi-Wei & Liu, Tung-Lin (2006). Joint source-channel video coding based on the optimization of end-to-end distortion. *Proceedings of Pacific-Rim Symposium on Image and video Technology,* 2006.

Lin, Shunan & Wang, Yao (2002). Error resilience property of multihypothesis motion-compensated prediction. *Proceedings of IEEE International Conference on Image Processing,* Vol. 3, pp.545-548, June 2002.

Reyes, Gustavo de los; Reibman, Amy R.; Chang, Shih Fu & Chuang, Justin C.-I. (2000). Error-resilient transcoding for video over wireless channels. *IEEE Journal on Selected Areas in Communications,* Vol. 18, No. 6, June 2000, pp. 1063-1074.

Ringuest, Jeffrey L. (1992). *Multiobjective Optimization: Behavioral and Computational Considerations.* Kluwer Academic Publishers.

Stuhlmuller, Klaus; Farber, Niko; Link, Michael & Girod, Bernd (2000). Analysis of video transmission over lossy channel. *IEEE Journal on Selected Areas in Communications,* Vol. 18, No. 6, June 2000, pp. 1012-1032.

Sullivan, G. J. (1993). Multi-hypothesis motion compensation for low bit rate video coding. *Proceedings of IEEE Int'l Conf. Acoustics, Speech, and Signal processing,* Vol. 5, pp. 437-440, Apr. 1993.

Sun, M.-T. & Reibman, A.R. (2001). *Compressed Video over Network,* Marcel Dekker, Inc. New York, Basel.

Wiegand, Thomas; Farber, Niko; Stuhlmuller, Klaus & Girod, Bernd (2000). Error-resilient video transmission using long-term memory motion-compensated prediction. *IEEE Journal on Selected Areas in Communications,* Vol. 18, No. 6, June 2000, pp. 1050-1062.

Xia, Minghui; Vetro, Anthony; Sun, Huifan & Liu, Bede (2004). Rate-distortion optimized bit allocation for error resilient video transcoding. *Proceedings of IEEE Int'l Symp. Circuits and Systems,* Vol. 3, pp. 945-948, May 2004.

Yang, Hua & Rose, K. (2005). Rate-Distortion optimized motion estimation for error resilient video coding. *Proceedings of IEEE Int'l Conf. Acoustics, Speech, and Signal processing,* Vol. 2, March 2005, pp. 173-176.

Zhan, R.; Regunathan, S. L. & Rose K. (2000). Video coding with optimal intra/inter mode switching for packet loss resilience. *IEEE Journal of Selected Areas in Commun.,* Vol. 18, No. 6, June 2000, pp. 966-976.

Zorzi, M.; Rao, K.R. & Milstein, L. B. (1997). ARQ error control for fading mobile radio channels. *IEEE Trans. On Vehicle Technology.,* Vol. 46, May 1997, pp. 445-455.

# Permissions

All chapters in this book were first published in MULTIMEDIA, by InTech Open; hereby published with permission under the Creative Commons Attribution License or equivalent. Every chapter published in this book has been scrutinized by our experts. Their significance has been extensively debated. The topics covered herein carry significant findings which will fuel the growth of the discipline. They may even be implemented as practical applications or may be referred to as a beginning point for another development.

The contributors of this book come from diverse backgrounds, making this book a truly international effort. This book will bring forth new frontiers with its revolutionizing research information and detailed analysis of the nascent developments around the world.

We would like to thank all the contributing authors for lending their expertise to make the book truly unique. They have played a crucial role in the development of this book. Without their invaluable contributions this book wouldn't have been possible. They have made vital efforts to compile up to date information on the varied aspects of this subject to make this book a valuable addition to the collection of many professionals and students.

This book was conceptualized with the vision of imparting up-to-date information and advanced data in this field. To ensure the same, a matchless editorial board was set up. Every individual on the board went through rigorous rounds of assessment to prove their worth. After which they invested a large part of their time researching and compiling the most relevant data for our readers.

The editorial board has been involved in producing this book since its inception. They have spent rigorous hours researching and exploring the diverse topics which have resulted in the successful publishing of this book. They have passed on their knowledge of decades through this book. To expedite this challenging task, the publisher supported the team at every step. A small team of assistant editors was also appointed to further simplify the editing procedure and attain best results for the readers.

Apart from the editorial board, the designing team has also invested a significant amount of their time in understanding the subject and creating the most relevant covers. They scrutinized every image to scout for the most suitable representation of the subject and create an appropriate cover for the book.

The publishing team has been an ardent support to the editorial, designing and production team. Their endless efforts to recruit the best for this project, has resulted in the accomplishment of this book. They are a veteran in the field of academics and their pool of knowledge is as vast as their experience in printing. Their expertise and guidance has proved useful at every step. Their uncompromising quality standards have made this book an exceptional effort. Their encouragement from time to time has been an inspiration for everyone.

The publisher and the editorial board hope that this book will prove to be a valuable piece of knowledge for researchers, students, practitioners and scholars across the globe.

# List of Contributors

**Yasuo Ariki and Tetsuya Takiguchi**
Kobe University, Japan

**Guifang Wu**
Electronic Information Engineering College, Henan University of Science & Technology, China

**Kazuki Nishi**
UEC Tokyo (University of Electro-Communication), Japan

**Mohammed Golam Sarver and Lai Man Po**
City University of Hong Kong, Hong Kong SAR, China
University of Windsor, Canada

**Q.M. Jonathan Wu**
University of Windsor, Canada

**Wei-Ta Chu**
National Chung Cheng University, Taiwan

**Chang-Duk Jung, Phd and You-Keun Park, Phd**
Korea University

**Woo-Young Ahn, Seo-Ha Lee and Gyeong-Seok Kim**
Faculty of Department of Civil & Environmental Engineering and Kongju National University, South Korea

**Tatsuya Yamazaki**
National Institute of Information and Communications Technology' Japan

**Songhao Zhu and Yuncai Liu**
Institute of Image Processing and Pattern Recognition, Shanghai Jiao tong University 800, Don chuan Road, Shanghai 200240, China

**Eduardo Martínez Cámara, Emilio Jiménez Macías, Julio Blanco Fernández, Féliz Sanz Adán, Mercedes Pérez de la Parte and Jacinto Santamaría**
University of la Rioja, Spain

**DongGyu Park, SangHunk Woo and MiRiNa Jo**
Dept. of Information and Communications Engineering, Changwon National University, Changwon City, 641-773, GyeongNam, Korea

**DoHoon Lee**
School of Computer Science and Engineering, Pusan National University, 609-735, Pusna City, Korea

**Wen-Nung Lie**
National Chung Cheng University, Chia-Yi, Taiwan

**Zhi-Wei Geo**
TECO Group Research Institute, Taipei, Taiwan

www.ingramcontent.com/pod-product-compliance
Lightning Source LLC
LaVergne TN
LVHW051046220926
848485LV00001BA/20
*9781639870127*